What readers say about the biography of Marvin Gilmore:

"There are many heroes in the story of Boston's remarkable revival, and one of them is Marvin Gilmore. In fact, his story should be an inspiration to every young person in this country who wants to do great things. A black kid from Cambridge, he overcame unbelievable obstacles in a racist America to succeed in business and, more importantly, as a tireless and relentless civic leader. He is also an inspiration to those of us who are approaching old age – still working, still pushing, still making the world a better place as he celebrates his 90th birthday."

- *Michael Dukakis, twice Governor of Massachusetts (1975-1979, 1983-1991) and the 1988 Democratic nominee for President of the United States*

"When you read this book about Marvin Gilmore you will learn a lot about history, a lot about Marvin Gilmore, and a lot about the progress that has been made in race relations. This book is important and should be read by everyone. You will be inspired and impressed by the life of Marvin Gilmore – an Army veteran, a community organizer, a businessman, a faithful and loyal citizen of Cambridge. I recommend this book with great enthusiasm."

- *Charles J. Ogletree, Jr., Jesse Climenko Professor of Law, Harvard Law School, and Founding & Executive Director, Charles Hamilton Houston Institute for Race & Justice*

"This book brings to life the qualities that make Marvin Gilmore a great citizen. Those of us who know and work with Marvin witness daily his labors to promote racial harmony and to heal communities. Marvin understands that racial harmony is underpinned by socio-economic success, and this book shows how Marvin learned that truth. It also showed me where Marvin got his guts and grit, his vision and his leadership. *Find the money,* Marvin says. *Create jobs... Nurture communities... Believe in the unbelievable...* Wonderful anecdotes that show how Marvin became Marvin."

- *Jeanette Clough, President and CEO, Mt. Auburn Hospital*

MARVIN GILMORE:

Crusader for Freedom

A Legacy of Battling Discrimination & Building Jobs

World War II Black Hero-Soldier, Entrepreneur, Civil Rights Activist, Musician, Community Builder and Defender

Paul Katzeff

Published by BookLocker.com, Inc., Bradenton, Florida.

Printed in the United States of America.

BookLocker.com, Inc.
2014

First Edition

Acknowledgements

This book would not have been possible without the generous help of a lot of people. My heartfelt thanks go to each of them. Special gratitude goes to two people: Marvin Gilmore, Jr., for sharing his story and his family's history, including his treasure trove of documents, and for participating in a colossal number of interviews and informal conversations. And my wife Janet, for her invaluable feedback and Job-like patience.

I'm also grateful to David, Lisa, and Marque Gilmore for sharing their memories and insights. In addition, Lisa provided key family records.

Further, I am indebted to the people who provided interviews for this book. Their voices helped turn what would have been a Gregorian chant into a stirring song filled with harmonies.

Marvin's story spans many generations. It weaves in and out of historical events large and small, some recent, some in the distant past. Retrieving details often required extensive research. Several professional librarians and researchers very kindly provided advice and tracked down documents. My special thanks to Michelle Romero, Assistant Archivist, Archives and Special Collections Department, Northeastern University, who contributed the power of her expertise and the depth of her institution's resources.

Others also were generous with their assistance: Richard L. Baker, MA (MSgt, USAF ret.), Senior Technical Information Specialist GS-11, U.S. Army Military History Institute, Army Heritage and Education Center; Anne Clark, Reference/Local History Librarian, Brookline Public Library; Misha Clebaner; Joellen ElBashir, Curator of Manuscripts, Moorland-Spingarn Research Center, Howard University; Cecile W. Gardner, Reference Librarian, Microtext Department, Boston Public Library; Clifford L. Muse, Jr., Ph.D., CA, Interim Director/University Archivist, Moorland-Spingarn Research Center, Howard University; Martha Reagan, Director of Library Services, *Boston Herald;* Natalie Savits, *Boston Herald* Research Librarian.

Important genealogical services were provided by Judy Baxter Osborne of Family Finder in Montgomery, Alabama; and Jan Hillegas of New Mississippi in Jackson, Mississippi.

I received precious feedback from Mack and Marcia Gordon, Harry Kluger, Geoffrey Precourt, Marshall Strauss, and Janet. They read with keen eyes and delivered candid comments.

Additional help in tracking down information was also offered selflessly by Katie Bell of Royal Conservatoire of Scotland; Dena Glasgow, Education Director, Boston-Area Jewish Education Program; Elisa Ho, Associate Archivist, The Jacob Rader Marcus Center of the American Jewish Archives; Ma'ayan Sands of the Grossman family; William Smith, founding Executive Director of the National Center for Race Amity; and Ellen Fitzgerald Watson, Executive Assistant, Cambridge License Commission.

In addition, Debra Englander was a sounding board for myriad topics. Carl Katzeff tackled manuscript coding challenges.

Writing this book required mental toting of tons of information. Libraries and librarians in Cohasset and Hingham, Massachusetts provided me with levers to ease my lifting on numerous occasions.

Again, my thanks to all of those people, who helped me create this book.

Table of Contents

Introduction
Defender of the Downtrodden

E ven before dawn's light leaked into the sky on June 6, 1944, 19-year-old Marvin E. Gilmore, Jr., knew exactly what was going on and so did all of his buddies. Any soldier could tell this was the real deal. It was D-Day. The invasion. None of them needed G.I. ESP.

Marvin was in a landing ship, steaming toward the beach of Normandy, France. Inside, the ship was shaped like a foxhole. It had sheer walls on the sides and steep ones front and back, made of steel. It offered a semblance of a foxhole's shelter, too. Below deck was jam packed with trucks and mobile artillery. A man could hunker down between those hulking vehicles and weapons and feel pretty safe, surrounded on all sides by thick steel machines, as far away as possible from the open sea air and the risk of enemy bullets and shrapnel and cannon shells.

But no one was taking cover in the bowels of this ship. Marvin and his buddies – the guys who had trained together as the all-black 458[1] Anti-Aircraft Artillery (Automatic Weapons) Battalion[1] – were all gathered on deck, along the rail, exposed to whatever might come so they could see the historically large fight unfolding all around them. They were surrounded by hundreds – no, *thousands* – of American and other Allied ships. On some, heavy deck guns were pounding the German beach defenses. Each time they fired, a flash of flame bloomed for an instant from their barrels. Moments later each gun's report reach him with a thunder clap – some loud, the distant ones soft – punching into Marvin's ears.

When morning light finally appeared, it revealed a cross, storm-tossed sea with a low, tight cloud cover. Ocean and air and clouds and the distant beach all looked gray and grim to Marvin. And minute by minute, the sullen scene grew more clamorous.

Marvin saw snub-nosed landing boats packed with assault troops plowing through choppy, ashen waters toward the beach. Soon a steady, fierce shower of German fire and metal began to greet them, raking them from cliffs above the beach. He could make out the muscular humps of some of the concrete bunkers shielding the Germans. Smoke and mist and distance obscured Marvin's view. The roll of the ship also made it hard to see details far away on shore. But even from here he could see that amphibious landing boats were swimming into a shooting gallery.

The time for Marvin and his buddies to hit the beach was getting near too. But despite the angry weather and choppy violence exploding all around them, no one was ducking for safety into the ship's foxhole of a hold. Hide out below deck? These guys were young. They were a primed fighting force, itching to see action. Avoid trouble? These guys *were* trouble, trouble for the enemy, part of a giant maul that was smashing down on the Germans defending this string of beaches in northwestern France.

"We had been in our ship a good 10 or 12 days," Marvin said decades later, recounting that long day of the landing.[2] "We had been waiting for orders, waiting for something to happen. Now all of a sudden you could not even see the water. There were so many other ships around us. We had all crossed the English Channel toward France. Now the water was black with ships. There were so many ships, you couldn't even see the water. We were anchored. But we all knew what this was without getting the word from officers. So we were waiting for orders to move forward, waiting for our turn to land."

There was one ominous sign. "My skin had turned white from the salt spray after so many days on the ship," he said. "I looked like a ghost."

Stinging salt saturated the sea air, whipped up by wild water and wind, the inclement weather that top Allied commander General Dwight D. Eisenhower was using as a brilliant screen. *Invade Normandy?* the German high command asked itself. *In this weather? Impossible!* Besides, the Germans *knew* the invasion would come in Pas-de-Calais, about 130 miles to the northeast. The town of Calais overlooks the Strait of Dover, the narrowest part of the English Channel. This was the shortest, quickest route across the Channel for an invasion force. And the town itself was a port, whose facilities would be vital for landing men and war supplies.

And so at this moment, Marvin had a front-row seat to history in the making. His outfit was lined up to land on the stretch of Normandy codenamed "Utah," one of five beaches in a row targeted by the Allies. He was about to become one of 1,800 African-American soldiers to storm the virtual fortress that Germany had erected on France's Atlantic coast.[3]

"We couldn't see much on the beach even as we got closer," Marvin said. "There was so much smog and smoke. But we could hear everything! There were constant loud noises and explosions, shooting and firing."

Like the lower deck, the open-air upper deck was crowded with vehicles except along the rail, which is where the men were gathered. From where Marvin watched, the Germans' reinforced concrete walls and massive-walled bunkers had low profiles. "We couldn't see much. But I could make out some of their gun turrets," Marvin said. "And in the air we saw German and American airplanes. I could see dog fights."[4]

The overall seaborne assault began at 6:30 in the morning.[5] For Marvin, waiting seemed to take forever, but he recalls that it was actually still morning when his ship nosed towards the beach.

When the ship was well into its beach approach, Marvin and the other men manned their vehicles. Drivers revved their truck engines. All conversation died.

"We had no sense of how good or bad things were going on the beach," Marvin said. "We started our trucks when we got orders. Then no one was talking. We were all listening for orders from our commanders. There was no talking as we got near the beachhead."

When the landing ship got close enough, it dropped its trailing anchor. This was the ship's lifeline. The vessel was built with a nearly flat bottom, and was designed to beach itself to offload its cargo. Later, when that job was done, a shipboard winch would strain on the anchor, buried in the shallow sea bottom far enough astern so the ship could haul herself back to sea.

Now the ship finally skidded up onto the Normandy mudflat.

A Door to War

The next minutes fused together like hot molten metal, like time compressed in an explosion. The ship's bow doors parted with a gasp as loud and startling as a starter's gun. They kept opening, spreading apart like the wings of an angel about to take flight. But they were accompanied by a hellish sound. Motors squealed as gears and chains slid heavy steel ramps forward. The ramps clattered and screamed as they slid over the ship's thin steel skin. The men of the 458th had practiced this debarkation dozens of times, but no rehearsals could capture the pressure on them now as the battle howled all around them, with the course of the war itself hanging in the balance.

Inside the belly of the ship, trucks and caissons lurched forward, wheeling their way down the steel ramps. "When that ramp went down, we hit the beach like lightning!" Marvin said.

There was scant room for error. Vehicles and wheeled weapons had to be steered straight and true down the ramps. Veering mere inches to either side would send heavy equipment careening off a ramp, fouling the disembarkation, delaying anti-aircraft weapons urgently needed to rake enemy fighters and bombers from the sky, now and in the hours, days, and months ahead.

As Marvin's truck plowed onto the beach, he heard the murderous music of war. Drum rolls of machinegun fire came from several directions. The booming kettle drums of artillery pressed air into his ears. Aircraft engines overhead whined like out-of-tune trombones.

"Off in the distance I saw American and German planes in dog fights," Marvin said. "Over us I was really glad to see barrage balloons. That helped keep German airplanes from strafing the beach. I was told later the balloon outfit was another all-black unit."

Metal cables tethered the balloons to a winch truck or some other vehicle. Enemy aircraft couldn't strafe the men, ships, and equipment on the beach without being sliced and diced by the cables. That forced them to fly ineffectively high, or avoid what would have been their deadliest maneuver, low altitude aerial runs along the length of the shore.

The balloons shielding Marvin's section of beach probably were floated by the 320th Barrage Balloon Battalion (VLA) – for very low altitude.[6] Military author Jonathan Gawne wrote that the 320th was the first barrage balloon unit in France and the first black unit in the segregated American Army to come ashore on D-Day.

Marvin's anti-aircraft artillery outfit began to move its heavy gear up the sand dunes and beyond. They followed the path punched through the German defenses by American infantry at great cost in lives and limbs.

The outcome of this Allied invasion was by no means certain. It could still be stopped cold, the beachhead transformed into a congested killing ground, a bloody bottleneck awash with the gore of young Americans and Britons and Canadians. Marvin knew he could easily end up dead, drowned, and dismembered at any instant. But he was free of fear.

"There was no fear in any of the soldiers," Marvin said. "We were too young. We were too fired up. Even as the day moved on and we had to pick up a lot of dead soldiers and put them on trucks, that fear never existed."

Months of practice kicked in.

"We spent a lot of time in England training, practicing what we would do," Marvin said. "Now it was time. All the men were fired up to get there and attack the Germans. There was no sense of fear. We were all too busy doing our jobs, moving to the fight, protecting ourselves."

Did he know how much peril he was in? "Yes, it was dangerous," Marvin said. "But I was too busy to think about it. In a way it was either kill or be killed. You didn't stand around thinking about whether you'd be alive or dead. You were fired up to move forward and kill the enemy. It never dawned on me I could be dead in the next day or the next hour or the next minute. Or the next second. That's why the Army chooses young men! They never think about dying."

Marvin was in an anti-aircraft battalion, but like any soldier he had endured harsh months in boot camp and later training, training with weapons and in hand-to-hand combat. He had been toughened by long marches, by oppressive heat, by fierce swamps, by mad-man drill instructors.

His outfit had moved its heavy guns forward, off the beach and toward the adjacent countryside, which was divided into a checkerboard pattern of farm plots delineated by hedgerows. Each hedgerow was an earthen embankment roughly six and a half feet tall, with a flat top surface. Beech, oak, and chestnut trees sprouted from the crown of each embankment. Thick, tall, and steep, the hedgerows formed walls that would make the advance of Allied tanks and artillery and anti-aircraft guns extremely difficult in the hours and days ahead. They would slow the American-led rescue invasion. German machine-gunners could mow down infantry daring to enter a field at a corner, where there were gaps in the hedgerows.[7]

The main duty of Marvin's outfit was to shoot German warplanes out of the sky. But Marvin and his brothers in arms were also ready to defend themselves from German foot soldiers. Marvin carried two handguns, a carbine, a bayonet, and a dozen hand grenades. "In all of our training leading up to that day, we were never trained to be afraid," he said. "You were trained to be a victor and win. I never thought I wouldn't see my mother or father or America again. It *never* entered my mind. As bad as the war and the situation was, I never thought about that. If I had, *then* I would be afraid."

Then, somehow, the day came to a close. The day was all mad order, it was all angry chaos. It had ended moments after it had begun. It had taken an eternity. Everything had gone as planned. Nothing had gone right. Finally, Marvin's sergeant, Edward O. DeWitt, ordered, *Get some shut-eye*. Marvin had a small pup tent, but instead he looked for a tree on top of the nearest hedgerow. Deliberately, he sat on the ground with his back against the trunk. His back covered, he checked one .45-caliber handgun, then the other. Both were loaded. On both, the safety was off. He holstered them. He fingered the bayonet sheathed on his belt. It was still there. He prayed he would not abruptly find himself in a wrestling match to the death with a stranger in the blinding darkness of night. But if some such horror occurred, he wanted every weapon possible.

He took a deep breath to calm himself, then checked his M1 carbine for the umpteenth time that day.[8] A magazine of bullets was still properly clipped in place. Without looking, he brushed the fingertips of his right hand across several hand grenades that were clipped to a bandolier across his chest. It was a quick act of reassurance. Just checking to make sure they were still there. There was no need for him to actually do anything with them. It was all part of a routine that had become second nature, a sort of combat countdown in the dark French night. Marvin was armed and primed.

Fighter for Freedom

Marvin's biography is the story of a fighter. He has fought to win a better life for himself and his family. That struggle has been all the more difficult because Marvin had to battle bigotry every step of the way. Yet those challenges have never kept Marvin from fighting for other people as well, helping them escape oppression and improve their lives, whether it is his black brothers and sisters in America or the victims of German tyranny during World War II.

Marvin was born in 1924. His story traces his ancestry back through generations of slaves in Alabama and South Carolina. Marvin's success and achievements are the fulfillment of his forbearers' hopes and dreams. So is his freedom to fight discrimination, a fight he comes back to again and again.

As a boy, Marvin heard his grandparents' stories about the brutality, beatings, rape, poverty, and fear they had endured as Southern slaves. His parents exercised stern authority at home as they sought to instill discipline in him. They wanted to forge in him the self-control they were sure he would need to study hard and achieve the financial freedom that had been denied to previous generations of Gilmores and, on his mother's side, O'Neals.

When Nazis threatened to enslave Europe, Marvin joined the Army before he reached enlistment age. He was young, but he recognized racist fanaticism when he saw it in newsreels and newspaper stories. He understood exactly where it led, to the same sort of suffering, violent oppression, and slavery his grandparents had suffered. He understood that Hitler's rabid ideology of racial hatred was his family's old enemy, back again, a menace not only to Europeans but also a threat to throw Marvin back in time to an evil place of pain and suffering, fear and deprivation that his grandparents had warned him about.

Still, Marvin was steeling himself to fight for more than racial justice. He had grown up in a multiethnic neighborhood. His friends were a Noah's Ark of different ethnicities, skin colors, and religions. Everyone was different. But they treated each other the same.

Marvin knew this new tyrant in Europe was a menace to black Americans. He also knew he was a threat to his home, to his entire country. This mustached maniac was a danger to his neighborhood and his buddies. America was a place Marvin loved, the nation he would fight for. Enlisting was a no-brainer. It was only in a distant recess of his mind that he admitted maybe, just maybe, he might have to pay some horrible price.

Fighting Several Wars

Like so many other African-Americans, Marvin embraced what black America called the Double V Campaign: victory against dictatorships abroad and victory against racism at home.[9] He would willingly risk life and limb in foreign lands to secure his opportunity to win full citizenship rights at home – for himself and for his fellow African-Americans.

He held to those convictions in southern Army training camps as he came face-to-face with organized discrimination far more severe than anything he had experienced back home in Cambridge, Massachusetts, where he had grown up in a racially and ethnically mixed community. Despite the bigotry that he encountered, Marvin was instrumental in calming a race riot at Camp Stewart in Georgia, one of the military's worst instances of racial conflict during World War II.

From the moment he found himself barred from an Army bus because he was black, Marvin was fighting several wars at once. He battled white segregationists. He skirmished with poor Southern black G.I.s, who resented Northern black soldiers who were better educated and had not been raised to fear whites, even armed whites. And once he got to Europe, he was in combat against the German war machine – the *wehrmacht*. From his first day in France – D-Day, the Normandy invasion – he slept with his weapons so that he would always be able to defend himself, whether the foe was American or German.

In one battle, Marvin suffered severe wounds that landed him in a field hospital. Here too he had to fend off attacks by fellow soldiers. He escaped harm because he had his handgun handy. Once he was healthy enough to return to action, rather than risk random assignment to an unfamiliar outfit he stole a jeep, then two more, as he scouted his way back to his old unit at the front.

During most of the war, Marvin was attached to Gen. George Patton's Third Army, fighting its way across northwest Europe. Periodically, his outfit got moved around to fill gaps in manpower. For a while Marvin was conscripted into the Red Ball Express, the emergency trucking shuttle the Army set up to move war supplies to the front. The conveyor belt on wheels became an urgent need when gung-ho generals like Patton and the First Army's Courtney Hodges outran their supplies of bullets, gasoline, cannon shells. Three quarters of the Red Ball's drivers and mechanics were black G.I.s.[10]

German soldiers certainly were not the only threats to Marvin during the war. War-time tensions could turn a "routine" clash with a racist G.I. into a fatal encounter. Danger lurked even away from the front. In Glasgow, white military police tried to ambush Marvin simply because he was black. Black marketers, both in the Army and outside its ranks, were willing to kill honest soldiers like Marvin rather than risk letting them foul up their lucrative underground trade.

Marvin had tumbled into a nightmare world. Many of its denizens were vicious men who hated and feared him, some because he was black, some because he was honest, all because he was not one of them. It was a world of chaos. It was a world where a man like Marvin could be killed and his death might not even be noticed amid the rampant carnage. It was a world overflowing with armed men trained to maim and kill, many driven mad by the horrors of combat. They would slay or cripple someone like Marvin just because he was there.

And racism did not disappear once the European war was won. Marvin was turned away from the troop ship that was supposed to transport him and other soldiers home. He was barred from boarding with the admonition that only white solders were allowed onboard.

Finally, Marvin returned home. But his battles were certainly not done.

The Fight at Home

On the personal front, Marvin fought to complete the education he had interrupted to join the war effort. He worked part-time to earn money while he finished high school. He took odd jobs, performed house cleaning, and washed and polished cars for wealthy whites. The drudgery and put-downs with not-so-subtle racial undertones convinced him that when he was done with school, he would only work for himself, never for other people.

He went through a similar routine in college at the prestigious New England Conservatory. Marvin studied piano and percussion at the music-oriented school. He added catering and playing in bands to his income-earning sidelines. He also worked the graveyard shift at a mental hospital as an orderly. There, he found himself caring for Sam Langford, a black boxing champion who had gone blind and broke. Langford was not mentally ill, but the aging, broken down black man had somehow been swept into the facility, like something society had thrown away.

Marvin realized who the old pugilist was, and he was happy to comfort him. But Langford's sorry state was another life lesson for Marvin. It was important for a black adult to be financially independent, able to take care of himself and his loved ones.

Marvin developed into an excellent musician – and an outstanding caterer. He ran social functions in suburban Boston, several of which the president of prestigious Brandeis University attended. Impressed by Marvin's panache, he offered him a job as his campus-residence butler. Marvin was flattered but he declined. He had loftier goals in mind.

He was already at work on one of them. Years earlier, in the depths of the Depression, his family lived in a modest Cambridge rooming house. When their landlady fell into foreclosure, Marvin's mother purchased the building. Basically, she swapped her meager bank account for the building. Through the following years she slowly added to her rental real estate holdings. She did it by creating a market for herself.

She heard that ambitious young black students at Harvard University could not obtain campus housing; the Ivy League school discriminated against them. So Marvin's mother spread the word that she would provide housing. Through church groups and the rest of her social network, she promoted her rooms and apartments as housing for worthy students. Sure enough, she attracted tenants (a few of whom were white) who went on to include a Nobel Prize winner, judges, a Presidential cabinet secretary, two U.S. ambassadors, a Nieman Fellow at Harvard, and a future wife of singer Nat "King" Cole. Among her non-student tenants briefly: Martin Luther King Sr., father of the civil rights icon.

Marvin made friends with many. The expertise of several proved invaluable in helping to solve problems during Marvin's decades as an adult businessman.

Meanwhile, as a young adult, Marvin helped his mother run her properties. He continued to learn business lessons from his mother. She emphasized the value of fiscal caution and never taking on debt. He applied those lessons as he began to buy his own properties. Those became the foundation for his financial self-sufficiency.

The Boston Battler

The family to which he would devote so much of his energy began with his 1959 wedding. Lorna Langer, a brilliant Harvard-educated biochemist who happened to be white and Jewish, was the love of Marvin's life. Marvin was her first black friend. Their wedding took place despite the strident opposition of Lorna's mother. Their marriage lasted until death parted them after 48 years.

The 1960s were the decade of civil rights battles and flower power. Marvin blossomed in the fight for racial equality.

He was chairman of the life-membership committee of the Boston branch of the NAACP. Marvin could have invented the Boy Scouts' slogan, "Be prepared." He's had a lifelong habit of working long hours and starting his labors early. He was routinely early to NAACP branch meetings so that he could review notes and organize his thoughts for the upcoming session. That passion for preparation paved the way for a chance conversation with Charles Evers, brother of slain activist Medgar Evers and an NAACP official in Mississippi. After their brainstorming session, Marvin teamed up with professional basketball superstar Bill Russell to visit Jackson in the state of Mississippi – the heart of segregationist darkness – within days of enactment of the Civil Rights Act of 1964. Their agenda was to seek service in restaurants and hotels, which under the new law could no longer bar customers due to their race. The duo spent five days in Jackson, in a constant game of cat-and-mouse with armed segregationists who were out to scare them out of town – or kill them.

But despite the risks, their mission was a success. They broke the color barrier in several places. They brought the light of publicity to a community that had used intimidation and violence to repress its black residents. They delivered hope to an oppressed black citizenry.

Later that same summer, Marvin – who had spent enough time as a jazz musician to know his way around a performance hall – took a train to Philadelphia and talked his way backstage and into Sammy Davis, Jr.'s dressing room in the theater where he was rehearsing *Golden Boy*. Marvin's mission: talk the headliner into performing for free at a fundraiser for the Boston branch of the NAACP. Would his gambit work?

In business, the 1960s saw Marvin diversify his activities and sources of income. The bonus was that he did it in a way that enabled him to combine work and pleasure. He had been forced to abandon a career as a musician as a young man because it was an unreliable way to earn a living and because of bias against black talent. Now, in his forties, he recognized a way to get back in. Driving his red Jaguar through Cambridge one day, he was struck by a neighborhood that was pockmarked by seedy bars.

They were the neighborhood's lament. But to Marvin they suddenly looked like an opportunity. Could he buy one and turn it into a high-class nightclub, showcasing top-notch bands, welcoming mixed audiences of blacks and whites? Would he have tried if he had known in advance how he'd be harassed and hassled by city authorities who couldn't bear to see a black man succeed?

Discrimination was a never-ending plague in all of his businesses. Repeatedly during the 1940s, '50s, and '60s, banks refused to lend him money. Banks always seemed more concerned with his black skin than the fact that his balance sheets were written in black ink, not red. His solution sprang from his entrepreneurial vision. He organized a campaign to establish the first minority-owned commercial bank in New England.

Marvin was a hot commodity. Governors and mayors appointed him to public boards that counseled the state and big cities on issues ranging from housing for the poor to racial harmony. Charities vied for his presence on their boards of directors. Michael Dukakis, a rising politician who would eventually run for President, became a friend.

At the outset of the 1970s, Marvin's growing reputation led to his being hired to head the nonprofit Community Development Corporation of Boston. His appointment occurred just as President Richard Nixon was dismantling the federal Model Cities Program, which had supported CDCs around the U.S.

During a cross-country tour of CDCs around the country, Marvin realized that the only way his CDC could survive was by reinventing itself. Marvin's guiding principal was that the best way for the CDC to help any struggling community is with jobs. Their benefits are longer lasting than handouts. But *how* to reinvent itself? What roadmap for resurrection did he find?

Marvin's community activism did not stop there. Community groups blocked a huge interstate highway from plowing through a black neighborhood. The highway would have enabled white suburbanites to leapfrog the neighborhood on their way to jobs in downtown Boston. After consulting with community groups and people like Marvin, city and state officials approved a multimodal project. It would modernize mass transit, providing black inner-city residents with better access to the rest of Boston and the metro area. It would also improve long-distance and commuter rail facilities, create a useful local road, build new residential housing, and bring in a community college and a job training program.

There was just one problem. Federal transportation officials stonewalled. They had legal dibs on the land, which had been taken for a federal highway. And they held the purse strings for the federal funds that would pay for the bulk of the replacement project.

The logjam was broken only when Marvin phoned an old friend, who had the authority to order the recalcitrant federal big-wigs to sign-off on the new project. Who was he, and why did he help Marvin?

New Activities

Still going strong as he approached his ninetieth birthday, Marvin remains active in his various businesses.

"Marvin is not only still active in business and public affairs; he's also still the best dressed man when he enters any room," said a longtime female friend who asked not to be named. "He has tremendous charisma. People think of him as a ladies' man. The truth is that he is simply a very stylish gentleman, who lights up a room with his smile and spirit."[11]

Also, time and success have enabled him to devote more of himself to philanthropy. He supports a number of good causes, including hospitals and schools.

Brandeis University could not land Marvin as a butler back in the 1940s, but Marvin has returned to campus, having endowed a scholarship in his and his wife's names in the Transitional Year Program, which helps prepare youths from disadvantaged backgrounds for college studies. At the University of Massachusetts' Boston campus, Marvin is a member of the Board of Visitors, an advisory group to the Chancellor. At his alma mater, New England Conservatory, Marvin is a member of the Board of Overseers and he mentors individual students, who are all young musicians with outstanding promise.

And Marvin has received some belated honors for his Army service. In 2000, Marvin represented black World War II veterans at the Day of Honor 2000. The event's ceremonies at Arlington National Cemetery and the White House paid homage to veterans who were minorities – African-American, Native American, Japanese-American, Latino – whose service in World War II has often been overlooked and underplayed.

That same year Marvin was highlighted in an NBC News feature with Tom Brokaw, "Home of the Brave," which paid tribute to black World War II servicemen.

Ten years later, in a ceremony at the Massachusetts State House, the nation of France awarded Marvin its Legion of Honor with highest distinction for his service. Marvin became the first African-American in New England to receive the decoration. Prompted by France's recognition, in a better-late-than-never action the U.S. Army awarded Marvin several medals he had earned six and a half decades earlier but which the Army had never bestowed.

The momentum from those French and American honors continued. Marvin recently returned from France, where he participated in the June 2014 ceremonies marking the seventieth anniversary of the D-Day Normandy invasion. He shared a stage with President Barak Obama, the United Kingdom's Queen Elizabeth, and French President Francois Hollande. For two weeks he mingled with joyous Europeans, mainly French, who were not shy about expressing their gratitude to this elderly veteran who had helped liberate them and their parents and grandparents.

Marvin's success has enabled him to encourage his sons, David and Marque, to pursue careers in music, the career that eluded Marvin. They have achieved global distinction as modern jazz musicians. His daughter, Lisa, perhaps reflecting her medical-researcher mother's influence, is a consultant in federal asthma control projects.

Marvin is a fighter. Marvin is an entrepreneur. Real estate, music, night clubs, catering, the CDC...there's even a commuter airline and a limousine service on his resume. Marvin has been able to achieve things his forbearers never could have dreamed for themselves or their descendants. His story is unique. It spans centuries. It leaps from the chasm of slavery to the heights of self-determination. His uphill battle is the story of every person, of any color, creed, race, or religion, who wants to live freely, unfettered by the ignorance of others. Yet the heat of battle never distracts him from helping others.

Marvin's story is not just about his life. It is also about the development of civil rights in the United States in the 20th and 21st centuries. And Marvin was not merely a bystander, an African-American who lived through those events. He has been a participant and often enough a mover and shaker.

Marvin's story is not just for African-American readers. People of all colors and backgrounds can relate to Marvin's struggles to better himself and make a better life for his family. People of all colors and backgrounds can understand Marvin's fights against injustice. "Marvin is one of those people who has helped make America better – for everyone," said Michael Dukakis, former governor of Massachusetts and the 1988 Democratic nominee for President.[12]

Marvin has an entrepreneur's x-ray vision. His fertile mind can see golden nuggets where most other people see only dusty slag. But as eagerly as he builds one enterprise after another, he is never too busy to answer an injustice. Whether a challenge is in business or civil rights, time and again Marvin has seen that the solution is to fight to assure everyone equal access to the promise of America, the chance to pursue your own dream.

Part of what makes Marvin marvelous – as one magazine headline labeled him – is that seemingly infinite capacity for multitasking. Marvin builds his own businesses. At the same time he steers the CDC of Boston on a course designed to lure businesses to Boston's black community and create jobs for the Hub's have-nots. "People want jobs, not handouts," Marvin said. "They want to earn money and feel independent." Also at the same time, he crusades for civil rights.

"Marvin's a force of nature. He's led five or six lives, any one of which would be an interesting, honorable life," said Andrew Szanton, a longtime friend of Marvin and memoirist of civil rights activist Charles Evers. "I asked him once how he did it. He said he barely sleeps. He also made clear to me he is always thinking. He is like a master problem solver. He is like one of those chess players who plays 50 people at once – and wins. He tackles a lot of problems all at once."[13]

And so many of the problems involve helping other people. As a businessman, he takes time to reach out and help people. As head of the CDC, his entire focus is helping people. As an active citizen of Cambridge, he helps people. As a musical impresario he helped people. As a benefactor of universities and other worthy entities, he helps people. As a knight jousting for black civil rights, he certainly helps people.

He helps people even when others try to block him from contributing. Marvin the fighter.

Why does he care so fervently? It's because Marvin, this grandson of slaves, knows exactly where he comes from.

Chapter 1
Family Tree

Sometimes Sophronia O'Neal told her horror stories while sitting on a sidewalk bench. Her favorite spot was outside the Pill family's hardware store on Massachusetts Avenue in Central Square in Cambridge, Massachusetts. Her young grandson Marvin Gilmore was with her.

Sophronia had been born shortly before the outbreak of the Civil War.[14] Now, nearly four score years later, in the 1930s, she visited her daughter and her daughter's family whenever she could. She made this family pilgrimage as often as 10 summers in a row, including years when Marvin was in grade school. She traveled to Cambridge from her home in Alabama, starting each journey by bus, then switching to a train at a depot along the route. Each trip north from the hot, humid South took several days.

Once she had arrived, it was common for her to babysit Marvin and his younger brother Lester. Whether it was day or night, Sophronia watched after the boys while their mother worked, cooking and cleaning for white couples or working in a store. Many days Marvin sat with his grandmother while she relaxed on that sidewalk bench, taking in the sun, saying hello to people, watching the swirl of daily life in the college town. "She enjoyed it," Marvin said. "She did it a lot. She was a fixture. She got to know local people."

Sophronia also told stories to Marvin, there in Central Square and sometimes at her daughter's home. Some were too chilling for Marvin to ever forget. His grandmother was a small woman, but when she told certain stories, they made the small hairs stand up on the back of Marvin's neck.

Sophronia talked about her life in the South, including her youth. Some of her stories were casual reminiscences, just ways to pass the time. Others were far more than that. They were oral histories. She told them with a purpose in mind. They were meant as a kind of psychic inoculation. "She wanted to raise us so we would know how bad things could be, so we would never go through the same things she did," Marvin says quietly. "She came out of the era of President Lincoln. She knew how blacks were treated in the South because she had gone through it herself."

Sophronia's sagas included tales of terror.

"I remember especially while I was in the seventh and eighth grades, she would tell us stories about when she was a slave girl in Alabama," Marvin continues in a quiet, solemn voice. "She lived in a hut. They had kerosene lamps for light. No electricity."

That was not the only power Sophronia and her family lacked. They were helpless against attacks by their white overseers, both before the Civil War and after. "My grandmother told me about being raped and beaten. All the women were."

Sophronia's stories have stayed with Marvin. They are a mental tattoo.

They are key cogs in his motivation for getting ahead in life while, at the same time, dedicating himself to civic service. Anything less, he senses, and he risks sinking backwards, risks letting others slide back.

The memories help define him. In his mind, he will always remain the grandson of a slave girl. That identity weighs on him like a manacle and chain. It is heavy, cold, and hard as steel. Yet Marvin's successes and his service not only liberate him, his family, his community. They also liberate Sophronia and his countless kin who preceded her in bondage. Marvin's accomplishments become theirs. His achievements become a pinnacle for their history. Having endured their sufferings, they enabled him to climb high. Their dreams are realized in Marvin. He gives their lives new meaning. He never forgets them.

To understand Marvin, start by understanding his family tree.

Scraping Out a Living

Marvin built much of his reputation and success by developing land and putting property to productive uses. That's quite a turnaround for a man who had ancestors shackled to land.

Jerimiah Rowell,[15] Marvin's great grandfather on his mother's side, was a sharecropper or tenant farmer in rural Alabama, right after the Civil War.[16] Either occupation was a tough way to wrestle a living out of land. Its pay was almost always very poor. But it was one of the few ways a black man could eke out a living in the South after the war. And it was better than the previous life he had known.

Rowell had been a slave prior to Emancipation.[17]

He lived just outside Notasulga, Alabama. The community is roughly 44 miles east-northeast of Montgomery, towards the border with Georgia. It is a few farm fields north of Tuskegee. Auburn is a short 12 miles to the east. Today, Notasulga is north of Interstate Route 85. Almost the entire town is in Macon County. Its northeast corner pokes into Lee County.

Rowell's Notasulga was a productive farming community, a fertile cornucopia whose soil gave rise to an enviable variety of produce. Nearly every farm harvested corn and churned out barrels of butter. Local output also included wheat, rice, tobacco, peas, beans, and sweet potatoes. The Alabama earth blossoomed with corn and oats, which could feed the area's livestock – horses, mules, asses, milk cows, oxen, other cattle, sheep, and pigs. A small number of farms produced wool. A slightly larger number – mainly the biggest farms – kept beehives for production of wax and honey.[18]

An individual farmer like Rowell would turn out just a fraction of that bounty. He undoubtedly began to save his money as soon as he was a free man in 1865. Penny by penny, dollar by dollar, he held fast to the profits of labor that was finally for himself and his family after decades of fruitless, grinding servitude for callous owners. By 1870 he had scraped together $125. Saving anything was all the more difficult for a black man in a region still struggling to rebound from the ravages of war.

Compare his circumstances with those of Burrell Barrow, who lived down the road from Rowell. Barrow was one of the wealthier white farmers in the area. In July of 1860, nine months before the Civil War erupted, Barrow was 43 years old, and his land was valued at $8,000. His personal estate – movable personal property (including any slaves he owned), everything other than land and buildings – amounted to $20,050.[19]

In today's dollars, his farm was worth $223,000.[20] His personal property, also in today's dollars – which means after adjusting for nearly a century and a half of inflation – was worth $560,000. That's more than 252 times more than Jerimiah Rowell's personal property was worth. Burrell Barrow was not the richest man in the region, but he was better off than most white farmers there. And he was vastly more affluent than Marvin's great-great grandfather.

Life during Tough Times

Then came the war's devastation. By 1870, having had five years to rebound after General Robert E. Lee's surrender at Appomattox Court House in Virginia, Barrow's farm had inched up in value to $9,000. Jerimiah Rowell still did not own a square inch of land. All he had was that $125 of money and other worldly goods. Barrow's possessions, from clothes to farm tools, livestock, jewelry, furniture, and cash, had fallen to a value of $18,000.[21]

That was a loss of more than 10%. Barrow was still far wealthier than Rowell. He had never felt the cut of an overseer's whip. He had never suffered the humiliation, pain, and sorrow of slavery. But his standard of living had taken a hit. It was a relatively small price – especially for someone who had prospered and benefited for decades from owning slaves – but it was a price nonetheless. Just for a moment, try to put aside your contempt for someone who had been a slave owner. Of course he gets no sympathy for suffering a hit to his standard of living by losing the economic benefit of owning slaves and because he was on the losing side in a bloody war. But imagine his gloom! Look at only the dollars and cents. Think how you would feel having endured a war if, despite five years of recovery, your 401(k) account or IRA was still worth 10% less than it had been 10 years earlier. A big chunk of your life savings had vanished.

Tough times had come to Notasulga, even to its one-time slave-owning overlords. Some white land owners simply could no longer cut it and gave up. Albert Henry Rowell – yes, same last name as Marvin's great-great grandfather – had owned nine male slaves and six females in 1860.[22] He was building a good life for himself in the Notasulga area. His farm was worth $8,000. His personal property totaled $25,115 – more than $700,000 in modern money. He was 40 years old, with a wife 10 years his junior and a bevy of 10 children, ranging in age from two years of age to 14.[23] But in 1866 he relocated to Jefferson in Marion County, Texas.[24] Unable to make his Alabama farm pay without the forced sweat equity of black slaves, he up and left.

Even without free labor, making money off land is never a sure thing. Persuading property of any kind to yield you a living is a valuable skill. Marvin's earliest lessons came from his mother, Lee Augusta O'Neal.

"My mother's first property was a home she bought from a bank that had foreclosed on it," Marvin says. "Then she used the income from that to help pay for the next, and again for the one after that. She never lived off of her properties. She continued her other jobs, like cooking for rich white people. The rents from property went into the bank.

"She never owned a car. She never took a vacation. She never went to a movie. She used her own money to furnish every apartment she owned. She worried about paying for repairs and upkeep. She worried about finding good tenants. She worked hard to pay off her mortgages. When she died, she didn't owe anybody anything. Nothing. She never thought of her properties as a source of wealth. She always looked at her properties with financial caution. She didn't want to bite off more than she could chew. And she trained me that way too."

Marvin's family tree has stood and grown for 200 years. The trunk and branches that we can see, including Marvin's children and grandchildren, span seven generations.

The earliest ancestor identified so far is Kizzie Rowell, Marvin's maternal great-great-great grandmother. She was born in Virginia in 1812.[25]

Paternal Side

We can also trace Marvin's ancestry back through his father. Marvin Gilmore Sr. married Lee Augusta O'Neal, Marvin's mother, on Nov. 29, 1923.

Just as Marvin's mother' side of the family has a strong identity with Alabama, starting with the decades that Kizzie and Jerimiah spent there, Marvin's father's family has a South Carolina linkage.

Marvin Gilmore Sr. was born in 1900, in or near Columbus, South Carolina.[26] Marvin Jr. says his father was part Seminole. He was one of five brothers and four sisters. He appears to have been the third oldest sibling. He trailed his sisters Minnie, born in or around 1892, and Bessie, born in or around 1897. We don't know when his sister Narva was born.

21

Simplified family tree, showing Marvin's parents and maternal ancestors back to his great-great grandmother Kizzie.[27]

Source: U.S. census reports; family papers

Marvin Sr.'s youngest sibling was Lottie Lee, who was born in or around 1914.

His parents were Samuel M. Gilmore and Lottie. Lottie presumably was the namesake for Marvin Gilmore, Jr.'s aunt Lottie Lee Gilmore.

Samuel M. Gilmore was born in 1867 or 1868[28], shortly after the close of the Civil War, in South Carolina, apparently in Poplar Township, Orangeburg County, where he was still living with his parents, five brothers, and four sisters in 1880.[29] Lottie was born in South Carolina in about 1878, also apparently in Poplar.

We can trace this trunk of the Gilmore family tree further back one additional generation, to John Gilmore and his wife Lousea. John Gilmore – Marvin E. Gilmore, Jr.'s great grandfather on his father's side – was born in 1834 or 1835 in South Carolina, evidently in Poplar Township in Orangeburg County, where he still lived in 1870.[30] John's nickname appears to have been "Sank" because that's the name the census taker used to tally him as head of his household in 1880.[31]

Lousea – or Louisa in some records – was born in 1840.[32]

Marvin's family tree is large. Each generation of ancestors was fruitful. His grandfather Samuel M. Gilmore had five brothers and four sisters. Marvin's father had eight siblings. Marvin's mother plus no less than nine of her siblings were alive in 1900. Eight still lived at home with mom Sophronia and dad Ruse, ranging in age from baby Agusta, one year old, to oldest brother Jones, 22.

That year, 1900, Sophronia told the census taker that she had mothered 19 children in all! So two living children had moved out of the nest and were living on their own. Presumably, they were older than Jones.

The family is now very widespread. One of Agusta's (Lee Augusta) siblings, for example, was Jettie Lena O'Neal, who married Charlie White. Most of Marvin's cousins in that branch of the family – the Whites – live in Alabama and Kentucky, says Marvin's cousin Denise White. A few are in Georgia, Massachusetts, and New York.

In rural 19th century America, a large family meant parents had enough offspring to help run a farm and to care for them in their own old age. But life could be cruel. Sophronia explained to the census taker that she had mothered 19 children. But only 10 were still alive in 1900.

Death at an early age was common. In the mid-eighteenth century, more than one-third of all black infants perished, succumbing to a host of afflictions, including malnutrition as well as infectious and parasitic diseases such as a typhoid and cholera, spurred by lack of sanitation and health care. Black infant mortality was 57% greater than for whites.[33] How bad was that? By the year 2000, black infant mortality had declined to 14.1%, far lower than in the mid-1800s but still more than double the rate for white infants.

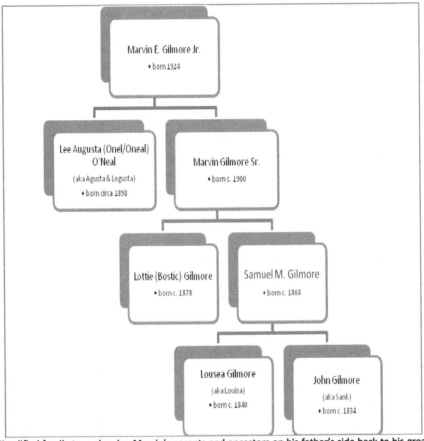

Simplified family tree, showing Marvin's parents and ancestors on his father's side back to his great grandparents.
Source: U.S. census reports; family papers

Prior to 1865 the trail of records needed to trace the family back in time evaporates. Pre-1865 records that name blacks are hard to find because few existed. Slave-owning society simply refused to treat African-Americans as human beings. Earlier in this chapter we pointed out that federal census records, for example, rarely identified slaves by name. The 1790, 1800 and 1810 censuses show only the total number of slaves an owner held. The next three censuses listed slaves by sex and age range.

The 1850 and 1860 censuses added slave schedules. Slaves were still rarely named. Instead, the schedules customarily showed how many slaves of each gender and age the slave holder owned. Some schedules also detailed whether any of slaves were fugitives on the run from their owner, had been released from slavery (known as "manumitted"), and were deaf or mute ("dumb"), blind, insane, or "idiotic."

The refusal to acknowledge a slave's humanity was endemic, extending to nearly all forms of record-keeping. Exceptions were made only for the convenience of slave owners. For instance, one or more particular slaves could be identified by name for the sake of clarity in some business or legal transactions such as the sale or bequest of a black person.

So the fog of slavery, that absence of records, obscures the names of Gilmore family members who came before Sank and Louisa as well as ancestors who preceded Kizzie on Marvin's mother's side. But of course they were there. And they had to have been strong and resourceful to have survived, first their capture and restraint in Africa, then the terrifying loading of transatlantic slave ships, next the infamous Middle Passage, and finally decades or centuries of enslavement in America.

The greatest testimony to the toughness of Marvin's ancestors on both his mother and father's sides is the determination they have passed along to their offspring, to Marvin and his children and his grandchildren, to recount their story so that it does not vanish, and so that its lessons are passed down not only to successive generations of family members but to their friends and acquaintances and even total strangers – to anyone who reads this, their story. It is a story of people who refused to give up, refused to concede defeat. In their son Marvin they shaped a man who so valued freedom and dignity that he could not help but labor to secure it for others.

It is a proud legacy that shines light where others tried hard to cast darkness. It is a proud legacy that stamps its name on its community, despite earlier efforts by others to trample it into dust. It is a proud legacy that wins high honor, all the time conducting itself with selfless humility. It is a proud legacy of community building and giving to others, of taking up sword and shield in the face of the dragon time and again, of risking life and limb to secure life, safety, and liberty for those less able to fight for themselves.

Despite slave owners and hate-mongers at home and abroad who would have erased Marvin's name, Marvin gets to tell his story, and you get to read it.

Unraveling the Mystery

In this chapter we've traced Marvin's family tree back through time. But an irresistible mystery remains: Who owned Marvin's great-great grandmother Kizzie Rowell, her son Jerimiah, and Jerimiah's wife Milly?

Solving that mystery takes detective work. See whom the evidence points to in Appendix A: "Who Owned Marvin's Ancestors?" at the end of this biography.

Also, please turn to Appendix B: "Slavery's Brutal Enforcement" to read stories about the day-to-day lives of slaves and to learn about the drastic measures used by slave-owners to control slaves. Much of the material comes from the same university archive that preserves some of the earliest editions of the memoir, *Twelve Years A Slave,* by Solomon Northup, the free black man who was kidnapped and shanghaied into slavery. More than a century later, that memoir was made into a 1984 Public Broadcasting Service TV movie. Nearly three decades later, it was the basis for a 2013 Academy Award-winning cinematic film.

Passing the Torch

Marvin, the grandson of slaves, has become a philanthropist and an influential voice in local civic chambers where weighty decisions are made, public policy is set, and opportunities to pursue fortune are created or crushed.

None of this was handed to Marvin. He was not born with any silver spoon in his mouth or a trust fund to prop him up. He was handed only new opportunities, greater than those known by his forebears, and he has used those openings not only to better himself but to build a better world for all Americans

Building is a theme in Marvin's life. He has built buildings, businesses, jobs, and opportunities, for himself and for many others. He has built a better life for himself and has done the same for others. He has embraced the builder's hard hat even when it put him into harm's way. He joined the Army in World War II to help build freedom. He found himself fighting to safeguard America and its friends and to free millions of men, women, and children who were enslaved in Europe and Asia and threatened by mad butchers around the globe. In the process, he also found himself fighting to change racist attitudes of some of his own fellow countrymen, who felt African-American were not fit to serve.

He kept fighting those prejudices at home after the war. Decade after decade, he found himself fighting the same battle, again and again. On one occasion in the 1960s, he took the fight into the heart of Dixie. He did not have to do that. He could have stayed safely at home, focusing on difficult challenges in his own work, overseeing the day-to-day needs of his family. Instead, he and basketball star Bill Russell took one of life's most daring detours, veering 1,500 miles out of their way to Jackson, Mississippi, plunging into the smoldering, simmering, violent heart of America's civil rights civil war. (Please read Chapter 10.)

It was the summer of 1964. Congress had been embroiled for months in rhetorical fisticuffs, debating landmark civil rights legislation and voting rights laws. Many cynics in America warned that enactment of such bills would be utterly intolerable to a wide swath of white America. They forecast a backlash of domestic violence not seen since the Civil War itself.

In parts of the South, white supremacists were already using violence to discourage blacks from demanding reform, to scare blacks out of accepting help from potential allies among Southern whites and Northerners whether white or black. It was a year of appalling mayhem, violence, and tension. Homes, churches, and businesses were fire bombed. Beatings, kidnappings, and killings exploded into the nation's headlines and nightly newscasts. Victims included civil-rights advocates and daring idealists who criss-crossed counties as they struggled to help blacks enroll as voters. Some victims were virtual bystanders, blacks who were total innocents, not activists, who happened to be in the wrong place at the wrong time. Some were felled by accident. Some were slain because they had witnessed an assault or murder. Almost all were cut down because of the color of their skin.[34]

When Marvin and Russell journeyed to Jackson, they did so to dare establishments such as restaurants and hotels to defy the recently enacted federal law that prohibited such facilities from barring patrons on the basis of race. Every day, armed men threatened Marvin and Russell to leave the city...or else.

The Boston duo spoke to local residents in a number of local places, including churches and gyms.

"We spoke about freedom, how you stand up for your rights. The fear of God was in their minds. They were afraid. But us just coming down there gave them hope. They could see that black men were free to travel around this country and do what they wanted.

"But we didn't stay in any one place very long," Marvin says. "We had to keep moving. The crackers[35] were after us all of the time. When we went into hotels, we saw white guys parading around with guns. Guys with guns edged up to us in restaurants."

Marvin felt as vulnerable as he ever had on the front lines in Europe, facing open combat.

"Only in America had I allowed the armed enemy to get that close to me and say, 'Nigger, don't move.' I fought World War II to protect this cracker's life, and I almost got killed by him, trying to go into a restaurant to get something to eat. It was very frustrating."

And that was just one of the battles Marvin entered. This life story details others as well. Starting on the day he first heard his grandmother Sophronia's stories about slavery while sitting on a bench in Central Square, Marvin took a torch that was passed to him by his forefathers. Marvin's lifelong fight is a reminder that freedom is something that must be repeatedly won by men who are unafraid to stand up for their rights and the rights of others. And Marvin is telling his story especially to young men and women in the hope that they too will stand up when the time comes and be ready to help protect and perfect the freedoms that we all hold dear.

Chapter 2
Migration to Boston

The tin can emblazoned with the logo of Calumet Baking Powder practically jumps off the edge of Marvin Gilmore's desk. The red, white, and black can's colors are distinctive. So is its design, showing the profile likeness of a Native American wearing a feathered headdress. It spends a lot of time swaddled in a soft chamois cloth bag, locked for protection in a safe. But sometimes Marvin displays it on the desk in his master bedroom, in his home just outside Porter Square in Cambridge.

He does that when he feels the urge to reconnect with his past. It has been decades since the last of the container's original contents, its powder for leavening baked goods, was used up. Its importance now is that it's a sort of time capsule. It's a reminder of where his family came from, how he got to where he is.

Marvin brought the tin can home from Geneva, Ohio. It had belonged to his uncle Isaac Gilmore and Isaac's wife Minnie. Isaac had been a man of simple means. He and Minnie lived in a flimsy wooden shack in an industrial part of the city. Their home was close enough to railroad tracks that everything in the house shook whenever a train rumbled by.

The tin can was Isaac's safe. In it, Isaac – who had little wealth – hid his tiny trove of silver dimes, secreted beneath the floor boards of his home. Under nearby floor boards, Isaac concealed silver dollars. Next to that he concealed hand guns.

After Isaac died in December 1977 at age 80[36], authorities notified his brother, Marvin's father. But Marvin Gilmore Sr. was in his own late seventies, and had little experience dealing with legal matters and property. In contrast, Marvin Jr. was in the prime of life and in the prime of a career that focused on real estate. He also had direct experience in this very situation. He had traveled to Opelika, Alabama, a dozen years earlier on his mother's behalf to bury his uncle Crawford, one of his mother's many siblings, and to settle his worldly affairs.[37] Over the years, Marvin would repeatedly perform the same sad task for several of his father's brothers and a sister. So on this occasion in 1977 Marvin Sr. and his son agreed that Marvin Jr. would go to Ohio to sell Isaac's home and make final arrangements for what little property he had owned.

Marvin was 53 years old. His mother had introduced Marvin to real estate investment. He had embraced his mother's guidance and was carrying on her tradition. Now he was the owner of real estate in Cambridge and Boston. He was in his fourth year as president and chief executive officer of the Community Development Corporation of Boston. He was an obvious choice to be his father's proxy in tending to Isaac and Minnie's estates.

"Most of this had to do with real estate, and Lee Augusta always said the best way to learn how to handle things was to grab them and figure it out first-hand," Marvin said, citing his mother's words of wisdom. "It simply made much more sense for me to travel to Ohio than for my father to do it."

Marvin flew to Cleveland, then drove about 45 miles northeast along Route 90 to Geneva, where he checked into a local motel.

Call from the Sheriff

Isaac and Minnie had been dead many days. County Sheriff Vettel had already entered the home. Marvin was angry to find that the sheriff had exercised his authority under Ohio law to take custody of various pieces of property of someone who dies as Isaac had without leaving behind a will.

"Some neighbors used to bring food sometimes to Isaac and Minnie," Marvin said. "That's how one of them found my uncle and aunt. It was winter. It was very cold. The neighbor found both of their bodies frozen. The neighbor called the sheriff. The coroner could not even say who had died first."

The neighbor also read some of Isaac's paperwork, which was scattered around the house. He was looking for anything that would give him a clue about family members. "He found some letters from me," Marvin said. "He called and asked if I was Eugene. When I said I am, he said, 'Well, your aunt and uncle died. You need to come out here immediately.'"

Marvin, some neighbors, and the sheriff subsequently tried to figure out what had happened. In fact, it was a situation reminiscent of the deaths of Romeo and Juliet. Shakespeare's famously tragic lovers were so devoted to one another that they committed suicide because they could not bear the thought of living without each other.

"The house had heat, but it was turned off," Marvin said. "We finally figured that one of them was ill and about to die. Whichever one was healthy could not stand the idea of going on without the other one. So they got all dressed up in new clothes. Then they turned off the heat, laid down, and froze to death."

The sheriff had already confiscated rings. He was planning to take possession of more valuables – some lamps, a stove, and a shotgun. His intention was to have them appraised and, once the probate court gave its consent, sold. When Marvin said the heirs wanted those items, the sheriff said the heirs could buy them when they went on public sale. He predicted that the heirs would be able to land them for $150. That should be sufficient, he predicted, to reimburse the county for gathering the goods, appraising them, and then selling them![38]

When Marvin arrived in Geneva shortly after Isaac's death, the sheriff was polite but set firm limits.

"I had to go to the sheriff's office to find the house and to get the key," Marvin said. "The sheriff's office gave me a key and said I could go in but that I couldn't take anything."

Because Isaac had died without a will, the sheriff was arranging the disposition of Isaac's property. State rules for doing that trumped the wishes of surviving relatives like Marvin and his father.

"Our lawyer, Stephen Angel, said the sheriff had the right to do what he was doing," Marvin said. "The sheriff, a white guy, had already ransacked the house."

Marvin decided to execute an end run. As he puts it now, "I decided to make it simpler for the sheriff. I decided to help him."

Marvin returned to Isaac's home under cover of a cold, dark, winter, night sky. He was armed only with a flash light. "I was nervous," Marvin said. "And I was scared." Once inside his late uncle's home, he looked around. Nothing worthwhile was in open sight. But surely, Marvin thought, his uncle had left things behind that the sheriff had not found.

What would his mother do?

"My mother tied stuff into stockings and hid them under floor boards in Cambridge," Marvin recalled. "She tied paper money together with stockings and hid the bound wads of cash under the wooden floor. Sometimes she used corsets."

So Marvin went digging indoors. Working at it about an hour, he finally found Isaac's red, white, and black Calumet tin can. He lifted it up from beneath the bedroom floor. It was surprisingly heavy. Prying it open, he found it full of coins. Under another floor board he found silver dollars wrapped in cloth. Some of them dated back to 1878 and 1881. Nearby, behind the boards of a wall Marvin found a shotgun and one pistol.

Uncle Isaac had not lived in a gentrified neighborhood. "If you live in a rural area like that, isolated, you always have guns," Marvin said, explaining his uncle's precautions for self-defense. "It's for protection. You're out there alone mostly."

Marvin had to decide which items to reclaim. "I took out what I could. But I had no way to carry a lot of heavy things. So I had to pick carefully," he said.

A Chilling Lesson

He salvaged that baking powder tin as a keepsake. Some of its hidden treasure of coins turned out to be silver dimes. Marvin sold those at a local bank, fetching $10 each because of their precious metal content. The bank paid a premium for some because of their age and the year they had been minted. Days later, Marvin brought the silver dollars back to Cambridge. He still protects them inside a locked safe. He also eventually returned home with the pistol, which he had hidden in his luggage. The shotgun he gave to the sheriff.

In the days before he returned home, Marvin tackled the sad necessities of his journey. He got the process of settling his uncle's affairs rolling. And he arranged for the burial of Isaac and Minnie.

In addition to the coins and gun, Marvin brought something else back from Ohio. It was not a tangible memento. But it was just as memorable. It was a chilling lesson learned in how cruel society could be. Isaac and Minnie had died in the cold. And they had died poor.

"I learned lessons about dealing with the law, about dealing with government agencies. But it really hit me how poor they were. It showed me some family who had come far from the South and slavery but still did not have much money or anything else of their own. When I was a boy one of the reasons my mother pushed me so hard to learn and improve myself was so I could fend for myself in life and help those around me too."

It's a lesson Marvin had taken to heart for himself, his family, and his community.

Lee Augusta had learned similar lessons decades earlier when she had lived in Alabama. She had seen how the poor suffered, were victimized, and all too often died tragically. Now Marvin had seen that same fate imposed on Isaac and Minnie.

North or South, it didn't matter. The poor were downtrodden. So Lee Augusta pushed herself to find ways to make a better living. She would discover that path in the world of real estate. (See Chapter 4.)

She also pushed Marvin to raise himself as high as possible too. Following her footsteps into investment real estate was one route. She prodded him to be entrepreneurial in all of his work endeavors. She succeeded. Marvin splits his time between running his own properties and helming the Community Development Corporation. Until he recently sold his night club, the Western Front, he also devoted time to overseeing that music venue too. His hard work has meant a better, safer life for his family than his Uncle Isaac and Aunt Minnie knew. And his efforts as the head of the CDC have brought jobs to Boston's black community and raised property values where the CDC has been active.

"No question about it, Mother Lee was the biggest influence on my life," Marvin says quietly. "She taught me the importance of standing on your own two feet. And she showed me ways to earn a living so I could do that, do that for myself, not want for anything, and not owe nobody nothin'."

In his youth and into adulthood, Marvin heard Mother Lee's stories about life in the South, about how cruel life could be, how tough life could be for those unable to fend for themselves. Life in the North had its share of bitter times too. Marvin would see some of those miserable moments for himself. And his trip to Ohio was a reminder of all of that, of the potential suffering that life could impose on people of modest means. As president and chief executive officer of the CDC, Marvin was already in full stride in his career as an advocate for others, helping those least able to help themselves. Being forced into battle to see that Isaac and Minnie were sent to a better place with dignity quietly reinforced his determination to fight that same fight on behalf of the Boston constituents of the CDC.

Great Migration North

Early in the twentieth century, huge numbers of African-Americans began to move out of the South to flee repression and seek better lives in the Northeast, Midwest, and West. This exodus became known as the Great Migration.[39] Between 1915 and 1970, more than six million blacks relocated in this mass movement. Black populations in cities such as New York, Chicago, Detroit, and Cleveland soared by about 40%, according to Pulitzer Prize-winning journalist Isabel Wilkerson.[40]

Lee Augusta was an early pioneer in that South-to-North passage. Escaping from Alabama to step up in life, she moved to Cleveland, Ohio in 1923.[41] The northeast Ohio city sits on the southern shore of Lake Erie. Lee Augusta went to work as a housekeeper[42] at Lakeside Memorial Hospital.

In November of 1923 she and Marvin Sr. married. A Reverend Clark presided. Descriptions of why she and Marvin Sr. moved to Cambridge, Mass., vary slightly. Family tradition says that when Lee Augusta developed goiter, an enlargement of the thyroid gland, she had surgery and her doctor advised her to move east to a wetter climate.

Her autobiographical essay says that she was advised to travel to Boston for medical treatment of her goiter at famed Massachusetts General Hospital.

Marvin says the family-tradition account is the explanation his mother always gave to him. It was in 1929 that Lee Augusta and Marvin Sr., who were now proud parents of their sons Marvin Jr., age five, and four-year-old Lester, relocated to Boston.

Their move required pluck and planning. The great stock market crash that signaled the start of the Great Depression occurred in 1928. So Lee Augusta, having abandoned her job in Cleveland, now had to bounce back from surgery at the same time that she was out of work, lacking a paycheck, when the nation's economy suddenly was running low on fuel. Fortunately, Marvin Sr. worked at the Fanny Farmer candy factory on Sidney Street in Cambridge.[43] He had worked for the same company in Cleveland. The candy maker had allowed him to transfer to Cambridge so Lee Augusta could obtain her medical needs.

Still, Lee Augusta faced a desperate challenge in replacing her lost income. Even in the North, African-Americans found it tough to land jobs as employers discriminated against them more than they did against other ethnic groups, such as those from eastern and southern Europe.[44]

Racial discrimination made African-Americans' jobs jam worse in the Great Depression. Unemployment rates were much higher for blacks than whites. Among men in 13 large cities in 1931, the jobless rate was a staggering 52% for blacks in comparison to a bad 31.7% for white. By the spring of 1933 50% of black workers still couldn't land a job. That was double the rate for the overall work force. This widespread unemployment forced a far higher portion of African-Americans onto the welfare rolls. In 1935 25% of the black population was receiving government relief dollars. Only 15% of whites were.[45]

As the economy contracted, jobs vanished. Meanwhile, more and more people were looking for fewer openings. Countless souls were flooding into the North's shrinking job market. And many employers would not even consider many black job seekers simply because of their skin color. Lee Augusta was forced to swim against an onrushing tsunami of joblessness. She had to battle despair. Yet she never let her dignity diminish. Slowly, she made progress. In a brief passage, her memoir captures her grit:

"While I was recuperating [from goiter surgery], I had to seek employment which was hard to find, since it was [during] the time of the depression. The only income we had was [from] my husband's job at Fanny Farmer[']s, which paid him only twenty dollars a week."

Work Ethic

Lee Augusta kept up her brave spirit despite going through the demoralizing routine of getting benefits checks at her local unemployment office.

"Even though the unemployment office was always crowded, that did not bother me," she wrote. "I walked from house to house, knocking on doors for work, and as I walked, I also prayed because I would rather pray and walk than pray while sitting in an unemployment office.

The first job she found was with a Mrs. Peabody in Cambridge. "I did domestic work two days a week and was paid [t]welve dollars and fifty cents. Sometimes I received a bonus of seventy five cents more."

Mrs. Peabody was Mary Elizabeth Peabody, mother of Endicott "Chub" Peabody, who was born in 1920 and who in 1962 would be elected Governor of the Commonwealth of Massachusetts. Mrs. Peabody was a well-heeled Cantabrigian, who could well afford Lee Augusta's services. She also stood out from her own social class, who tended to be old-money, conservative Republicans. Her son would win election as a liberal Democrat. He would distinguish himself as a champion of ending racial housing discrimination. Mary Elizabeth herself made headlines in 1964 when, at age 72, she was arrested while attempting to integrate a segregated restaurant in St. Augustine, Florida, with a group of white and black companions.

In fact, Mrs. Peabody was the first of a long list of future movers and shakers that Lee Augusta befriended, worked for, or – soon – provided housing to.

Lee Augusta and her family lived in residences far more modest than the spacious dwellings of blue bloods like the Peabodys. But the family kept moving on up. Each time, Lee Augusta found a bigger apartment or a better street. She was determined to improve her family's situation. Again and again she found more comfortable or safer locations. And she was determined to teach her sons how to fend for themselves, how to make sure they would never slide back into the poverty and oppression she and her ancestors had suffered in the past.

Chapter 3

Boyhood in Cambridge

In the winter of 1944, Jim Thornhill was a young G.I., barely old enough to vote but already growing worldly. He knew he was in the middle of a shooting war. He knew he was in harm's way. And on this particular day in Liverpool, England, he knew he was much farther away from home than he wanted to be. Still, this was a moment to try to relax, to try to take his mind off the danger he and his buddies faced. As he stepped forward in a line of other American soldiers, he was about to enter a local dance hall run by the USO – the United Services Organization, the nonprofit group which famously provided a home away from home for American soldiers, sailors, airmen and Marines.

When Thornhill got to the head of the line and looked down at the sign-in sheet, he was surprised to see Marvin Gilmore's name on the same page.

"I knew right away it had to be my old pal Marvin," Thornhill said.[46] "Marvin even wrote, 'Cambridge, Mass.' next to his name. I thought, 'It's Marvin! It's got to be the guy from my old neighborhood. How many Marvin Gilmores from Cambridge were our age, Army age? It has to be him!'"

Thornhill scouted throughout the hall. He actually ran into another old buddy from Cambridge, but he never spotted Marvin. He wouldn't see Marvin again until after the war back in Cambridge.

Thornhill and Marvin had been boyhood pals. The two grew up in Cambridge and lived in the same neighborhood. Now, decades after that chance wartime near-encounter far from their familiar haunts near Harvard Square and Central Square, Thornhill is in his late 80s. Today he is seated at the kitchen table of another longtime friend, Lou Myers. They are in Hyde Park, one of Boston's southernmost neighborhoods. Jim is sipping cold juice from a tall glass. It's been a longtime since he was a boy in Cambridge, but he remembers those carefree days clearly.[47]

Thornhill was born in 1924, the same year as Marvin. Every day after school, Thornhill and the other neighborhood boys congregated in an open grassy field formed by the unfenced backyards of homes along their streets. Homes had very narrow side yards; they nearly touched each other. So the grassy area was the neighborhood's makeshift ball field. The boys would play ball. There wasn't enough room to play real baseball, but the boys played stickball and catch, or they just ran and shouted.

Neighborhood girls would watch, talk, try to converse with the boys. And most every youngster from the neighborhood was there. Attendance could not have been higher if it had been legally mandatory and enforced by the police.

Except for Marvin. Thornhill recalls that Marvin was never there, at least at the outset of each day's recreation. And to this day he remembers exactly why. "Eugene's mother had him practicing music every day," Thornhill said, using the middle name that Marvin was known by as a boy. "She wanted her son to learn how to play music. She wanted both of her boys to know music. So Eugene and his brother" – Lester – "were never in the field with us, because they were practicing."

Marvin remembers the same thing. "My mother bought me a second-hand piano," he said. "It was an upright piano, which we kept in the living room on the first floor. She bought a violin for Lester. And, yes, I practiced every day. She'd sit there and listen. It was after school, from three to four or 4:30, when we had to start home work. Mother said she worked too hard for the money to waste it. There were times I wanted to play ball, but she made sure we practiced and studied."

Marvin's weekly lessons were mostly at Cambridge's prestigious Longy School of Music, on the outskirt of Harvard Square and which is now part of Bard College. One of his teachers was a Ms. Shurcliff. In Boston's South End he studied voice under Elizabeth "Priscilla" Sprague.

Mother Lee let Marvin take two days a week off from piano practice, Monday and Wednesday. But she did not do it to give him time to goof off. "We had to do homework instead," Marvin said.

So like most kids who learn a skill that is not first acquired on a playground, Marvin was forced to sacrifice hang time with his pals. And piano was not the only thing he learned. He learned the virtues of dedication, sacrifice, and discipline. He discovered that attaining a new talent came at a price. It took time. It required giving up other pleasures. On some level, the price tag must have made sense to Marvin. No kid sticks with music lessons forever just because his mother wants him to.

"I liked it. I liked the creativity of it," Marvin said.

And Marvin discovered rewards that made up for at least some of his sacrifices. "We played for the Christian Hour at church. That started at five on Sunday evenings. We met girls at church when we played."

The gatherings were for the church's young members. Marvin and Lester would play two or three songs, then another musician would play several songs, then a third musician would play, and so on for an hour or two.

Music not only became imbedded in Marvin's life, it became a huge part of his world. It would be a source of emotional and intellectual pleasure. It would influence his path for higher education. It would become a means for earning a living, not once but twice in his career. Through music Marvin met wealthy clients who would introduce him to commercial real estate. And music would be a source of satisfaction, fulfillment, and artistic expression that he could pass on to his sons David and Marque, who have carved out distinguished careers as musicians on global stages. Along the way it would even be Marvin's escape hatch out of the carnage and mayhem of front line combat in World War II.

"In every phase of my life, music has played an important role," Marvin said.

Cambridge itself was another big influence in Marvin's life. He is the product of his upbringing in that university city, which faces Boston to the south, across the Charles River.

Neighborhood with Cohesion

Marvin's neighborhood was poor and heavily African-American. The Cambridge schools were decent. Youngsters who applied themselves and had opportunities could advance in life. William Beckett, a retired software engineer for Raytheon who was another boyhood neighbor of Marvin, also recalls their old neighborhood.

By high school, Beckett's family lived at 53 Dana Street. Marvin lived at 51 Dana. Dana Street runs north-northeast from Massachusetts Avenue to Cambridge Street. The Becketts and Gilmores lived near Dana's intersection with Broadway, about a block and a half from the public library, which then as now abuts Cambridge Rindge & Latin School, the city's high school. (When Marvin and Beckett were students, Cambridge Latin and Rindge Technical were separate high schools.)

Beckett is eight years Marvin's junior. From time to time a young Marvin babysat for his younger neighbor.[48]

"I don't want to use the term ghetto," said Beckett. "Now we would politely call them black neighborhoods. But it was not dangerous like some black neighborhoods in Boston, like the South End and Roxbury. We're not even talking about [Boston's] Grove Hall. [Boston's] Franklin Park, which is black now, was still middle class although Jewish families were moving out. There were even tougher parts of Cambridge, like Western Ave. and the 'Port'" – two areas south of Massachusetts Avenue and north of the Charles River.

Beckett had a direct pipeline to an expert on the relative toughness of city neighborhoods. His dad was a Boston police officer, one of the earliest black cops in Boston, he says. And before living on Dana Street, his family had lived in Boston's Dorchester neighborhood.

Beckett also remembers the open field formed by back yards of homes along Dana Street. "We learned quickly you don't play hard ball or softball," Beckett said. "We learned it the hard way by breaking people's windows."

Still, the neighborhood triggers nothing but fond memories for Beckett, who in the 1960s went on to a career writing online diagnostic software for the Apollo 11 lunar lander. "We had a miniature garden of Eden. People had grape vines in their yards. In season, they produced big bad purple grapes. You could smell them everywhere. And the adults didn't care if the kids helped themselves, so we did. We snacked on grapes. And some people had pear trees. When the trees were ripe, we could get pears. It was pretty much a middle- to upper-class black neighborhood."

As a boy, Jim Thornhill lived on Broadway, a short 13 blocks from Dana. Broadway, which is roughly parallel to Massachusetts Avenue, runs southeast, away from Harvard University. Before he was drafted into the Army, he worked in an armaments plant in nearby Watertown, Mass., making 16-inch gun barrels for naval warships. After the war, he worked in housing construction, in an automobile factory, and as a taxicab driver. He remembers Cambridge overall – not just the Dana Street neighborhood – as ethnically mixed.

"There was every nationality there," he said the day he reminisced in Lou Myers' kitchen. "By their names I could tell you their nationality.

There were Lithuanians, Poles like Smerlas, and Greeks like Populos. It was a melting pot. There was a Kelly, a Sullivan.

"Everybody did name calling. But it was a joke, just ribbing. There were so many nationalities that no one group was dominant. The name calling was good natured. We called some kids grease balls, wops. It meant nothing. People got along. We kids didn't really care what anyone was. People learned to help each other regardless of nationality."

The things people shared seemed more important. Limited incomes were something the residents had in common. "People didn't have telephones because they couldn't afford them," Thornhill said. "No one had a TV. People couldn't afford radios!"

Low incomes of course meant people lived without frills. Life was simpler. Life was often tougher. Many of the social safety nets we take for granted today did not exist then. Thornhill, for example, was one of 13 children in his family. Three died very young. Like many people in the neighborhood, he was born at home. "Nobody went to hospitals then," he said. His grandmother was a midwife and a seamstress.

Many families in the neighborhood were immigrants. Many black families had roots in the Caribbean.

And when times were tough, they were tough for everyone. The Great Depression was an equal opportunity demolisher. "I remember everyone in the neighborhood got laid-off during the Depression," Thornhill said.

Families in the neighborhood struggled financially. But few gave up altogether. People tried to keep their heads above water. They tried to get ahead. Beckett said, "I got my Social Security when I was eight years old." That was in 1940. That's how young he was when he looked for his first "real" job.

Despite their different heritages and the inevitable frustrations arising from low incomes, the neighborhood had cohesion. People stuck together. By and large, they were friendly with each other. Adults cooperated. There was a sense of community and of shared values.

"As kids, we knew we could never get away with anything in the neighborhood," Beckett said. "You never knew which grown up was watching from an upper-story window or a doorway. If you got into mischief and were spotted, you'd be reported. They'd tell your parents.

Heck, we didn't even try to get away with stuff.... I never gave my mother any trouble. And I never got into any scrapes or problems with the police."

Marvin also recalls the old neighborhood as a peaceful place.

"Families looked out for themselves," he said. "And neighbors looked out for each others' kids. There were none of the problems that came later. There were no drugs. That came later. It was [an ethnically] mixed neighborhood. And people didn't lock their doors. They didn't have to.

"My mother and father could go to work because neighbors looked out for the kids after school. Parents would watch us in that field playing ball. And we all had to be home by 7 or after the sun went down. If you weren't, you got a whoopin'."

And Marvin may not have spent as much time hanging out as his school mates did, but he was not absent 100% of the time. He got to spend time with the other youngsters on weekends, school vacations, and the occasional Monday and Wednesday afternoon, as well as during the summer. He remembers youngsters dealing with the temptations of adolescence's onset.

"The boys seemed younger than a lot of the girls, who were in young bloom," he said. "But if a girl tried to play with the boys, her parents would beat her."

The boys of course found ways to misbehave even on their own.

"Those were all three-family houses, and we kids could hide beneath the back porches," Marvin said. "The boys under a porch would smoke ground up corn silk in a corn-cob pipe. Or they would roll ground up corn silk in cigarette rolling papers. Real cigarettes were too expensive. They'd try to be young men before they were young men." Marvin himself never smoked, he says.

Crawl spaces under those porches were a world within a world. It was the kids' realm. "If you stood in the field, there were no secrets in that neighborhood," Marvin said. "There were no secrets unless you went under a porch. Then our mothers couldn't see what you were doing."

And religion was a large part of neighborhood life. "Everyone belonged to one church or another," Marvin said. His mother was an avid, active member of Union Baptist Church on Main Street, then the Baptist church in Cambridge's Porter Square. Marvin Gilmore Sr. was a member of the Christian Science church. His parents handled their divergent church affiliations smoothly. It was not a source of any conflict between them, Marvin says.

Marvin's Daily Routine

Marvin recalls his neighborhood as an idyllic, nurturing environment. His daily routine reflected how less-urbanized Cambridge was back then. Now the brainy university city is a hotbed of high-tech innovation and bio-tech research and manufacturing. Burgeoning businesses in those fields employ armies of young professionals, who make the city a fast-paced epicenter of urban chic, a city that moves at warp speed. But in Marvin's boyhood, Cambridge was a slower place. It was less modern in an age when the whole world was less modern. And the economically modest Gilmores certainly did not have access to fancy appliances and safe, efficient, sleek, time-saving utilities. Some of Marvin's daily tasks sound like things he would have done if his family had stayed in rural Alabama or South Carolina.

He woke every morning at 4:30. Starting around age eight, one of his household jobs was to start a fire in the kitchen stove. The flame warmed up the house for everyone, and it prepared the stove for any cooking that was to come. It was a responsibility that Marvin shared with his brother Lester, alternating weeks.

"We started with pea coal, small pellets of coal," Marvin said. "It burns faster. Then we'd put larger, slower burning lumps of coal in, called egg coal. Coal was delivered by horse and buggy. It could be real cold in the morning. The idea was to have a fire ready for when father woke up at 7 a.m."

The boys also stuffed old newspaper and wood into the stove for fuel. And they were responsible for cleaning out the stove. "We took the old ashes outside in the yard and buried them," Marvin said.

In cool-weather seasons, once the Gilmores owned their homes, the boys also stoked and tended coal-burning furnaces in the basement.

Marvin worked outside as fast as possible because he had to wear knickerbockers – known as knickers – which are baggy-kneed trousers that stop just below the knees. Many parents did not let their youngsters wear long trousers until they reached puberty or hit their teenage years. Marvin's socks were tall, covering his knees. But especially in the winter, his knickers exposed him to the crisp outdoor cold despite wearing a coat and bundling up with a scarf. "I was cold, my brother was cold, the house was cold," Marvin said.

Ice was also delivered by horse and buggy. The Gilmores put a block into their zinc-lined, nonelectric refrigerator. "It was on the side of the kitchen opposite the stove," Marvin said. "The zinc kept the cold inside." And of course ice-melt could not make zinc rust. Electric refrigerators with chemical coolants became more widespread in homes of the wealthy during the 1930s. Less affluent families, like the Gilmores, lagged in their ability to afford modern refrigerators for years, sometimes decades.

Mother Lee expected Marvin and Lester to wear knickers at school too. But when the boys got old enough to realize that knickers were a symbol of immaturity, they rebelled.

"I switched into long pants every day on the way to school," Marvin said. "I used to buy the long pants and hide them behind a fence near my house. Then I hid long pants in a bag in bushes. On the way to school I took out the pants and changed into them. I changed back on the way home after school. I had to do this until I was 12 or 13 years old."

By high school, the Gilmores lived on Dana Street at No. 51. Marvin and Lester lived on the first floor. Their room had bunk beds. Their parents were also on the first floor. The family's kitchen was in the basement. Mother Lee's tenants lived in rooms on the upper two floors.

Lee Augusta bought 69 Dana Street while Marvin was in the Army during World War II. When he came back, he was the only member of the family with a bedroom on the third floor. He had a desk, bureau, desk lamp, and a radio. When he turned it on, he listened to jazz. The house was just a block away from Marvin's old high school.

After starting each day with household chores, Marvin had breakfast. "The typical breakfast that mother made was hominy grits and biscuits, things like that. They were Southern meals. Or corn flakes. Sometimes she made pancakes. When we asked for it, she made egg soufflé or scrambled eggs," he said. "Mother was a very good cook. Remember, she was cooking and cleaning for rich families too."

Marvin was on the high school track team. In those day track events were still measured in yards rather than meters. Marvin ran the quarter mile and the half mile, and he says he was an average runner. After practices he went home, practiced piano, and studied.

Dressed for Success

Mother Lee's standing order for Marvin to wear knickers and Marvin's defiance seem quaint now. It was the sort of clever but mild act of adolescent mutiny that we'd expect to find in *The Adventures of Tom Sawyer*. Its harmless disobedience is from a bygone era.

It really says more about Mother Lee's sense of propriety than anything about Marvin. By the 1930s, knickers had been falling out of fashion for about a decade. They were imposed on two young boys, Marvin and Lester, by a mother who couldn't afford the latest hip styles, but who remembered what had symbolized good taste and upward mobility in the not-too-distant past. Mother Lee also dressed to impress. She dressed well because it suited her aesthetics. It was also because she felt if you wanted to be rich, you should look rich.

"Mrs. Gilmore was one stunning woman," recalls Carolyn Yarde Roland, who grew up a few blocks from where the Gilmores lived.[49] She remembers visits to her home by Lee Augusta who, ever the entrepreneur, sold ladies undergarments door-to-door in Cambridge. Roland's grandmother was one of Lee Augusta's regular customers. And they were friends, belonging to a ladies' church group together.

"Mrs. Gilmore came regularly," said Roland, who is a little more than two decades younger than Marvin. "I was always in the dining room when my grandmother would be fitted for corsets. Corsets were strange, and I was fascinated with how Mrs. Gilmore would fasten and tighten them so grandmother would be comfortable.

"I remember that Mrs. Gilmore always dressed the part. She was not matronly. She dressed in business suits.... Mrs. Gilmore always wore herringbone suits and she had tweeds on. She dressed very differently than my grandmother, who was a smart but traditional dresser. My grandparents were island people, from Barbados."

Similarly, Marvin's father was a sharp dresser. "He always dressed well. He wore a chesterfield," said Marvin, referring to a knee-length overcoat with a velvet collar.

But while Marvin Sr. dressed to kill, Mother Lee dressed for success. "My dad had only a third-grade education and didn't appreciate real estate," Marvin said. "He didn't have a head for business. He would have sold Mother's properties for next to nothing."

Mother Lee was not in her Brooks Brothers mode all the time. She owned about a dozen cats, and she fed them in high style. "She loved them!" Marvin said. In relatively casual attire suitable for marketing, she took a streetcar from Cambridge into Boston, then switched to the elevated Orange Line branch of the metropolitan area's subway system for the ride to Dudley Square, a commercial center in the heart of the city's black community. There, at a favorite fish market, she bought fresh fish heads for her beloved felines.

"She usually got them for free," Marvin said. "Stores had to get rid of them because people didn't want to eat them." In other stores right there, Lee Augusta bought her other groceries. In the 1930s and 1940s, before all-in-one supermarkets were common, consumers bought food at specialty stores – fish markets, butcher shops, bakeries, produce markets. Many stores, especially those selling fruits and vegetables, stacked produce outdoors, where most shoppers made their purchases.

These shopping excursions were colorful, boisterous occasions, where a shopper like Lee Augusta might run into friends and neighbors. But Dudley Square was not near Lee Augusta's home, so the trips were not convenient. "She'd buy enough vegetables for a week or two," Marvin said.

"When they shut that Dudley Square fish store down, Mother Lee shopped for fish heads in Haymarket," Marvin said, referring to Boston's popular open-air market near historic Faneuil Hall and Quincy Market. "She'd go alone or with her children. She'd buy fish heads, then boil them for the cats. She usually got haddock."

Accompanying his mother, Marvin was participating in an old-time shopping routine, patronizing a number of individual vendors. There was an additional way in which Mother Lee was emphatically old-fashioned. Marvin Sr. shared her views on this. When it came to making sure their children applied themselves in school, did their chores at home, were obedient, and stayed out of trouble, Marvin's mother and father were on the same page. Both were strict disciplinarians.

For what they considered bad behavior, the Gilmores – Mother Lee far more often than Marvin Sr., Marvin says – would punish Marvin or Lester with a severe spanking with a fearsome length of rawhide rope. The whip-like rope even had a name – "Charlie." Marvin remembers being on the receiving end of Charlie's bite for not doing chores on time and for rough-housing. "If we fooled around and knocked a hole in a wall, knocked things over, or broke stuff, we got it," Marvin said. "And that rawhide left marks on your body."

In Mother Lee's mind, boyhood misbehavior was a short one-way street leading to a life of wrong. "I understand why she beat us," Marvin said. "She tried to make us into something. Make us shape up. She said, 'I want no jailbirds in my house. I'll kill you first, before you can embarrass me.' She promised to put the fear of god into us. She said she would make us somebody."

In a separate interview Marvin said, "Sometimes my mother believed we were bad kids." He added, "Mother did not want us to be lazy. She wanted us to be honest. She wanted us to be truthful. Mother wanted us to speak the truth. She wanted us to become somebody. She never wanted us to steal anything. 'All you have is your word,' she said."

Her harshness was not limited to Marvin and Lester. Occasionally an argument with her husband escalated to the point where she wielded Charlie against Marvin Sr.

"Mother was a powerful, strong, dominant person," Marvin said. "She attended night school at Cambridge High & Latin. She was smart. She got nothing but As for grades. She studied math and business. She was hard working and an excellent learner. She set high standards for herself, and she set high standards for us."

Mother Lee's willingness to use corporal punishment stemmed in large part from her extreme concern for her children's well-being. It was tough enough for African-Americans to achieve a comfortable life with a decent standard of living. She knew that reaching such a plateau took smarts and schooling and hard work and stick-to-itness. And she knew the penalty for falling short could be catastrophic. After all, she was the first generation in her family not born into slavery. And her mother and grandmothers' stories of life under an overseer's whip would always be fresh and sharp in her mind. In her lifetime, even outside the abyss that was slavery, it was all too easy for whites to bully and dominate blacks. She was painfully familiar with life on the lower rungs of society's economic ladder. She wanted to save her boys from sliding down to a life she had fought mightily to escape. She had sacrificed far too much for far too many years to let her boys fritter away the opportunities she had accumulated for them. If it took a little disciplining now and then delivered by the stroke of a strop, well then that was a small price to pay in her mind for being reminded that life is not easy and that you had to play by life's rules to win life's game. Heck, that's what it took just to avoid losing the game.

At times it even seemed that Mother Lee was motivated by bitterness, by regret that her own life had not turned out exactly as she had hoped, even in her modest dreams.

"Lee Augusta was the eighteenth child of her mother Sophronia," Marvin said. "When she had her goiter operation, she had two children, who were boys – me and Lester. She didn't have any more children after that. She wanted to have a little girl. That little bit of disappointment, she took it out on us as boys by whippings and things like that."

Marvin suspects that Lee Augusta was also often frustrated by Marvin Sr.'s lack of interest and acumen in business. "She had to deal with my father," Marvin said.

Charlie hung from a peg next to his parents' bed. "When she got angry at us, Mother could point to it and say, 'See Charlie? If you aren't good, you know what's coming!'" Marvin said. In their defense, he says that his parents' generation and their ancestors were far less talkie-feelie than today's parents. They had to be.

"In the South, kids got beaten before they got talked to," Marvin said. "You knew what you did wrong. Now parents talk first."

On rare occasions "when I had been real bad," he said, he would get a double beating, lashed first by one parent, then the other.

Marvin's lashings were serious. He had a cousin, Rupert O'Neal from Alabama, who lived with the Gilmores two or three years so he could attend the Cambridge schools, which were far better than the schools for blacks back home in rural Alabama. The boys – Rupert, Marvin, and Lester – attended the Roberts School together. Rupert witnessed several of Marvin's whippings at home, and he thought the thrashings were too much. The cousins were close friends. And being a big, powerful youngster – Rupert already stood well over six feet tall – the Alabama boy from time to time took the heat for Marvin. "Sometimes Rupert took beatings for us by claiming he did the things that brought on the beatings – punching a hole in a wall or breaking something or not doing a chore," Marvin said.

Out of love and loyalty, Marvin defends his parents', especially his mother's, methods. Marvin points out that his mother's determination to prevent her boys from turning wayward in fact paid off. "That did happen," he said. "I certainly have not been to jail."

Finally, a family member who had seen blacks whipped and beaten by whites intervened. Marvin's grandmother, Sophronia, demanded that the beatings must stop. It happened during one of her summer stays in Cambridge.

Marvin described the sudden end of the whippings. "One day she said, 'Gussie, you're not going to put your hands on those kids no more. Enough's enough.' Grandmother told my mother not to beat us anymore. Grandmother took Charlie and cut that rope up."

Like an armistice that abruptly interrupts the violence of war, at that moment the beatings stopped.

But also like a victim of war, Marvin had to grapple with the repercussions of the violence for years afterward. Lashing into Marvin's psyche, the rope beatings left emotional scars. In the sixth grade Marvin began to stutter. It took years of speech therapy, including some when he was an adult, to remedy his impediment.

"In the sixth or seventh grade I took a special class with a Miss Shore. That went on for a couple of years. She taught me how to breathe while speaking. How to relax, how to relax while speaking. It gave me my confidence back. I got rid of my fear of speaking. I took lessons for about a year."

As a adult, Marvin took more pointers from his friend and mentor Kivie Kaplan, a longtime president of the National Association for the Advancement of Colored People (NAACP). "I was in the NAACP and doing fundraisers, and I didn't want to have difficulties speaking."

Marvin claims that even to this day he occasionally stutters. But no friends or family interviewed for this book recall witnessing any such thing.

Summers in Cleveland

Marvin's extended family was close-knit. His father still had siblings in Cleveland. They loved one another, and these relatives wanted to know their nephews. The Clevelanders included Sammy (Samuel M. Gilmore Jr.) and Bessie (Bessie M. Ewell). Isaac and his wife Minnie lived in nearby Geneva. Like Marvin Gilmore Sr., all had migrated from South Carolina.

Starting when Marvin Jr. was around age five, as soon as school let out for summer break his father and mother sent him and his brother Lester on a long-distance trip to stay in Cleveland with various relatives. Marvin and Lester made the excursions eight or nine years in a row.

"Every year, the aunts and uncles fought over us," Marvin smiles. "Sometimes we'd stay with Uncle Sammy one or two nights, then Aunt Bessie."

Marvin and Lester traveled by train and bus. The youngsters traveled alone but they never got into trouble enroute or experienced difficulties because a social service organization called Travelers' Aid Bureau watched over them. The Bureau kept track of youngsters traveling without adults and functioned as a sort of mother-hen outfit. "They made sure that we got off at the right destination and watched after us until family picked us up at the station," Marvin said.

Marvin remembers the journey taking about a day and a half in each direction. When Mother Lee learned that trains with sleeping cars staffed by black Pullman porters were available on the Boston-Cleveland route, she switched the boys to rail travel from Greyhound busses. The trip by train was faster of course and it was interrupted by fewer stops.

The boys started each visit by leaving Boston in the morning, arriving in Cleveland the following evening.

"It helped us grow up fast," Marvin

A Changing U.S.

Black History

Pullman Porters

When Marvin and his brother Lester began their visits to relatives in Ohio and Alabama, they traveled by bus. But as soon as their mother could afford to send the boys by train, Lee Augusta did. The trains typically featured Pullman Cars. Those were seating cars that were converted into sleeping quarters at night. The porters who performed the twice daily makeover were African-Americans, mostly men.

Despite low pay and difficult work conditions, those porters helped create America's black middle class.[i] They also played a key role in the American civil rights movement.

The seeds of that legacy were planted in

said. "Mother Lee trained us to take care of ourselves."

Mother Lee gave the boys money for living expenses, maybe $15 or $20. Their aunt and uncle took the money when the boys arrived. "They gambled with it. They bought 'policy' numbers," Marvin said, using a nickname for the numbers racket, the illegal lottery that was common in low-income urban neighborhoods and which was even more common before state lotteries became so widespread. "They never won."

Their relatives lived in a neighborhood of brick tenements. "I still remember the alleys and the gambling out in the open," he said.

Marvin and Lester quickly learned to conceal as much of their travel booty as possible before their aunt and uncle could confiscate any. In their earliest visits, the boys put their cash into a bedroom bureau drawer. When their aunt and uncle discovered this hidden treasure and helped themselves to some, the boys would demand it back. "We wanted to protect our money so we could get candy and ice cream," Marvin said.

At the start of later visits, Mother Lee sent the boys off with orders to bring home a smoked ham on their return. Marvin was too young to know whether Cleveland's African-Americans had brought recipes from the Deep South for the delicious delicacy, or whether this culinary treat was common in Cleveland due to its proximity to slaughterhouses

1867, when Chicago industrialist George Pullman invented the railroad sleeping car.[ii] Part of his brainstorm was to rent the rolling stock – railroad cars – as well as staff on board to railroad companies.[iii] But the appeal of sleeping cars was not just in making long-haul journeys easier by allowing passengers to sleep at night.

George Pullman also was creating a fantasy for travelers. Most could not afford servants at home. But on Pullman Cars, they could enjoy a temporary, short-term version of that life of ease. Pullman porters, wearing friendly smiles and neatly pressed uniforms, were on hand to provide a wide range of services in simulated luxury, all delivered politely and graciously.[iv]

Porters made beds, shined shoes, brushed lint and dirt from passengers' coats, wiped steam-engine cinders and meat processers in Chicago and hog farms in the South and Midwest. But his mother's eagerness for the delectable dish was something that only had to be explained once. Marvin got it.

Each visit at any age, Marvin and Lester immersed themselves in their relatives' routines. They even made pocket money by selling glass to a local recycling company. "This went on way back in the 1930s and '40s," Marvin said. "We separated the colors. We could sell clear glass for $4 a bushel and colors for $2 to $3. We'd collect a bushel or two each week and sell it once a week."

The rest of the time, the boys played with other kids and enjoyed their relatives' companionship.

Visiting Family in Alabama

For the same reasons of family bonding, the boys also visited their grandmother Sophronia, Aunt Addie, and Uncles Crawford and Edmund in Alabama a few times. Crawford lived in Opelika, about 17 and a half miles from Sophronia and Addie in Notasulga. Crawford had moved there from Florida, where he had a farm. Every December around the holidays he had sent the Gilmores gift packages. The boxes were filled with produce he grew. He sent pecans, sugar cane, raw peanuts, tobacco leaves, and cotton.

Why did he send cotton? "It was his way of showing us what he produced on his farm," Marvin said. "One year he sent

from handrails, served ice water, lugged luggage, and answered passengers' calls at any hour of the day.[v] Each porter was a butler, maid, and hotel concierge rolled into one.

And they did this for paltry pay, especially in the early decades of the job. "Pullman demanded 400 hours a month or 11,000 miles — sometimes as much as 20 hours at a stretch – and paid ridiculously low wages (in 1926, an average of $810 per year…)," reported Public Broadcasting System station WTTW. Those $810 are worth $10,300 today.[vi]

The wages were not enough to live on, but porters got by thanks to tips.[vii] Still, conditions were harsh. The company demanded that porters pay for their own meals, supply their own uniforms, even buy their own shoe polish to shine passengers' footwear.

a sugar cured ham."

The Gilmores enjoyed the gifts, including the tobacco. "Sophronia chewed tobacco," Marvin said. "She had a spittoon and never missed. The odor of tobacco was very strong. She kept a spittoon next to the front door."

Addie, Crawford, and Edmund were three of Lee Augusta's siblings. They were among Sophronia and Reese O'Neal's 18 children.

Edmund's life illustrated two of Marvin's own key traits –his devotion to learning, whether it was in school or at the piano, and his energetic ambition. Edmund's drive for education came from seeing the handicap that a lack of education was for his father Reese.

In a 23-page memoir, Edmund wrote, "My mother and father both were born slaves and had little opportunity for an education. When [I was] a small child I used to go about with my father a great deal, and was greatly grieved because he could not write his name. I would ask him questions about this and he tried to explain to me, as best he could, that he did not have an opportunity for an education. I was too young to understand it all then, but when my struggle began for an education, it was quite plain to me."[50]

No doubt Lee Augusta saw the same difficulties stemming from her father's lack of education, and that was why she pushed Marvin to do well in school.

Edmund came to recognize that lack of education sharply limited Reese's

The company only permitted porters to take short naps on couches in a smoking car. And porters could be fired for speaking up about work conditions.[viii]

Also, porters were often subjected to the added indignity of being addressed as "George," apparently after the company's founder George Pullman, regardless of their real names.[vix]

To staff his sleeping cars with men who knew how to wait on people and do it with a smile, all the while accepting low pay, Pullman knew just where to turn: to the ranks of recently freed slaves.[x] Alternative job opportunities were still scarce for blacks by the 1920s. In fact, compared to work as a sharecropper or housekeeper, a job as a Pullman porter was prestigious in the black community.[xi] The job provided steady work.

options for earning a living. It manacled him to the land. And in that time and that part of Alabama, it condemned Reese to scratching out a living as a sharecropper. He didn't own his own farm. He had to pay a portion of his crop to the white farm owner. When the amount he owed the white farmer was based on some sliding-scale, Reese would still owe a hefty levy even after a poor harvest.

The arrangement was painfully close to a life sentence of poverty.

"Although my father was not successful at farming and could not provide us with sufficient clothing, my mother usually found some way out of the situation," Edmund wrote in his memoir.

Edmund wanted to escape from the cycle. To do that, he had to earn an education. But to pay for advanced schooling, he had to save money from what he earned on the farm, where it was hard enough to make a living, let alone earn extra to set aside as savings. It was a vicious circle, and he fought hard to break out.

The energy he displayed and refusal to give up are reminiscent of Marvin's own drive to succeed.

Despite his distaste for farming, Edmund managed the family farm for his mother, four sisters, and a brother. "I had to take charge of the farm because my father could not get along with the white man for whom we were working," Edmund wrote. In fact, Reese O'Neal abandoned his family. Edmund wrote,

Porters dressed well. And porters got to travel around the United States. And so the Pullman Company became the largest single employer of African-Americans in the 1920s.[xii] At its peak, the Pullman Company employed 20,000.[xiii]

Still, the workers grew increasingly disenchanted with their long hours, low pay, and peril for protesting their conditions. In 1925 the porters formed a union called the Brotherhood of Sleeping Car Porters (BSCP). It took another 12 years for the union to reach its first contract with the company.[xiv] This was the first successful black labor union in the United States.[xv] Along the way to signing its 1937 contract with Pullman Company, the BSCP in 1935 became the first African-American union to receive a charter from the American Federation of Labor, the labor umbrella group that had

"After my father left we continued to live with this [white] man because we were tired of moving to a new home every year. Two of my sisters were young women and I did not want to see them hauled about."

Besides, Edmund added, he was a better plough hand than his dad.

The family found it impossible to get ahead. In 1907, Edmund (who was born Feb. 28, 1891[51]) hoped to enter Tuskegee Institute.[52] He was intent on educating himself and pursuing a career in education. But he came down with typhoid fever in May. The doctor's bill was huge, and the farm's crop was disappointing. Unable to afford the doctor's bill, he had to negotiate a settlement. His school plans were "blasted," he wrote. The year's net income from farming: 81 cents.

Edmund continued to take advantage of free courses in agriculture offered by Tuskegee. Eventually, after an absence of two years, his father rejoined the family. The following spring Edmund cultivated a cotton patch, and he used income from the successful harvest to pay for more classes. He squeezed every available penny out of the farm. He even "borrowed" several baskets full of cotton from his father's cotton patch.

"The next year father decided to move again," Edmund wrote. "I would not agree to go with him this time until he had promised to let me make my own arrangements with the new landlord."

Reese agreed, and Edmund cut his

traditionally excluded blacks from its membership.[xvi]

The porters' union was led by A. Philip Randolph and Milton Webster. PBS station WTTW's report noted that the union's triumph in dealing with the Pullman Company taught its many members invaluable lessons about perseverance and sticking together, which would soon be applied to the broader civil rights movement. The successful contract campaign also knocked down the racism stereotype of blacks as incapable of organizing.[xvii] And the union provided leadership and money to that struggle, the *New York Times* pointed out.

One instance occurred during World War II. "Union leader Randolph pressured President Franklin Roosevelt into issuing Executive Order 8802 in 1941," the National Museum of own deal to become a sharecropper for the white farm owner. When Edmund's crop came in abundantly, Reese also tried to charge him a share – rent on the patch that Edmund worked. Reese's view was that he had not given the patch to Edmund; he had leased it to him. Edmund saw the situation differently. Father and son argued, and when Sophronia took Edmund's side he won.

For the next few years Edmund labored to earn a living. He never could set aside enough money to afford full-time tuition at Tuskegee, so he paid for less expensive classes – including night courses – at other schools in the area. When he fell ill, he was hospitalized. His doctor, Dr. John A. Kenney, allowed him to pay his bill after returning to work. Eventually, incredibly, he studied at the business school of Boston University and at Harvard.

His first teaching job paid a salary of $30 a month. Edmund went on to become a leading educator and minister in Selma, Alabama, and Albany, New York. (Selma is about 77 miles west of Notasulga.)

Also in his memoir Edmund explains that he was named for an uncle, Edmond Rowell, who had crippling rheumatism. He got his middle name, Judson, when he bought a mail order "talking machine" for 15 cents. The device probably was an imitation Victrola, an early record player, but only a nonworking toy version. He described it as a toy tin box with a little speaker horn. It was delivered to "Judson

American History observed.[xviii] "It barred discrimination in defense industries and created the Fair Employment Practices Committee."

E.D. Nixon, a Pullman porter and leader of a local chapter of the Brotherhood of Sleeping Car Porters, helped plan the 1955-1956 Montgomery, Alabama, bus boycott, one of the key battles in the post-World War II civil rights campaign.[xix] And it was Nixon who selected Rosa Parks to refuse to give up her seat on a public bus to a white passenger in defiance of local segregationist rules – a refusal that sparked protest marches, violent racial confrontations, blacks boycotting the bus system, and finally integration of the public busses. Press coverage of the boycott helped galvanize political support for passage about a decade later of the Civil Rights Act of

O'Neal," so he used that as his middle name after that. Crawford revealed his sense of humor in describing why he thought the toy was worth the price even though it did not produce sound. "Through the incident,...I got a name which, I think, is worth the fifteen cents that I borrowed."

Over the years there was occasional friction between Lee Augusta and Edmund. "There was jealousy between them," Marvin said. "Mother was Baptist. Uncle Edmund was Methodist. Mother went along the path of investment and owning property. Uncle focused on spiritual goals and the importance of education for blacks. And he was her older brother. It was a jealousy to see who was going to get ahead of the other. My uncle tried to influence me to be like him."

An Uncle "Cap" was another Alabama relative, another one of Sophronia and Reese's children. "Cap" was Marvin's cousin Rupert's father. "Cap" brought Rupert to Cambridge for one of his stays, but otherwise Marvin rarely saw him and recalls little about him – except the nickname he wore as proudly as the scally cap he liked to wear. Sure enough, he's wearing just such a flat-top, snap-brim cap in an old photograph. "Cap" passed away when Marvin was relatively young.

So Edmund, Sophronia, Addie, Crawford and possibly "Cap" were the relatives that Marvin visited in Alabama. But reinforcing family ties was not the only reason Mother Lee sent the brothers South. She also wanted Marvin and Lester

1964 and the Voting Rights Act of 1965.[xx]

The strategy behind selecting Parks was to choose a figure whose plight would illustrate and humanize the injustice that was the crux of bus boycott.[xxi] "Because Nixon was often out of town attending to his duties as a porter, he enlisted the help of a young black minister new to Montgomery to run the boycott in his absence: the Rev. Martin Luther King Jr."[xxii]

Less than a decade later, Randolph also helped plan the watershed 1963 civil rights march on Washington,[xxiii] in which Martin Luther King, Jr. delivered his stirring "I Have A Dream" speech.

Sidebar notes
[i] Steve Inskeep, *Morning*

to see the hard life that would have been theirs if their parents had not clawed their ways North, up out of the South. She wanted the boys to sample life in the South. She wanted them to come close enough to the deadly flame of Southern bigotry that they could learn it was something to be avoided. She hoped they could do that without making a misstep that would get them burned. She wanted her boys to experience something that would motivate them to work hard and earn better livings than any of their Southern relatives. She wanted them to know what poverty felt like and to understand how nearby it was.

She also wanted the boys to learn lessons about self-sufficiency. And she wanted them to learn the humility that comes from seeing nature and life and death in a rural setting.

Much about the trips to Alabama resembled the boys' excursions to Cleveland. But key details changed. Chiefly, the Gilmores were doing better financially, thanks in large part to Mother Lee's rental housing business. And Marvin and Lester were older. Marvin recalls visiting Alabama after the war. So now, instead of modest pocket change, Mother Lee gave the boys much more traveling money.

"Every time I went my mother put $1,000 in my hand," Marvin said. "When I visited, it was for a week or two. Mother Lee sent me so I'd know what the South was like, what she went through, so I'd

Edition, "Pullman Porters Helped Build Black Middle Class," http://www.npr.org/templates /story/story.php?storyID=1038 80184, accessed Jan. 21, 2013.
[ii] *Chicago Stories,* "Pullman Porters: from Servitude to Civil Rights": http://www.wttw.com/main.ta f?p=1,7,1,1,41, accessed Jan. 21, 2013.
[iii] *Chicago Stories,* "Pullman Porters: from Servitude to Civil Rights": http://www.wttw.com/main.ta f?p=1,7,1,1,41, accessed Jan. 21, 2013.
[iv] "Facing Freedom," http://facingfreedom.org/work ers-rights/pullman-porters, accessed Jan. 21, 2013.
[v] *America on the Move,* "Lives on the Railroad": http://amhistory.si.edu/onthe move/exhibition/exhibition_9 6.html, accessed Jan. 21, 2013.
[vi] From the money-value calculator at: http://www.measuringworth.c om/uscompare/relativevalue.p hp, accessed Jan. 21, 2013.
[vii] *Chicago Stories,* "Pullman Porters: from Servitude to Civil Rights": http://www.wttw.com/main.ta f?p=1,7,1,1,41, accessed Jan. 21, 2013.
[viii] "Facing Freedom," http://facingfreedom.org/work ers-rights/pullman-porters, accessed Jan. 21, 2013.

never have to go through that. That's why she escaped. She followed my uncle Edmund, to have a better life. That's why so many of my uncles and aunts left the South, to escape the life they lived as slaves, the life their parents had lived."

Sophronia's home was simple. Marvin recalls, "There was no bathroom. She had an outhouse. Her house had a kitchen with a wood-burning stove, a couple of bedrooms. People lived right next to each other. Just wooden boards separated one room from another. You could hear everything in the next room. The stove provided the only heat, and it was used for cooking. She used kerosene lamps for light. There was no electricity.

"My aunt Addie, her daughter, Uncle Crawford, and grandma Sophronia lived there. There was no such thing as privacy. If someone wanted a bath, you had to heat water with buckets on the stove. There was a round tub that you sat in to bathe. It was very primitive living.

"Even in the 1940s parts of the South were still like that. I had a girlfriend when I was in the Army in World War II. Her parents' house was like my relatives' house.

"At my relatives' house, we'd cut the head off a chicken so we could have fried chicken for dinner. The chicken would still run around after its head was cut off! So I was raised as a Southerner, at least some, even though we lived up North. We still had Southern ways of tending goats, killing our own chickens, milking cows. Mother

[ix] Jennifer Lee, "The Last Pullman Porters Are Sought for a Tribute," *New York Times*, April 3, 2009: http://www.nytimes.com/2009/04/04/us/04porters.html?_r=0&adxnnl=1&pagewanted=print&adxnnlx=1358795048-or2uygg0g+5IpIrZtYFEuQ, accessed Jan. 21, 2013.

[x] *Chicago Stories*, "Pullman Porters: from Servitude to accessed Jan. 21, 2013.

[xi] "Facing Freedom," http://facingfreedom.org/workers-rights/pullman-porters, accessed Jan. 21, 2013.

[xii] *America on the Move*, "Lives on the Railroad": http://amhistory.si.edu/onthemove/exhibition/exhibition_9_6.html, accessed Jan. 21, 2013.

[xiii] Jennifer Lee, "The Last Pullman Porters Are Sought for a Tribute," *New York Times*, April 3, 2009: http://www.nytimes.com/2009/04/04/us/04porters.html?_r=0&adxnnl=1&pagewanted=print&adxnnlx=1358795048-or2uygg0g+5IpIrZtYFEuQ, accessed Jan. 21, 2013.

[xiv] *Chicago Stories*, "Pullman Porters: from Servitude to Civil Rights": http://www.wttw.com/main.taf?p=1,7,1,1,41, accessed Jan. 21, 2013.

[xv] Jennifer Lee, "The Last Pullman Porters Are Sought for a Tribute," *New York Times*, April 3, 2009:

didn't want us to be city boys. She wanted us to respect and understand what it was like to come out from the country."

Marvin paused in his description, then added, "My dad didn't. But my mother did."

Did he learn the lessons that his mother intended? "Yes," he said. "It's a frame of mind. She always said she didn't want me to become too big for my britches."

Marvin's Cambridge

No question about it, many people in Marvin's neighborhood were poor. Others struggled to maintain a handhold on the lower rungs of middle-income existence. But the neighborhood did not pose insurmountable barriers to its youths.

Unlike all too many communities of color in America, Marvin's swatch of Cambridge was not quicksand, swallowing young people, exerting a death grip on them.

On the contrary, a sense of community prevailed. Adults kept a critical eye on youngsters outdoors. Schools functioned. Streets were safe. Back alleys were playgrounds, not shooting galleries. Boys and girls could aspire to improve their lots in life. William Beckett could rise up to distinguish himself in a notable career in America's space program, playing a key role in landing a man on the moon. Jim Thornhill could live a long, industrious life as a patriot and productive citizen. Marvin Gilmore could also rise, cultivate his skills

http://www.nytimes.com/2009/04/04/us/04porters.html?_r=0&adxnnl=1&pagewanted=print&adxnnlx=1358795048-or2uygg0g+5IplrZtYFEuQ, accessed Jan. 21, 2013.

[xvi] "Facing Freedom," http://facingfreedom.org/workers-rights/pullman-porters, accessed Jan. 21, 2013. Richard Wormser, "Brotherhood of Sleeping Car Porters," *The Rise and Fall of Jim Crow*, http://www.pbs.org/wnet/jimcrow/print/p_stories_org_brother.html, accessed Jan. 21, 2013.

[xvii] "Facing Freedom," http://facingfreedom.org/workers-rights/pullman-porters, accessed Jan. 21, 2013. Richard Wormser, "Brotherhood of Sleeping Car Porters," *The Rise and Fall of Jim Crow*, http://www.pbs.org/wnet/jimcrow/print/p_stories_org_brother.html, accessed Jan. 21, 2013.

[xviii] *America on the Move*, "Lives on the Railroad": http://amhistory.si.edu/onthemove/exhibition/exhibition_9_6.html, accessed Jan. 21, 2013.

[xix] Steve Inskeep, *Morning Edition*, "Pullman Porters Helped Build Black Middle Class," http://www.npr.org/templates/story/story.php?storyID=103880184, accessed Jan. 21, 2013.

[xx] Nell Irvin Painter, "Mother of the Movement," *New York*

as a musical artist, serve his nation with distinction in the military, carve out successful and diverse careers for himself, bring jobs to Boston's impoverished minority precincts, fight for civil rights, raise a family, mentor young musicians, and act on his sense of responsibility with philanthropic generosity.

Marvin's is a classic American bootstrap story. Growing up, his advantages consisted far, far more of parental guidance than material goods. And at every stage, he had to fight forces of racial prejudice, which avidly sought to suppress him.

The more he fought for himself, the more battles he won on behalf of others.

Times, March 29, 2013, review of biography by Jeanne Theoharis, http://www.nytimes.com/2013/03/31/books/review/the-rebellious-life-of-mrs-rosa-parks-by-jeanne-theoharis.html?pagewanted=1&ref=rosaparks&adxnnlx=1367762562-JbJrDSUiw49bSPvBTrtpcw&_r=0, accessed May 5, 2013. Painter describes Theoharis' account of how on Dec. 1, 1955, Rosa Parks left her job as a seamstress at the Montgomery Fair department store and took a seat in the middle of a public bus. A Jim Crow policy required blacks (no

matter what age or gender they were) to give up their seats to any white person they were) to give up their seats to any white person who needed one. On Parks' bus that day, when seats in the white section filled up the driver ordered blacks to surrender their seats. Parks refused. The driver called the police, and Parks was arrested. She knew beforehand that Claudette Colvin, another black women, had been manhandled by the police after being arrested, Theoharis wrote, and others had been beaten or shot. Parks eventually suffered hate calls, death threats, and loss of her job for her resistance. President Bill Clinton awarded her a Medal of Freedom in 1996.

[xxi] Jennifer Lee, "The Last Pullman Porters Are Sought for a Tribute," *New York Times,* April 3, 2009: http://www.nytimes.com/2009/04/04/us/04porters.html?_r=0&adxnnl=1&pagewanted=print&adxnnlx=1358795048-or2uygg0g+5IplrZtYFEuQ, accessed Jan. 21, 2013.

[xxii] Steve Inskeep, *Morning Edition,* "Pullman Porters Helped Build Black Middle Class," http://www.npr.org/templates/story/story.php?storyID=103880184, accessed Jan. 21, 2013.

[xxiii] *America on the Move,* "Lives on the Railroad": http://amhistory.si.edu/onthemove/exhibition/exhibition_9_6.html, accessed Jan. 21, 2013.

Chapter 4
Lee Augusta Discovers Real Estate

L ike the Israelites wandering the desert in search of their true home, the Gilmores kept on the move in Cambridge. Lee Augusta was the family Moses.

Each time the family moved, it was because Lee Augusta had found a larger apartment or a safer street.

The Gilmores lived in a series of apartments, first on Pleasant Street, south of Central Square and north of the Charles River. Next, they moved to 13 Pine Street, which was north of Central Square and Massachusetts Avenue. That was followed by 25 Market Street, and 261 Columbia Street after that.

Marvin attended the Boardman School while he lived on Pleasant and Pine streets. When the Boardman burned down, he switched to the Roberts School, which he attended through moves to Market and Columbia streets.

He attended Longfellow School in the sixth, seventh, and eighth grades. His family lived on Columbia, and then Dana Street when he entered high school in 1939.

Through all of the relocations, Lee Augusta and her family lived in residences far more modest than the grand homes of rich people like Mary Elizabeth Peabody – mother of a future governor of the Commonwealth of Massachusetts – who hired her to clean, cook, and tend house.

Property had never been kind to Lee Augusta and her ancestors. Her mother Sophronia and many uncles and aunts had shared first-person stories about the horrors of slavery and of being tied to a piece of land, forced to wrestle with the land to scrape out a living. Family member lives in Alabama had been little better after slavery ended, but segregation and oppression still reigned.

Lee Augusta's family had long been servants to land. Her move to Cleveland had been a first step toward hard-won freedom. She won even greater liberation in Cambridge, when she pulled off a wrestler's reversal.

Flipping her relationship with land, she learned how to make property work for her instead of the other way around.

She made this new opportunity possible with her hard work and disciplined savings. But the opportunity was a total surprise. She had no way to see it coming. In fact, the roots of this upturn in the family's prospects arose from a frightening family crisis.

A New Beginning

The Gilmores were living on Columbia Street when both Lee Augusta and Marvin Sr. fell ill. Marvin does not know what was ailing his father. "He was so secretive," Marvin said. His recollection is that his mother was battling lingering aftereffects of her throat surgery. His parents were admitted to Cambridge's Prospect Hospital, which was run by a black physician, Dr. Burnett. The Gilmores had just enough advance warning to arrange for their boys to stay at a rooming house at 51 Dana Street, which was owned and run by Mrs. Mabel Brown.

"It was a three-story building," Marvin recalled. "We slept in bunk beds. Lester and I woke up every day at 6:30 or 7 o'clock. Mrs. Brown made cereal for breakfast. School provided lunch. Later, Mrs. Brown made dinner. It was good but nothing special. Mrs. Brown was a poor lady. I know it cost $9 a week for the two of us. Mrs. Brown didn't charge much more when Mom and Dad moved in."

When Marvin's parents got out of the hospital, they too moved in to Mrs. Brown's rooming house. Marvin remembers that his mother liked the Dana Street neighborhood more than Columbia Street.

Despite her new tenants, Mrs. Brown was on shaky ground financially. It was the 1930s. The Depression was crushing people's ability to pay for anything, including room and board. And Mrs. Brown was falling behind in making mortgage payments to East Cambridge Savings Bank. All too soon she found herself facing foreclosure.

The Gilmores wrestled with their own nightmares. As the Depression worsened, people grew increasingly worried about losing their jobs. Investors raised cash that they desperately needed to pay bills by selling stocks, which forced down the value of shares. That reduced investors' wealth and made them edgy. As more bills came due, they'd be quicker to sell additional stock. It created a vicious cycle.

Consumers tightened their belts. That decline in spending forced businesses to lay off workers. Work hours shrank. Incomes fell. Many people such as business owners and home buyers who had borrowed from banks had trouble making their loan repayments, and defaults rose. Banks failed. Depositors worried that more banks would fail. There was no insurance on bank deposits, and newspaper headlines screaming about each bank failure reminded citizens that the federal government – which today has many powers it can use to prevent bank panics – had few such safeguards in the late 1920s and early 1930s, and it was not using the regulatory muscle it did possess.[53]

Knowing that the money in their accounts was not insured, depositors around the U.S. panicked more and more often. Even if a bank was technically sound, it could be wiped out by jittery depositors demanding to withdraw their funds. That's because banks kept only a fraction of their total cumulative deposits on hand in actual cash.

And that very thing happened time and again all around the nation. The mere fear that a bank might not be able to make good on its deposits often became a self-fulfilling disaster. Empty rumors that a bank was in trouble or about to suffer a run could spark a run.

About 650 banks failed in 1929.[54] That number jumped to more than 1,300 in 1930. By the end of the Great Depression, a staggering 9,000 banks out of the nation's total of 25,000 had run out of money and collapsed. Nearly half of those failures occurred in 1933 alone.[55]

And in the earliest part of the panic it happened to a bank in Cambridge where Lee Augusta had kept her meager savings.

"Savings Holocaust"

"I remember standing in line with my mother," Marvin said. "We were outside. It was in Central Square. The line snaked out of the bank and down the sidewalk. It was cold. It must have been winter. And we had to just stand there. The line didn't move. There were lots of people in line, all waiting to get their money out of the bank. Everyone was scared and nervous."

Finally, after what seemed like an endless wait, Lee Augusta and Marvin were at the head of the line. When Lee Augusta asked to withdraw her balance, she was told the bank had practically zero cash left.

"It was a savings holocaust," Marvin said. "My mother got a few dollars from her account. The bank took the rest. She got only pennies on the dollar. She lost several thousand dollars. The bank wasn't kind to us at all. In those days there was no FDIC protection. My mother cried. Her hard earned savings went out the door. I'll never forget it. And she never let me forget it."

The disaster reinforced Lee Augusta's instincts to be self-sufficient. Always, she only bought what she absolutely needed. She only bought what she could afford. She rarely piled debt on her own back. The less overhead she was responsible for, the easier it was to make ends meet. And Mother Lee relentlessly hammered Marvin with lessons about the absolutely essential nature of education, self-sufficiency, and frugality.

"She pushed me hard to get educated and be able to support myself," Marvin said. "Even now, with the housing market so bad and all of these foreclosures, I see people buy things they can't afford. They don't realize they never owned it from the beginning. The bank owned it. When people live above their means, they lose things that are valuable, like their homes or a car. I still avoid doing that. If I don't have the money for something, I don't buy it."

Still, after losing her savings life went on. Lee Augusta tirelessly sought employment and income. She was as hard-working as before. And she kept stitching together a quilt of jobs, sometimes as a housekeeper and cook and occasionally as a clerk, usually in one or another retail store in or near Cambridge's Harvard Square.

Marvin recalls walking to the Square along Massachusetts Avenue, Cambridge's main thoroughfare. In the winter especially, a hike to rendezvous with his mother could be a boyhood adventure.

"Sometimes I would walk to the store," Marvin said. "In the winter, I walked through snow. I was young, so the snow could seem like it was 10 feet deep. In those days, Mass. Ave. was all cobblestones and people still rode horses and buggies. The trolley" – today long since replaced by a subway – "rode down the middle of the road on the surface."

Like Massachusetts Avenue in mid-winter, the economy was in a deep freeze. The Great Depression blew its chill wind with stubborn persistence. Yet incredibly Lee Augusta managed to squirrel away pennies, nickels, and dimes from her own meager income and from what Marvin Sr. gave her for groceries, rent, and other family expenses. Keeping the family on a careful budget, she accumulated surplus cash. She opened an account at another bank, East Cambridge Savings Bank. In those hardest of hard times, she managed to visit regularly to make deposits.

"The bank began to like her," Marvin said. "She had a style and she made friends. As properties became available, they told her about them. Finally, when the bank foreclosed on 51 Dana Street in the early 1930s, the bank president knew she lived there. He asked my mother if she wanted to buy the house. Mother said okay. She bought 51 Dana for $2,000 or $3,000."

The bank officer was Fred B. Wheeler. Marvin, who was then still a young boy, slightly misinterpreted Wheeler's power to grant a loan to Lee Augusta. Wheeler was on the bank's board of investment but was not the bank's president. Gustavus Goepper held the title of president. Still, Wheeler was a savvy loan officer. He was also president of another nearby bank in Cambridge, Lechmere National.[56] He knew Cambridge. He knew his customers. He knew how valuable a trustworthy depositor like Lee Augusta was. Without a doubt, he needed no reminder of the importance of a customer like her in the midst of the depression.

So, in 1935 – three years after moving to Dana Street – Lee Augusta bought No. 51 from Mrs. Brown. Marvin's mother described in her memoir how she put the house to work for her right away. "At that time many of the houses in Cambridge were neglected and in need of repairs," she wrote. "The house we purchased had twenty two rooms [including nine bedrooms] and one bathroom. We converted it into a three family house for the purpose of obtaining income [from] two of the units."

Lee Augusta was off and running. Over time she added more properties to her portfolio. And she would try to use her purchases and management decisions into entrepreneurial lessons for her boys. No. 51 Dana Street was where it began.

Years later, after Marvin left the Army following World War II, he used $3,000 from his G.I. Bill money to help buy

---

A Changing U.S.

Black History

Higher Education for Blacks

In 1941 the U.S. Naval Academy barred a black player on Harvard's lacrosse team from a game between the colleges.[i] Harvard

---

the house from his mother for $5,000. "I still own it," he said. "It's worth millions. But the reason I keep it is in honor of my mother. I have it in my will; it will never be sold."

Creating a Win-Win Situation

After buying 51 Dana Street, Lee Augusta's next challenge was to avoid Mrs. Brown's dilemma. How could Lee Augusta find enough tenants, tenants with the ability to pay rent dependably?

She soon figured out the answer was all around her. She was immersed in a sea of prospective tenants. The region – Cambridge and Boston in particular – was awash with students. And African-American students especially needed private housing.

"Black students needed rental housing because Harvard discriminated against them," Marvin said bluntly. "It wouldn't provide them with campus housing."

Lee Augusta connected the dots. She saw that students needed housing. And she saw that not enough rental rooms and apartments were offered to them. "Mrs. Mamie Eastland, who owned a house on Dana Street[,] could only accommodate a few students," she wrote in her memoir.

Other sources confirmed the size of this unmet market. Mother Lee's sharp mind grasped the implications.

"She began to hear about problems that [black] students had finding housing," Marvin said. "She heard about it through allowed its team to play anyway.

Overt racism was rampant at America's elite colleges and universities in the first half of the twentieth century.

Lee Augusta catered to young blacks and black students, especially at Harvard, who were victims of that bigotry. Discrimination in college housing was simply one facet of a multi-decade history of campus bias. Since the start of the century, schools had openly restricted admissions for blacks and denied them housing.

It was part of a shameless campaign many American institutions of higher education had waged against anyone who was not a son of the nation's business or political Establishment. The campaign picked up steam after World War I. Until then, colleges had admitted all interested her church. And she heard about it through a dental student who was one of her tenants, one of her first tenants." Equally important, black students began to hear about Lee Augusta's apartments.

The apartments were simple and a mirror of their vintage. Sinks were built onto walls without counters or vanities. Tenants cooked on old iron stoves. As quickly as she could afford to, Lee Augusta added bathrooms and kitchens to apartments that lacked them. A few years later she built an extension onto the rear of 51 Dana. She bought more buildings over time. At the peak, she owned half a dozen apartment buildings with dozens of apartments.

They were magnets for college students. "Harvard wasn't ready to have black students on campus," Marvin said.

Mother Lee's transformation into a rental housing landlord was a win-win situation. Black students and other young blacks on the rise needed housing. Lee Augusta needed tenants and relished the idea of helping ambitious young African-Americans as they built foundations for their careers. And the simple but sound character of her apartments attracted quality tenants. Her roster of tenants over the years included young blacks on the rise such as Charles Stith while he was a student at Harvard Divinity School. After earning his degree, he took the pulpit of the historic Union United Methodist Church in Boston's ethnically mixed South End. His voice quickly became one of the students.

"Before World War I, institutions of higher learning matriculated essentially all interested young people," David O. Levine wrote in "Discrimination in College Admissions."[ii] A prospective student's parents, principal, or headmaster wrote a letter of recommendation to the college he wanted to attend, Levine added. The boy showed up in September, took the entrance examination, and enrolled. "The student inquired about only one college; there was no admissions office, no formal application process. As late as the second decade of the twentieth century, all American colleges were still seeking as many students as they could persuade to come, whatever their academic qualifications," Levine wrote.

That arrangement

city's clearest bells on issues like voter registration and affirmative action. Later, President Bill Clinton appointed Stith United States Ambassador to the United Republic of Tanzania. Now he is director of the African Presidential Archives and Research Center at Boston University and adjunct professor of international relations.

Lee Augusta's other tenants included William Coleman, Jr., former U.S. Secretary of Transportation, while he was a student at Harvard Law School. Samuel Slie, pastor emeritus of University Church at Yale University, lived in one of Lee Augusta's apartments while he performed pastoral duties in Boston in the mid 1950s. Martin Luther King Sr., father of the slain civil rights leader, was one of her tenants while he received medical treatment in Boston.

Reporter Simeon Booker was a Lee Augusta tenant while studying at Harvard on a Nieman Fellowship in 1950-1951.[57] After that he became the first fulltime African-American reporter for the *Washington Post*, then Washington bureau chief for *Jet*. Booker went on to rack up a number of professional awards in a distinguished career. In 1961 he served as the sole journalist accompanying the Freedom Riders on their historic, terror-filled bus odyssey through a gauntlet of Southern states, where segregationists greeted them with violence as they attempted to integrate bus terminals.

Clarence Ferguson Jr., a World War II veteran who went on to serve as U.S.

contrasts sharply with today's elaborate routine. Now we take it for granted that students must apply for admission, imploring a school to admit them on the strength of factors such as high school grades, competitive test scores, extracurricular activities, and geographic origins. Recognizing that there is a good chance of rejection by the school they desire most, the bulk of students apply to several colleges.

College admissions became competitive after World War I. Colleges became more selective as the number of applicants rose. That happened because the ranks of America's middle class expanded, thanks to a growing economy after the war and in the Roaring Twenties.

But blacks shared very little in this shining new world. They got stuck with more than their own share of the economic ambassador to Uganda, U.S. ambassador-at-large and coordinator for relief efforts in the Nigerian civil war, was a professor of law at Rutgers, dean of Howard University law school, and member of the Harvard law faculty. He had been a Lee Augusta tenant while earning his law degree from Harvard, which he got in 1951.[58]

As a girl, Maria Hawkins was yet another tenant. Later, she became a professional singer. During her career she performed with Count Basie, Fletcher Henderson, and the Duke Ellington Orchestra. She eventually met and married superstar crooner Nat "King" Cole, becoming his second wife. Cole became the first African-American to host a variety television series.[59] Hawkins and Cole became the parents of several children, including Natalie Cole, who went on to achieve pop-music stardom in her own right.[60]

Lee Gilmore's galaxy of tenants included non-blacks too. Herbert Hershfang, now retired as a Boston Municipal Court judge, was a tenant while he was enrolled at Harvard Law School. Judge Hershfang's roommate was Robert John Aumann, another student at Harvard, who in 2005 won the Nobel Prize in Economics. Hyman Minsky was an economist who was an authority on the causes of financial crises and who taught at Brown University; the University of California, Berkeley; Washington University; and Bard College. He was a

misery in the following decade's Great Depression.

Among men in 13 large cities, the jobless rate in 1931 was 31.7% for whites and 52% for blacks. By the spring of 1933, unemployment had fallen to 25% of those white men. It was still 50% for blacks. In 1935 25% of the black population was receiving welfare. Only 15% of whites were.[iii]

Discrimination at colleges sprang from a desire by the nation's dominant social group to reserve college education, a key to upward mobility, for their own offspring. Jews, Catholics, and blacks were victims. By the time of the Great Depression, motivation for the restriction got more desperate, more ugly. Concern about upward mobility morphed into fearful hoarding of a key to outright economic survival.

tenant while earning his Ph. D. at Harvard.[61]

"She usually got to know her tenants," Marvin said. "She developed relationships with them. If they had children and needed a babysitter, she did that sometimes."

Lee Augusta also kept washing floors in her buildings – even stairs – years after she could afford to pay people to perform custodial services. Marvin asked her why. "She said this was how she kept an eye on her properties. She saw things. She heard tenants talking about things."

Marvin made the most of his own interactions with these tenants. Many became Marvin's friends and sometimes role models. Later, as Marvin created his own successes in adulthood, these former tenants of Lee Gilmore became part of Marvin's network of movers and shakers.

Take William Coleman. As U.S. Secretary of Transportation in the 1980s, Coleman okayed payment of $680 million to the Massachusetts Bay Transportation Authority for construction of a new subway line through Roxbury, Boston's black community. Creation of that mass-transit branch was a key component of Boston's Southwest Corridor Project, which would also eventually include an Amtrak train line, Roxbury Community College, and mixed commercial, retail, and residential development.

It capped the defeat of an entirely different project known by the same name. Starting in the 1960s the state had

Levine wrote: "Racial and ethnic bias flourished in the American college of the 1920s and 1930s.... Faced with the self-consciously determined opportunity and challenge to prepare a generation of leaders for a technological age, college officials and alumni – predominantly white Anglo-Saxon Protestant (WASP) and often anxious about the loss of status and power of 'native' American stock in American society in general – created the model student in their own image."[iv]

More and more young blacks wanted to attend college. And they were prepared for college studies in ever larger numbers. But white schools severely restricted the number accepted.

In 1899-1900, no more than 88 blacks graduated from white colleges, according to various head counts.

begun to acquire homes and businesses in this same area for construction of the Southwest Corridor, an interstate highway that was going to cut like a knife through this part of Roxbury. "Basically, it was going to destroy black people's homes and businesses to build a road for white commuters," Gilmore said.

For two decades people of color in Roxbury organized themselves and fought the highway version of the Southwest Corridor. Marvin, whose Community Development Corporation of Boston was headquartered inside this battleground, became a key figure in the opposition. He eventually became a mover and shaker on the Parcel 18 Task Force, a community organization involved in planning the reuse of Corridor parcels. That placed him in the vanguard of formulating alternative proposals that replaced the highway. His allies came to include Boston Mayor Raymond Flynn and Governor Michael Dukakis.

Coleman in effect signed the check that was the final fatal blow, forever killing the community-crushing highway. Marvin had taken part in countless meetings with fellow citizens, politicians, and public officials to build community, state, and federal consensus, backing the transit version of the Southwest Corridor. Federal financial backing was essential. Coleman's door was one of very many that project advocates like Marvin had to knock on, he says.

And for Marvin, getting to Coleman's

Most of those were from one college, Oberlin. In addition, an estimated 475 earned degrees from mainly black colleges. "By the mid-1930s, the number of black students attending college had grown to 19,000, the vast majority of whom were now enrolled in public black colleges, fewer in private black colleges, and only a very small percentage attending predominantly white institutions," wrote education historian Christopher J. Lucas.[v] So over those three-plus decades, the percentage of blacks studying for degrees from white colleges actually seems to have gone down.

The predominantly white school with the highest proportion of black students in the early decades of that century was Oberlin, a liberal arts college in Ohio founded by abolitionists. The school lays claim to being the door was made a little bit easier by a relationship that had begun with Lee Augusta.

Mother Lee was an American success story...a feisty, female, black Horatio Alger. Her own mother had been born a slave. She had to rally from illness with only the treatment available to a poor black woman. She relocated and established new homes several times. Yet rather than succumb to self-pity or wander through life aimlessly or surrender to self-destructive behavior, she was sharp and kept a sharp eye peeled for opportunities.

She trudged through unfamiliar streets to knock on white strangers' doors in search of paid work. She further advanced her prospects by fearlessly selling herself to shop proprietors one after another until finding one willing to take on her services.

In the late 1930s, one of her jobs as a sales associate was at the Window Shop in Harvard Square. The store was a consignment shop where refugee women could sell handmade crafts and Viennese pastries. It was founded in 1939 by four wives of Harvard professors.[62]

In the depths of the Great Depression, when despair stalked America and ravaged its poorest communities, when every dollar she earned was urgently needed to help feed and clothe and shelter her young family, she denied herself an extra serving of food, a bus ride when she could walk, a new pair of gloves

first U.S. college to regularly admit women and blacks. Yet even there blacks made up a paltry 4% of its student body.[vi] That was well below the prevalence of black students nationally. Throughout the U.S., African-Americans accounted for more than 25% of all students below college level in the 1930s.[vii]

One Oberlin teacher laid the blame squarely on intolerance among white students. The faculty member lamented that "it [was] impossible...to uphold old Oberlin's ideals because of student prejudice."[viii]

At Harvard, the administration blocked blacks from campus housing. "At Harvard in 1914 President Abbott Lawrence Lowell closed the freshmen dormitories to blacks, explaining later on that though the buildings originally had been built to reduce

MARVIN GILMORE: Crusader for Freedom

when holes wore through old ones. She scrimped and saved precious pennies and desperately needed dollars. She built her nest egg and financed a business enterprise of rental housing buildings that brought cash to her family, taught Marvin life lessons, and exposed him to ambitious young men who became lifelong friends and models of how to build a better life for himself.

She never relented. Her drive was unlimited. Even as she accomplished more, she was not satisfied. By her fifties she had accumulated a small group of apartment buildings. But she wanted to keep expanding her housing assets and handle those she already owned more efficiently. No matter that she was at an age when most people who could afford it thought about preparing to retire. No matter that this was a dark era when most people were happy to hold any livelihood. In contrast, Lee Augusta took on more.

She enrolled in night school at Cambridge High & Latin School to study math and business. Classes were three nights a week, from 7 to 9 p.m.

"She did her homework at the kitchen table," Marvin said. "She had a hunger for knowledge. She did it after working her job during the day and after feeding me and Lester. I don't know how she did it. That's why she brought her mother up during the summer. To look after us. She would never leave us alone. Sophronia's visits started when we lived on Columbia Street or Dana Street. Sophronia would

students' social segregation, he felt it was important not to offend whites by introducing a black within their midst. A rule was passed stipulating that no one was to be excluded 'by reason of his color,' but in the same breath it declared that 'men of the white and colored races shall not be compelled to live and eat together.'"[ix]

Harvard clung to its bias. One key reason was that Harvard was afraid of losing business. The school was afraid that forcing whites and blacks to live together would alienate potential white students from the South, wrote American education historian Harold S. Wechsler. "[A]nd [Harvard] did not wish to acquire a reputation for forced 'race mingling' or for 'social equality.' As a result, Harvard's dormitories remained segregated de facto until the early 1950s."[x]

visit for the entire summer. But she couldn't take the cold, so she did not stay in the fall or winter."

Rental housing was not Lee Augusta's last big idea. Dr. Charlotte Hawkins Brown owned a house at 69 Dana Street. Like No. 51, it had 22 rooms. And it was for sale. Dr. Brown needed to spend much of her time in Sedalia, North Carolina, where she had founded Palmer Memorial Institute, one of America's most prestigious prep schools for African-American girls in the first half of the twentieth century.[63]

Lee Augusta bought No. 69 in 1942. (Maria Hawkins Cole, the singer who married Nat "King" Cole, was Dr. Brown's niece and lived at No. 69, first while her aunt owned the property and then after Lee Augusta became owner.) The Gilmores lived there for eight years.[64]

But Lee Augusta's real game plan was to convert the address into a nursing home. From working at Cleveland's Lakeside Memorial Hospital, and from her bouts of hospitalization, she had learned to appreciate the need for convalescence homes. She had taken special training to be a diabetic cook. She was also aware of the steady income their long-term residents paid to proprietors. So in 1954, Lee Augusta turned to the city for the necessary permits. Dr. Joseph Brusch of Brusch Medical Associates in Cambridge had agreed to serve as house doctor. But the city turned her down.

Was the building too small? Did it require too many renovations for use as a nursing home? Nothing so innocent,

And Harvard had been practicing its prejudice for decades.

William Edward Burghardt "W.E.B." Du Bois — the famous sociologist, historian, civil rights activist, and a founder of the National Association for the Advancement of Colored People (NAACP) — had encountered it in the 1890s, while on his way to becoming the first black to receive a Ph.D. from Harvard.

"I was in Harvard but not of it," he said.[xi]

Sidebar notes
[i] Timothy Davis, "The Myth of the Superspade: The Persistence of Racism in College Athletics," Fordham Urban Law Journal, vol. 22, issue 3, article 4, 1994, p. 626: http://ir.lawnet.fordham.edu/cgi/viewcontent.cgi?article=1664&context=ulj, accessed Nov. 20, 2012.

Marvin says. "Cambridge was not ready for my mother. It was because she was black."

Being female didn't help either. Lee Augusta was stung by her rejection. But she wasn't deterred. She had psychological calluses that got their start from listening to her mother's tales of life in human bondage, calluses that grew under the impact of decades of living in the South, calluses that hardened further each time she shrugged off racist dirty looks up North.

She treated Cambridge's prejudicial snub as a mere speed bump. She plowed forward, making 69 Dana Street into her second rental-apartment property. She was building her mini empire of real estate. And she did it despite charging less than what she knew the market would bear. "It was my policy to charge less than the full rate for rooms and apartments, so long as I could operate and maintain the properties in good comfortable condition, because I wanted to help students who were trying to further their education," she wrote in her memoir.

She also taught her son Marvin to help others, not just with ordinary life challenges like paying for housing, but with life's fiercer challenges.[65] She taught Marvin to help others avoid the setbacks and injustices she and her family had been forced to endure. She pushed Marvin in a direction where he could help make a world in which no one would be subjected to such setbacks and injustices.

[ii] David O. Levine, *The American College and the Culture of Aspiration, 1915-1940* (Ithaca, N.Y.: Cornell University Press, 1986), p. 137.

[iii] New Jersey State Library, "Unit 11 The 1930s: The Great Depression": http://slic.njstatelib.org/NJ_Inf ormation/Digital_Collections/A AHCG/unit11.html, accessed Nov. 26, 2012.

[iv] David O. Levine, *The American College and the Culture of Aspiration, 1915-1940* (Ithaca, N.Y.: Cornell University Press, 1986), p. 136.

[v] Christopher J. Lucas, *American Higher Education: A History* (New York: St. Martin's Press, 1994), p. 207-208.

[vi] David O. Levine, *The American College and the Culture of Aspiration, 1915-1940* (Ithaca, N.Y.: Cornell University Press, 1986), p. 159.

[vii] Encyclopedia.com, "Education for African Americans": http://www.encyclopedia.com /doc/1G2-3468301124.html, accessed Nov. 20, 2012.

[viii] David O. Levine, *The American College and the Culture of Aspiration, 1915-1940* (Ithaca, N.Y.: Cornell University Press, 1986), p. 159.

[ix] Christopher J. Lucas, *American Higher Education: A History* (New York: St. Martin's Press, 1994), p. 209.

[x] Harold S. Wechsler, "An

A Disney Character

Lee Augusta had an engine that never ran out of gas. She avidly sought positions as a domestic for wealthy homeowners despite her growing roster of rental properties.

In the late 1930s she found work keeping house and cooking for Robert D. Feild. The assistant professor of fine arts at Harvard lived with his wife in Cambridge near Harvard Square, in a home with an expensive view of the Charles River.

Academic Gresham's Law: Group Repulsion as a Theme in American Higher Education," *The History of Higher Education,* second edition, edited by Lester F. Goodchild and Harold S. Wechsler (Needham Heights, Mass.: Simon & Schuster Custom Publishing, 1997), p. 425.
[xi] U-S-history.com, "W.E.B. DuBois": http://www.u-s-history.com/pages/h1613.html , accessed Nov. 20, 2012.

"Mom got a job on Hawthorne Street, cleaning house and cooking for a Mr. and Mrs. Feild," Marvin said. "Feild was a writer. He taught at Harvard. And he did some sort of work for Walt Disney Studios."

Marvin's boyhood impression was close to the truth. In 1942 Feild would publish a book about Walt Disney, the iconic Hollywood mastermind and creator of Mickey Mouse. From June 1939 to May 1940 Feild immersed himself in the Disney Studio, researching his book. Allowed to roam freely, he visited every department, watched films as they were made, studied Disney's techniques and procedures, and interviewed animators, technicians, and Walt Disney himself.[66]

In his book, Feild characterized Disney as a new kind of American artist. Remember, elaborate cartoons were new. Disney's *The Sorcerer's Apprentice* – an animated short film based on a poem penned by Johann Wolfgang von Goethe, set to orchestral music, and starring a mischievous Mickey Mouse – had debuted only a few years earlier, in 1936. *Fantasia*, a feature-length animation running 124 minutes and showcasing classical music conducted by Leopold Stokowski, would appear in 1940. It was a demanding creation. The breathtaking multimedia entertainment cost about four times more than the average live-action movie.[67]

Steven Watts, a later Disney biographer, wrote that Feild's book was "the first extensive assessment of Disney's creative achievements. Feild believed that Disney's films had pioneered a new type of creative expression, undermining the outworn assumption that 'music, painting, sculpture, and architecture...alone are *art*.'"[68]

Unfortunately for Feild, his Harvard colleagues did not agree. Harvard was a cathedral for worship of High Culture. Feild's fellow faculty felt Disney and cartoons were the epitome of low-brow mass media. *Cartoons,* for god's sake! Sure, a lot of what Disney produced was clever. But it was as much about – gasp! – *commerce* as art.

For his salute to the prince of popular culture, Feild was drummed out of the high temple of high brow.

Watts wrote: "Even before his book was published, Professor Field's teaching appointment at Harvard University was terminated. The situation became something of a minor scandal. Details of the case were never released, but it seems clear that many of Feild's academic colleagues viewed his foray into the realm of popular art with considerable suspicion. Both *Time* and the *Harvard Crimson* reported that he was dismissed by 'Harvard's conservative art department because of too much enthusiasm for modern art, particularly Disney's.'[69]

Feild was not sacked for lack of teaching skills. Watts wrote that the Boston *Evening Globe* described him as one of the most popular teachers on campus. His lectures were jam packed. In fact, after his firing fine arts majors denounced his dismissal and campaigned for his reinstatement, Watts wrote. But their efforts were futile. Feild was forced to continue his teaching career far from the Ivy covered walls of Harvard.

Feild was a real person who actually lost a job in a citadel of academic freedom because of cultural bias. For the Gilmores, Feild's exile meant the loss of a source of income and the destruction of a stable routine for Lee Augusta. It reinjected uncertainty into the lives of Marvin and his family. It was not the first Marvin would feel some sting stemming from prejudice. But it was a vivid, up-close-and-personal lesson to Marvin of the cost that people's narrow-mindedness can have.

For Lee Augusta, the incident was another challenge to be overcome.

Doing Well by Doing Good

Harvard's tradition of housing discrimination created an opportunity for Lee Augusta to do well while doing good. She provided housing to African-American students whom Harvard would not allow in its front door. She helped them prepare for higher-income careers in business and the professions. She enabled them to feel less pressured and outcast. Further, by providing something necessary that Harvard would not, she generated a return on her own investments. And it was a way she could teach valuable life lessons about hard work, the value of investing, the importance of economic independence to her son Marvin.

"I don't remember her ever taking a penny out of the properties," Marvin said. "I do remember her preaching about the importance of controlling the land under your own two feet. It's your home. It can be a source of jobs and work for others. It's a foundation for financial security. She never let me take any of that for granted. And she warned me to keep my eyes open for anyone trying to take land away from you."

Chapter 5
You're in the Army Now

On December 14, 1942, Marvin took a short walk from his home. He traveled less than one mile, but when he reached his destination he had left behind his boyhood and stepped into the world of adults.

"I never had a teenage life," Marvin said. "I spent my teenage years in the service. But in a war, you grow up or you get taken advantage of really quick."

That short walk also led Marvin to a crucible. He emerged, having passed the test with distinction. Many men around him did not. They were all in a Southern Army camp when racial tensions exploded in a deadly riot between white and black troops. In the aftermath, units were broken up. Careers were shattered. Many black men were court-martialed and imprisoned in a military prison. Marvin got promoted and went on to a fine military stint. He served in England, Scotland, and Belgium. He fought in Normandy, elsewhere in northern France, and in Germany. For all of that, he was eventually awarded France's Legion of Honor – the prestigious decoration awarded by a grateful Gallic nation as its way of saying thank you to foreign military heroes.

Marvin's journey began that December 14 with a walk down the front steps of his family's home at 51 Dana Street. He turned right and walked three blocks to the end of Dana Street at Massachusetts Avenue, Cambridge's main thoroughfare. There, he turned left, heading toward Central Square. He was carrying a small suitcase, filled with a few clothes, a toothbrush, tooth paste, and some shaving gear. At the small Army recruiting station about half a dozen blocks away, he joined a small group of males. Probably all of them were older than Marvin, who was only 17 years, two months, and three weeks old. After a short wait, the group boarded a bus that took them about 35 miles west, into an area of old factory towns, to Fort Devens in Ayer, Massachusetts.

Shortly after arrival, Marvin enlisted in the U.S. Army.

Call of Duty

Marvin had risen that morning, still a high school senior. He was an average quarter-miler and half-miler on the Cambridge Latin track team. He was also an avid and skilled young pianist. And he had talent as a percussionist. The military draft did not touch youngsters under age 18, so Marvin knew he could remain in high school until the end of the academic year that spring. He could even enroll in college the following autumn and still be too young for the draft.

Yet that's not how Marvin wanted to play his hand. Sure, he could stay in school. "But it would be wasted time and money," he said. "I could be drafted in my first year."

More importantly, America needed him and so did Europeans. The U.S. was in a fight, and Marvin was not about to hide out in college.

"Germans were crossing Europe at a fast pace," he said. "The U.S. had to put a stop to it."

Marvin weighed other factors as well.

Chief among them, his father had made it clear he wanted Marvin to move out. "I was at odds with my father," Marvin said. "He felt I should be out of the house, that I shouldn't be dependent on him. His attitude was that when you turn 16 you're a man. He thought it was time for me to move on. The house was too small for two men to live in."

Marvin chooses his words diplomatically. He does not speak with disrespect of his father. But once his father had decided that it was time to kick Marvin out of the nest, Marvin knew it would be pointless to try to change his mind.

"My father was a tough, opinionated man," Marvin said. "When he made his decisions, he never looked at what he was saying. And he never changed his mind. He had a third-grade education. You have to understand what I had to deal with in him. It was what my mother had to deal with too. It absolutely was part of why I wanted to join the Army. I made up my mind to join the Army a week or two after my father opened his mouth."

And Marvin kept coming back to the crux of this situation. There was a war on.

"That was a time when Hitler was crossing the entire continent. America needed every able bodied young man in the service," he said.

Marvin decided that not only could college wait, high school graduation could wait too.

Graduation would be only months away, in the spring. But on this winter day, with the holidays approaching, Marvin's path looked increasingly clear. His diploma could wait. Stopping the rapid spread of Adolf Hitler's malignant racism and ideology of oppression felt more and more important. Stopping Hitler's brutal crushing of one European democracy after another, his growing threat to America itself, was the clear priority.

Marvin could envision a world ruled by repression and tyranny if America fell. He could see the world growing dark, taken over by pitiless dictators. He could picture a world in which people deemed inferior races by a fanatical despot named Hitler and his dictatorial allies Hideki Tojo of Japan and Benito Mussolini of Italy were doomed to subjugation and death. And Marvin could visualize this nightmare reality looming in the not-too-distant future because he knew his own family had already suffered something similar, the world of slavery in the American South.

They had escaped this horror only two generations earlier. This was not some dusty, distant history lesson involving other people. It was real and recent. His own grandparents and great aunts and uncles had lived through it. His grandmother Sophronia had repeatedly told Marvin of her bitter experiences, witnessing brutality, herself tearfully enduring whippings and rapes, humiliations and deprivations even in the years shortly after emancipation. Marvin's father had passed along stories he had heard about his grandparents Lousea and John's brutal bondage.

Marvin was merely a high school kid, but he was old enough to know the chilling truth. Blacks were among those whom Hitler viewed as inferior people. Conquest by Hitler would mean a return to the frightful plight of his ancestors' past.

This terrible threat was reinforced by recent events. Just a few years earlier, 12-year-old Marvin had followed black superstar Jesse Owens' campaign into and through the 1936 Olympics, held in Berlin, Germany. Germany was, even then, in the grip of Hitler and his Nazi political party. Hitler had mega-rock star status, and his ample influence was still rising thanks to the Nazis' relentless, persuasive propaganda. The Nazis' terrifying red-and-black swastika emblem was everywhere – on flag poles, on banners dominating the sides of buildings. Also relentless was Hitler's storm-trooper militia. These brown-shirted thugs stomped opponents into submission and waged domestic war on Jews and others they regarded as inferior.

In those summer Games, Owens transfixed America as he won an astounding four gold medals in the 100-meter sprint, the 200-meter dash, the long jump, and the 4-x-100-meter relay. Like virtually every African-American old enough to listen to radio, read a newspaper, talk with friends, family, and pals, and hear adults comment on the day's events, Marvin's heart swelled with pride. And Marvin was painfully aware that Hitler had refused to congratulate the heroic black athlete for his epic achievement.

Owens was black, and Hitler was peddling a segregationist doctrine that insisted that Aryans – white northern Europeans – were the master race. More than any other non-German champion of those Olympics, Owens – the son of a black sharecropper and grandson of slaves – had dramatically demolished Hitler's monstrous mythology.[70]

"My history teacher in high school made it clear to us what was going on," Marvin said. "We knew all about Jesse Owens. And we knew all about Hitler. Our teacher told us how Hitler had invaded the Nordic nations and kept them like slaves, then kept invading more European nations and making them slaves too. We saw the stories on the front page of the newspaper every day. And we saw news reels in the Cambridge movie theater. It was all very graphic. We saw the bombings, the shooting. We knew exactly what was going on."

So, to Marvin Hitler was not some abstract, distant person in the news. He was a real person, posing a direct threat to the world Marvin knew, threatening to unravel the hard-won progress achieved by Mother Lee and his grandmother Sophronia and all those who had come before and given life to Marvin. America may have been imperfect, but it was Marvin's home and a place that gave him a family, a life, friends. Heck, America had given him the opportunity to learn to play piano.

Marvin knew his own life was a heck of a lot better than his grandmother's had been. America was allowing Mother Lee to scale heights never before reached by his ancestors. Marvin was a relatively free young man, and America was offering him a better life day by day. Sure, Marvin had encountered his share of jerks and bigots. But as his neighborhood pal and fellow black Jim Thornhill put it (in Chapter 3), the racial and ethnic slurs that occurred in their Cambridge were little more than good-natured ribbing. The put-downs and slurs were dished out evenly in every direction. Lithuanians, Poles, Greeks, Irishmen, Italians – everyone got it. It was equal opportunity one-up-manship. It was boyish assertiveness, the ages-old spectacle of young males seeing who was top dog. It certainly was not an organized war on any one group based on skin color or national heritage.

Marvin's life had its tough moments. But he was basically a happy kid in a decent place. His America was blessedly free of the sort of brown-shirted paramilitary goons who were goose-stepping through one European capital after another. He knew it was the duty of every American to fight that maniacal menace. And he knew that if he wanted to keep the white-hooded Klan, America's kissing cousins of the Brown Shirts, at a safe distance, the fight was here and now.

Marvin had come to Fort Devens to join that fight. That's exactly what he did.

The Vanishing Deal

Marvin's enlistment took place at Fort Devens. He had decided weeks earlier to make this move. And he wanted to use the fact that he could not be drafted as a bargaining chip for how he would serve. He did not want to join the infantry. "I did not want to volunteer for long marches and for foxholes – digging foxholes, fighting in foxholes, sleeping in foxholes. I was ready to fight. But I wanted a little distance between me and hand-to-hand combat," Marvin said.

Instead, Marvin wanted to be in a military band.

He thought he could pull off that arrangement based on his age and based on conversations he had had with the recruiting officer at the recruiting station in Central Square near his home in the past two weeks.

The key was Marvin's age. Barely one month earlier, Congress had lowered the age of eligibility to 18.[71] It had been 21 for a little more than two years. But Japan's attack on the United States' Naval base at Pearl Harbor, Hawaii, on December 7, 1941 had turbocharged America's preparations to fight in World War II.

Still, Marvin had nine months to go before he could be drafted and pressed into whatever type of service Uncle Sam desired.

Another reason Marvin could dicker with the Army was that he could sign up with another branch of the service, either now with a parent's consent or when he was old enough. Marvin said, "A bunch of guys from Cambridge had decided they were going to join the Air Force[72] and go to Tuskegee [Army Air Field in Alabama] to become pilots.[73] But I didn't want to fly. I wanted to keep my feet on the ground. And I didn't want to go to Alabama, period, because of what I knew about it."

What Marvin knew about Alabama was that it was the state where his mother's side of the family had been enslaved for as long as anyone in her family could remember, possibly stretching back centuries. His grandmother Sophronia's first-hand accounts were still vivid in his memory. Sophronia had repeatedly told Marvin of her toil as a slave, of being raped and beaten, of her fear and horrors, and of witnessing the agonies of other slaves including her own kin. Tales of bondage were the worst. Nearly as discomforting were stories told to Marvin by his aunts and uncles about their lives as blacks in the segregated society that was post-Reconstruction Alabama. So this was an easy choice for Marvin. He had no desire whatsoever to travel to Alabama for any purpose, no matter how patriotic.

Ironically, Congress and the military's own Jim Crow attitudes bolstered Marvin's ability to withhold his military service. In December 1942 the draft still excluded African-Americans.[74] Congress and the military claimed that blacks were not fit for service, and they felt that a racially mixed Armed Forces could not succeed. That did not change until 1943, when a quota was imposed, allowing a limited number of blacks to be drafted.

A large part of the reason for that change was because African-Americans were demanding the opportunity to prove their patriotism, their fighting mettle, their courage, their ability to learn military jobs, their ability to take and give orders – all of the things that racists said blacks could not do.[75] Another reason for opening the door in 1943 was the wartime demand for manpower.

Meanwhile, Marvin did not want to serve in just any capacity. As an enthusiastic young musician, he wanted to be in a military band. So he decided to use his right to delay joining the military as a way to negotiate for what he wanted. If the Army would let him join a music outfit, he'd sign up right away.

He even had a form signed by his mother, giving her okay to Marvin's underage enlistment. With that consent, the law would allow Marvin to join the Armed Services at age 17.

On the other hand, the particular recruiting officer that Marvin had been talking with wanted Marvin to sign up. The officer may not have shared the bias that was barring blacks from the draft. The officer may have been more concerned with impressing his superiors by swaying large numbers of young Cambridge men to enlist. He may have wanted to take credit for Marvin entering the military. He certainly wanted Marvin to be able to join. And the officer was much more experienced at enticing men to join than Marvin was at negotiating the terms of his enlistment.

So the officer agreed to Marvin's demand to be assigned to a band.

But their handshake meant nothing to the Army. There was no signed, binding contract. There was nothing that obligated the military to put Marvin into a music unit. Marvin had no right to simply walk out of the service if the recruiting officer's pledge was not kept.

So Marvin got on the bus that December 14 and was driven along with other young men to Fort Devens, and there Marvin signed up to serve in the U.S. Army. That very same day, Marvin recalls being put on a train with others from New England, heading south to Camp Wallace in Texas.

Marvin was being railroaded in more ways than one.

In a Swamp

Camp Wallace was on the inland side of Hitchcock and Texas City, Texas. Across Galveston Bay sits Galveston, Texas. When Marvin arrived in December 1942, it had only been open since February 1941 as a training site for Army anti-aircraft units. In 1944 it would be transferred to the U.S. Navy.[76]

Marvin had been outfitted in a uniform at Fort Devens. His civilian clothes were shipped home. "By the time I got to Camp Wallace, I was definitely a G.I.," Marvin said.

But he was not a G.I. making music to entertain troops. Instead, Marvin found himself being taught how to make war. The Army ignored its recruiting officer's phony assurance that Marvin would be assigned to a music outfit. Marvin's only consolation was that he was not being trained to be an infantry soldier. Still, there were many days and weeks when it was hard for Marvin to tell the difference.

He was taught how to shoot a rifle and a handgun and a machinegun. His prowess earned him status as a rifle sharpshooter.[77] And he learned how to handle himself in hand-to-hand combat, including how to fight with a bayonet. "You learned how to fix a bayonet on your rifle, how to put it into somebody, and how to pull it out," Marvin said.

The Biggest Jerk He Met

Drill sergeants were merciless. "They yelled at us a lot, and tried to toughen us up," Marvin said. Some sergeants did it to prepare the soldiers for the rigors of war that lay ahead. Some were harsh because they were white and disliked black soldiers.

"The sergeant who trained us was the biggest jerk I ever met," Marvin said. "He had us march on a parade ground that was covered with seashells. The shells were very uneven and hard to walk on. They'd crack as we walked on them, and guys would twist ankles. The sergeant would yell at you for not marching right. He'd swear at us. He'd yell at us for falling down. I remember his name – Sgt. Sorrell. He was from the South. They were all racists. He'd make you march until you dropped dead. We had to march in hot weather with packs that weighed 30, 40 pounds. He had no pity, no sympathy. He'd punish guys who didn't march right by making them stay behind and keep marching after he sent everyone else back to their huts."

Nothing appeased racist drill instructors. "They hated black soldiers," Marvin said. "They hated the ignorant ones. They hated dirty black soldiers. They hated blacks who were educated, who were neat and clean. It made no difference."

The overt racism was a jolt for Marvin. It was like nothing he had experienced in Cambridge. It was like being thrust back in time in one of his grandmother's stories.

The racially tinged abusiveness of sergeants was no accident. The Army was an officially segregated organization. At the level of Camp Wallace, deep in the sweltering South, there was no mistaking that it barely tolerated blacks within its ranks. Like a human body's immune system attacking an infection, the Army seemed intent on isolating blacks. There were essentially two armies – one white, the other black. And the black one had white officers foisted on it.[78]

"Being in a black outfit, with white commanders, was a whole new bombshell for me," Marvin said.

And racist verbal abuse was commonplace. "White soldiers called me nigger all the time," Marvin said. "Back then, no one called you black. In the South, you were a nigger. I heard that all the time."

At this stage of the war, the Army was still determined to keep blacks out of frontline infantry outfits. The Army knew that unit cohesion was invaluable. In combat, men would fight for themselves and their buddies – the self-preservation instinct of a band of brothers. And all too many of the Army's top brass – white men – persisted in believing that white and black Americans could not forge that brotherhood together. So, many black soldiers were shunted into service jobs as cooks, janitors, and waiters, which often placed African-Americans into roles resembling that of servants. They were also restricted to menial and dangerous labor, such as loading and unloading ammunition and explosives.[79]

But growing political pressure in America and the cruel dictates of warfare were gradually forcing the Army to bend.[80] In 1942 the Army activated the war's first all-black foot-soldier outfits, the 92nd and 93rd Infantry Divisions.[81]

And more black soldiers like Marvin were placed into noninfantry combat units. As part of Camp Wallace's mandate to train men to work anti-aircraft guns, some men were taught how to operate big search lights. Men who excelled at aiming lights were taught how to fire artillery at airplanes in the next stage of training, at the next camp.

"At Camp Wallace, everyone started out on search lights," Marvin said. "We had to learn to use a spotlight to track German planes in the sky. If you could aim a light, they trained you on 40-millimeter cannons."

That training with anti-aircraft artillery would come next, at Camp Stewart in Georgia, to which Marvin was transferred roughly eight months after arriving at Wallace. Firing a 40-millimeter cannon was not the only thing Marvin would learn at Stewart. Bad as racism was at Wallace, it was worse at Stewart. In fact, it spawned one of the Army's worst wartime race riots. And Marvin found himself right at ground zero.

Deadly Serious

News reels sometimes made Army camps look like summer camps for big kids. You slept outdoors in pup tents a lot. You made friends with a few of the guys in your bunk house – at first, anyway. The guys you didn't like, you called them jerks and profanities behind their backs, and it was okay. It was just guy stuff. Funny. Then you went back to making camp fires and eating chow. You learned to box, and often the instructor actually encouraged you to hurt the other guy. Not kill 'im. Just punch him hard and hurt him. You learned to take care of yourself. You organized into teams and played something like capture the flag.

But in reality training camp was a lot more deadly than any summer camp. Guys got hurt, maimed, and killed.

"I cried several times in Stewart," Marvin said. "I was a fledgling coming out of the North. I was naïve. I came there clean, decent, and found myself in a swamp. A lot of the men were filthy, uneducated, cruel, thieves, who were covered with lice and didn't seem to notice or care. Stewart was a hell hole. One day we were on a training march in a swamp. We were always on a buddy system. You and your buddy watched out for each other. It was summer. It was hot, humid, sticky, stinking. We were wearing forty-pound packs. We were soaking wet from the heat and humidity and marching."

The men were in a column, wading through a swamp. Marvin was two or three steps behind and to his buddy's left. A bug or mosquito or a snake – *something* – distracted Marvin and he looked away for an instant. When he turned back, his pal was gone. "He walked into quick sand. It sucked him down. The ground was so soft, it would just pull you down. He went down so fast, there was nothing I could do. I didn't even see it."

The outfit organized a search party. But Marvin's buddy was never found, which put a chill through most of the men.

The here-one-moment-gone-the-next experience toughened Marvin up. "Now I don't even remember his name. But after that, I didn't try to learn anybody's name. He could be here today, then gone tomorrow. I didn't want to lose more friends. So I didn't try to make friends."

The fear factor has stayed with Marvin to this day. "I still don't go in water. I'll go near it, but not deep. Maybe up to my ankles. That's it. I never learned to swim. Those swamps had snakes and alligators and bugs and nothing good in them. I don't want no part of that water."

Danger, even death, was not restricted to the swamp. It saturated Camp Stewart. It was random and struck without warning.

"I learned to shoot. I was good at it. You lay on the ground and trained with a rifle or carbine. Everybody learned how to shoot a Tommy gun," Marvin said, referring to the popular Thompson submachine gun. When fitted with a drum bullet magazine, it was a staple of hoodlums in the 1920-1933 Prohibition era and in gangster movies.

"Even though we were in an anti-aircraft outfit, you learned to shoot everything the Army gave you," Marvin said. "But not everybody could handle them. Some guys – not my own unit, some other unit – got killed on the shooting range. They were training on a big machine gun. They didn't know how to handle it. They were probably using it for the first time. When they started firing, it jumped out of their control and spun around and killed some guys. About three or four men got killed. Another four or five got wounded."

Work and Play at Camp Stewart

Marvin had proven himself a marksman with guns and rifles back at Camp Wallace. Seeing his true aim, instructors had selected him to put a bead on aircraft using searchlights, which was preparation for becoming an anti-aircraft gunner. Graduation to firing anti-aircraft guns came at Camp Stewart, where Marvin was assigned to the 458th Anti-Aircraft Artillery (Automatic Weapons) Battalion.

Learning to fire anti-aircraft artillery became part of Marvin's training routine, along with continued training with guns and rifles and in hand-to-hand combat. "They were getting us ready to be an anti-aircraft outfit," Marvin said. "But the Army knew we'd be in combat areas close to the enemy, so we had to keep training to protect ourselves from German foot soldiers."

In addition to the hard training, Marvin also dealt with the drudgery and pettiness for which military life is often infamous.

"When men got a pass to leave camp, they had to be back by a certain day and time," Marvin said. "If you were late, you got punishment duty."

One time, Marvin was late. He had gone into a nearby town. He was due back by 7 p.m., he still recalls. He did not return until hours after his deadline. Ruefully, he still recalls his punishment. "I had to dig a six-foot-deep hole. They taught us to dig holes for the wheels and feet of anti-aircraft guns, so they wouldn't move when they were fired. But a hole like this wasn't used for anything. It was just a hole. It was hard work. And it could take you a whole evening to dig a hole like that. People walking by would laugh at you. Once you dug the hole, the sergeant would come by and order you to fill the hole up. If the sergeant was in a bad mood, he might order you to dig it out again and fill it up again."

The chore was intentionally unpleasant. And most of the time it had the intended result. "Usually," Marvin said, "if you got punishment duty you'd never be late again."

Still, sometimes a man could not help being late. Work and life in the camp was hard and boring and sometimes dangerous. There were fights. There was that buddy who drowned on a training march through a swamp, and those shooting range deaths. But in the soldiers' off hours, the nearby towns offered entertainment and relaxation.

Hinesville was the camp's neighbor to the south. It had bars. And the woods surrounding the camp had makeshift bars.

"And girls," Marvin smiled. "Men went into town to meet girls. There were little shanty barrooms in the woods, where people danced and drank beer. These were little wooden shacks. Most didn't have lights. Most served wine and beer but no liquor. We reached the shanties on foot along rutted, dusty dirt roads. Sometimes you had to walk a mile or two."

Like the Army itself and the South, these dance joints were segregated. "The black shanties were on one side of town," Marvin said. "White ones were on the other side."

Going out at night into uncharted rural back roads could be perilous. "You never went to a shanty alone," Marvin said. "You'd get rolled and robbed. Being alone was the kiss of death. If you were alone, a bartender would put something in your drink and roll you. We seemed rich to a lot of those people. We got paid $20 a month. Back then, you could buy cabbage for one cent a pound. So you'd never go out alone. If you did, you'd always be a target. Instead, it was always the buddy system for soldiers. And you'd try to go to safer bars. You'd stick with the ones you knew. But for a lot of guys there was temptation everywhere. A lot of the girls were prostitutes."

Even if an evening out was uneventful and peaceful, Marvin would come back dusty and filthy from the dirt roads.

And what would happen to a black soldier who dared to step into a white bar? "He'd be killed," Marvin said.

Visits to Savannah

Many Saturday nights, Marvin and other soldiers would make the 39-mile trip to Savannah, a good sized city to the northeast.

The journey was yet another reminder of how racially divided the Army and Georgia were.

The Army provided buses coming and going in a non-stop relay. The buses were strictly segregated. "If you went on a bus, they'd only allow two or three black guys, and we had to sit in the back. And we weren't allowed to sit near whites. We had to sit on a wide seat in the back of the bus. If you were heading out with 10 buddies, only a few could get on a bus. Here we were in the Army, fighting for them, and they were treating us like that. It was humiliating. I had to swallow my pride many times."

When there weren't enough buses, Marvin and other black soldiers had to take Army trucks.

"You had to wait in line," Marvin said. "Then you got on a truck, with the canvas slaps on the side rolled up. You'd start out with a clean shirt and pants, but by the time the truck got to Savannah you were filthy dirty."

Marvin always took pride in looking sharp. Once he made a female friend in Savannah, he learned to leave clean clothes where she lived. "I always left a suit in town because clothes quickly got dirty from traveling in the truck," he said. "I left the suit at a woman friend's house."

Getting back to camp could also be a chancy proposition. "There might not be a regular bus where you were going, so there was no bus coming back either," Marvin said. "Even if there was a bus, the schedule was not reliable. It didn't matter. If you missed your ride back to camp, it was no excuse. You were still late."

And in Savannah, Marvin had to remember where he was. No admiring looks at white women. No sass to white cops or military police. "Fear and hate were always there," Marvin said.

Racial protocol was sternly enforced. "If you complained about sitting in the back of a bus, the driver and an MP would kick your butt right there," Marvin said. "If you opened your mouth, the MP might arrest you. If you objected, you'd get bloodied."

And woe to the black soldier who failed to address a white officer, especially a Southerner, as sir. "I was at an Army dentist," Marvin said. "He asked me if my tooth was giving me trouble. I said, 'Yes,' but I didn't say,

'Yes, sir,' and he cracked my tooth a pair of pliers and scolded me for not addressing him as sir! I was bleeding. I had to do something. I reported it to my commander. You know what happened? The dentist got a promotion! I got the message. I was an uppity nigger!"

Coming to Blows

Troops in the camp were a cross-section of civilian society: bad guys and good guys. The bad guys were the same as they had been before enlistment – toughs, thugs, thieves. Putting on an Army uniform didn't change them. Camp Stewart was just a new neighborhood for them, a new place to steal, harass, and gamble.

Marvin was practically a different species. He was an educated, civilized kid who knew right from wrong. And he had been taught to stand his ground. "Mother taught me never to run from a fight," he said simply. That was a rule he did not abandon in the camp. But he was a tempting target. He was young, stood just five-foot-ten-and-a-half, and was a slim 125 pounds.

Still, he was no patsy and he wasn't scared. "If you let someone push you around or take advantage of you, he'd keep doing it. It would get worse. And others would start doing it too. So you either stood up for yourself or you got taken advantage of. It could get very ugly," Marvin said.

Late one afternoon as he returned from drills, several older guys jumped him. They pinned him to the rough wooden floor and poured whiskey down his throat. This was their idea of fun. Just rough-housing. And teach the young punk from up North a lesson, too.

"I was a kid. I wasn't a drinker," Marvin said. "I never drank before. I didn't touch anything except maybe beer. So one day several of the older soldiers jumped me. They roughed me up and held me down and poured booze into me. It was like an initiation, a hazing. It was their way of forcing me to be like them. They poured so much booze into me that I got sick. They poured a whole quart down my throat. It was deadly poison. I ended up in the infirmary for a few days."

There was little Marvin could do about what happened. "I couldn't go to my commander," he said. "I couldn't squeal. Squealing was the kiss of death. They'd kill you. *Lit-er-ally*. But I grew up real fast. The lesson was that I wouldn't let it happen again. I kept a gun on me and I kept it cocked.

I don't know how many times I cocked my carbine in Georgia," Marvin said. "This was a whole other world. This was no Cambridge. I had to learn to defend myself. You can't be no coward, no pussy. You'd be robbed and killed."

The idea to standing up for yourself was to teach the other guy a lesson. If the price for picking on you was too high, he wouldn't do it again. There were plenty of other guys to pick on.

One day out of the blue, Marvin got into a beef with a soldier who was much bigger than him. "You could not be weak," he said. "It was like being in prison. Bullies always challenged you. If you gave in, they'd never stop bothering you. He was a real ---hole. So we fought. He was big, so he won. But I was smarter. I had a couple of my boys tell the sergeant that they saw him doing such-and-such; you know, something he wasn't supposed to do. So he ended up having to dig a six-foot ditch during dinner."

Marvin isn't proud of his ruse. But the ploy was essential to survival. He said, "Training camp was like a giant, chaotic, crazed fifth grade, except everyone was carrying guns."

In his barrack, Marvin organized his personal things around his cot. He kept his mess kit – his Army-issued, metal food plate with cutlery – handy by hanging it on a nail in the wall below a window. He hung pants and a shirt from a nail higher on the wall. He stored everything else – fatigue jacket, shirt, tie, boots, shoes, underwear, long johns – in his duffle bag, secured by a padlock.

"One time, some guy – I think he was from Puerto Rico – stole my mess kit," Marvin said. "He never washed his own. Mine was washed and clean and polished. One day I came back to the barrack and it was gone. This one guy looked really guilty. He didn't know it, but I had scratched little X's into my kit with the edge of a spoon to mark it as mine. If I just treated it as lost, I'd have to pay a couple of bucks to get a new kit. That was a lot back then. So we got into a fight. I was wrestling with the guy, but I couldn't get a grip on him. He was oily and slippery. It was so hot in the swamps, your upper body was naked. He was slippery as an eel. Every time I thought I had him, he slipped through my hands. I finally got so exhausted I gave up."

But that soldier never touched Marvin's mess kit again.

War within a War

Marvin trained as a gunner on the 40-millimeter anti-aircraft gun, a weapon that commonly was transported on a four-wheel carriage. Big guns, small guns – Marvin demonstrated skill with a variety of weapons, and he knew how to handle himself in hand-to-hand combat.

Marvin does not portray himself as some G.I. Joe. He makes no claim to having been a one-man Army. He was just learning to be a soldier. Day by day, week by week, month by month, the Army was teaching Marvin how to fight for liberty and how to keep himself alive in a war zone. His outfit learned not only how to aim and fire the automatically loading 40-mm anti-aircraft cannon, but also how to hook its carriage to a truck and move it and how to set up the rig for firing in the field. Marvin's black outfit took great pride in knowing that their growing skill refuted the smug expectations of racists, and they took satisfaction in knowing that they were increasingly ready to turn the sky above Europe into a no-fly zone for Nazi airmen. "We learned to move fast, shoot straight, and move out," Marvin said.

Days began early in the morning, when a bugler rallied sleeping soldiers from their small metal cots with an abrupt blast of reveille. "He played at 4 or 5, depending on what we had to do that day," Marvin said. "It was 4 o'clock for marches through a swamp or drill on land. They'd wait until 5 o'clock for everything else."

If you didn't get out of bed, the sergeant would turn you and the cot over, Marvin says.

After reveille, men had five minutes to dress. Then they hit the latrine and went to the mess hall for breakfast. "We had half an hour to eat," Marvin said. "The food was plain. But I never thought about food in those days. We went back to the hut, then the latrine, and outside, where we got orders."

It was at Camp Stewart that Marvin found himself caught up in a war within a war.

Battle at Camp Stewart

Hollywood war flicks rarely depict the race-based conflicts that occurred between black and white troops as well as white civilians, mainly law officers in areas adjacent to military camps. But there were hundreds of such clashes, ranging from minor small brawls to serious large disturbances, according to an official Army history of what African-American troops endured in World War II.[82]

Army historian Ulysses Lee wrote, "[The fights] were a continuing cause for concern within the War Department and in the Army's higher commands. They continued to be a threat to discipline, to relations between Negro and white troops, to relations between the Army and civilians, and to unity in the war efforts on the home front. As fodder for propaganda against the Army and, in the hands of the enemy, against the nation, they were unsurpassed."[83]

The U.S. was a different nation in those early years of World War II. Many whites, especially in the South, felt threatened by the mere idea of arming and training black men.[84] Many whites feared the war would foster black militancy at home, and that blacks would use their military training and weapons to avenge or end their second-class citizenship with armed insurrection at a time when many white men were away from the home front, a Mississippi historian wrote about his state.[85] And steadfast in the pretzel logic of their bigotry, many Southern whites insisted on perpetuating racial discrimination in their communities surrounding military posts with large numbers of black troops. They saw no reason why the military itself should not continue its own Jim Crow rules.[86]

Surrounded by hostility, black servicemen felt threatened with discrimination, physical abuse, even murder, Lee wrote. The black public back home, whether in the North or South, "was convinced that the life of the Negro soldier was one of constant fear and danger while his unit was still in training," Lee added.

Blacks' fear was fueled by incidents such as the death in April 1941 of Private Felix Hall, an African-American soldier who was found hanging from a tree in a wooded section of Fort Benning, Georgia, with his hands tied behind his back. The Army suggested Hall's death might have been a suicide. Blacks decided it was obviously an old-fashioned racist lynching.[87]

The white public, especially in the towns near heavy troop concentrations, also felt constantly threatened, Lee wrote.

The number and size of racial disturbances throughout the war was in reality relatively small. But, Lee wrote, the screaming newspaper and radio reports of incidents that did occur persuaded many people among both races that the very next clash would spark a racial Armageddon.

It made no difference that incidents, hinging on serious racial animosities, occasionally sprang from circumstances that would be fodder for late-night TV talk-show comics if they happened in our own day and age and involved people of the same race. Exhibit A: A gun battle at Fort Dix in New Jersey on April 2, 1942, between white military police officers and black soldiers erupted out of an argument over the use of a telephone booth.[88]

When Marvin arrived at Camp Stewart in Georgia, racial animosity had turned the base into a powder keg, ripe for a deadly spark. The danger had been growing since 1941, Lee wrote. In fact, the War Department had received anonymous letters, petitions from civilian organizations, and other communications warning about conditions at the camp. Still, the Army had not taken adequate action. How could it? The Army's own segregation policies made it part of the problem.

Racial ill will was fueled by the large size of the populations involved. That increased the opportunities for race-based rows between black troops and everyone else.

Camp Stewart itself had a force of 40,000 to 50,000 men. It was near Savannah, a prominent Georgia city with a population of about 95,000. Two shipyards close by employed around 75,000. The Army air base at Hunter Field was worked by approximately 9,000 men. All of these men descended on Savannah for recreation. So did Marines from nearby Parris Island and the area's Coast Guardsmen on liberty.

Especially on Saturday nights, Savannah was inundated by men from all of these facilities and services. Camp Stewart alone sent a convoy of about 100 trucks, which carried 1,200 to 1,500 men. Sometimes 75% of them were blacks, Lee wrote. All together, this was simply too many young men often whooping it up for the city and military police to handle, even if they had been prepared to do so in a racially even-handed manner – which the vast majority were not. Black troops had been complaining for months about the treatment they received from white civilians and military cops in Savannah and at Camp Stewart alike, Lee wrote.

In the spring of 1943 the situation soured quickly. There were 14 black anti-aircraft units training at the post. Their men were mainly from the North. Many of them were well educated and had recently arrived from serving in areas where civilians and customs on their posts had been friendlier and less racially hostile, Lee wrote. At Stewart, they objected to the racial segregation of latrines and other facilities, which at this point even the War Department had barred. They reported being harassed by white MPs when they left and returned to the base. The complained about inadequate recreational facilities at Stewart. They beefed about everything from inferior bus transportation to their treatment by military and civilian police. They objected "to the lack of overnight lodging and meals at reasonable prices in Savannah in comparison with those available for white soldiers," Lee wrote.

African-American G.I.s were restricted to using blacks-only busses. Even though approximately 40% of the camp personnel were black, the Army provided six times more busses for white soldiers, the *New York Age*, a black newspaper, reported.[89] And taxicabs in Hinesville, the nearest town to Camp Stewart, refused to take black passengers.

Black troops also resented the attitude of white officers. And *New York Age* sneered in a news story that two of the offending officers, Colonels Gross and Ochs, were "of German extraction." No reader would have missed the implication that racist Nazi attitudes were in the blood of those men. But just in case anyone did not get the insinuation, the newspaper spelled out that black enlistees and officers characterized one white commanding general "as being 'definitely in sympathy with the whole policy of discrimination.'"

The list of black grievances mounted. African-American MPs were token puppets with no authority. All of the MPs stationed in Savannah were white, including those who patrolled black neighborhoods. There was no recreational facility in Savannah for black officers. The USO club for black soldiers could accommodate no more than 50 men. The white USO had nearly nine times more floor space, and white officers had a club of their own. *New York Age* spared no details in its recitation of gripes. The camp provided only "meager facilities" for treating venereal diseases among black soldiers. White civilian nurses refused to touch black G.I.s. "[A]nd in Savannah there is only one prophylactic station for colored soldiers," the newspaper said, citing an NAACP report.

This lengthy catalogue of complaints was no baseless whining by a corps of idle, undisciplined misfits posing as soldiers. On the contrary. Lee wrote that the black gunnery teams were considered well trained and sharp. "[T]he commanding officer at the training center said, 'They have the snappiest gun crews that I have ever seen in this whole place, and I go out [to observe crews] every day.'"

The accusations by blacks finally triggered a response. Army Inspector General Virgil Peterson recommended improvements in recreational facilities at the camp. He also advised staggering pass privileges to prevent overcrowding of latrines and buses, the use of more black MPs, and closer coordination among staff and commanders.

But before his recommendations could be implemented, this powder keg exploded.

On the evening of June 9 a rumor swept through black troop barracks that a black woman had been raped and murdered by white soldiers after they had killed her husband, Lee wrote. One version of the rumor specified that some of the murderers were military policemen.

This shocking story was made all the more believable by the callous violence shown to a black soldier in an actual incident just days earlier. MPs had quelled a disturbance with a viciously heavy hand. The new outrage they were hearing about MPs partaking in the rape and murder of a woman reminded black G.I.s of the excessive force against a fellow black soldier many had witnessed.

In the earlier occurrence, military policemen in vehicles armed with machine guns had stormed up to an off-post service club during a dance to break up a crowd gathered outside. At that moment, a black soldier happened to ask for a drink of water at a nearby ice plant. Instead of receiving a cold wet glass, he was battered on the head with ice tongs.

That incident had left many black troops at Camp Stewart primed to respond to any subsequent racial injustice. As Lee depicted it, "The majority of the Negro soldiers were convinced that justice and fair treatment were not to be had by them in neighboring communities and that the influence of these communities were strongly reflected in the racial policies of the command at Camp Stewart."

The troops' edginess was further fueled by fright. "Many Negro troops feared for their personal safety," Lee wrote. "Others, gripped by a feeling of desperation, had determined to fight back against existing abuses without regard to consequences."

So on the night of June 9, when the rumor of a black woman's rape and murder tore through black barracks, many African-American troops exploded in rage.

Around 8:30 nearly 100 soldiers, some armed with rifles, charged out of barracks housing several battalions, including the 458th. Lee wrote that officers tried to quell the agitated mob. "A wild shot was fired," Lee wrote. "Military police and vehicles were ordered to the area. The first crowd moved back and broke up but a second mob, tense with excitement and anger, formed later. Gun racks and supply rooms of several Negro battalions were broken into and ammunition, rifles, and submachine guns were removed. Some troops, bent on revenge, joined the mob; some went into the nearby woods in fear; others remained to 'fight it out' and to defend their areas. To add to the confusion of the evening, gas alarms rang out in nearly every battalion area."

Around 10 o'clock a military police vehicle approaching the disturbance was fired on. The shooting came from the 458th battalion, Marvin's battalion. Hell had just broken loose. More gun fire erupted in this and other battalion areas, and the shooting went on for two hours. Before long, four military policemen had been wounded, one seriously, Lee wrote. A civilian bus driver, fired on as he approached the area, was slightly wounded. The worst occurred shortly before midnight. A military police detail crossing a small parade ground on foot was fired on. One of the MPs was killed.

Marvin's Move

As mayhem erupted outside, Marvin was inside his barrack.

Each barrack was a simple wooden building the men called a hut or hutch. Each one housed the 10 men who constituted a gunnery crew. Marvin's was a microcosm of the camp. Some of the men were screaming and shouting, eager to join the riotous hysteria outside. Others were quiet and passive; pushed the right way, they would become mob followers, pulled out the door in the loudmouths' wake. Marvin felt alone. He felt surrounded by rabble rousers.

He was sitting on his cot. He had no intention of joining the flock that was psyching itself up to head outdoors. Five things were clear to Marvin.

First, joining a vigilante mob simply was not his style.

Second, the men who were baying the loudest about joining the riot were a gang of slackers. "They had been looking for a way out of the fight since Day One," Marvin said. "They were cowards who didn't want to be part of any invasion and didn't want to risk their lives for anything. They were always looking for excuses to get out. They were more concerned about fighting the Army than about getting ready to fight the Germans. If this riot hadn't come up, they would have gone AWOL [absent without leave] rather than ship out to join the fighting. If they had gone to Europe, they would have deserted."

Third, one of the loudest inciters was the guy who had stolen his mess kit. The guy was a natural born crook, Marvin thought. He was a trouble-maker, who was always on the side of the bad guys.

Fourth, what did all of this boil down to? Revenge for a black woman who had been raped and murdered by white soldiers after they had killed her husband, right? But what woman? Which soldiers? Said who? Where was the proof? Now some people wanted to grab rifles and shoot up the MPs...based on a rumor? That would be just as crazy as what the white soldiers had supposedly done.

And fifth, the Army was bigger and tougher than these punks. When this hot summer night cooled down, the Army would seek revenge. "The Army had spies," Marvin said. "They knew everything that went on. There was no way you could join the mob, then pretend you hadn't been part of it. There would be a day of reckoning."[90]

Amid all the shouting and chaos inside his barrack, Marvin shared his thoughts with anyone who asked.

"It was a shameful riot. It was cowardice," Marvin said. "It was a warped way to get out of going to Germany for the real fight."

Marvin remained in his barrack. Some of his gunnery mates stayed with him. The mess-kit thief and several of the others joined the riot outside.

Around 12:30 security reinforcements arrived in the disturbance area. Marvin was watching from his barrack just as half-tracks armed with .50-caliber machineguns and carrying troops barreled down Harmon Avenue alongside the parade ground to disperse the demonstrators there.[91] Shortly after that, the gunfire ceased and the conflict died down.[92] An astounding 5,000 rounds of ammunition had been fired.[93]

In the aftermath, it was determined that the story about a raped and murdered black woman and her homicide victim husband was in fact fiction. No such double slaying had taken place, Lee wrote.

A review board of officers tried to blame the eruption on the stationing of Northern blacks on this Southern base. They also attempted to blame the "average negro soldier's meager education, superstition, imagination and excitability."[94] Those factors made many of the black troops vulnerable to being "easily misled."

Segregationist attitudes certainly did not vanish overnight. Just seven weeks later, Brig. Gen. E. A. Stockton issued a directive, urging Camp Stewart's many Northern black soldiers to respect the traditions and laws of their host state, Georgia. "'The laws of Georgia provide for segregation,' the directive said, and added: 'Which means different places to sit on trains and busses, different hotels and cafes, and so on.'"[95]

Stockton even argued that slavery itself could not have been so bad. After all, "'[m]ost slave owners were good-hearted Christians, who liked for everybody around them to be happy. They were, as a rule, good to their slaves."

Heck, black soldiers should be grateful that Georgia does not treat them worse, Stockton seemed to argue. "The American colored man has come a long way since the days of slavery,'" he wrote.

Black newspapers, civic leaders, and organizations such as the Urban League and NAACP exploded with ridicule and condemnation of Stockton.

William R. Jackson, head administrator of the Newark, New Jersey, YMCA wrote, "'Nazism is the same, whether practiced by a German dictator or an American army officer.'"[96]

In the end, the Army review board recognized that the disturbance was a result of long pent-up emotions and frustrations by the black G.I.s.

The board recommended a list of remedial actions, including disbanding the 458th battalion. Army high command overruled that recommendation. For one thing, the 458th was too good.

"This unit appears to have had an excellent record of accomplishment prior to the riot," the Army higher-ups conceded, Lee wrote. And it would be a shame to waste all the money, time, and effort expended on the outfit's training. So the 458th was kept intact. But a lot of new soldiers were brought into the battalion. And the battalion itself was slapped with an official, severe reprimand.[97]

Besides, group guilt — guilt by association — is an idea repugnant to most Americans. Instead, Army command said only proven individual offenders should be punished.

Among those punished for participating in the riot: the man who had stolen Marvin's mess kit. "He was sent to Leavenworth," Marvin said, referring to the military prison located at Fort Leavenworth in Kansas.

Marvin got the exact opposite treatment. For keeping a cool head during the disturbance and apparently helping some of his barrack mates decide to steer clear of the violent turmoil, he was promoted to corporal.[98]

Chapter 6

Marvin's War

As if exhausted by the exertions and sacrifices of D-Day, the sun began to sag into the ocean late on June 6. Marvin and his outfit found themselves about a quarter mile inland from the beach. It had been a day of lethal mayhem. Marvin had seen torn bodies of fellow GIs on the beach and in the dunes. Gun fire and the bark of artillery had stung his ears. Fighter planes had screamed overhead. Several had twisted and gyrated. Marvin had been sure he was watching life-and-death aerial dog fights. Now, among the soon-to-be notorious hedgerows, which frustrated the advance of American armor and funneled GIs into the gun sights of German troops, Sgt. Edward O. DeWitt spread the word that it was time to dig in for the night.

Looking for a safe spot to sleep, Marvin did something that he calls one of his smartest moves in the war. It was also in violation of Army regulations.

"I found a piece of rubber from one of the [barrage] balloons," Marvin said. "It was a real nice piece of rubber. It was big enough to cover a pup tent or to wear like a poncho, and it didn't have any holes. I wasn't supposed to keep it because it wasn't regulation equipment. But it was way too good to throw away. So I kept it. That little piece of rubber helped me survive the war. But I had to keep it a secret – from the officers, not from the other guys. So I folded it during the day and tucked it under our truck. At night I pulled it out and covered myself or my tent with it. That's how crazy war was. This was the best piece of gear that I had. And it was illegal. I had to hide it. That's war."

Marvin had found the sheet of rubber because he happened to be in the right place at the right time. It also fell into his hands because he kept his eyes open and his wits sharp. That sheet of rubber became a symbol of Marvin's war-time experience. To survive the war, you needed to be lucky – and smart. Marvin was both.

War-Time Romance

After the riot at Camp Stewart in June 1943, military authorities dropped the hammer on individuals they found at fault. Marvin remembers some soldiers being sent to military prison. Others were assigned to other units. Marvin remembers men being transferred to units at Camp Atterbury in Indiana. The bulk of Marvin's outfit continued training.

"The worst of the cowards from the riot got sent to the stockade," Marvin said, referring to soldiers who were imprisoned. "The ones they couldn't prove anything about or who weren't good with anti-aircraft artillery were put into other units at Atterbury. The rest of the 458 they kept together."

That shake-up was just the tip of an iceberg that was aiming straight for Marvin's 458th battalion, but it would not hit for another 10 months. Meanwhile, Marvin had no way to see it coming.

All Marvin knew was that the war was heating up, and his outfit kept training. They were one of many blades that the Army continued to hone in anticipation of the D-Day invasion and taking the ground war into Hitler-held Europe.

Marvin and his buddies had no way to know, but the Army was getting ready to ship them overseas. Step one was to transfer the 458th to Camp Lee (today known as Fort Lee) in Virginia on February 8, 1944. The camp was named for Virginia-born General Robert E. Lee, the main military defender of the slavery stained Confederacy. "I don't think any of us realized it was named for him," Marvin said in hushed tones. Then he brightened, indulging in an uncharacteristic moment of ribald humor: "But if we had, I'm sure it would not have taken long for someone to make a crack about where they hoped wastes landed when they used the latrine."

On April 14 the 458th was moved to Camp Patrick Henry, also in Virginia. At some point while in Virginia, Marvin remembers the 458th setting up a tent encampment, which the men called Camp Pollack Shield, on a college campus.

"It was a cold winter," Marvin recalled. "That's where I met a girl, who went to college there. Her name was Helen."

Baltimore native Helen Green was attending Virginia State College for Negroes (now Virginia State University) in Ettrick, Virginia. She and Marvin began to date, and they grew close. "On dates we went for walks," Marvin recalled. "But there was nowhere to go. There were no movies in those days. And we were getting ready to go overseas."

Helen kept writing to Marvin after he shipped out to Europe. Her letters lend color to this long-ago relationship between two black teenagers in a time of war.

Helen starts a May 17, 1944 letter by writing, "Dearest one, I know you think I am no good at all, because I have waited so long to write. Please forgive me but I have been busy. I didn't write anyone. You know I always think of you and write [to] you first."

Helen was in turmoil. She was having a tough time in school and at work. She told her aunt that she would not be returning to school, and it upset her aunt very much. She also wrote that she was growing more and more fond of Marvin, whom she addressed as Eugene, the middle name that Marvin went by from boyhood until after returning from Army service at war's end.

"I know you have probably lost all faith in me now, and honestly I don't know what to say," Helen wrote. "But Eugene you know no matter what happens it's always you. Please forgive me. Examination will be over next Friday and then I go to work.

"When I think how long I waited to write after you asked me to I really feel bad. There are so many things I would like to tell you but I can't put them into words. Each day I think of you more and more. As you told me I had to grow up and I am growing. Growing to like you more and more. Know why I like you? You are so sweet to me. I'll care for you until you tell me to stop."

The letter continues for another paragraph. Helen signs it with a poetic, romantic flourish: "Forever thine, Helen."

In later letters, Helen begs Marvin to write more. But Marvin was distracted, to say the least. In the midst of combat, he was preoccupied with trying to stay alive.

End of the 458th

Romance was not the only thing that happened to Marvin in Virginia.

In the wake of the riot at Camp Stewart in June 1943, the Army had resisted suggestions by some officers that the 458th be disbanded (see Chapter 5). But Army records show that the outfit was disbanded on April 24, 1944.[99]

The 458th's written history summary is brief and concise. It lists what happened and when, but not why. It shows that the Army had planned to break up the outfit about two weeks earlier, but changed its mind. No reason was given.

It may be that the outfit was disbanded simply because other units needed its men more.

Or it may have happened because white officers up the chain of command had bitterly resented the racially oriented riot at Camp Stewart and had wanted revenge on the all-black battalion. When the Army refused to disband the battalion back in 1943, those officers may not have abandoned their anger against the black troops who had shot back at a segregated Army. Now, nearly a year later, with the battalion hundreds of miles away from Camp Stewart and on the verge of being shipped overseas, amid a blinding bureaucratic storm of paperwork, general orders from Washington, and troop movements around the nation and into the war zones of Europe and Japan, while the Army was thoroughly distracted by its own preparations for what would be the largest wartime invasion ever, those resentful white commanders may have acted on their last best chance to wipe out the memory of the black battalion that had defied them.

A third possibility is that the 458th was disbanded not out of revenge for the riot at Camp Stewart but as part of a broad, more general campaign by the Army to use black troops in service roles rather than combat. Many of those service tasks were the responsibility of quartermaster units.[100] This stemmed from lingering stereotypes. Many white officers and politicians continued to believe that African-Americans were not smart or brave enough to be entrusted with complex weapons and strategies. The War Department's policy of converting black combat troops to service tasks actually became a hot political issue as black voters back in the States complained about it more and more as the war progressed.[101]

For bland bureaucratic reasons or due to hostile racial attitudes, the 458th was disbanded. Yet the motives did not keep Marvin and his buddies from waging war against the Nazis and battling cracker discrimination, and doing so with the determination, honor, bravery, brains, skill, and inventiveness that their enemies refused to credit them with.

New Identity, Same Lethal Skills

Marvin was never told that his 458th had been buried. Life in that wartime Army was very different from life today in, let's say, a mom-and-pop business on Main Street or even a large corporation. Memos were not sent to staff. G.I.s might hear about a bureaucratic change like this through the grapevine. But officers in the World War II-era Army felt no obligation to share information with rank-and-file troops, certainly not merely for the sake of being polite. The troops had no need to know. And the white Army command for the most part was even less concerned with cozying up to black troops. Further, if organizational information fell into enemy hands, it could lead to U.S. deaths and battle losses.

As the war progressed, Marvin knew he was being shuttled among many different outfits. He always thought this was simply a matter of the Army making spur-of-the-moment decisions in the field to use whatever men were handy to get certain jobs done, even if the tasks were not what they had trained for. After all, this was war and chaos reigned. And being shuffled from one role to another contributed to his growing awareness that the Army could be callous in how it treated black soldiers. But Marvin was never informed that the 458th had actually been formally disbanded.

Another thing that masked the dissolution of the 458th was that Marvin's Battery A and apparently other batteries in the battalion were kept together in the U.S., then moved intact overseas.[102] It was only once they were overseas that Battery A (possibly with other units from the 458th) was attached to another outfit – in fact, maybe a succession of outfits. There's paperwork that seems to show Marvin spent time in three Quartermaster Truck Companies, the 4266th, the 3985th, and the 3390th.[103] Each was an all-black outfit.[104]

Restricting African-Americans to all-black units reflected the military's official segregation during the war. It also reflected the extent to which blacks were shunted into servant-like jobs such as cooks, waiters, and bus boys as well as low-prestige and unpleasant assignments to mortuary crews and truck drivers.[105]

Ending up in a quartermaster outfit may have been coincidence, or it may have stemmed from the time he spent at Camp Lee. In October 1941 Camp Lee had become the new home for the Army's quartermaster school. This was where the Army trained officers and soldiers in the arts of military supply and service.[106] As home of the Quartermaster Replacement

Training Center, the Army taught soldiers how to store, transport, and dish out essentials ranging from fuel, food, and other supplies, as well as handle mortuary affairs and laundry services. The center trained more than 300,000 officers and enlisted soldiers for service in both the European and the Pacific theaters, says Encyclopedia Virginia.[107]

Meanwhile, in the States and in England, Marvin and his buddies continued to train as an anti-aircraft artillery unit. Once they reached the war zone, they fought as anti-aircraft soldiers, even though they were technically attached to a truck outfit. And that was not unheard of. In the pressure cooker of a war zone, men often were called on to perform tasks for which they had not been trained.[108]

The Navy, for example, created 17 segregated construction battalions, known popularly as CBs or "Seabees." In the Palau Islands of the Southwest Pacific, "200 black Seabees with no previous combat experience joined in the assault against the Japanese [who held the island]. In the first week of the attack, half of the blacks in this stevedore unit were either killed or wounded. On many occasions, black Seabees suffered casualties performing their duties under artillery and mortar fire," says a Department of Defense study.[109]

Marvin's outfit had in fact been trained – and had distinguished itself – as an anti-aircraft outfit. Sure, bureaucrats had attached them to a trucking company. But the fact that they were kept together as a trained group with their equipment, ammunition, vehicles, and their officers shows that the Army – even white officers who may have hated them – had every intention of making use of their deadly skill at swatting enemy aircraft from the sky.

Shipping Out

In April or May of 1944, Marvin and his comrades were packed like sardines into the Queen Mary. Marvin always assumed the ship departed from Norfolk, Virginia. But for the sake of wartime security, the Army rarely spelled out operational details to rank-and-file troops. The force Marvin was in may have been switched to a different ship. Even if they went on the Queen Mary, that ship's departure point likely was kept secret and may even have been changed. Most of the Queen Mary's departures were from New York City, and Marvin says his outfit took a long truck ride from its encampment to the ship.[110] That drive probably was to New York.

"We got orders to get out of the camp real fast," Marvin said. "We got on trucks. We were ready to fight."

Modified for use as a troop transport, the Queen Mary was Spartan – quite a change from her look at birth. At her launch in September 1934 by Cunard/White Star Lines, she was the largest and fastest cruise ship in the world.[111] In her early years as a luxury liner, she boasted features such as two swimming pools, outdoor paddle tennis courts, children's nurseries, beauty salons, libraries, music studio, lecture hall, dog kennels, elevators, and a three-story tall main dining room.

After war erupted, the ship was transformed for war service. She was painted camouflage gray. Her luxury fittings and furnishings were removed in Sydney, Australia. Oil paintings, plush rugs, draperies, and crystal chandeliers were taken ashore for storage. So were cases of dining china and crystal and silverware. Stateroom beds and furniture were replaced by bunk beds and hammocks. Dining rooms were converted to medical areas and mess halls, where meals were served to some troops around the clock. Anti-aircraft guns, cannons, and machine guns were installed on decks. The ship was even fitted with torpedoes and depth charges. But the ship's main defense was her speed. She had been built to carry civilian passengers speedily as well in luxury. On each troop crossing, Queen Mary's speed and zig-zag maneuvers made her too difficult for any U-boat and aircraft to attack successfully, despite a huge bounty placed on her by Adolf Hitler.[112]

Passage was not comfortable, but the ship made up for that by being an efficient war machine. She was now able to carry up to 15,000 troops plus 2,000 crew, all at once. In a single voyage she could transport an entire army division. On crowded voyages, troops slept in relays, rotating in and out of bunks and hammocks every eight hours.[113]

From 1940 to 1945 810,000 people – mostly troops – traveled aboard Queen Mary, which logged 600,000 nautical miles altogether.[114]

Marvin's outfit, the remnant of the old 458th, was berthed in a large space near the bow, seven or eight levels beneath the top deck. "There must have been a thousand guys in there," Marvin said.

On their first day aboard ship, the men were shown how to rig their hammocks at night from ceiling hooks. At night they slept as close together as bats in a cave. Their initial debarkation was well after sunset. "The ship pulled out at night," Marvin said. "It was dark. The ship was quiet. The men were quiet. Very few people moved around the ship, to keep things quiet. London had been badly bombed, and it was a wartime mentality. We didn't want to take chances."

The idea was to avoid detection. "It was for safety, to avoid being seen or heard by German submarines or planes," Marvin said. "We were happy to get underway. But there was no cheering or noise or anything like that. We were warned not to laugh or talk because German submarines would pick up the sound."

The trip took a week or two, Marvin recalled "It was a big convoy. "We had smaller ships around us the whole way," Marvin said. The escort ships were positioned to make it harder to a u-boat captain to see the Queen Mary through a periscope. The smaller ships were also sacrificial pawns that could take a fatal torpedo hit to spare the big troop carrier.

Soldiers were generally quiet due to nerves and an all-business attitude. But soldiers were also repeatedly told to make as little noise as possible. Sound can carry far across water and travel fast through water, so being quiet was a defense against enemy submarines and surface warships. Crowding was a third reason for silence. With recreational facilities having been removed to make room for troops and medical areas, there was little if any opportunity for men to whoop things up.

During the day, men passed the time talking softly in smaller groups. Some men smoked. Many sat on their duffle bags and played cards on top of boxes. When the brass showed movies, the men were allowed to have beer. The films were popular ones featuring Hollywood stars. Many were news reels and propaganda. "They showed news reels about London being bombed to show what Hitler was doing, to remind us what we were fighting for and what we were getting into," Marvin said. "Some of it was scary."

Very few men were allowed to roam around the ship. Other outfits, some white, some black, were spread throughout the ship, but men did not circulate and there was virtually no interaction among different outfits. There was also lots of gear and weapons.

Marvin's outfit was in a cargo hold. In the middle of the space a large, wide shaft rose up through all of the ship's levels to the top deck. During daytime the lid at the top of that opening was removed to let fresh air and sunlight in. Any time Marvin looked up he saw a safety net covering the huge skylight.

When it was meal time, Marvin ate either C rations or K rations. C rations consisted of cans of precooked meat, vegetable or potato, and crackers, sugar and soluble coffee. K rations were separate containers of breakfast, lunch, and dinner concoctions.[115] No mess area was set up for Marvin's outfit. There was no hot food. Guys ate wherever they liked. And if hot meals were served to other troops elsewhere on the ship during this crossing, Marvin's outfit was not invited.

The worst pitching and rolling was during the first day or two, but the ship never stopped its stomach-churning motion the entire voyage.

"It was very hard to sleep. I never slept," Marvin said. "I was afraid I'd fall off the hammock, and the motion of the ship never stopped. It wasn't comfortable. It wasn't set up to be comfortable. They took everything comfortable off the ship, and they didn't do anything to make us comfortable. And there were a lot of men packed in there. We were trying to ship as many men and guns over to stop Hitler as possible. It made us feel like we were expendable, especially if you were black."

The ship's movement not only made sleeping hard, it also made men sick. "A lot of guys got seasick," Marvin said. Sometimes the raw stink of vomit hung in the air. And the crowded, tough, young men kicked off a lot of body odor. "There was no air-conditioning. You just lived with it. You lived with all of it," Marvin said. "I got seasickness pills. But the only way to get away from the feeling was to get off the ship, and you couldn't do that. When men got sick, they cleaned up after themselves. And there were doctors and nurses aboard ship for the guys who felt worst. Most of the time it didn't smell that badly. Well, most of the time."

Practice, More Practice

Marvin was lucky. Neither the ship nor the convoy was attacked during the crossing. The ship docked in Liverpool, England. "We switched to small ships, then rode up to Gourock, Scotland," Marvin said. "The small ships carried just 300 to 400 troops each. From there, we traveled by trucks to outside of Glasgow, where we bivouacked. It took a day, maybe a little more to get there."

Marvin remembers his outfit "reforming" for training purposes. This was probably a result of the 458th's being disbanded. The "reforming" was actually a matter of troops being divvied out to their new units. When Marvin's outfit reached Glasgow, he found the city filled with black troops. The next time Marvin saw Glasgow, the next year, it was bustling with white G.I.s. Many treated him as an enemy. He often felt as hated as a German soldier.

But for the moment, upon his initial arrival, Glasgow was a peaceful place for Marvin. His outfit stayed a couple of weeks, then began to travel south in England.

"We went to Nottingham, near Sherwood Forest," Marvin said. "We bivouacked and trained there. Then we went to Cambridge. Next we went to Birkenhead. We bivouacked and trained on the golf course." Birkenhead is on the western shore of River Mersey, opposite Liverpool.

At each stop, Marvin's outfit rehearsed. Again and again they practiced hitching their artillery to trucks, then driving trucks up narrow ramps and down those same ramps.

On D-Day, precision would be crucial. The men would have to perform their tasks with literally precious room for error. If a driver veered an extra few inches off to either side, his truck, weapons, ammunition, and buddies would slide off the ramp. That would jam up the parade of men and material. The finely choreographed dance would grind to a halt, delaying debarkation from the ship, wasting precious time. Under fire, men in Marvin's outfit would be exposed to injury or death. One of their artillery guns that would save some other G.I.'s life might be too late or never make it. So it all had to become second nature to Marvin's outfit. Through repeated rehearsals, they had to master their maneuvers so they could nail the tasks whether they were under fire, in sloppy rain, shrouded in the smoke and fog of a battlefield, unable to hear each other because of the din and chaos of combat all around them.

And off-loading from their floating transport wasn't the only thing they practiced time after time. They rehearsed racing to a spot in an open field, unhitching their artillery, setting up a battery, spotting enemy aircraft, and firing at the target.

And everything was rehearsed at double time. Fast, fast, fast.

The tone of training changed in Birkenhead. Suddenly, sergeants and lieutenants focused on training the men to waterproof their weapons. Men were taught to cram greasy gunk down the barrels of guns, rifles, and artillery and into any nook or cranny in a weapon that would be fouled or jammed by salt water. They were taught similar precautions with their vehicles. The men learned to plug exhaust pipes and air intakes. The men were also taught how to clear the gunk out of weapons and vehicles. And the men were taught to how to hold their handguns and rifles above their heads, to keep them out of any beach surf they'd shortly have to wade through.

"No one said anything to us, but we knew we were getting ready for the invasion," Marvin said.

The outfit's movement southward through Great Britain, the back northwest to Birkenhead and Liverpool, was like a boxer closing in on an opponent, slowly, deliberately, making the ring smaller and smaller. All of the training, all of the travel, was to position the outfit for boarding ships once again, this time in Liverpool, for what the Army hoped would be one final journey across a body of water – the trip to Normandy, for the invasion of France. The drills performed by Marvin's outfit were like a boxer's jab, jab, jab.

By June 1944, the historic final voyage was only days away. A ferocious enemy awaited them, determined to slaughter these men wherever they dared to put foot on German-held soil.

Plane Spotting

When Marvin's outfit got to Liverpool, it began to load onto transport ships. Officers said nothing about the invasion being near. But the men could feel it. "Nobody said *noth*-ing to us," Marvin said. Marvin's transport moved out to sea. Days went by. The ship pitched and rolled. The salt water spray turned Marvin's skin ashen white. "I looked like a ghost," he said.

The ship was on the water well over a week. To kill time, Marvin wrote letters to home. He deleted details for the sake of security, but told friends and family his transport had been at sea a long time. More than a month later Priscilla Sprague, Marvin's former voice instructor and an older family friend, wrote back. "So you are a sailor instead of a soldier!" she joked. "I have been trying to puzzle out where you are, whether it is somewhere between England and France, or in the Mediterranean."

Priscilla had no inkling that Marvin had written while he was in the midst of the world's greatest invasion fleet.

On the morning of June 6 Marvin awoke to see that his ship was surrounded by other ships. There was a traffic jam in the Channel. "There were ships everywhere," he said. "We knew we were going to land in France."

Finally, the landing he and his buddies had practiced countless times began to unfold in front of Marvin. Smog and smoke curtained his view of much of the action on the beach. But he caught glimpses of an occasional bright flash on land – the result of cannon shells landing or German artillery fire or other detonations. And the soundtrack of explosions and gunfire became clearer the closer his ship got to the shoreline. Overhead, he could hear and see German warplanes. That is what he had been trained to look for – enemy aircraft to shoot from the sky.

Starting back in the States, part of Marvin's training had focused on identifying German fighters and bombers. "Once we got to Europe, they didn't want us shooting down our own airplanes," Marvin chuckles, one of his few war memories that is not somber. "They taught us to recognize all the different types of military aircraft in Europe, and recognize the German ones as quick as possible. We were training on those big 40-milimeter anti-aircraft guns to shoot down German planes. But friendly fire is no joke. You don't want to realize you've just shot down a U.S. plane or an English plane."

Now, off the Normandy shore, by far most of the action was on the ground and in the water all around. But Marvin could not stop looking skyward. His training would not let go.

"We were in a segregated army. It was segregated by Congress," Marvin said. "The myth was that we didn't know how to fight, that we were cowards. That's what the crackers called us: cowards. But I knew one of the reasons I was there in that ship heading for those beaches was to fight what those people said about us. We were there to fight the Germans. And we were there to fight what the crackers said. I never thought about getting killed or wounded. I was too ready for the fight."

Surrounded by Enemies

At the end of the crazy first day ashore in France, Marvin's sergeant gave his outfit the order to dig in for the night. Marvin sat with his back to a tree, then checked his weapons – carbine, handguns, grenades, bayonets. He just wanted to be ready to defend himself. Enemies surrounded him.

He cradled his rifle in his arms and tried to doze off. But it was impossible. He could not fall asleep. He was too nervous, too jazzed, too alert.

Marvin had no way of knowing it then, but this was the start of a stretch that would last for months when his body refused to relax enough to let him slumber. He was on guard permanently now. He was a stew of nerves, fear, fatigue, adrenalin, aches, and pain. His spiced-up senses would not allow both of his eyes to close simultaneously, not by choice anyway.

The rest of his time on the continent he did not remember falling asleep even once until he was hospitalized with a combat wound. Still, on this first night in France he embraced his carbine, keeping it at the ready, guarding himself. He would take the same precaution every night after that in France.

"I didn't know how close or far the Germans were," Marvin said decades later.

His prayer was that the tree at his back and his handy weapons would help protect him from any German patrol infiltrating this area. But Germans weren't the only threat Marvin was guarding against.

"Crackers would try to kill me," Marvin said, using a slang put-down for bigoted whites, especially those from the rural South. "They were as much of a danger to me as the Germans were."

Marvin also had crazed enemies among Southern black soldiers. In his earliest days of boot camp Marvin had discovered that many of those young men resented Northern blacks who, like Marvin, were better educated, more articulate, more optimistic about their futures. Marvin was just one of tens of thousands of young African-Americans from the North sent to training camps in the South, and many proved to be cocky, confident competition for the affections of young black Southern girls. Marvin found that young Southern black G.I.s were also jealous of the way that Northern blacks were not cowed by crackers. "We hadn't been raised to fear Southern whites the way Southern blacks had been," Marvin said. "And Southern black soldiers could see it!"

Yet Marvin had no delusions about being immune to the very real danger of physical harm, even death, posed by white bigots, especially from the South. He had grown up in an America where racism was overt and widespread, even if not universal. His own grandparents had been slaves, and he had heard their harrowing stories dozens of times. "Before I went into the Army and before I went south for training, my parents had warned me over and over to remember my place in the South."

Still, the dynamic between Northern black soldiers and Southern white G.I.s was unmistakably different than the one that Southern blacks had. The Southern blacks could see it. Marvin could see it. So for many young Southern black soldiers, there were more than enough reasons to resent and despise the Marvin Gilmores of their world.

At War

Marvin E. Gilmore Jr. was in a war zone. And he was fighting on three fronts against three separate enemies, each equally dedicated to his destruction. There were Germans, members of the *wehrmacht*. And since his earliest days at boot camp, shortly after joining the Army, he had also been battling some American soldiers who were devout racists, offended by any other black man, woman, or child who failed to show satisfactory subservience.[116] Their bigotry took on an even sharper edge when it came to Marvin. They were especially opposed to his being armed and trained in martial arts. Those un-American Americans went out of their way to discourage him and other African-Americans from serving their country. They did that through a wide array of actions, ranging from insults and intimidation and inconveniences to physical threats and, on occasions, attempts to physically injure – or kill him.

Incredibly, just as deadly were those young Southern black soldiers who saw Marvin as some sort of class enemy.

So on this first night in France, Marvin was on alert for all of his potential mortal enemies. He may not have thought about it at the time, he may not have put it into so many words as he sat against the base of that tree close to the beach in France, exhausted by the day's ardor and hoping earnestly for nothing more than a night's precious rest. But at least in the case of the Germans and home-grown white bigots he was fighting these wars not just for himself, not even just for other people of color, nor even just for France, but for all Americans of all races, all colors, all creeds.

He may not have expressed it. But Marvin knew it. He knew it the way any black person knew it. He knew it the way any thoughtful American knew it. He knew it the way any U.S. soldier, sailor, flyer, or Marine knew it in those moments when he wasn't preoccupied with the intense struggle to survive.

Marvin's dedication to the cause of democracy and liberty was total. He was a volunteer, a young man who had eagerly left school so he could enlist in the Army while he was underage, needing a parent's signed consent. He had stepped up to the plate of his own volition, well before any draft board had come calling. And he was here despite being painfully aware that the Army was officially segregated. The rationale for that discrimination was the widespread slur that blacks were inferior fighters, undisciplined, and incapable of leadership.[117] Many whites embraced the tortured logic that blacks had no interest in defending a people who treated them as second-class citizens – not that there was anything wrong with oppressing blacks, that screwball reasoning went.

Even after accepting African-Americans into its ranks, the Army reflected biases in much of white society by embracing segregation, which remained official policy until 1948 – three years after the war's end.[118] The Army funneled black servicemen into all-black units – not to nurture pride and cohesion, but to spare white servicemen from having to mingle with blacks, share facilities with blacks, and compete with blacks. Yet black outfits were typically commanded by white officers. In the Navy, blacks were restricted to service jobs as cooks, janitors, and waiters. The Marines refused to admit blacks until 1942.[119]

Military base chapels, mess halls, and entertainment facilities excluded or segregated black soldiers.[120] Military bus services also either excluded blacks or were segregated. Jim Crow discrimination was a fact of life on bases and in many surrounding communities, historian Jerrold M. Packard wrote. "Jim Crow-style discrimination was by no means confined to the South, black service members experiencing overt racial discrimination in military towns in every section of the country. But the South housed a disproportionate percentage of military bases through the war years, and throughout the region the humiliations of racial discrimination were brought to a high and sometimes deadly degree of malignancy."[121]

Black servicemen repeatedly saw German prisoners of war treated with more respect than they got. African-American military police officers in the South often were barred from restaurants where their German prisoners were being served a meal.[122]

"German prisoners of war held in United States military bases were commonly permitted to dine with white U.S. soldiers in facilities that excluded black U.S. soldiers. When Lena Horne, an African-American songstress, performed in a southern GI camp, German prisoners of war were given front row seats while black servicemen were relegated to the back of the theater. Horne delivered her performance in the aisles before her fellow black Americans, but, shaken by the experience, she ended her military tour."[123]

For Marvin and other black servicemen, life in the military was often colored by painful irony.

"The world's greatest democracy fought the world's greatest racist [Adolf Hitler] with a segregated Army," wrote Stephan Ambrose, probably America's best-known World War II historian.[124]

So why did African-Americans like Marvin wholeheartedly join a war in support of a nation whose laws treated them with disdain, and many of whose citizens subjected blacks to discrimination that was often enforced with violence? Why did Marvin and others like him put themselves in harm's way for people who often seemed to resent their mere presence?

The vast majority of African-Americans agreed with heavyweight boxing champion Joe Louis, who was black, who said, "America's got lots of problems, but Hitler won't fix them."[125]

America was home. For Marvin, Cambridge, Massachusetts, was home. And Marvin and millions more African-Americans reasoned that this war, this colossal disruption that was erupting all around them, was an opportunity wearing a cruel disguise. On street corners, in churches, in schools, in bars, in food stores, at kitchen tables, on the pages of black newspapers, African-Americans talked it out among themselves. And overwhelmingly they concluded that they could make war on bigotry at home at the same time that they made war against hatred and repression abroad.

As the New Jersey Historical Commission explained in public-school educational literature, "African Americans ... saw fit to 'close ranks' once the United States entered the war in 1941, not-withstanding their treatment as second-class citizens and the siren call by the Japanese [for unity among people of color]...against the United States as World War II approached. But while they viewed Germany and Japan as the aggressors, they also saw the elimination of racial discrimination as a war aim."

In fact, many African-Americans were inspired by the President of the United States, Franklin D. Roosevelt. In his State of the Union speech in January 1941 – as America continued its fight to climb out of the Great Depression – FDR had proclaimed four fundamental freedoms that Americans and others should be able to enjoy. The freedoms were of speech, of religion, from want (like hunger and unemployment), and from fear (of war). The public quickly nicknamed Roosevelt's address the Four Freedoms Speech.

Like other Americans, America's blacks wanted those Four Freedoms. Rallied by black leaders and publicized by the black press, America's black community embraced what it called a Double V Campaign: victory against dictatorships abroad and victory against racism at home.[126] African-Americans who were risking life and limb in foreign lands wanted to receive full citizenship rights at home.

"I never had to think about it," Marvin said. "It was natural. I was an American. Of course I was going to fight to defend my country. But I could see the bigger picture. I knew what was at stake. Blacks had just as much at stake as America itself did. I was fighting for those goals too."

Chapter 7

A Swiss-Army-Knife Soldier

Reality slapped Marvin's outfit hard. The invasion, which had seemed to start well, bogged down. After their first day ashore, Marvin's outfit moved inland, but they couldn't get far. They found themselves in a countryside that was divided into a checkerboard pattern of farm plots. Each plot was delineated by trees and bushes growing from the top of hedgerows. The hedgerows penned the men in.

Each hedgerow was an earthen embankment roughly six and a half feet tall, with a flat-top surface. Beech, oak, and chestnut trees sprouted from the crown of each embankment. Thick, tall, and steep, the hedgerows formed walls that would make the advance of Allied tanks and artillery and anti-aircraft guns extremely difficult in the hours and days ahead, slowing the American-led invasion. German machine-gunners could mow down infantry daring to enter a field at a corner, where there were gaps in the hedgerows.[127]

"The worst thing was the Germans shooting at us, Messerschmitts strafing us, and Germans who were still nearby," Marvin said. "They were sneaking around, especially at night when you couldn't see.

"One day a Messerschmitt came screaming in low along the hedgerows. We couldn't hear the engine until it was right there. Flying low somehow concealed the sound. The plane was only eight or 10 feet in the air, just above the hedgerows. We were in farmland. We had more than half a dozen jeeps. It was still summertime. I don't remember the plane shooting any of us, but it scared a few of the fellas."

Mortuary Detail

Marvin and his buddies followed whatever orders came down, even if they had nothing to do with anti-aircraft artillery. Sometimes Marvin and his fellow G.I.s got an order because they were the handiest G.I.s. Sometimes, Marvin wondered whether it was because he and his buddies were black. That's what he wondered in the first days after the D-Day landings. As the battle for Normandy expanded, Marvin was assigned to put the dead and wounded onto jeeps and trucks.

"When guys in our outfit got shot, we radioed back to camp for a truck," Marvin said. "When guys got killed, we never looked at the dead. If you got shot, you got badly chewed up. It's not like TV or the movies. So we never looked at the head because that strikes fear into you. We had no time to cry. We were trained not to. But we had guys who couldn't handle it. They were dealt with later on. And that's why some guys went AWOL [absent without leave]. Fear."

Slogging It Out

For Marvin, the days and weeks after the landing became a blur of tasks. He would end up criss-crossing the northwest European battle zones, performing a dizzying lineup of soldier's duties. Artillery. Truck driver. Mortuary detail. Clerk. He became a Swiss-army-knife soldier: one G.I. able to perform a wide variety of jobs. The one constant was danger.

In Caen, France, he was assigned to a group of British officers for a couple of weeks. "I drove a jeep for them," Marvin said. "They were looking for [artillery] guns. We drove all around the front. It was dangerous. We were out there alone. We could have been shot or hit a land mine."

Back with his outfit, the men moved west to Cherbourg. Cherbourg was a major port just to the west of the D-Day Normandy beaches, fronting the English Channel. In their retreat, the Germans destroyed 90% of the port's harbor facilities. The Allies took Cherbourg on June 30, and the Americans immediately began to restore the port and its harbor works so that the Allies could use it as a landing point for soldiers and material, feeding the Allies' push eastward, further into France and towards Belgium, Holland, and Germany itself.[128]

Yet the battle front was still close by. Fighting remained fierce, and the outcome of the overall invasion was uncertain. Cherbourg's value to the Allies was absolutely clear to the German army and air force. With its vulnerability to attack, the allies wanted to set up anti-aircraft batteries as quickly as possible.

A similar need arose when the Allies liberated Le Havre on September 12, 1944. Le Havre was another big port opening to the Channel, even better positioned to feed the Allied surge eastward. It sat at the mouth of the River Seine. Like Cherbourg, it flanked the Normandy beaches area. It was situated on the far eastern tip of the Bay of the Seine, facing Cherbourg 78 miles away in a straight line across the big bay, or 95 miles by land.[129] "We bivouacked in Mayville, a little island outside Le Havre," Marvin said.

Marvin's outfit set up anti-aircraft batteries on a small island off Le Havre. With the passage of weeks, the seasons had changed and the weather turned freezing cold. "It was so cold, ice was coming out of my nose," he said. "My water canteen froze solid."

The sheet of rubber that Marvin found on his first day on French soil was a lifesaver. Every night in the field he slept outdoors. "I kept it under a truck," Marvin said. "At night I used it to cover my pup tent. I kept the rain and snow from running into the tent. I dug a trench around the tent to keep water from coming into the tent. I made a little moat. That rubber kept me dry and warmer than I would have been."

The sheet measured about five feet by five feet. It was jagged, heavy, and grayish black. "It kept me dry even with snow or rain," Marvin said. "I found stones to hold the rubber in place."

Marvin turned pitching a tent at night into an art. "You had to learn where to pitch your tent. I tried to pitch mine under a tree. That gave me protection in case the enemy snuck up on us, and if I leaned against the tree it helped my back."

The rubber sheet was one of the few layers of protection that Marvin had against the elements. "I had two pairs of socks, long underwear, a short jacket, an overcoat, a couple handkerchiefs, two shirts, two pair of wool pants, my hat – and that was it," he said. "You slept with your clothes on."

When he could, Marvin would wash his underwear in any nearby river or stream. Sometimes he used a traveling Army laundry truck. Sometimes he'd pay a French civilian to wash his clothes. It was a special treat when an Army shower truck rolled through camp. "Didn't seem to be there much," he said.

There was nothing fun about sleeping outdoors like this. He was not on a recreational camping trip. "I never really slept," he said. "I kept my guns ready and loaded. I never kept pictures of my family on me. Officers never wore their insignia. There was no glamour to this. My only bed was the dirt ground. It was cold and hard and dirty. The warmest thing I had was my long woolen overcoat. I never got a leave to come home. You *forgot* about home. Remembering home would upset you too much. The Army was my home."

Food contributed to Marvin's misery. Most of it was bland at best, awful tasting at worst. For most of the war, he lived on C rations and K rations, those meals in small containers. None were contenders for any culinary awards. As one modern Web site puts it: "The field rations of the 1940s were a compromise between caloric and nutritional specifications, suitability for mass production, and need for compact packaging. Most GI's would suggest that flavor and variety were way, way down on the list — if there at all."[130]

Becoming mentally tough had begun in boot camp and follow-up training camps in the U.S.

"It was not easy to survive in World War II, I don't care who you are," Marvin said. "The buck sergeant's job was to harden you.[131] He kicked your ass to toughen you up. Those sergeants trained us to become tough and hard. They knew that war was no joke, and that you had to be tough to survive it. Not just the shooting and the marching, but the constant threat of danger, the loneliness, the tough conditions. No one talked nice to you in the Army, not in boot camp, not in France. The sergeants would beat the hell out of you if you were weak. That strengthened me to fight for existence every day, back in the States and then France and Germany.

"At that level, you didn't give a damn. The only rule was survival. That's what you were trained on. The quickest way to end the misery was to kill the enemy as quick as possible and get myself home. There was no shortcut, no sugar-coating it."

Only the most basic necessities were important in the field. In letters to Marvin from friends and family back in the States, warm clothes are one of the most frequent topics. In letter after letter, people ask Marvin if the socks or mittens or scarf or hat they knitted had reached him. And once they did, Marvin was sure to send his thanks when he got around to writing, which was never often enough, judging by his repeated apologies.

"People sent knitted head gear, gloves, sweaters," Marvin said. "My mother and friends and the church back in Cambridge sent me items in winter to keep me warm. They bought olive green colored yarn and knitted the clothes. I loved getting the clothes! It was freezing cold in the winter, so the clothes were a big help. The Army told us to wear our helmets all the time, so the knitted caps had covers on the eyes and ears. And people sent us long johns too. They had a trap door on your bottom!"

He and his mother had both worked for Mr. and Mrs. H.H. White, a wealthy couple with homes in affluent Brookline and Marblehead. "I asked Mrs. White and my mother to send me long underwear to keep me warm, and they sent me a nice, warm knitted scarf. They sent me soap and handkerchiefs."

Washing and keeping clean was a top concern in the field. When some soldiers got lice, others kept their distance. Keeping clean was a challenge. "If you used your helmet to wash or shave, you could get court-martialed," Marvin said. Still, that wasn't as much of a problem for Marvin as it was for guys who were two or three years older. "I was too young to shave."

Priscilla Sprague, his old singing teacher and family friend from home, wrote to Marvin. She was dumbstruck by a grim letter he had written to her. She wrote, "Of course war isn't easy wherever you are. What a terrible slice of life you are getting all in one gulp. And things aren't moving as fast you wish they were, as we all wish they were."

Roll Call

Every day was a duel with death. "Sgt. DeWitt took roll call every morning at 6 and again at night, maybe 8 o'clock," Marvin said. "Sometimes guys were gone. They didn't answer. They had disappeared. Some guys might be AWOL. Other guys thought they were on Fifth Ave. Stupid. They'd sneak out of camp at night to go into town. If they snuck out with no gun, they could get killed. They might get jumped or grabbed by German infiltrators. Or someone in the underground might kill you to get your boots or money. You've got to remember a lot of soldiers were uneducated, and they did stupid things that could cost them their lives. Our company commander had to remind them this was war; we weren't there as tourists.

"You didn't wander far at night. If you had to go someplace, you went with other soldiers. There was strength in numbers.

"After a few guys disappeared, the sergeants had to post more people to take guard duty. They'd change guard every two to three hours, and you better not sleep."

Visiting nearby towns was a way to cope with boredom and stress. But venturing away from your outfit was dangerous. Life near the front was not like a Hollywood war movie. It was not glamorous. It consisted of bouts of brutal combat and tedious labor separated by boring pauses. Its random violence could be downright medieval.

"Sure, I took chances," Marvin said. "And I'm very fortunate. Sometimes you do things I shouldn't have done. Fortunately, I didn't get killed. Every day we were warned and cautioned, don't leave camp. Wherever you go, carry your guns. But a lot of soldiers were stupid and never came back. I'd look around and say, 'What happened to John?' Guy left camp and never made it back. I don't know what happened to him. Somebody probably killed him. Could have been a knife. Could have been with a gun. Those situations went on. War is unpleasant.

"But you couldn't keep the men from going to town. Sure, we liked the French women. The American Army provided women for the men. Men would line up. Most men were crazy in the war, going out of their minds. So the Army had to provide those necessary situations. I was a kid. My naiveness kept me on the path of righteousness. I was fortunate. I didn't get caught in that whole rough way of life."

Discovering the Black Market

One day Marvin was told to drive his sergeant to a local field headquarters. "I was sent with our sergeant to headquarters to get new orders," Marvin said. "I drove a jeep there. We came back outside a couple of hours later. The jeep was gone. You know, they charged me for that jeep. They charged me and the sergeant."

That was Marvin's introduction to the wartime black market. "There were black markets run by our own soldiers," Marvin said. "Some were very dangerous men. And the French underground had a black market."

War of course disrupted commerce, creating huge demand for many goods and services that were in painfully short supply. Black marketers on all sides were all too willing to profit from that distorted imbalance, and they had no qualms about stealing equipment – or paying unscrupulous soldiers or civilians for stolen goods. Including jeeps.

The U.S. Army reimbursed itself for the purloined jeep by docking Marvin and his sergeant.

"After the war, my sergeant applied for a refund and got it," Marvin said. "He told me how to apply. I wrote to the War Department and described what happened, and they sent me a check for $200 or $300. They kept a portion, $25 or $30, for loss of the jeep. It was the only time I got a check from the government quickly."

Marvin Gilmore, Company Clerk

Like members of civilian society, soldiers banded together based on shared interests. Honest soldiers who wanted no part of criminal activity banded together for mutual protection. Some found themselves involved in coping with criminal elements within the Army.

Marvin's sergeant, Edward O. DeWitt became something of a guardian angel to the young soldier from Cambridge, Massachusetts. DeWitt simply liked Marvin, who strikes people as friendly, charming, and energetic.

DeWitt also needed an aide who was honest and could read and write, so he could handle paperwork that DeWitt needed to delegate. Marvin more than fit that bill.

"I had two jobs in the Army," Marvin said. "Firing guns and being company clerk. I became clerk because I knew how to type."

But being company clerk could be perilous. One of Marvin's responsibilities as clerk was to keep the minutes of court-martials and other formal justice proceedings. Some defendants and suspects figured they could erase disciplinary proceedings by eliminating the record of the hearing or trial – or by eliminating Marvin himself.

"DeWitt told me where to sleep and not to sleep out in the field," Marvin said. "He kept me separate from other men who were not clean, who had lice, who would kill me at night if they could."

Some defendants and suspects were doubly dangerous. They were not only criminally inclined. They were also trained to fight and kill. "During court-martials, some defendants were kept in cages to keep them from jumping on judges," Marvin said. "Imagine what they would do to me!"

Cases involved serious crimes such as rape and murder. And thieves stole anything they could carry. "They set up companies where they sold stuff on the black market," Marvin said. "You could stumble on black marketers selling ammo, guns, fuel, you name it. It was unbelievable what they had. Some had very large organizations, so they had a lot at stake. They could lose a lot. They could be sent to the stockade."

So those defendants were highly motivated to avoid prosecution, and were not above intimidating or killing judges, prosecutors – and Marvin, the guy taking notes of proceedings. "I wasn't looking for trouble," Marvin said. "I minded my own business. I tried not to see anything that could cause me trouble. War was rough. In those court-martials, I was isolated next to my sergeant."

Red Ball Express

In late 1944, Marvin, who had been a runner for his high-school track squad, got conscripted into the Red Ball Express, the soon-to-be famous relay team of truck convoys that hauled urgently needed materials to the front. The nonstop supply circuit was desperately important to the war effort, bringing everything from fuel to bullets, cannon shells, food, medical supplies, lubricants, spare parts, and other vital supplies to front-line outfits. The work was also dreadfully dangerous.

And it was one of the least publicized stories of heroism by African-American troops. Three-quarters of the drivers, infantry, and mechanics were black.[132]

Driving trucks was one of those supposedly menial service jobs to which the segregated Army consigned black troops. But the Red Ball Express performed its vital task well despite adverse conditions. The men of the Red Ball Express excelled by demonstrating precisely the skills and qualities that many whites accused them of lacking, such as courage, smarts, energy, and teamwork.

The Army realized it needed to cobble together a makeshift supply line right away when the Third Army's General George Patton and the First Army's General Courtney Hodges began to achieve unexpected breakout victories in the late summer of 1944. But their tanks began to grind to a halt in the field due to shortages of fuel, cannon shells, and other necessities. The Yanks were frantic for a way to resume their pursuit of the retreating German forces. But they could not use French rail lines to transport the needed war supplies. The rails had been reduced to ragged steel tooth picks by the Allies' pre-invasion bombing attacks.

In an emergency brainstorming session, Army brass conceived of an alternative strategy: a barrage of truck convoys.[133]

One key problem was a dire lack of drivers. To make up for that, the Army cannibalized its own forces. Drivers were drawn from quartermaster and transportation companies and battalions. They were also pulled from infantry, artillery, and anti-aircraft units like Marvin's. Short of trucks as well, units that had their own vehicles were combed for drivers and vehicles. Men and vehicles that weren't in fire fights at the front at that very moment or that weren't in some other critical activity were most likely to be dragooned for this new supply campaign.[134] Marvin's outfit met all of the requirements.

The supply circuit got its name from railroad jargon. Back in the States, rail cars that carried perishable goods that needed right of way to speed them along for years had been referred to as "red balls." The Army adopted that practice, slapping signs with bright red balls on the sides of trucks in its high-priority convoys. Signs with red balls were erected along the roads used by the convoys.[135]

Glitches cropped up right away. When the first convoys headed east, they got bogged down in civilian and military traffic. The Army instantly took over two parallel highways between the Normandy beach head, where supplies were piling up, and the city of Chartres, outside Paris. As the front progressed eastward, the Red Ball Express' priority route was extended too.[136]

Ironically, the convoys also became a conveyor belt of merchandise for black marketers, like those who threatened Marvin. The thieves grabbed goods that fell from trucks. They filched from trucks at stops for fuel, maintenance, food, and rest. Many formed gangs to hijack supplies. Unscrupulous drivers also delivered cargo to underground buyers.[137]

The Army tried to stamp out the widespread theft by positioning masses of military police along routes, especially at intersections. Convoy crews posted their own guards when they stopped.

But those measures could not stem the tidal wave of stolen military goods heading to the black market. The enticements were simply too big. In a year when gasoline cost 21 cents per gallon back in the States, bootleg gas sold for $5 a gallon in France. With the U.S. minimum wage pegged at 30 cents an hour, a hot U.S. Army truck could fetch $1,000. A pack of cigarettes selling for 5 cents at a post exchange stateside could bring $2.40 in France. And a 5-gallon can for gas was worth $100 on the French black market.[138]

Working on the Red Ball Express was dangerous for other reasons too. Trucks were supposed to stick to a 25 miles-per-hour speed limit for safety and to cut down on wear and tear on vehicles. But officers at the front constantly pressured drivers for faster deliveries. In addition, many drivers couldn't resist the thrill of barreling down highways. So convoy crews stripped out their carburetors' speed governors, reinstalling them only for inspections, writes historian David P. Colley.

Trucks overloaded with supplies careened down the Express' special highways. Top-heavy vehicles swayed back and forth, cargo boxes bouncing, hitting speeds up to 70 miles per hour. The road was like a race track jam-packed with exhausted drivers, ferrying vehicles laden with highly explosive ordnance and gasoline. Truck tires frequently blew out as they ran over sharp-edged remnants of artillery shell fragments, C-ration cans, and barbed wire. Drivers crowded the center of their highways to avoid land mines along road shoulders.[139]

Some convoys came under fire from German troops. Convoys could be strafed by German fighter planes. Some convoys ended up in the middle of fire fights or in the midst of German troops. German infiltrators strung piano wire at night across roads, aiming to behead Red Ball Express drivers. To defend themselves, many drivers equipped the front of lead jeeps with angle-iron hooks to shield drivers and passengers from piano-wire garrotes. Sometimes, those hooks were all the protection jeep occupants had. Many drove with windshields down near front lines to avoid reflecting glints of light that could trigger a murderous volley of German fire.[140]

Piano-wire guillotines were the first things Marvin had to worry about on most trips. That's because he got to ride in the lead jeep, which was supposed to be more comfortable than riding in a truck – so long as your head didn't get torn off! A seat in the jeep was one of Marvin's small rewards for being company clerk.

"I had a higher status than a lot of the other soldiers, so I mostly got to drive jeeps," he said. "It was little less dusty up there in front, and there was no truck in front of you to bump into. Other times I drove a truck or sat on a bench in the back of a truck. We sat on benches on both sides of the back and had a tarpaulin over us."

But garrotes were not the most common threat Marvin faced. Crashes, sleepy drivers, gun fire, artillery, and mines were constant threats. The standing order was to keep 60 feet between vehicles. Each convoy was supposed to have at least five trucks, and a lead as well as trailing jeep. The trucks were mostly General Motors two-and-a-half ton vehicles, known as deuce and a halfs. Convoys protected themselves from gun fire and artillery by making themselves hard to spot. They did that by running with "cat eyes" – narrow slits over their headlights.[141] But that maneuver made it harder to avoid crashes and running off the road.

Marvin remembers that in some risky combat areas, trucks ran without *any* headlights, just slits that narrowed their red tail lights. "The only way you knew where the road was was to follow the truck in front of you," he said. "Even driving through mud and water and dust, all we had to follow were those tiny cat eyes."

Marvin understood why they took such precautions. That didn't make him feel any better. "We had those little cat eyes so enemy planes and gunners could not spot the vehicles. But you could get just as killed hitting the truck in front of you or running off the road, and it was tough not to hit the truck in front of you – or to go off the road."

As if dealing with the German army was not daunting enough, occasionally convoys like Marvin's got into games of chicken with motorcades of white soldiers. When a white convoy would suddenly swerve to the middle of the road to prevent the black convoy from passing and showing them up, trucks could be forced off the road and into a ditch at dangerously high speeds.

Jittery nerves got wound up even tighter by routine security precautions. Convoy crews did not get their orders until just before pulling out. "That way, if a guy got captured before, he wouldn't know any future orders," Marvin said. "He couldn't give out any secrets even if he was tortured."

Sometimes, after a long haul to the front, Marvin's convoy would arrive in the dark of night, exhausted. Rather than unload and head back in the dark, the crew was ordered to bivouac. "We could be in a battle area. It didn't matter. We settled in for the evening," Marvin said.

On some return trips away from the front lines, convoys had the additional grim task of transporting the remains of dead G.I.s. Blood and gore fouled the cargo bays of trucks, and the awful odors of maimed bodies lingered. "War was gruesome," Marvin said. "I did that back in

Cherbourg, moving dead bodies. And we moved dead bodies, mostly Germans, away from Aachen."

Aachen, on the doorstep of Germany, was the scene of fierce fighting later in the war.

Sometimes Marvin drove a truck. He still has his old dog-eared Army driver's license. But he quickly credits other drivers for getting his convoys through the campaign without ever crashing or getting shot up. "Blacks were very skillful drivers," Marvin said. "They got us out of a lot of tight spots. It was like everything else in the whole war: They did a lot better than the crackers said they would. They pushed it. They got to the front faster than people expected. They fixed trucks along the way. If one guy got killed, other guys knew how to do his job, and they did it well. They did everything better than the crackers expected. They were real heroes."

Overall, not just in Marvin's convoys, accidents and injuries mounted as brave but exhausted drivers, hauling explosive fuel and ammunition day and night, in all weather, pressed themselves to maintain their proud pace.[142]

Then, suddenly, the Army stomped on the brakes of the Red Ball Express. The campaign was as potent as it was short. The Allies had liberated the crucial Belgian port of Antwerp on September 4, 1944. But it took many weeks to clear German forces from the Scheldt estuary, which blocked access to the open sea, and to remove mines from the harbor. The port reopened on November 28.[143]

Meanwhile, the Allies had been repairing key segments of the French rail lines. They also had installed temporary gasoline pipelines. The rails and pipelines were much cheaper, faster ways for moving war supplies.

"Between late August and early November [of 1944], the men of the Red Ball Express traveled from Cherbourg and St. Lo, France, to points east, moving more than 410,000 tons of gasoline, ammunition, and food to the American Army and covering more than 120 million ton-miles. By the end of the offensive, the Red Ball Express had supplied the 3rd and 1st Armies at the rate of 3.5 tons a minute and had contributed greatly to the liberation of northern France," military historian Robert F. Jefferson wrote.[144]

The operation was an Allied victory, thanks in large part to African-American troops like Marvin.

Spilling Blood

Mission accomplished, the Red Ball Express was discontinued on November 16, 1944. Marvin switched back to work in anti-aircraft artillery. He had no way to know that he was highballing toward the greatest mortal danger he would face during the war.

He returned to his outfit, which was near Yvetot, France, about 36 miles east-northeast of Le Havre. Marvin's crew had dug in their 40-millimeter gun, positioning the piece's feet – extension levers and support pads to keep the gun steady while firing. The men received word by radio that a German aircraft was approaching.

Marvin's crew was ready. Their artillery was loaded. Marvin as usual was the gunner, the triggerman.

"I was shooting at an enemy airplane," Marvin said. "It shot back and shrapnel flew off."

A shard slashed Marvin's left eye. Another sharp piece knifed into the left side of his gut. He went down. He was stunned, likely in medical shock. A medic probably gave him a stab of painkiller in the field. And he was rushed to a field hospital.

"They took me to some field the size of a baseball field," Marvin said. "It was filled with Army hospital tents. As far as you could see, there were soldiers with wounds. All you saw was blood, guys with legs missing, head and eye wounds, leg and arm lifts. The hospital was not where you wanted to be."

Marvin continued: "They took the shrapnel out of my stomach. You can die from bleeding. You can die from getting poisoned from the metal. And they worked on my eye. I still see a doctor for trouble with my left eye. I still have pain. All the time."

The heart of the hospital was some sort of building. This whole site, which should have been a safe haven, quickly proved itself to be the opposite. It was another stage where angry, violent, ruthless men, who were trained to kill, acted out their furies. Whatever predatory instincts some soldiers had when they joined the Army were amped up by the sights and sounds of war, the rage and frustration of being wounded.

"I saw craziness that makes men wild," Marvin said. "You were subject to attack everywhere there, in the building, in your tent, everywhere. There was no security in the hospital. Inside the building, people solicited sexual stuff from unsuspecting soldiers. They'd work in teams. One would come after you in a bathroom while the others stood watch outside.

"This one guy was a giant, six-six. How could you go up against men like that who were crazy? War bred animals. I was young. I was scared. Everyone there had been on the battlefield and was shot. The war makes you crazy. They all wanted to go back to the field and kill Germans, kill whoever had wounded them. Their wounds bred more fanaticism. I had never seen anything like this in my life. I was a little kid from the North, facing all of this. It was all beyond my imagination."

When he was accosted in the bathroom, Marvin could see his attacker's lookouts in the hall. Another time he was confronted in a hallway or bunker. A third time, it was inside a tent. "There was no security," Marvin said. "There was nobody you could call for help from."

Each would-be rapist seemed bigger and more intimidating than the one before. Only one thing prevented Marvin from falling prey. "I had my pistol with me," he said. "In fact, I had two guns. I had my .45. And I had some other handgun, I don't remember what kind. I never shot anyone or hit anyone, but I cocked the trigger on my gun several times."

The hospital was Marvin's first chance to enjoy a bed since leaving the United States. It also could have been his first chance to actually fall asleep at night. But just like in the field, Marvin didn't date fall asleep in the hospital. "I couldn't sleep because men were waiting to rape anyone they could," he said.

Decades later, Marvin says he still applies lesson he learned in that hospital. "In all of my business dealings, I have kept the attitude I learned there: Watch your back, and watch your front."

Meanwhile, while Marvin was still hospitalized, his guardian angel was still watching over him. Sgt. DeWitt had sent some notes to Marvin while he was in the hospital, letting him know how far the outfit had gone. They were moving east-northeast toward Belgium, then Germany.

DeWitt wanted his friend and company clerk back.

"Let me be more specific," Marvin said. "My outfit, Battery A, had some dumb soldiers. They weren't bright, but they were dangerous. I was close to Sgt. DeWitt. I knew how to handle the company records. I knew how to operate the anti-aircraft guns. I was young, sharp. He could trust me. I was an asset to him. I helped him keep track of guys. In return, he kept me away from uneducated, dangerous soldiers. He protected me."

Sgt. DeWitt did not stop looking out for himself or his young corporal just because Marvin was hospitalized. And Marvin was gung-ho about rejoining his outfit. He knew what the alternative was, and he was determined to avoid it no matter what it took.

"Once I left the hospital, they would send me to a repo depot," Marvin said, using his old Army slang for the manpower pools called replacement detachments. "I didn't want to go there because they'd ship me out to an infantry outfit, not my own outfit. I wanted to go back to my own outfit and fight the war with guys I knew."

If he ended up in a new unit, he'd be an outsider, a stranger. No one would watch his back. "I'd be dead within days," Marvin said.

After a few weeks in the hospital, Marvin was discharged. He had an eye patch, which he would continue to wear for eight or nine months. Meanwhile, it was decision time. He could take the designated truck to the repo depot. Or he could get creative.

"I walked out of the hospital and stole a jeep," Marvin said. "I drove in the direction Sgt. DeWitt had described. When one jeep ran out of gas, I switched jeeps. Trucks and jeeps were abandoned along the roads. Sometimes a jeep would still have gas if the occupants had been killed. If I didn't, I kept looking until I found another that did have gas."

He wouldn't need a key. Army jeeps started with the turn of a knob on the dashboard. "Each time, I hoped and prayed it had gas and more gas in the spare tank. You wanted to find one fast, before the enemy saw you and killed you."

Marvin kept motoring back to the front. That's where his old outfit would be. After about one week, he found his buddies from the old 458th. The unit had traveled roughly 325 miles.

"We were a gunnery outfit," Marvin said. "I followed the trail that DeWitt gave me. And I asked other units along the way."

"Superman" Meets Kryptonite

After Marvin found his buddies, he noticed a very welcome sign of the war's direction. German soldiers, whom Nazi ideology had boasted were supermen, incapable of being defeated, were appearing in ever greater numbers as prisoners of war, humbled by doing menial labor for G.I.s. – *deeply* humbled by doing scut work for blacks, whom they had been taught were their racial inferiors.

"We had captured German officers and storm troopers," Marvin said. "Back in their army they had been big shots. We had them doing KP," Marvin said, using a term that stands for "kitchen policing," which refers to the tedious, demeaning work of cleaning pots, pans, utensils, tables, floors – everything – as well as peeling potatoes, cutting vegetables, and performing any other tasks the cook orders. "That was a big come-down for German officers.

"Our guys would heckle them. The G.I.s would swear at them. They had to clean latrines too. Some had to dig trenches. There was no love lost. They were treated roughly, although I never saw any physical abuse. Just rough in terms of being ordered around, sworn at, that sort of thing. Our kitchen guys got a kick out of ordering the German officers to do this or that. Our black guys had someone below them, and I gotta say they got a kick out of it.

"I never got involved in that stuff. I was happy not to.

"They were put into a stockade at night. They slept on the ground. Most of our guys slept outdoors too. Most of them had pup tents. The KP duty started at 5 in the morning. When the Germans handled food, a G.I. would watch them. At night, the Germans made souvenirs for G.Is. They made ashtrays out of the bottom of artillery shells, cigarette lighters, that sort of thing.

"But the thing that struck me how there were so many of them. Regiment [command] or divisional gave us about half a dozen. At least four were officers. I remember thinking, these guys were smart and yet they were *happy* to prisoners. That's when I knew we were going to win the war, and the end wasn't far off."

Finding His Outfit

The best part about having found his old outfit was that Marvin was back with his buddies. He had avoided going to repot depot and being dished out to some infantry squad, filled with strangers who wouldn't care whether he lived or died. He even found his protective rubber sheet wedged into the undercarriage of the same truck he had left it in weeks earlier, before being hospitalized.

The drawback to being back was that his outfit was on the outskirts of Aachen, the westernmost city of Germany, located along its borders with Belgium and the Netherlands. Marvin didn't have to be a military historian to know that this meant German troops would be more impassioned now. They were defending their own homeland from invasion. It would be the first German territory hit by a ground attack in more than a century. And it was strategically vital. It was home to an air base for the German air force, the *luftwaffe*. And from Aachen, Germans could attack Allies advancing toward the Rhine River from the west.[145]

The city had enormous symbolic significance too. "Capturing the city was tantamount to ripping out the heart and soul of National Socialist [Nazi] mythology," Peter C. Xantheas wrote. German dictator Adolf Hitler had promised that his reign, which he dubbed the Third Reich, would last one thousand years. Germany's First Reich, Hitler had declared, was the Holy Roman Empire. The Empire had been created in 768 by Charlemagne, who soon made Aachen his unofficial capital, and it had endured for one thousand years.[146]

The Allies, then, had every reason to flatten Aachen and root out all remnants of armed resistance. The Germans had every reason to fight for the city. As ugly as the war had been up to this point, it was about to get uglier right here.

Marvin had arrived as the Allies were well into six weeks of bombing Aachen. The horror escalated as foot soldiers on both sides advanced and retreated time after time in the city. Assaults were measured in city blocks or mere yards, Xantheas wrote. Allied soldiers often had to scour not only the city's streets but also its sewer system and underground bomb shelters for German soldiers who were hiding, he added.

The pummeling took its toll. The city was flattened. Streets were littered with shattered glass. Telephone, electric light, and trolley cables dangled from poles. Wrecked cars, trucks, and armored vehicles were strewn about like a giant's broken toys. Shattered weapons were scattered everywhere.[147]

Marvin's nose stung from the stink of dead horses, many blown open. "Aachen was filled with dust and debris," Marvin said. "The city had been pounded by bombs and artillery. And there was a stench from dead horses the Germans used to pull artillery caissons. The dead horses were on both sides of the road. There were dead bodies. It was unimaginable."

Other soldiers gagged on the reek from ruptured sewers, fractured gas mains, and worse.

The outfit finally got through Aachen, and it kept moving forward. The group was not a frontline infantry outfit, but it was close enough to the front to suffer casualties. By the time the outfit reached Altenau, about 80 miles northeast of Aachen, all of the unit's officers – its lieutenants and captains – had been killed, picked off by snipers and assorted *wehrmacht* gunners.

"The captain got killed by machinegun fire," Marvin said. "He was nearby, but I didn't see it happen. It was sudden. I never knew what happened. Medics came out. I was thinking I could be next. We were artillery, but I was armed up like infantry. I was carrying bayonets, my guns. I was carrying so many grenades, I was a walking bomb. I had my M1 carbine, a small rifle. I also had a machinegun. All the men were armed like me, all the time now."

Suicidal Order

The outfit was maybe one mile from *the* front. Also nearby, some American units had bigger anti-aircraft artillery than Marvin's unit. The 90-mm artillery, known as heavy guns, were used to swat planes from the sky and to blast German tanks. "When those 90-millimeter guns went off, the ground shook," Marvin said. "It put fear into your heart. We were in hell."

Being this close to a hotly contested front was purgatory even when the heavy guns were silent. "We were close enough that you could *hear* the fierce fighting ahead of us. You could hear guns and mayhem. We were so close that a German infiltrator could kill you with a bayonet at night," Marvin said.

In one area close by, German commanders were doing their best to bloody the advancing armies under generals Patton and Hodges. They turned woods and roads into a network of lethal roadblocks. Felling trees, they barred passage on some key roads, reinforcing the barriers with tanks positioned farther back. When American infantry and tanks pushed through the woods rather than approach directly by road, the Germans would pull back and set up a new roadblock farther east.[148]

In a German counterattack in Altenau, the Germans used a captured American tank. "During the first few days German infantrymen sometimes used the concealment of the woods to infiltrate back into towns and villages. In some cases they laid mines or erected log barriers behind

140

American columns, and occasionally they counterattacked with perhaps as many as a hundred men;..."[149]

While Marvin's outfit waited for replacement officers to arrive, he and Sgt. DeWitt ran the show. Marvin was his battery's gunner, he was more educated than most of the men in the outfit, and as company clerk he had an aura of authority. DeWitt was the person who relayed orders from the officers to the G. I.s anyway. "Until the 90-day wonders arrived, DeWitt and myself took command of Battery A," Marvin said, using the derisive term for fresh replacement officers, newly minted first and second lieutenants straight out of school, with no field experience . The nickname mocked these assembly-line officers for supposedly having a scant 90 days of training.

One of them in particular struck Marvin as being especially pompous. "Lt. Floyd Inyeard was light-skinned and short," Marvin said. "He carried a swagger stick – can you imagine? – and had a high-pitched voice." The fact that Inyeard and the other 90-day wonders were black just made things worse, Marvin said. "They acted like they had to prove themselves to the rest of us, so they acted bossy. They acted like know-it-alls."

Those young lieutenants were self-conscious about how inexperienced they were. They felt they had to prove themselves to their new troops. And they felt they had to prove themselves to the Army, as new black officers. To establish their authority, they were determined not to display any form of weakness. They were careful not to be pals with their troops. When they gave an order, they demanded immediate compliance. When they gave an order, they stuck to it.

The trouble was that they lacked the currency most in demand by their troops: experience under fire. "They were not battle-tested," Marvin said. "I resented that. I had been in the war so long that I knew more about what needed to be done than these 90-day wonders did. And I had seen what happens when someone made a mistake."

Since landing in Normandy, Marvin had seen buddies chewed up by war. "I saw buddies with their heads blown off. Literally. I saw guys with holes blown right through their bodies. I remember loading bodies on trucks, with blood still coming off their bodies. Body parts. It was awful. These were guys I knew. This was very real. I saw so much death in France, then Germany," Marvin said, pausing before he continued. "Outside

Aachen the dust was red from bodies getting blown to bits. There was no room for mistakes."

A clash came quickly. Lt. Inyeard ordered Marvin to advance to the front and find a spot for the rest of his battery to set up their artillery. Marvin thought Inyeard was nuts. The outfit was already in a combat area, taking fire. Men had been killed – the captain, the lieutenants. Ordering one man to head out on his own was tantamount to ordering him to commit suicide. It wasn't done. It reflected Inyeard's inexperience. And Marvin did not want to provide the young lieutenant with a field lesson by getting captured or coming back in a body bag.

"He wanted to send me to the front lines without any backup, without any men who knew how to fight," Marvin said. "It was stupid. It would get me killed. I told him I wouldn't go without others who could help me scout the area. These 90-day wonders were giving orders that would get people killed. I wasn't afraid to fight. I just wanted support to do it. I wanted to do it the right way."

In Marvin's mind, he was having a strategy session with Lt. Inyeard. He was sharing the hard-won experience of his weeks and months on the beach, among the hedgerows, in the field, in combat.

"In a war zone, we're equal," Marvin said. "It had nothing to do with rank. We fought together and depended on each other. We could both get killed. And he was sending me to the front without help. But he wasn't using my experience. He wasn't being smart."

Lt. Inyeard also wasn't having a strategy session with this corporal. Not in his mind. The young lieutenant saw this exchange of words in an entirely different light than Marvin did. He wasn't brainstorming with Marvin. He was giving the corporal an order.

Furious, Lt. Inyeard tore off Marvin's buck corporal stripes. He told Marvin to return to his barracks. "That made no sense," Marvin said. The outfit was in the field, far anything as luxurious as a wooden hut. Inyeard's choice of words shows how rattled the young officer was by the confrontation. Inyeard wheeled around and stomped away.

Ticket to the Stockade

The rest of the afternoon became a blur to Marvin. The outfit got a lull in combat action. Marvin hung around and thought about what had happened. He was, he realized, in trouble. He had defied an officer's order. He could get court-martialed. He could get end up imprisoned in a stockade. The only good thing was that Lt. Inyeard had not taken any official action yet.

The next morning Marvin went to division headquarters on his own. He wanted to speak with the one higher authority he could think of. Col. Albert Baron was the outfit's commanding officer and had been Marvin's C.O. since back at Camp Stewart in Georgia. He had seen it all. He had seen Marvin stay cool during the race riot at Camp Stewart. He had seen Marvin talk barracks mates out of joining the fray. When Marvin got his promotion from private, Baron almost certainly had signed off on it – if not recommended it himself. He had been in charge of the outfit when Marvin demonstrated his skill as an anti-aircraft gunner. He had been in charge of the outfit during its Normandy landing. He was the boss when Marvin and others had been strafed by a Messerschmitt in French hedgerow country. He knew Marvin had helped make the Red Ball Express a success. He knew Marvin's value as clerk for the outfit. He was the C.O. when Marvin nearly got his head blown off while firing ack-ack – anti-aircraft rounds – at that German fighter plane. He was as happy as anyone when Marvin made his way back to the outfit from the field hospital.

Marvin had grown from a teenage boy into a trustworthy young man under Baron. They had served together. They had seen heroism and tragedy together. Together, they had seen men in their outfit bleed painfully for their country. Together, they had demonstrated willingness to die for their country. Now he had Marvin standing in front of him, a dilemma in uniform.

"Baron was top dog," Marvin said. "He was the boss. He was head of the entire division. I didn't go the stockade yet because the first lieutenant had no brains. I was just a field corporal, but being company clerk I knew what to do if I was stepped on. And I was doing it.

"I took my case to Baron. I felt I was stepped on and mistreated, and I felt the first lieutenant was without cause. But the colonel had a sympathetic ear. He was a white guy from the South, a Southern white officer, but he was always fair with me, *always!* Now I was in a state of shock that the colonel took time to see me. And I was in a state of shock that the lieutenant had busted me. The fact that I was now a private really pissed me off."

Col. Baron gave Marvin a chance to describe what had happened. A war against the Germans was raging around him. A war between two of his own men had also erupted. But the colonel was quiet and calm.

"The colonel asked another lieutenant, one of his own, to look at my record," Marvin said. "Then he asked me what I wanted to do. I told him I wanted to go to Paris and study cosmetology. I will never understand what made me say that. I just wanted to be in Paris. I had been through Paris during blackouts, and I was fascinated. I had never seen Paris in daylight, only at night. I was 17, 18 years old. He asked me what I wanted to do and all I could think of was cosmetology. You know, hair and beauty. It was the first thing that came to my mind. Maybe I just wanted to be with women." Marvin chuckled at the memory.

The colonel, still cool and collected, shook his head slightly as if saying no. Then he actually did say, *No, I can't send you to Paris. I can't send you there to become a women's hair stylist.* Marvin's heart sank. He was not making progress. And Baron was bound to send him to the stockade. Baron's lieutenant mumbled something and handled him Marvin's record. Baron read the paperwork, then looked up at Marvin again. "You're a musician," he said.

"I said, 'Yes, sir, I was.' See, I learned my lesson. I said, 'Sir.' I said, 'When I joined the Army I wanted to be in special services, in a band for soldiers,'" Marvin said.

Without missing a beat, Col. Baron nodded and said he was going to send Marvin to Glasgow, Scotland, to a school for musicians. He made Marvin a corporal again, giving him back his two chevrons plus a T for technician, and said the lieutenant would see to the paperwork.

"I have no idea why the colonel took an interest in me," Marvin said. "But right then he saved my life."

As generous as Col. Baron's order was, it broke no rules and solved a problem. It was actually shrewdly nuanced. He was not handing Marvin a ticket home. He was sending Marvin to learn musical skills needed by the Army, in a program the Army was already participating in. He was nudging Marvin toward the special services program – a military band – that a recruiting officer in Cambridge had promised years earlier. And the music-school training would have a specific starting date and an ending date. After music school, Marvin would end up in a military band or back here in

Germany, in his old outfit or another one, in combat, as close to the action as he was now.

Col. Baron had come up with an ingenious way to help keep his outfit running smoothly. He was going to separate Lt. Inyeard and Cpl. Gilmore. He was going to put a lot of real estate between the two of them. If Lt. Inyeard wanted to, he could tell himself he had won; he had gotten Marvin kicked out of the outfit, at least temporarily. Marvin didn't need anyone to translate what happened. He had been handed a wonderful gift: a legitimate ticket out of the corner of the war run by Lt. Inyeard.

Col. Baron certainly could not single-handedly determine the outcome of this war. But there in his regimental headquarters he had the power to keep Marvin's life from taking a terrible wrong turn. Amid the chaos and random cruelty of war, Col. Baron committed an act of random kindness.

In the war, some soldiers by chance stepped on land mines and suffered grievous injuries or mortal wounds. Some soldiers by chance got shot and killed. Entirely by chance or not, Marvin had just been sent to military heaven. And he didn't even need to die.

Good-Bye to Germany

"Within a week I was out of there," Marvin said. "I was the happiest fellow you can imagine."

Within days or weeks, a lot of other people got happy too. On May 5, 1945, the war with Germany ended. There was still the business of occupying a defeated Germany. And Marvin was told his outfit might be shifted to the Pacific for what was then the widely expected invasion of Japan. That invasion would be horribly bloody, and men like Marvin knew it. Japan still had a frightening 5 million men under arms. Tens of thousands of Imperial Japanese soldiers were already building daunting defenses. "Old men, women, and children were trained with hand grenades, swords, and bamboo spears and were ready to strap explosives to their bodies and throw themselves under advancing [U.S.] tanks," wrote historian John T. Correll.[150]

Marvin was out of Germany. But he was hardly out of danger. Yet for now Marvin's orders stood. He was bound for the Royal Scottish Academy of Music, in Glasgow, Scotland.[151] His joy was short-lived, though. Rather than be sent directly to Glasgow, the Army sent Marvin to Belgium first, where connecting transportation would be arranged. Marvin's rollercoaster ride continued. He found himself in Blankenberge, a coastal resort. A stopover that was supposed to last just a few weeks turned into months. And since Marvin was an able-bodied soldier rather than a tourist on vacation, the Army expected Marvin to work. He was assigned to a quartermaster truck company.

"This was a huge comedown, delivering goods," he said. "When I first transferred there, they had me changing tires on huge trucks."

Marvin being Marvin, his entrepreneurial instincts kicked in. He looked for a way to use his time in ways that appealed to him. "I spoke to the captain," he said. "I told him I had been company clerk. So they put me into general headquarters for one day a week. I was typing and keeping records. The rest of the week I just socialized, but I got tired of that, so I started a band. We performed for the USO."

Marvin bivouacked in an abandoned local school house that was being used as a barracks. "I even worked with the French underground to find Germans."

These French resistance fighters were not shy about expressing their thanks to American G.I.s. Guys like Marvin had helped liberate them from beneath the crushing hobnailed boots of their cruel Nazi conquerors. Many had seen friends captured, tortured, and murdered by the German occupiers. So, very soon after arriving in Blankenberge, the grateful underground members gave Marvin a bottle of cognac.

"That bottle was just a pint, but it was delicious and I nursed it for a month," Marvin said. He liked the excellent brandy so much that he resorted to a white lie. "I told them I lost the bottle and could they send me another." His French friends, no doubt perfectly aware that their young American liberator had enjoyed his introduction to the luscious distilled liquid, were only too happy to go along with his innocent request. They gave him a second bottle. Marvin, they must have figured, had just become a future customer for this popular French export.

On September 6, 1945, Marvin's seaside resort reverie ended. He was finally ordered to Glasgow. His orders, from Brig. Gen. Koenig, were to report to Field Center V, American Red Cross, 350 Sauchiehall Street in Glasgow by 1700 hours – 7 a.m. – on Sept. 8, ready to start classes on Sept. 10.[152] Marvin flew to Glasgow from Antwerp.

"It was morning when I got on the plane," Marvin said. "It flew to Gourock. It took a couple of hours. From there I took a jeep or a bus to Glasgow. I stayed at the Red Cross facility in Charing Cross, which is in the center of Glasgow."

A buddy back in Germany had told Marvin to look up his girlfriend, so as soon as Marvin settled into the Red Cross building he contacted Betty Timofei. "She had a child, a little black child, with my buddy," Marvin said.

Timofei's apartment was at 35 Mair Street, on the southern side of the River Clyde, less than three miles away. Marvin liked Timofei's apartment and the neighborhood right away. "It was much quieter where she lived," Marvin said. "The Red Cross was in the center of Glasgow, and I couldn't take the traffic noise, so I asked Betty if I could rent a room in her building. It was nice even though it was in a poor section of Glasgow, maybe the suburbs, a section called the Plantation. It was the poorest part of Glasgow. She had a single-room apartment. There was no central heat, just a fireplace. The only way to try to keep it warm was to keep the fireplace going. But it was always freezing cold and misty."

Marvin took an apartment, which like the others was a cold-water flat. The bathroom was a communal one in the hall outside the apartment. It had one tiny toilet, which all the renters on that floor shared. The only shower for the entire building was in the building's ground-floor courtyard. But this bare-bones arrangement suited Marvin. His apartment was one room with a kitchenette. And another neighbor owned a piano. She let Marvin use it for practice every day.

"The people were very nice," Marvin said. Just like his first visit to the city, upon first arriving in the United Kingdom as part of the big pre-Normandy invasion buildup, the Scottish people Marvin met were friendly and free of bias against African-Americans. They had struck him as very nice people back then, and they were still friendly and open.

That was a very good thing, too, because something else about Glasgow had changed dramatically, and it had changed for the worse.

When Marvin had passed through Glasgow on first arriving in the United Kingdom, he had been part of a large contingent of black troops. The only soldiers he had seen or encountered were black. He characterized Glasgow as a black city.

But now the city was filled with white G.I.s – and white military police. And unlike the Scots, many had imported their racial biases from back in the States. "Now the city was being used by white soldiers who were recuperating from war," Marvin said. "The MPs were white. And the city was no longer controlled by black soldiers."

One of the clearest lessons Marvin's experience in the Army had taught him was that bullies would take advantage of the weak. Marvin had seen Hitler do it to the European continent. Marvin had seen big black soldiers do it to smaller black soldiers in military camps in the South. He had seen big white soldiers do it to smaller white soldiers. And he had certainly seen white soldiers do it to outnumbered black soldiers. That lesson had been reinforced in the Army field hospital where Marvin had been treated for his eye wound.

But the big difference between now and back then was that Marvin no longer had a weapon to protect himself with. When he left Germany, he had been required to turn in his weapons. Now he felt naked. "I was a sitting duck," he said. "I knew from earlier that the MPs would give me a tough time, and they were everywhere. They directed traffic in Glasgow. They were just everywhere."

Marvin befriended a number of white Scots. In addition to liking Marvin, they had made friends with several black G.I.s early in the war. "African-American soldiers came to Glasgow first," Marvin said. "They made friends. And I was a symbol of those African-American soldiers. The white American soldiers who came later didn't make as nice of an impression. They were surprised when Scots told them they had liked us. The white Americans described us as monkeys. The Scottish people were offended by it."

So Marvin had found it easy to make friends among Betty Timofei's friends and acquaintances. Several also became Marvin's new guardian angels. And even though guns were illegal, the war had widened whatever black market had existed previously. Marvin's new friends knew where he could buy a weapon. "I was able to buy a gun for self-protection," Marvin said. "I could get a gun for just a few dollars even though it was illegal to carry a weapon in Scotland."

Marvin's fear came to pass. As one of the few African-Americans in a city filled with white Scots and white soldiers, he caught the eyes of several MPs when he went to school each morning. Soon enough, Marvin found himself playing the role of the prey in a game of cat and mouse with MPs. "A single soldier was always a target for harassment," Marvin said.

When Marvin told his Scottish friends that MPs were shadowing him, sometimes stopping him and making threatening comments, the Scots came up with a defensive plan. "When I left the apartment, five or six walked on the other side of the street parallel to me to make sure I wouldn't be harmed by military police. It went on for months. I also carried my gun."

And a new threat arose.

"One night one of my women friends [Timofei] said don't carry your gun for a while, give it to me. The MPs got wind of the gun and they were planning to stop me in the street, search me, find the gun, and throw me into the stockade." Marvin fully expected a severe beating in the process.

Looking back, Marvin thinks too many people knew he had bought a gun. Either the seller squealed or one of the Scots shared Marvin's secret with the wrong person. Either way, Marvin was not about to ignore this new danger. He gave his gun to Timofei, who hid it.

As usual, he headed to school that night for a concert rehearsal. Also as usual, he had his entourage of witnesses close by. Sure enough, just three blocks away from his apartment, a white MP ordered him to stop. "He frisked me," Marvin said. "He was angry he didn't find a gun on me. He warned me he'd toss me into the stockade if he caught me with a gun."

Another night a white soldier attacked Marvin near the Academy library. "It was just a random white soldier who had one drink too many that day," Marvin said. "But I was vulnerable. There were no black soldiers. And it got so bad that Scottish people were afraid to talk to me. White soldiers threatened Scots who socialized or talked with blacks."

Royal Scottish Academy

Marvin put in regular work days. Classes started at 9 in the morning and ran until 5 p.m. He'd be home by about 6 p.m. If he had a concert, he'd go back to school for extra rehearsals at night. He took classes in piano, which was the instrument he concentrated on at this stage of his musical life. His other classes were in harmony and counterpoint, history of music, and sight singing.

He ate lunch at school. "I had very little money," Marvin said. "I lived on about $10 a week, which was like having $100 today. Food was cheap. We bought it off of street carts or went to any of the saloons on street corners for a mug of beer and a sandwich. I had rabbit a lot. In a stew. I learned not to like it. An American dollar would last a week. At night I ate fish and chips a lot. Being alone, I wasn't interested in going out on my own."

Marvin was a solid student. In his report card for the September-December session, piano teacher A. Ramsay Calder wrote, "Mr. Gilmore has proved himself a keen and painstaking student. He has made quite outstanding progress in technique and has added very considerably to his musical understanding."

His sight singing instructor, Arthur J. Irvine, reported, "Mr. Gilmore made very good progress. A very keen student, good in sol-fa and in staff. His attendance was perfect."

A high point of the school term was a concert for the Duke and Duchess of Montrose.

Marvin participated in other musical programs as well. He sang in the American Red Cross Glee Club's Thanksgiving Day concert. The performance was a marathon, 12-hour, nonstop recital. And it was a thanksgiving performance both literally for the holiday and a public showing of the joy everyone in attendance felt now that the war was over and won.

The Glee Club had 24 singers. Nearly all of the girls were Glaswegians. Some were married to American service men. Glasgow's *Evening Citizen* newspaper said the performance, which included Handel's *Largo*, attracted a large audience of 500 people. The concert was well received. So was the other highlight, a traditional Thanksgiving dinner with all of the fixings – hors d'oeuvres, Du Barry soup, turkey, cranberry sauce and dressing, giblet gravy, roast potatoes, Brussels sprouts, pumpkin pie, oranges, tea, and coffee. The entire feast had been brought to Scotland by the U.S. Army.[153]

A photograph on page three of the *Evening Citizen* shows Marvin in the second row of the Glee Club while it performed *Largo*.

By the time the school term ended, Marvin knew he'd be shipping out for home – and then possibly on to his death in Japan.

Discrimination Not Vanquished

When his written orders arrived, Marvin followed them by trying to report to a particular ship on a certain day in Glasgow. Returns to the United States were based on a sort of merit system. The more time you had logged overseas, and the more combat zones you had served in, the earlier you were scheduled to ship out back to the States. "It was all based on battle stars," Marvin said. "I had four major ones, so I got to the head of the list."

But other, more sinister rules applied too. Marvin was accompanied to the dock by a bon-voyage entourage of about 35 Scottish friends and fellow students. "I was supposed to go back on a ship with a refrigeration outfit," Marvin said. "I think it was the 313th." At the check-in depot on the dock, Marvin handed his paper to a white sergeant, who glanced at them before handing them back. "'You can't board,' the sergeant said. 'This ship is for whites only!'"

Marvin was stunned. He protested that he had written orders to board this ship. "'You're reading your orders wrong,' the white sergeant said. 'You're reading them wrong. You're black. You can't come on this ship. This ship is for whites only!' I had written orders, but he wouldn't let me on. I felt humiliated. This was in front of my Scottish friends, who came to see me off. 'But I have my orders,' I said. He just shook his head and said, 'Only white solders can board this ship.'"

Embarrassed and angry and depressed, Marvin left the wharf with his friends. In silence they went to a nearby shop for a lunch of fish and chips. Returning to the Plantation district, he remembers having rabbit for dinner later that night.

The silver lining to being barred from a whites-only ship was that it saved Marvin from preparations for participating in the expected invasion of Japan. He would have spent little if any of the next several months at home. And he would have been burdened with the prospect of being wounded or killed in the invasion. Estimates of U.S. casualties alone ranged from about 250,000 to more than 1 million.[154]

Instead, Marvin spent additional months in Glasgow with his Scottish friends.

Japan surrendered on August 15, 1945. The Army finally got around to scheduling Marvin for a return trip to the U.S. the following winter. The ship came up the Firth of Clyde toward Glasgow. This time when Marvin reported to the dock, instead of the large cruise ship he had been barred from months earlier, he was processed for boarding a much smaller ship.

"This was a small boat," he said. "There were only a couple dozen soldiers going on board. We played poker all the way across. The ship was small and it bobbed on the water all the time. We played poker inside a cabin. We played all day. There was nothing else to do. It was boring. You couldn't sleep because the ship moved around so much. We lived on sandwiches or K rations or C rations. The ship had an open hold, like a freighter. We had hammocks there. America was not kind to black soldiers. We had no luxury on that ship. Crossing the North Atlantic in a small boat in the dead of winter – America loves us!

"It was cold, freezing cold. A good thing in those days was that the Army gave us heavy woolen coats and blankets. We wore those all the way across the Atlantic.

"Four or five guys at a time played poker. I must have lost money. Lots of guys did. But nobody minded much. The guys got along. We were finally on our way home. I was looking forward to getting home after arduous fighting. All of us felt lucky to be alive. Some of the men were wounded. Half of the group onboard was intelligent. I could tell from the way people talked and what they talked about. One of them was a sergeant. I went out with his sister, Rachel Diggs, for a little over a year and a half when I got home. She was from Winston-Salem, North Carolina, but she was in Cambridge, attending Radcliffe. Everyone onboard the ship came from different outfits and different places in the United States.

"The ship took one or two weeks to cross the Atlantic. Everyone's spirits were high from having survived the war and being on the way home. The ship went to Boston. From there I went to Fort Devens, where I was discharged January 16, 1946. Then I went home. I got a hero's welcome from my family."

About a week after Marvin got home, he received the sad news that Betty Timofei had died of bronchitis. Timofei's fate symbolized what had happened to the United Kingdom. It had exhausted itself in its effort to survive the war and defeat Nazi Germany. Timofei too had defied her enemies, racists who could not tolerate the presence of blacks like Marvin in the city of Glasgow, racists who harassed her for having had a child with a black G.I. She defied those enemies by helping Marvin and by staying true to herself. But the effort had weakened her. And in a U.K. depleted by war, she lived in a drafty cold-water flat, where she could not stay warm and healthy. "It was raining all the time," Marvin said. "It was a good thing I was young and strong, or I would have died too." Timofei survived the enemies she could see, but could not the invisible microbial ones.

Marvin mourned her passing. He and his mother tried without success to track down Timofei's baby to make sure she was all right. Now Marvin was caught up in the unseen currents of time, moving forward in life. He was four years older than when he had joined the Army. He went in a boy, he was discharged a man. The war had prepared him for adult life. Having survived the guns and bombs and artillery of the Nazi regime, no challenge could scare him now. Having survived the taunts and threats of crackers in the military, he understood better than ever the danger pose by bigots. Having fought the good fight, he understood the necessity of fighting back against evil.

On the hard anvil of war, Marvin had been forged into a man determined never to ignore hatred, inequality, and discrimination. He had seen for himself that turning your back on evil did not make it go away. Marvin had learned the value of taking initiative. In the following decades, he would apply that lesson to business, to romance, to racial justice.

Chapter 8
An Entrepreneur Rises in the Postwar Decades

Back from war in Europe, back to Cambridge, back in civvies, Marvin commenced life as a discharged soldier the same way many veterans did, by returning to school and by finding work. Marvin's work was for a Mr. and Mrs. H.H. White, for whom he had worked part-time before the war. Mr. White was a sort of Great Gatsby to Marvin. Marvin, who was young and a hired hand, had no idea what White did for a living. All Marvin knew was that he had money to burn.

The Whites were wealthy and had big, high-priced homes in Brookline, a wealthy suburb just west of Boston, and in Marblehead Neck, a posh peninsula in picturesque Marblehead, a cushy coastal town 17 miles north of Boston. Like many denizens of the Neck, the Whites owned a sailing yacht. Their adult playthings also included eight expensive automobiles.

Before the war, Marvin had worked for the Whites as a chauffeur and a cook. Sometimes he functioned as a servant. "They taught me everything about how to be a good butler," Marvin said. "A lot of what I learned came in handy when I started to work as a caterer [after college]."

During the war, his mother kept Marvin's *toque blanche* – chef's tall white hat – warm by taking over his kitchen responsibilities as a cook. She was far more skilled than Marvin in the kitchen anyway. Her presence helped deter the Whites from giving away Marvin's job. And Lee Augusta was always on the lookout for an income opportunity.

When Marvin returned from the service, he worked mainly as a chauffeur for Mrs. White and washing their fleet of cars.

"They had cars like a Packard and a LaSalle," Marvin said. "They were huge, heavy cars. They cost a lot and used a lot of gasoline. They sent me to a school to learn how to drive those cars."

Marvin worked occasionally on week days after school. On weekends he lived with the Whites in Marblehead, especially in the summer. After demonstrating his reliability, when he had to return home after a long day Marvin was allowed to take one of the Whites' cars. Sometimes, like after helping to clean up following one of the Whites' late parties, he found himself driving home at four in the morning. Marvin could deposit the car at a garage in Cambridge's Harvard Square, where the Whites had parking privileges. Then Marvin could walk home just a few blocks away.

But there was a dark side to this work. From time to time Marvin drove the Whites to a country club in Ogunquit, Maine.

"Because I was black I wasn't allowed inside," Marvin said. "For lunch, someone brought out a sandwich, and I ate inside the car or sitting on the side board."

And Marvin hated the menial aspect of his job. "They wanted me to polish their cars, but I didn't want to. I always said I wouldn't polish their damned cars in their back yards. I am not a polisher. When they really condescended to me, they had me do their children's cars, which were dirty and filthy. That's what caused me finally to say good-bye."

Marvin was young but he was a man, and doing grunt work for rich white kids, work that they could do for themselves, rubbed Marvin the wrong way. Times like that reminded Marvin of the overt segregation of the country club in Maine and the Whites' acceptance of it. Indeed, they were participants. Working for the Whites was a far, far cry from the outright slavery his grandparents and earlier forebears had suffered. There were certainly no whips, no confinement to ramshackle quarters, no armed overseer on horseback. But the Whites clearly felt that Marvin was not their equal, and there was no denying the racial aspect of the inequality.

When the Whites ignored Marvin's distaste for polishing cars and repeatedly pressed him to do precisely that, to their cars and their children's under a hot summer sun, Marvin could hear his grandmother Sophronia recounting her brutal days doing tedious labor against her will under a not-so-different hot sky like this one above Marblehead. And Marvin thought, *This Gilmore is not going through that again; not me, no more.*

And yet the Whites would ask him again and again. It was as if they weren't listening to him. In those moments, it was clear that the Whites felt superior to Marvin, felt that their children were superior to Marvin, felt that it was Marvin's role in life to serve their kids. In those moments, it was clear to Marvin that the Whites regarded him as their houseboy. And Lee Augusta had not raised Marvin to be anyone's houseboy. The U.S.

Army had not trained Marvin to be anyone's houseboy. And the streets of Cambridge had not taught Marvin to accept being anyone's houseboy.

So in those moments under a steamy summer sky in Marblehead, Marvin chose his future path. He could not know the details in advance. But he resolved that he would never be anyone's houseboy.

The Whites were the first of many whites who would attempt to pigeonhole him as cheap black labor. Marvin refused to be stereotyped each time. Marvin knew that not too far in the past, his ancestors had been there, done that. Sophronia, Lee Augusta, and the others had worked too hard to get beyond that, and Marvin was not about to backslide.

He also wasn't about to ignore his own entrepreneurial instincts. He did not want to be someone else's employee. He wanted to build things, build a career, build wealth – his own and for others. He could only do that by working for himself, not for others. He wanted to own his own fancy cars. And he wanted to be able to pay someone else to clean and polish them.

Step by step, that's what he did.

Finishing High School

Fresh out of the Army, Marvin wanted to start college. He couldn't do it right away, though. Colleges were flooded with applications from returning G.I.s who had finished high school before the war and were ready to start college. Unlike those regiments of returning veterans, Marvin had not finished high school before joining the Army.

Leaving Latin early to enlist also had deprived Marvin of a chance to take several courses that could help him get into college and help expand his mental tool kit.

But he could not return to Cambridge Latin. He had been gone too many years. So he looked for an alternative. Manter Hall, a private school in Cambridge's Harvard Square, fit the bill. It was located just blocks away from his home outside the Square. Best of all, the U.S. government would help pay for it through the Servicemen's Readjustment Act of 1944— better known as the G.I. Bill of Rights, or G.I. Bill for short.[155]

That was in addition to Marvin's mustering out pay, which had been $300. His monthly military benefit was $38, which included $20 extra for the eye wound he suffered in Europe.

"I got a little extra money because I had been wounded. My eye wound. But rather than just hang around, I went to Manter Hall, which prepared me for college," Marvin said. "I buffed up on English, French, algebra, maybe a few other courses. I wanted to get ahead, and sitting around was not going to do it. I went to school, I cut grass, I played with my 18-piece band, I worked for the Whites."

About four years later, the government ended its program of compensating veterans like Marvin for wounds that it deemed insufficiently serious. To this day, Marvin is angry about being cut off.

At the time, though, Marvin's priority was completing his education and earning money. Commuting to classes was simple. He would ride a bicycle the nine blocks from Dana Street to 67 Mt. Auburn Street in the Square. "I didn't need to lock the bike when I got there," Marvin said. "We didn't have the thievery there is now. We never even locked our doors."

Marvin was living with his parents again at 69 Dana Street. Why had his father allowed him to return to the nest? With her income rising from student tenants, Lee Augusta was more assertive. "My father was very old-fashioned. But at that point my mother ruled the roost," Marvin said.

Reconnecting with Helen Green

Earning his diploma and moving back home to 69 Dana Street were steps one and two in Marvin's push to return to normalcy. Reconnecting with Helen Green, his wartime girlfriend from Virginia, was also part of the process. "We kept in touch through the war," Marvin said. "After the war, things went well. We wanted to get married, so I invited her to meet my mother."

Lee Augusta was delighted by the prospect. She was looking forward to meeting her future daughter-in-law. She arranged to throw the young couple a party, and she was eager to introduce Helen to friends and relatives.

Helen arrived. Everything went well. Then, one evening shortly before the party, she asked to see the guest list.

"She saw names of white people on the list, and said she did not like white people. She attacked me for having white friends. I talked to her, but she was adamant. I could not change her at all. I couldn't handle that. I didn't know she was prejudiced. She demanded to know why I had relationships with white folks. I explained I was in a white community with white friends. They were my *friends*. She said she hated them, all of them. She was from a very rural part of Virginia, and did not like white people. She said she felt the pain of slavery. I told her the difference between us was that I was trying to change people's attitudes, and you couldn't do that by not talking with them. And, besides, these people invited to the party were my friends."

Helen Green did not budge. Her anger did not abate. "I had to tell her right at that moment that we couldn't get married. I cancelled the party. After about a week I put her on a train and sent her back home. And I haven't spoken with her since."

Shattered Souls

As Marvin got on with his education and with preparing for the future, he was tight-lipped about his combat experiences, like many veterans. Having been in harm's way and having spilled the blood of others was something he wanted to put into the past. "I did some killing," he said. "I don't talk about it. I didn't kill hand-to-hand. It was by artillery. I went through hell. I don't talk about it."

His parents did not press him. They never asked about the war. They recognized that this was not a topic fit for small talk or bragging or sob-sessions. "They were so happy to see me back," he said. I was back alive. That's all that mattered. So many sons of other parents never came back. My mother was thrilled. She knew several of my classmates had been killed. My classmates. Kids from high school! It was sad."

The one topic Lee Augusta could not resist was Marvin's enrollment at the Royal Scottish Academy of Music, in Glasgow.

"Oh yeah, she was very proud of that," he said. "She asked me about it. The classes. What I learned. Where I played music."

For treatment of his war wounds, Marvin visited the Veterans Administration medical clinic in downtown Boston regularly. There, he talked with fellow veterans. Some were having a tougher time readjusting to civilian life than he was.

"Some of them stole, robbed, never made anything of themselves," Marvin said. "The war affects you, but I had good, hard training from my parents. It paid off. You can blame the government, you can blame other people, whatever. You can blame your own weakness. I survived that.

"I was happy to be home. I was determined to get ahead. I did a lot of jobs. I took any job I could. I cleaned dead bodies in a hospital. I worked hard.

"I had an uncle, a grandmother, who taught me so much. It stayed with me. I'm fortunate to have had the parents that I did. I am not happy that they beat on me, but it paid off. I kept to the straight and narrow path. I never veered from that. I weathered the storm. I didn't get weak. I got stronger."

Uncle Edmund

The uncle who taught Marvin so much was his Uncle Edmund (see Chapter 3), the educator and minister. Edmund realized early in life how lack of education made it easier for whites to take advantage of his parents economically. He focused like a laser on boosting his own education. And he always challenged his sister Lee Augusta, Marvin's mother, to make sure her kids were making the most of school. He was preaching to the choir. All on her own, Lee Augusta was an ardent advocate of education. She pushed Marvin and his brother Lester relentlessly to hit the books and get good grades.

Edmund pushed too from afar. And Marvin resented it. "He was strict," he said. "And I didn't like that when I was young."

Edmund's attitude began to change once Marvin got into the Army. He began to appreciate that Marvin was a talented, ambitious young man.

Edmund, who was a Methodist pastor, became an officer and minister in the Women's Army Corps, whose female members were the first women other than nurses to serve in the Army.[156] The corps was created to help the military cover all of the tasks that were needed to wage a two-front war in Europe as well as the Pacific, while also giving war supplies to allies.

Edmund figured he might as well serve side-by-side with his nephew. He may also have calculated that Marvin's odds of surviving the global war were better in the WACs, as it was known, than in a front-line outfit. He urged Marvin to transfer, and he lobbied his own commanding officers to arrange for a transfer of his bright young nephew. Nothing came of Edmund's campaign, though. The Army had its own plans for Marvin.

Lester's War

Marvin's brother Lester also made it home alive after having served in the Marines. Like Marvin, Lester had also found himself fighting a war within a war. The Marines had refused to admit African-Americans until 1942. And Lester had gone through the gory gauntlet of front-line action against a stubborn enemy.

"He saw a lot of combat in the Pacific," Marvin said. "He was in the invasion of Iwo Jima, stuff like that. I think the war had a profound mental effect on him."

Marvin says that Lester may have been hit with even more belligerent racial discrimination in the Marines than he did in the Army. "It was their whole attitude," Marvin said. "The way they trained. They were tough and rough on you."

When Marvin was training at Camp Stewart, he took some multiday passes to visit his brother. "Lester was stationed at Montford Point [in North Carolina]. I visited him. Georgia was not that far from North Carolina. It was a real morale booster when I visited," Marvin said. "Whenever I arrived, the guards at the gate saluted me."

Camp Montford Point was adjacent to Camp Lejeune, the large Marine training base along the coast, in Jacksonville, North Carolina. Once President Roosevelt issued a directive ordering the Corps and other branches of the armed forces to open their ranks to African-Americans, the Marines admitted blacks but remained segregated. Montford Point was an all-black training facility, where some 20,000 black Leathernecks trained from 1942 until 1949, when the military finally integrated. Thirteen black Marines lost their lives in the fierce World War II island-to-island fighting against Japan. Montford Point's Marines plunged into combat on Iwo Jima, Okinawa, Saipan, and the Marianas Islands.[157]

So Lester Gilmore was among the Corps' earliest black recruits. He joined in 1944 and became part of the 52d Defense Battalion, which in the 1942 invasion of Saipan had been the first black Marine unit to engage the enemy. "Cool In Combat" was how *Time* magazine applauded the black Corpsmen, who beat back an attack with professional discipline despite taking casualties. Stubbornly, they advanced even though they were under fire from mortars, cannons, machineguns, and handguns.[158] They did exactly the opposite of what segregationists had sneered they would do. They did their jobs. They remained organized. They were smart. And they prevailed. Once he joined the battalion, Lester served in the Philippines and survived the bitter carnage of Iwo Jima.

The battle for Iwo Jima was a key to victory in the Pacific war. It was essential for the U.S. to take possession of the eight-square-mile spit of land, which was only 600 miles from Japan. The United States needed the island's air base for fighter planes to escort long-range bombing of Japan itself. The airstrip would also serve as an emergency landing site for B-29 bombers returning to the Marianas from attacks on Japan and other Japanese targets. And seizure of the island would also permit U.S. forces to conduct sea and air blockades. Capturing the island was essential to the expected invasion of Japan itself, and ultimately to winning the war.[159]

Japan knew the island's value as well, and Japanese forces defended Iwo Jima as if Japan's existence depended on it. Japan poured a fortune into armoring the island with miles of deep, reinforced concrete tunnels and fortifications. When fighting erupted, it featured hand-to-hand combat, tanks, flame-throwers. And that sort of fighting went on for a sickening 36 days.

Even when American success finally appeared certain, Japanese soldiers preferred to die rather than surrender. In desperate, suicidal final counterattacks, Japanese soldiers wielded swords, automatic weapons, and hand grenades. The toll was terrible. Of the 20,000 Japanese defenders, only 1,083 survived. The U.S. suffered a shocking 26,000 casualties, including 6,800 dead. The island became a meat grinder. Many men were not simply killed. They were torn apart and pulverized.

By the end, the battle was the largest and most costly in the history of the Marines.[160]

Following the war, Lester worked as a railroad-car porter for one or two years. "In those days porters were a relatively high paying job," Marvin said. The job entailed making up sleeping berths, waiting on tables in the dining car, and even working as a chef.

After saving some money and thinking about what he wanted to do long-term, Lester started college at the New School of Social Research in New York City, where he studied drama and acting. He continued his studies at Emerson College in Boston, which is well known for its programs in the arts.

Following graduation in 1953, he taught in Boston and Cambridge, at Boston English High School and at Cambridge Rindge and Latin High and other Cambridge schools. He also taught acting at the Elma Lewis School of Fine Arts, a black cultural arts institution. And just as Marvin had enjoyed playing piano, Lester loved the violin. As boys, Lester and Marvin had given recitals at their church on Sunday evenings. The boys also performed at other venues in Boston and on Cape Cod. Now as an adult, Lester's passion for the performing arts expressed itself through theater. He began to direct and perform in many plays. Marvin remembers Lester in Shakespeare's "Othello."

"He became a brilliant theater scholar," Marvin said. "He could quote so many of Shakespeare's plays verbatim. Lester was super talented. We were almost parallel in terms of our interests. Lester was the intellect. I was more involved in business"

Unable to make a living at theater, Lester kept it as a sideline while he continued to teach. He also became a deacon at the North Prospect Congregational Church on Massachusetts Avenue in Cambridge, near Porter Square. As deacon, he performed administrative tasks for the congregation.

But everything was not serene in Lester's life. Turned down for a teaching job in Cambridge, he hired a lawyer. The city relented and Lester began to teach at the high school and elementary grades at the Fletcher School. At one point, his high school students included Marvin's children.

His wife left him. He also tried to boost his income from theater. "He got mother to invest in a play in the round church," Marvin said, referring to the then-Church of all Nations. "But it went nowhere."

Lester moved back in with his parents at 69 Dana Street.

The contrast between his lack of material success and Marvin's business accomplishments was weighing on Lester. As time went on, he began to drink more. Just as Lee Augusta had used "Charlie" the rawhide rope to discipline her boys until Sophronia had demanded an end to such severe corporal punishment, Lester began to lash out at the people around him.

"He was abusive," Marvin said. "He carried it to his children."[161]

Marvin had to intervene on some occasions, even calling in the authorities.

"Mother lost faith in him and began to pick on him while he was teaching," Marvin said. "I had to tell my mother to leave him alone, he was doing the best he could. She just didn't like his lifestyle. She felt he wasn't doing anything."

In response, Lester became belligerent. "I think it all came from the war," Marvin said. "It really got to him."

Like many veterans, especially of the World War II generation, Marvin and Lester remained closed about their war experiences. Neither discussed them. Neither vented about what they had experienced. "Lester never talked to me about discrimination in the Marines and he never talked to me about what he had seen and suffered in combat," Marvin said.

Marvin added, "It got to a point where Lester couldn't handle life. Like a lot of veterans, even though he taught school and kids liked him, he couldn't get over what he had been through and he took it out on his family, on mother, father, me, and his children."

Lorna was the lone exception. "People loved to talk with her," Marvin said. "She sacrificed her whole life socially and in every sense of the word. He understood that. He respected her and never bothered her."

Lester's sadness came to an abrupt end. The morning of May 28, 1985, a Tuesday, he died suddenly of a heart attack in his classroom while teaching at the Fletcher School. He was 59 years old.

"He got up that morning as usual and went to school at eight in the morning," Marvin said. "They called me from Cambridge City Hospital early in the

A Changing U.S.

Black History

Sam Langford, boxer

Shortly after starting work as an orderly at Boston State Hospital, Marvin Gilmore was enough of a boxing fan to recognize one of the patients, Sam Langford. Fighting professionally from April 1902 until August 1926, Langford had won the heavyweight championship of Mexico and the heavyweight title of Australia. But the five-foot-seven-and-a-half-inch tall native of Nova Scotia had not been able to land fame and fortune in the big market, the United States.[i]

"Sam Langford is regarded as one of the best boxers of all-time and arguably the greatest boxer to never win a world title," says the *Boxrec Boxing Encyclopedia*. "White morning. His body was still warm when I touched it."

Ironically, Lester had just started to share his feelings. Given more time, he might have gotten enough anguish off his chest to escape from his demons. He passed away on a Tuesday. "I talked with him until 4 in the morning on Saturday, maybe it was Sunday, at the club after we closed for the night," Marvin said, referring to the Western Front, a Cambridge night club he owned. "We just sat down, had some drinks and talked. I can't believe he died so soon after that." Marvin paused, gathering his thoughts. "I loved him."

College at New England Conservatory

After a year at Manter Hall, Marvin was ready for college. New England Conservatory was perfect. Marvin could focus on music, and its location in Boston near Symphony Hall, the Museum of Fine Arts, and Northeastern University was a short distance from his home in Cambridge, across the Charles River. He began classes in September 1947.

To commute, Marvin bought a car, a maroon Nash. "It was new," Marvin said. "I never bought a used car. It cost $600."

Marvin's purchase was a modest milestone for his family. "My family had never owned a car," he said. "My father didn't know how to drive."

Marvin used the car to reach classes at NEC, as many refer to the renowned music-oriented college. He also used his

champions drew the color line and Jack Johnson claimed a title defence against Langford wouldn't draw flies. Despite being under 5'8" tall the gnome-like Canadian was feared by even the giants of the fight game.

"After Jack Johnson won the World Heavyweight Championship in 1908, Langford claimed the World Colored Heavyweight Championship. With Johnson choosing to defend against white challengers, the top black fighters fought each other repeatedly. Langford fought Joe Jeannette 13 times, Sam McVea 13 times, and Harry Wills 18 times."[ii]

Langford was short of height, but his arm reach was a lethal long 72 inches. He defeated reigning lightweight titleholder Joe Gans by a decision in December 1903, but he was not

Nash to commute to yet another job he landed, this one at Boston State Hospital. The large campus-like facility straddled Boston's Mattapan and Dorchester neighborhoods, serving the mentally ill in Greater Boston. After its creation in 1839 it was seen as an enlightened facility that provided humane treatment for the mentally ill. When it relocated to its Mattapan-Dorchester location – at the time, a semi-rural area that had been farmland – one goal was to allow patients to work plots for the sake of exercise, fresh food, escape from the hazards of downturn city life, and the dignity that comes from productive work.[162]

Marvin's new job was orderly. He worked the graveyard shift, from 11 at night until 7 the next morning, His pay was $14 a night – better than the $12 per day he had earned from the Whites, scrubbing floors, washing and polishing cars, chauffeuring Mrs. White.

Marvin found that many Boston State patients were often ignored and the hospital could be a dangerous place – for staff as well as patients. That decline from its idealistic founding was an early warning sign of the negative changes that would lead to the hospital's closing in 1979 as part of a nationwide shift of mental health treatment and residential facilities to smaller, group settings.[163]

"It was not glamorous work," Marvin said. "I worked in two wards; one was ward K. In one ward, I washed and cleaned the bodies of patients who died. I wrapped

given the title because he had entered the ring two pounds over the weight limit. "[The next year he] fought the world welterweight champion, Joe Walcott, to a 15-round draw in a contest that the majority of [spectators] felt he deserved [to be declared winner of]," wrote boxing historian Clay Moyle.[iii]

Jack Johnson, on his way to the heavyweight championship, faced Langford in April 1906. Johnson was a strapping 28-year-old, who would become the controversial first black heavyweight champ. He weighed 40 pounds more than the 20-year-old Langford, which was a huge advantage in a sport involving fistic battering rams. And sure enough Johnson won a convincing 15-round decision. But Langford's punches made an impression.

Even after winning the title, Johnson refused

them in white cloth sheets, then took them to the morgue. In the other ward, I helped take care of living patients. It was a dangerous place. I was lucky I was not attacked and cut up or beaten up by patients. But I had to do it because I had to earn money.

"Sometimes the hospital matron would make me scrub floors on my hands and knees. She didn't like me because I was getting an education. She was going to be stuck there her whole life. I wasn't. So she would make me wash a floor repeatedly and do the cracks between floor tiles again and again. I remember she was a big woman. She was white."

The work was frequently sad too. "You'd talk to a patient one night, then the next night come back and they'd be dead," Marvin said.

One of the patients Marvin met was Sam Langford. Langford was in his sixties, short, and blind. But in their first conversation Marvin discovered that this diminished African-American was someone special. Sam Langford had been one of the most skilled and feared boxers of the early 1900s. In fact, he had been too talented for his own good. Sharing the fate of many skilled black boxers of his era, he could not land bouts with white champions and other highly ranked white fighters, who feared him and refused to fight him because of his race.

By the time Marvin found Langford wasting away inside Boston State Hospital, the once great athlete was indigent and

Langford's repeated pleas for a rematch. "Years later, Johnson confided to New England Sports Museum trustee Kevin Aylwood, 'Sam Langford was the toughest little son of a bitch that ever lived.'"[iv]

In June 1916, Jack Dempsey was building momentum, smashing his way up through the ranks of contenders toward his triumphant taking of the world heavyweight championship in 1919 from Jess Willard. The "Manassa Mauler" would go on to establish himself as one of the all-time great pugilists. But in 1916, as he racked up victories and rose in prominence, the 21-year-old future boxing hall of famer declined to take on an aging Langford. Years later in his autobiography he conceded, "...I feared no man. [But there] was one man, he was even smaller than I, and I wouldn't fight because I knew he would flatten blind. "I was assigned to care for him one night," Marvin said. "I don't know how he ended up in Boston State, which was for the mentally handicapped. He was blind, poor, and unable to care for himself. But he was not crazy. His mind wandered when he spoke sometimes. But he knew who he was, where he was. And he took a lot of pride in his boxing career."

Marvin treated Langford with special care. "This was a gentle man, who could teach people things – namely, the value of hard work and sticking to your goals. He was from an older generation, and he had made his living in a way that was very far away from my life. But I felt like I could learn from his dignity and stick-to-itness."

Nodding Off

Working from 11 o'clock at night until 7 the next morning at Boston State Hospital took a toll on Marvin. He often had to race straight from work to class at NEC in his car. Marvin always could get by on just a few hours of sleep each night, a routine that jibes with his nonstop work ethic. But he needed at least *some* sleep. And so, once he arrived at NEC and parked, he would nap in his car before sprinting into his morning classes.

But sometimes those naps weren't enough. Occasionally he could not help but nod off in class. When that happened one day in an orchestral conducting class taught by Malcolm H. Holmes, the distinguished musicologist took offense.

"He gave me a tongue-lashing in his

me. I was afraid of Sam Langford."[v]

Langford's long career took its toll. Born in 1883, he fought in more than 300 professional bouts.[vi] In a June 1917 bout against Fred Fulton, Langford could not come out for the seventh round. His left eye was closely tightly. This appears to be the fight in which he was blinded in his left eye, boxing reporter Kieran Mulvaney wrote for ESPN.com.[vii]

In 1922, at age 37, he knocked out future middleweight champion Tiger Flowers in the second round of their bout even after suffering an injury that all but knocked out the vision in his remaining good eye.[viii]

In desperate need of money from boxing purses, Langford fought on for years more. When he won the Mexican heavyweight title in 1923, his handlers had to guide him into the ring and to his corner.[ix]

office," Marvin admits. "He took it personally. I explained it wasn't meant that way. It wasn't that I didn't care and didn't want to listen. I was just tired from being up all night."

Marvin definitely wanted to remain in the good graces of Holmes, who not only taught the conducting class. He was also dean of NEC and conductor of the NEC orchestra (as well as orchestras at Harvard and Wellesley colleges). In addition, Holmes was himself a military veteran and NEC's veterans' counselor. "I tearfully explained that I worked all night to earn money for school and didn't mean to insult him, but I just didn't get enough rest. He was willing to let the matter drop when I promised to try not to fall asleep in his class."

> "How he used to fight, he used to feel his opponent, he used to go in close – and he was such a brilliant fighter, he could fight inside for the entire fight – and as soon as he was on the inside, he would instinctively know from his years of experience, he could tell where his opponent's arms were and so forth and he could do OK," boxing historian Mike Silver explained, according to Mulvaney.

First Marriage

The years after his discharge from the Army bubbled with events. One of them was Marvin's marriage to Louise Freeman, who had grown up on Cambridge's River Street, been a member of the congregation at St. Bartholomew's Church, and had been a classmate of Marvin in high school. They lived at 51 Dana Street, and had a daughter, Wanda. Their marriage lasted a scant two years. Nearly 50 years after they divorced, Louise succumbed to cancer. Marvin buried her.

Multitasking Musician

While still a student at NEC, Marvin had majored in percussion. He had switched to that from piano. "My teacher

Sidebar notes
[i] Tracy Callis, "Sam Langford: the 'Boston Tar Baby,'" Cyber Boxing Zone: http://www.cyberboxingzone.com/boxing/langford.htm, accessed Oct. 27, 2013.
[ii] Boxrec Boxing Encyclopaedia, "Sam Langford": http://boxrec.com/media/index.php/Sam_Langford, accessed Oct. 27, 2013.
[iii] Clay Moyle, "Sam Langford:

thought I could do better at percussion," he said. "It was more of a rhythm thing." He played marimba, an acoustic instrument which is a type of xylophone; vibraharp, which resembles a xylophone and uses electrically powered rotating discs to create tremolo in its sound; and xylophone. Marvin's marimba had mahogany bars. His xylophone had metal bars.

NEC's rigorous curriculum required Marvin's musical education to be well-rounded. He studied drums and bass as well as classical music.

Marvin still keeps some of his old instruments in the attic of his Cambridge home. David, Marvin's older son, is a professional jazz guitarist; when he was a young boy, his father occasionally played the marimba and vibraphone at home. "Dad played classical R&B pieces [on the vibraharp and marimba], David Gilmore said. He was rusty, but he did it from memory. He'd just rip it off, then he wouldn't play again for a year or so. The vibraphone was in the [basement]. He brought a marimba down from the attic. He plugged the vibe in. It still worked. Sometimes when he wasn't around, I started to teach myself things on it."[164]

Marvin said, "At NEC I switched to percussion from piano. Malcolm Holmes is the one who persuaded me to switch. Salvy Cavicchio, who used to play vaudeville shows at the Old Howard" – the most famous theater in Boston's old Scollay Square entertainment district[165] –

History's Forgotten Boxer," blackpast.org: http://www.blackpast.org/perspectives/sam-langford-history-s-forgotten-boxer, accessed Oct. 27, 2013.

[iv] Clay Moyle, "Sam Langford: History's Forgotten Boxer," blackpast.org: http://www.blackpast.org/perspectives/sam-langford-history-s-forgotten-boxer, accessed Oct. 27, 2013.

[v] Clay Moyle, "Sam Langford: History's Forgotten Boxer," blackpast.org: http://www.blackpast.org/perspectives/sam-langford-history-s-forgotten-boxer, accessed Oct. 27, 2013.

[vi] Clay Moyle, "Sam Langford: History's Forgotten Boxer," blackpast.org: http://www.blackpast.org/perspectives/sam-langford-history-s-forgotten-boxer, accessed Oct. 27, 2013. Boxrec Boxing Encyclopaedia, "Sam Langford": http://boxrec.com/media/index.php/Sam_Langford, accessed Oct. 27, 2013.

[vii] Kieran Mulvaney, "The greatest fighter almost nobody knows," ESPN.com, Feb. 7, 2007: http://sports.espn.go.com/espn/blackhistory2007/news/story?id=2755803, accessed Oct. 27, 2013.

[viii] Kieran Mulvaney, "The greatest fighter almost nobody

"and all over the country, taught me to play the vibes."

Also while Marvin was still in college, he demonstrated an insatiable appetite for hard work. Lee Augusta was slowly building the family income with rental real estate, but she never put Marvin in jeopardy of being spoiled. She insisted that he fend for himself financially and learn how to make his own way in the world. When he was fresh out of the service and living at his parents' home at 69 Dana Street, Lee Augusta required him to pay $9 a week rent for his room and board.

knows," ESPN.com, Feb. 7, 2007: http://sports.espn.go.com/espn/blackhistory2007/news/story?id=2755803, accessed Oct. 27, 2013.

[ix] Clay Moyle, "Sam Langford: History's Forgotten Boxer," blackpast.org: http://www.blackpast.org/perspectives/sam-langford-history-s-forgotten-boxer, accessed Oct. 27, 2013.

Once he was attending NEC and living at 413 Broadway, his expenses were even greater. He had tuition bills to pay. He had to keep gas and oil in the Nash. And Marvin had a social life.

So Marvin boosted his income by seeking out odd jobs for pay. He walked neighbors' dogs and mowed people's lawns. He also ran a catering business even though he was up to his neck in studies and already holding down a fulltime job at Boston State Hospital. Marvin even tapped into his experience working for the Whites of Brookline and Marblehead Neck by house-cleaning and washing and waxing cars for a businessman in Chelsea, a small city just north of Boston, across the Mystic River, who owned a car dealership.

But once again Marvin's path was made more difficult by the need to cope with a white employer's bias. The Chelsea businessman needed to feel superior to Marvin. And he needed to think that Marvin was so desperate for work that he would make the time-consuming and inconvenient trip by public transportation to and from Chelsea. That would reassure him that he could exploit Marvin financially. But Marvin refused to play his role in the Chelsea family's mind game. He drove his Nash to the job. In an effort to preserve this source of work and income, Marvin would park his car several blocks from the Chelsea man's home.

"The Chelsea people didn't want a black man who could afford a car," Marvin said. But Marvin's attempts to avoid a confrontation were doomed to fail. "When the Chelsea people found out I had a car, they didn't want me to work for them. They let me go."

Marvin still had his catering. "I did catering mostly on weekends, but sometimes on week days between classes or after classes," he said. "Whenever I could. Sometimes jobs came up two or three times a week. Sometimes none. I did whatever had to be done. I could cook. I scrubbed floors. I was a common work slave. But I needed the income. The money from the government wasn't enough to put me through NEC and pay for everything I needed. Plus, I was married part of that time. I had financial responsibilities."

Marvin often got by on just four hours of sleep a night. He was a whirlwind of productive activity. Incredibly, in addition to all of the other demands on his time, he formed a band. "Polka was in its hey-day so we did a lot of polka parties," he said. "If it was far from home and the party ended late, we slept on floors, on mattresses. We did parties, weddings, ethnic parties outside Boston. I pretty much did one party a week."

Marvin graduated from NEC in June 1951 with NEC's Diploma in Performance. The degree designates a focus on music and took longer to earn than a regular undergraduate degree. Marvin was 26 years old and brimming with the optimism of youth. He immediately ran right into one of society's brick walls.

"I was quite a percussion player," Marvin said. "I tried to get a job with the Boston Symphony Orchestra. That's when I found out the BSO did not allow black players. If you were like Marion Anderson and other great black musicians, you could be invited to perform there [at Symphony Hall]. But only members of the musicians' union Local 9 could get jobs, and Local 9 was the white union. I had to join Local 535, the black union."

Better Harmony

Decades later, on June 6, 2007, the Boston Symphony Orchestra took an indirect step toward making amends. Marvin was attending an evening performance of the Boston Pops Orchestra, which consists mainly of musicians in the BSO and provides light classical fare and orchestral versions of popular music. Symphony Hall's floor was reconfigured to banquet seating with tables, the customary arrangement for Pops performances there, switching from the auditorium seating that is standard for performances of the BSO itself.

The evening's theme was "Presidents at Pops," which is an annual event that gives corporate sponsors an opportunity to host valued clients, employees, and friends. It is also a giant networking event, giving Greater Boston's business bigwigs a chance to hobnob. That year's gala coincided with the 63rd anniversary of the D-Day landings on Normandy.

When regular Pops attendee Diddy Cullinane, a member of the BSO board of trustees, learned before the concert that her friend Marvin would be present, she spoke with conductor Keith Lockhart.

"I spoke with Keith before the concert," said Mrs. Cullinane, who would be attending with her husband John Cullinane, a renowned software industry pioneer and founder of Cullinet Software.[166] "Keith often speaks to the audience [between songs]. And that's what he did on this occasion."

Lockhart turned to the audience midway through the program. "He took time out to say that we have a very special person in our audience," Mrs. Cullinane continued. "Keith said that on this anniversary of the troops landing in Normandy, we have a member of the audience who was among those troops. He described Marvin's role in the community, and he asked Marvin to stand. They shined a spotlight on him. And the audience stood and applauded Marvin. Marvin had no idea this was going to happen. He was quite moved. We all were, really. And Marvin had tears in his eyes."[167]

Marvin recalls the event fondly. "Lockhart introduced me, talked about my war duties, and asked me to stand up," he said. "It was a thrill for me, and the crowd seemed excited. People were crying."

Marvin and the Cullinanes' tables were next to each other. Marvin and John Cullinane were within feet of each other. "What I clearly remember was standing next to [Marvin] when he was introduced and the spotlight shone on him (and me), and it was something to look up at the balconies and see everyone giving Marvin a standing O with great enthusiasm," said John Cullinane.[168] "It was June 6 and Keith made note of the day and landing at Normandy and that there was someone in the audience that was there, and that's when he introduced Marvin. Of course, what made it even better was that a black person was finally getting some recognition for fighting in World War II. [A]ll this was Diddy's doing. She put it all together."

Diddy Cullinane knew Marvin through Black & White Boston, a nonprofit organization that she had founded, which was devoted to easing

Boston's racial tensions by creating a forum in which black entrepreneurs could network with white business executives.[169] Marvin was one of the original 44 members – 22 black, 22 white.

Cullinane wanted to bridge the racial divide that had widened during Boston's public school bussing crisis in the 1970s. That racial tension had started to ease when it was reignited by the Charles Stuart murder case in 1989. Stuart, the white general manager of a Boston fur salon, had blamed a black man for the grisly fatal shooting of his pregnant wife. An ugly, racially impassioned manhunt ensued. Months later Stuart killed himself hours after his brother disclosed that Stuart himself was the killer and that the black suspect had been framed.[170]

Diddy Cullinane ran Black & White Boston for 19 years after its 1989 creation, initially as a Catholic Charities event, then as an independent group, with support from her husband John. The group sponsored golf outings for its members. The tournaments were opportunities to network. "Marvin did not play golf, but he came to the tournaments," Mrs. Cullinane said. "He showed his support by his attendance. His wife Lorna came with him. He was always very engaging. He was charming. He was always were dapper and loved by the black community and respected."

Making Music

Meanwhile, back when Marvin was a newly minted college grad, he looked for ways to make a living with music. He combined two services he had begun in college, catering and music. Here was Marvin's entrepreneurial flair. He absorbed valuable skills like a sponge. He used those new talents to pounce on fresh opportunities. His aim was nearly flawless, like a cat swooping in on a mouse.

"When I catered parties, I tried to perform as well," he said. "Why not own the whole gig? If the host was going to hire a band, I told him that I could provide music too. It meant more money, and why give away part of the night's business?"

Back in college he had studied cooking from his mother. "When I started catering, I could prepare the food myself. I could do it all," he said. "The catering was hard work. We had to lug in tables, chairs, linens, instruments, alcohol, silverware. Food. Everything. It was backbreaking work. After a party wound down, families who hired us would go to bed. I was still cleaning up. I performed or catered more than once a week. And I usually performed at every party I catered. Thank god I'm not doing this now. I did that for about 10 years. I *still* get calls from people asking me to run an event. But now I say, 'No.'"

Knowing When to Say No

Many parties that Marvin catered were for wealthy clients in Newton, Massachusetts, a suburb west of Boston and Brookline, home to many affluent professionals and business owners. Marvin still recalls the names of some of his clients – there were the Gordons. Another was a man named Cohen, who lived on Newton's Commonwealth Avenue, a wide, tree-lined boulevard winding its way westward; he owned a food market.

Dr. Abram Sachar was a guest at one or more of the Cohen gatherings. Sachar was the first president of Brandeis University. And as a guest of Cohen, Sachar recognized Marvin's ability to orchestrate fine food, luxurious layouts, good libations, and first-rate music. Conversations with Marvin broadened his appreciation for Marvin's skill at running an organization. Sachar quickly saw that he could use a man like Marvin.

The highly selective university in Waltham, Massachusetts, was in its early years, having been founded in 1948. Like any skilled chief executive, Sachar always was on the lookout for valuable talent. Also like any university president, he frequently hosted dignitaries at his Brandeis residence for fundraising, academic, or other institutional purposes. In addition, the home was an extension of his office; like his regular office, it needed a manager. Sachar offered Marvin a job as the house man or butler at his Brandeis residence.

"Sachar noticed I was a perfectionist," Marvin said. "You couldn't make mistakes at these parties. If you did, they'd find someone else. The women especially – god bless 'em – were perfectionists. I had to make borscht, the beet soup, the Jewish way, the way these ladies expected it, the way they would serve it at their own homes, the way *their* mothers made it. All of the food had to be that way. That's only natural. Any ethnic group wants their food done the way they're used it. You can't fake that. Either you learn to make things right, or you don't get hired. Sachar saw how I did things. He saw how the other guests liked it. And these were a lot of the same people coming to his events at Brandeis. So he asked if I would mind working for Brandeis."

Accepting Sachar's offer would mean financial stability for Marvin. It would relieve him of the small businessman's burden of having to sell himself and his service again and again to each new catering customer, music customer, house-cleaning customer, car-washing customer, day after day. There were just two problems. First, the job reminded Marvin of the servitude his grandmother had been thrilled to escape.

Sure, overseeing the home of a prestigious university president for a real wage and benefits was significantly different from being an enslaved house boy in mid-19th century Alabama. But there was still too much about the job that Sachar offered that plucked dissonant strings in Marvin's heart. If it *felt* like a giant step backwards, it *was* a giant step backwards.

"It would have been a good job," Marvin said. "But I said no. I didn't want to take off white folks' coasts, like I as in servitude. I didn't want to be saying, *Yes sir, No sir,* all of my life. And I had other plans."

Those other plans were the second problem. Marvin was an entrepreneur. Working for someone else simply was not his goal in life.

Marvin's wife Louise was furious. "My wife went crazy," Marvin said. *"Who was I to turn Brandeis down?* she wanted to know. But I was sure bigger opportunities would come around."

He was right. Marvin had the rare entrepreneurial gift of creating his own opportunities.

Building on Real Estate

One way Marvin created opportunities was by building on what he had been taught by his mother about rental property. Lee Augusta had handed the baton to Marvin, and Marvin ran with it.

Lee Augusta had shown him that rental residential real estate was something that even a person with very limited initial capital could invest in. And it could be done in a way that helped tenants badly in need of housing. Lee Augusta had created the family blueprint for doing well while doing good.

Starting in the late 1940s, Marvin duplicated his mother's success with real estate over and over. He used cash flow from one building to pay for another. Then he used cash flow from two buildings to buy a third. His portfolio of property kept multiplying.

Yet today Marvin has sold off the bulk of it. He focuses most of his time and energy on the CDC of Boston. He allocates some time to the Western Front. Two stories illustrate why his goals evolved.

From 1961 to 1968 Marvin was a member of the board of directors of the Rental Housing Association of the Greater Boston Real Estate Board. He was president of Council E, Brokers Institute of the Board, from 1971 through 1972, and its first African-American president. Council E designated a geographic area that included Cambridge and other large nearby suburbs such as Belmont. Before rising to those positions, one day in the 1950s he was talking with a fellow real estate investor. Marvin was describing how well he maintained his residential rental properties. Some were rooming houses. He did his own maintenance. "I painted halls and stairways. I did everything. I plastered rooms. I worked until 12 and 1 o'clock at night. I was young. I hustled. If a furnace broke, I called in plumbers to replace it, and I oversaw the installation. Like I said, I was young."

Marvin took such pride in his buildings and in how well he treated his tenants that he often spent Sundays in the spring and summer mowing lawns at his properties, cutting grass in front yards while his tenants socialized and barbecued in the back yard.

Proud of his commitment, Marvin expected a compliment from his friend. He was caught off guard when his Real Estate Board colleague took issue with him, saying it was not right for Marvin to work so hard. *What's the point of having an investment if it seems to own you rather than the other way around?* Marvin's friend asked. The friend continued: *The property should work for you; you shouldn't be a servant for the property.*

The friend urged Marvin to reconsider his strategy, and to shift his investments into larger buildings with more apartments. Buildings like that could have far better economies of scale, enabling the buildings to pay for maintenance men to do all the upkeep so Marvin himself would not have to.

Marvin took that advice to heart. Gradually, he replaced rooming houses with apartment buildings. He bought some in communities outside Cambridge. But his expansion beyond his home town was also motivated largely by what he describes as the city's hostile attitude. The city did not want him as a black man to get ahead.

"I had to look outside Cambridge," he said. "When I bought the Western Front, no blacks had liquor licenses in Cambridge. The Candlelight Lounge had a beer and wine license, but they wouldn't give me a full liquor license. You can't survive as a bar without one. They knew that. When I bought the Western Front, it was a rat trap. I put a ton of money into it, fixing it up. I ripped the old bar out. I put in a mahogany bar. I put a fortune into the club. But the city didn't care that I improved it. The police constantly harassed me. They tried to plant drug paraphernalia. They tried to break me financially by forcing me to hire lawyers. I went to court several times and was exonerated. But they'd blame me for individuals using drugs *near* the club. And the police didn't like that the club was racially mixed."

Marvin's zest for rental property took another hit one in the late 1960s. Marvin was standing atop a ladder, painting a hallway ceiling in a building he owned outside Cambridge. This was a larger building than Marvin's early properties, but Marvin still took a hands-on approach to maintaining it. He felt personally responsible to his tenants and properties. Yet some of his tenants in this location did not appreciate Marvin's dedication. One had radically different priorities.

While Marvin was up the ladder, a tenant came at him with a gun.

"I was young and strong, and I tried to keep it a beautiful building," he said. "It had 12 units, with a garage for each unit. But it was in a drug-infested neighborhood. And I was growing afraid of getting killed by drug dealers. I was afraid I would be collecting rents, and someone would shoot me. I would be found dead. When I thought about that at night, I closed my eyes and cried."

Soon after, Marvin sold the building for $1 to his tenants.

Rent control proved to be another bitter pill, shrinking Marvin's appetite for rental real estate. Cambridge – which some political pundits poke fun at as the "People's Republic of Cambridge" for its very liberal politics – introduced rent control in 1970. Landlords often found themselves barred from raising rents. Property owners also had to jump through hoops to justify expenditures for upkeep and improvements. Even then, after potentially expensive and time-consuming proceedings and paperwork mandated by the rent control board, requests for rent increases and maintenance reimbursements often were still rejected by the board. Landlords repeatedly felt unfairly treated.[171]

Fed up by what he saw as a discriminatory process, Marvin decided to cut his losses.

"Why was I running around with these buildings, working my butt off, then rent control stepped in?" Marvin wondered in hindsight. "Rent control would not let you raise rents. I wasn't even allowed to cover expenses. So I sold all of it. I had to. I could not maintain the properties. They hated landlords in Cambridge. So I had to sell them, and I had to sell them at a loss. I sold them below market value. Those buildings were worth over $1 million each. But I sold them for $200,000 to $300,000 each. A few went into foreclosure. I kept one or two for purely family sentimental reasons, because my mother had owned them."

Broker Business

Marvin knows only one speed: fast forward. He helps fill all of those hours when he is not sleeping with yet another business. He is co-owner of Urban Realty Group, a licensed real estate broker, based in Brookline, a suburb nestled against the northwest shoulder of Boston. Urban Realty specializes in commercial and residential real estate sales and rentals.

Demerits Debate

Whether it was by enlisting early in the Army or, decades later, fighting to create more economic opportunity as head of the Community Development Corporation of Boston, Marvin has made it a habit to stand up for other people.

One of his proudest stands for the little guy began in 1955. On February 26, Marvin was in a minor fender bender in Boston. Marvin did what he was supposed to. He reported the incident to the Registry of Motor Vehicles. Except for car insurance paperwork, he expected that to be the end of it.

Wrong. On May 23 the Registry notified Marvin that he had been assessed three demerit points for being at fault in an accident in which minor bodily injuries were caused. Under the state's insurance system, drivers were slapped with a $6 surcharge on their compulsory coverage for each demerit point received. And the surcharge was assessed not just once but each year for four years.[172]

Time out, Marvin thought. *Why is the Registry blaming me for the accident? Who had determined that? On what basis?* No one had asked

Marvin for any evidence. No one had given him a chance to respond to any evidence or claim against him. So, like many motorists who had been hit with the demerit surcharges, Marvin was angry. But unlike almost everyone else who had been hit with a surcharge, Marvin did something about it.

Marvin filed suit against the Registry, charging that the assessment of points was unconstitutional because it stole what should be the power of a court to determine who is at fault in an accident. Marvin pointed out that he had been blamed for the accident even though there had not been any court action, civil or criminal, nor any judicial judgment to determine anyone's fault, much less his. The Registrar's action was "arbitrary, capricious and without any cause or reason recognized by law," Marvin argued.[173]

Two other drivers filed similar suits. One of those cases was dismissed when another court subsequently cleared that driver of fault in his accident.

So Marvin's case and another man's were joined, and sent to the Massachusetts Supreme Court. Marvin had touched a raw nerve. The public hated the demerit law so much that the high bench's decision to consider the matter made front-page banner headlines.[174]

Sensing the Registry rule's imminent demise and recognizing the unfairness of the rule, local-court judges began dismissing traffic violators because they viewed the surcharges as inexcusably high. It simply would not be right to find anyone guilty of a traffic violation if the result could be this surcharge, which one judge called "too tough."[175]

The governor also jumped onto the bandwagon that Marvin had helped start rolling. He created a special commission to study the detested surcharge. That group quickly recommended suspending the penalty. The legislature piled on, repealing the surcharge by a nearly unanimous vote. Gov. Christian Herter signed the repeal on Feb. 8, 1956, killing the despised demerit.[176]

"I wasn't looking for a fight," Marvin said. "I just wanted justice for myself. That surcharge wasn't right. It wasn't right that the Registry was taking money out of my pocket and putting it into the pocket of some big insurance company without even giving me a chance to tell my side of the story. So I'm glad those other judges and the governor and the legislature all agreed with me. And I'm glad for all of the other drivers it helped too."

Marriage to Lorna Langer

As the weekend approached one week in 1956, Marvin lent his car –
by now he had replaced his Nash with a black and white Oldsmobile coupe
– to his girlfriend Winnie, a Native American, who drove it to New York
City, where she had a personal appointment. She would be gone through
the weekend.

After Winnie left for New York, a friend named Libby called to invite
Marvin to a party. With regrets, Marvin declined. "I told her I couldn't
make the party because I didn't have my car," Marvin said. Undeterred,
Libby said, *Come anyway. Take a cab. Oh, and bring your records.*

Party night rolled around. When Marvin still had not arrived by about
10:30, Libby called again. *Why wasn't he there? We're waiting for you and
your records,* she said. Marvin confessed he had simply gone to sleep
early. After all, he didn't have his car. *So what?* Libby countered. *Grab a
cab. And don't forget your jazz records.* Marvin had a superb collection,
including platters by Frank Sinatra and Nat "King" Cole, all excellent for
listening and dancing.

Marvin got up, dressed in a handsome herringbone suit, and took a
cab from his apartment at 423 Broadway in Cambridge to the address on
Park Drive in Boston that Libby shared with friends. Almost as much as it is
today, the tree-lined neighborhood of mostly three-, four-, and five-story
brick apartment buildings was heavily populated by college students and
recent graduates. It was a football toss from the Boston University
campus. It was a short walk from the Northeastern, Simmons, and
Wheelock campuses too. Also nearby was the Longwood medical area,
home to several of Boston's prestigious hospitals, which were affiliated
with many of the area's medical schools.

Shortly after arriving, Marvin noticed a girl named Lorna Langer. She
was a friend of the party's four hosts, who were all students at Harvard.

"Lorna was kind of quiet," Marvin said. "And I kind of liked her
because she was so quiet. We talked during the party, and at the end of
the party I asked if I could call her. She said yes, so I asked for her address.
But she wouldn't give it to me."

The mid-1950s were an era of far greater decorum than our 21st
century is. A respectable young lady might have seemed slightly over
eager if she gave her telephone number to a young gentleman she had
just met. Rather than commit such a breach of 1950s' etiquette, Lorna

deftly made Marvin responsible for any next step in courtship. He would have to do a little homework.

"Lorna said look it up in the phone book," Marvin chuckled. "It took me six weeks to get up enough nerve to call her. And when I did, I invited her over to dinner. I still remember what I served: an okra dish – with green, red, and yellow okra – with tomatoes and onions."

Marvin's dish was classic Southern cuisine. But meeting Lorna at that party may not have been pure kismet. The party hosts were hoping to introduce the two, says Marque Gilmore, who is the third of Marvin and Lorna's three offspring. "Dad didn't find out about it until later," Marque said.[177]

The two began to date and get to know each other. Marvin explained that he was a real estate broker. He learned that Lorna had been born and raised in the Bronx, New York. Her parents were Robert and Lillian. Robert worked for Knapp Engraving, a printing firm in New York City owned by his brother. Lorna herself, Marvin realized quickly, was brilliant. A 1952 Phi Beta Kappa honor society graduate of Vassar College, she was studying for her Ph. D. in biochemistry at Harvard University's Radcliffe graduate school. She would rank second in her class when she earned her degree in 1957, Marvin recalls.[178]

Lorna had a keen interest in helping to find cures for cancer. It was a prophetic concern. In the mid-1960s her mother began to battle postmenopausal breast cancer. She succumbed Oct. 8, 1968, around age 68. (Lisa A. Gilmore says Lillian was unsure of her year of birth due to loss to fire of a birth certificate and to conflicting records.[179] The 1930 U.S. census lists her year of birth as about 1903.[180] The 1940 census report says she was born around 1902.[181]) Lorna herself began her own battle against breast cancer decades later, in the mid-1960s. She licked the affliction and became a survivor.

Marvin and Lorna's courtship continued even as Lorna took a post-graduate fellowship in Copenhagen, Denmark. In her spare time, she and Marvin motored around Europe in Lorna's TR-3 sports car.

After studying abroad in 1957 and 1958, Lorna returned to the United States. She won a research fellowship in the pathology department at world famous Massachusetts General Hospital in Boston. And she and Marvin decided to marry.

But Marvin had to overcome a case of cold feet.

"Since I had a first marriage that did not work, I was not so eager," Marvin said. "So she was the one who really proposed. And I was no fool, so we agreed to marry. But she insisted that I agree to one condition. She said she was an only child, and she wanted three children. She was very clear about that. She was very serious. I agreed, and I kept my promise. Over the years we had three kids."

And what did Lorna see in Marvin? To her Marvin was more than a real estate broker. He was also a musician, a caterer, an entrepreneur. And she could see that he would expand on that resume in the decades to come.

"When I asked her, she smiled," Marvin said. "She said I could do many things, while she could do just one."

Lorna also appreciated the fact that Marvin esteemed her smarts, in a time period when women were still widely discouraged from seeking advanced academic degrees and careers outside the home. Her own parents had discouraged her from attending college. It was an Aunt Sadie who spurred her to attend college, Vassar in particular, said Lisa A. Gilmore, Marvin and Lorna's first of three offspring. "Mother told me she married dad because he was one of the few men who valued her intelligence," said Lisa, who is Lorna and Marvin's daughter.[182]

Marvin was Lorna's first African-American friend. "Mother didn't know any black people except the doormen at the apartment building in the Bronx where she grew up," Lisa said.

Marvin and Lorna's love had the makings of a storybook marriage. But there was a very big hurdle they had to overcome.

Lorna was white and Jewish, and her parents did not want her to marry a black gentile.

"My mother's grandparents came to the U.S. in the 1890s from Poland and Lithuanian, escaping pogroms," Lisa said, referring to the violent mob attacks on Jews that were rampant in the 19th and 20th centuries in Russia, Poland, elsewhere in Eastern Europe, and finally in Germany.[183] For generations, experiences with non-Jews and people outside their own community had taught them to be cautious.

Like many immigrants from a variety of backgrounds, Lillian's family stuck close to Jewish friends and acquaintances from the Old World. Every single one of their neighbors on New York's Madison Street told the 1900 census taker that both their mothers and fathers had been born in Russia.

The borders among Poland and her eastern neighbors have changed repeatedly in the past thousand years, including numerous redrawing in the past three hundred years.[184] Many immigrants who ardently regarded themselves as Poles or Lithuanians set out for the New World from territory that was technically Russia at that moment. It's also possible that the census taker, who may have been scornful of fresh-off-the-boat greenhorn immigrants, didn't bother to make distinctions among various Eastern European places of origin; instead, he callously labeled them all as Russia, the biggest country in the region.

In any case, this was a work-class neighborhood. Lillian's family's neighbors list occupations such as errand boy, messenger, printer, painter, tailor, box maker, and student.

Marvin continued his description of how his relationship with Lorna progressed. "When we started to go together, she told her mother about me," Marvin said. "And her mother gave her a hard time because of my race. She told Lorna, if you're not serious, don't get into a relationship.

"She saw blacks as no-good, people who took low-paying jobs."

The more serious Marvin and Lorna's relationship got, the more serious Lillian's defensive steps became.

"Her mother's law firm put a tracer on me," Marvin said. "[The private detectives] reported back to her. Her mother thought I was marrying Lorna for her money.

"Lorna was new school. She lived a separate, independent life. When she went to New York to tell her mother she wanted to get married, her mother blew a fuse. Her father was quiet."

Determined to prevent Lorna from marrying Marvin, Lillian came to Boston shortly before the wedding. "I had bought Lorna a beautiful satin dress," Marvin said. Lillian stormed into Lorna's apartment. "Lillian destroyed the wedding dress the night before the wedding. She tore it apart at the seams. I took it to a seamstress, who worked on it all night to restore it."

Lillian's fury extended into the wedding day, March 7, 1959. College buddies warned Marvin that his reluctant mother-in-law-to-be was asking invitees about the ceremony. She seemed intent on disrupting the event. So with little time to spare before the nuptials, Marvin changed the venue from Marsh Chapel at Boston University to a smaller chapel. He also arranged for two off-duty police officers to provide security. The wedding took place without a disturbance.

The couple was married by Dr. Howard Thurman, a renowned African-American preacher. Thurman had recently been named the first black dean of Marsh Chapel. He was the first black to be named tenured dean of chapel at a predominantly white university.[185]

But Marvin could not change the reception's location. When Lillian arrived, it took one of the police officers and a female guest to prevent her from entering.

"The detective told her that Lorna is a grown woman, who has a right to wed whomever she pleases," Marvin recalled sadly. "Lillian and Robert were put into a cab. Robert never objected to the marriage. And he was silent [while this confrontation played out]. He was powerless against his wife."

A year later the newlyweds honeymooned in Canada.

Lillian finally came to terms with her daughter's marriage a few years later, after Lorna and Marvin's daughter Lisa was born on Jan 10, 1962. "Lillian sent us a check for $15,000" – a sizable sum then – "when Lisa was born to make amends," Marvin said. "She visited us and she invited us to her home. We went several times. When [Lorna and Marvin's first son] David was born [Feb. 5, 1964] she sent another check. She did the same when Marque was born [May 29, 1966]. We became very close friends."

Lillian's relationship with Lorna and Marvin came full circle by the time she learned around 1967 that she would soon die from cancer. "She asked me to take in her husband," Marvin said. An aging Robert Langer was growing increasingly frail. He moved in with the Gilmores in 1968.

"He lived with us at 26 Mt. Vernon Street for three or four years," Marvin said. "He helped take care of the kids. I loved him! I took him to Hawaii for an American Bankers' Association conference. We took him skiing to Canada with us. The three of us drove to Canada in a VW bug, with a ski rack on the roof."

Meanwhile, Lorna made her own large mark in life. She had been elected to Phi Beta Kappa, the nation's oldest and best known academic honor society, in 1951 after three years of college. She had been awarded a James Ryland and Georgia A. Kendrick Fellowship in biochemistry at Harvard. Her research had been published in prestigious professional journals.[186]

Lorna's interests and talents were also diverse. She raised three children. She nurtured a lifelong love of reading. Over time, she became an avid gardener and animal lover. Family and friends relished her gourmet cooking. She also was secretary of the Cambridge Visiting Nurses Association for 20 years. And she lent her time and energy to many charities and causes. In addition, she served on the board of the Cambridge YWCA.

Lisa fondly remembers the joy of hearing her mother read the Br'er Rabbit folktales to her when she was a youngster. It was fun no matter how many times she had already heard the stories, which celebrate the triumph of wit over brute strength (and most of which originated in Africa).[187] "She treated all things with love and respect," Lisa recalls. And she recounts the human side of her mother. "As a child of the Depression, she also believed in not wasting anything. She didn't waste money on plastic sandwich bags for our school lunches when she could wash, and rewash, and rewash them. She didn't waste her breath by speaking negatively of anyone. And she didn't waste time, always doing what needed to be done when it needed to be done."

Further, because Lorna was a whiz at math she kept the books for many of Marvin's businesses.

"My mom was central to the accounting," said David Gilmore. "She handled all of the bookkeeping. It was tough at times because they didn't always see eye-to-eye. They had disagreements about what they should do. My mom was more conservative about finances. My dad was more of a risk-taker. For example, He wanted to buy some condos in New Hampshire or Vermont. She warned against it. They went ahead, and they flopped. They lost a lot of money in the investment.

"Another time my dad invested in a black-owned airline that flew to Martha's Vineyard and Nantucket. It flopped.

"Those setbacks created tension between them. It was a price they paid. He was goal oriented. His attitude was that the man is the breadwinner, and mom should be the nurturer. Dad saw his role as making sure the family's materials needs were met, which he did. But there was a price to pay for that. He was not always available on a deeper level emotionally."[188]

Like any entrepreneur, Marvin understands the inevitability of ups and down in business. He also sees Lorna as his most important partner, in life and business. She was a loving wife and mother and the bright star around which their family and household orbited. Lorna was Marvin's rock.

"Through it all, she stood by me and supported me," Marvin said. "I could not have been luckier."

Lorna passed away Feb. 17, 2007, two days shy of her 76th birthday, taken by one or more strokes. At her funeral, Rabbi Albert Axelrad praised Lorna for having earned what he called the crown of a good name. For her goodness throughout life, she had earned a reputation as a special person. Such a crown is worth more than money. It is more powerful than the crown of royalty. And it is a crown that does not fade with time.

Lorna Langer Gilmore's crown of a good name endures in the memory of her family and all others whom she touched.

Another First

One day in 1966 Marvin was at work in his real estate office on the street level of 409 Broadway in Cambridge. Marvin owned the entire block of brick buildings. In walked Wayne Hazard, a young black man, who introduced himself.

Glancing up from his desk, Marvin guessed the neatly pressed man was a graduate student at Harvard, looking for housing. Marvin was half right. The young man was indeed a student at Harvard, but he was not looking for housing. Instead, he explained, he was working on an academic paper about attempts by African-Americans to start banks in New England. Not one had succeeded, he said.

But he had done his homework. He knew who Marvin was and what he did for a living.

"He said I was the person who *could* succeed in starting a bank," Marvin said. "I laughed at him. I said I had no money. He seemed to think I was some sort of mogul. I was just a businessman in the real estate business. I kicked him out."

Marvin kicked the young man out when he came back two or three weeks later. But he did not chase him away when he returned for a third time. "By that time I had realized, *why not?* If he had confidence that I could do this, why shouldn't I? He gave me a copy of his thesis and I read it. His confidence turned me on. I got seven friends together and we started meeting at my house."

Marvin and his colleagues started searching for fellow investors. "I met with people in churches and synagogues," Marvin said. "We priced the stock at $10 per share, $5 par value. We finally found 3,300 stockholders and raised $3 million in operating capital." Early investors, including the founding incorporators, ended up kicking in amounts equal to several hundred dollars per share. Meanwhile, Marvin and his fellow founders worked to make their bank-to-be a reality. They addressed countless requirements, big and small, from the state banking commission. Marvin knew they were in the home stretch when they made arrangements for installation of a vault in their soon-to-open bank.

One of Marvin's proudest days as a businessman was when the group received its charter from state banking commissioner John B. Hynes. Even then, Marvin plowed forward. He enticed friends and prominent business owners like Murray Pearlstein, founder of the prestigious Louis Boston clothing store, to open accounts. Marvin alone brought in $13 million in deposits.

Quarterbacked by Marvin, the effort to organize and establish Unity Bank & Trust Company, in Boston's Roxbury neighborhood, took from 1966 until 1968. Unity became the first minority-owned commercial bank in New England. Marvin then served as vice chairman of the board of directors and first vice president, heading the bank's business development and marketing. He focused on his role as vice chairman from 1969 until 1971.

But while Marvin focused on persuading deep-pocketed business people to park their dollars with Unity, the lending side of the bank ran into trouble. Unity was forced to eat nearly $1 million in bad loans. That debt equaled 83% of Unity's initial capitalization of $1.2 million. Racked up over three and a half years of operations, operating losses totaled $1.3 million by 1972. The state commissioner of banking intervened and appointed an outside conservator to run the bank.[189]

Marvin remained on the board of directors. Soon, however, he became head of the Community Development Corporation of Boston. As his CDC responsibilities ramped up, his other business and family demands on his time also increased. Even Marvin, a man who got by on little sleep every night, was forced to choose. He decided it was time to move on from Unity.

"I'm still very proud of my role in starting Boston's first black-owned and black-operated bank," he said.

Public Service

Starting in the decades before he severely scaled back his investments in real estate, Marvin's involvement in housing for African-Americans made him a go-to figure for political office-holders who wanted to tackle minority housing problems. Marvin was an ideal resource. When a politician – a white politician, in all likelihood – wondered what questions to ask about housing, Marvin was already testing answers. He was at Ground Zero in the real world. He knew what the problems were, and he was uniquely positioned to help define solutions.

His list of appointments in this period alone speaks volumes:

- 1964-1965: Governor's Special Legislative Commission on Low-Income Housing.
- 1964-1970: Massachusetts Commission Against Discrimination, Advisory Council on Housing (M.H.F.A.).
- 1966-1972: Civic Unity Advisory Committee, City of Cambridge.
- 1968-1969: Governor's Special Commission investigating block-busting in Massachusetts.

Marvin's groups got things done. The Low-Income Housing Commission, for example, proposed legislation that gave birth to the Massachusetts Housing Finance Agency. Using low-cost loans, that agency's job was to help increase affordable rental and for-sale housing in Massachusetts.

Former Massachusetts Governor and 1988 Presidential candidate Michael Dukakis, who later appointed Marvin to the Metropolitan Area Planning Council (MAPC), a planning agency for the metropolitan Boston area, got to know him when they both served on the Low-Income Housing Commission. Marvin had been appointed by Gov. Endicott "Chubb" Peabody – whose mother had hired Marvin's mother to do domestic work in Cambridge in the 1930s (see Chapters 2 and 4).

Dukakis was not only struck by Marvin's creativity, he was also impressed by Marvin's logic. In fact, he says that Marvin's views helped shape his own vision on housing.

To solve the problem of insufficient decent housing for the poor, who included large numbers of blacks, in the 1960s politicians – especially in large cities – resorted to creation of public housing. But public housing got a bad reputation for isolating and concentrating large numbers of minorities in dour warehouses for humans. Some public housing projects were filled with minorities on welfare, many of whom were jobless. At their worst, some projects became magnets for crime and graffiti. Families lived in fear of being caught in the crossfire of drug wars, and of having their children recruited into gangs. Children were afraid to walk to school. Elderly tenants, fearful of mayhem and robbery in elevators and hallways, barricaded themselves inside apartments. Families were destroyed, said a National Housing Institute report.[190]

Marvin understood the flaws before most other people did because he had dealt them personally and up-close. He had done so as a black businessman trying to earn a living while providing housing for black tenants. His solution would combine compassion with a businessman's appreciation for the open marketplace. One key would be to avoid concentrating large numbers of poor, susceptible people in human warehouses, which is what many public housing projects were at their worst. Instead, spread out people who need housing assistance among many residences. The real question was how to do that. Marvin and his real-estate colleagues advocated doing that by mandating that certain regular, market-priced, non-public housing developments set aside some portion of their apartments for people who need assistance.

"I was in the legislature," said Dukakis, whose first of four terms as a state representative began in 1963. "I drafted legislation to create the special commission on low-income housing. We had legislators as members of the commission. And we three representatives of the real estate industry appointed by the governor: Mike Roberts, Alex Beal, and Marvin. Beal lived four houses away from us in Brookline. I didn't know Roberts. I had never met Marvin."[191]

Dukakis added that he assumed that some inner-city rental property owners were the cause of the problem. "I was a leader of young, rebel Democrats," he said. "I was not enamored of the real estate profession."

But as Dukakis drove around the state to conduct hearings and talk with potential developers, tenants in all demographic groups, and local officials, Marvin traveled with him. "I got to like him," Dukakis said. "I got to like him a lot. How could you not like Marvin? Here was a guy who trained as a classical percussionist, who was very good at that, but couldn't get a job in the BSO because he was black, so he started to clean houses, then buy houses, and put money into them."

On those car rides, Marvin and the rising political leader talked a lot about housing and how to deal with the problems. Marvin shared his insights, learned the hard way over many years as a black man facing discrimination and as a businessman offering rental apartments. Dukakis learned. And he shifted away from seeing public housing that sheltered only poor people as the sole solution.

"In point of fact, when it came to mixed-income housing, developing housing where poor people and middle-income people and the wealthy would live together, people were skeptical. But it was guys like Roberts, Beal and Marvin who said it would work, provided that you put a cap of 25% on really deeply subsidized units in a development."

Dukakis added, "One result was that the commission came up with the most thoughtful and far-sighted and far-reaching recommendations to provide affordable housing. It was well ahead of the federal government in terms of strategies like housing vouchers, mixed-income housing, and all that kind of stuff."

And so Marvin played a key role in Massachusetts' swing away from sole reliance on public housing projects filled with poor people to mixed income housing developments. And Marvin shaped the thinking on housing of Michael Dukakis, future presidential candidate.

Chapter 9

Recruiting "Mr. Show Business"

On a warm summer day in 1964, Marvin took the subway from Cambridge to Boston's South Station, a big, grand, neo-classical revival style train station, which opened New Year's day of 1899, linking the city to points south. He rode the rails through Providence, New Haven, New York, and then debarked in Philadelphia.

When he reached the City of Brotherly Love – Philadelphia – he took a taxi to the theater where famed entertainer Sammy Davis, Jr. was headlining the pre-Broadway production of *Golden Boy*.

Marvin knew his way around backstage in theaters, thanks to his own lengthy experience as a professional musician and to his recently begun career as an owner-operator of nightclubs in Cambridge, starting with his recent acquisition of the Candlelight Lounge (see Chapters 8 and 11). In fact, Marvin was embarking on what would turn out to be roughly half a century at the helm of popular music venues, turning the Western Front in particular into a major Cambridge entertainment destination. So it was as easy for the affable and knowledgeable Marvin to talk his way through that Philadelphia theater as it was for Davis to talk his way into the hearts of an audience. Marvin knew what to say to get inside through the stage door, then past the stage manager and other backstage authorities. Finally, he reached Davis' dressing room.

"I knocked on the door," Marvin said. "Sammy Davis was inside and said, 'Come in.' I remember the room was cold and plain."

Marvin introduced himself. Graciously, Davis asked how he could help this visitor. Marvin explained that he had come from Boston. He was chairman of the Life Membership Committee of the Boston branch of the NAACP, and he had come to invite Davis to perform at a fundraising show back home. Davis would *be* the show. Marvin would make all of the arrangements. All Davis had to do was show up and do his thing – sing and dance.

The show would be sold to a racially mixed audience – a rare arrangement in the early 1960s. Some NAACP officers would briefly address the audience. The main benefit was that it would raise money for the Life Membership Committee. And the cash was desperately needed. The branch was facing several difficult battles, including brawls over bias in public housing and discrimination in public schools. All of these fights would be on behalf of people who were not in a position to fight for themselves. Many were poor people. All were isolated individuals. And the fights would take time and money. Further – surprise, surprise – money was in short supply.

But Marvin was not in Philadelphia to hit up Davis for a contribution, he said. The branch would pay for its own campaigns, stand on its own feet. And one key to doing that was to attract more financial supporters. That why lifetime members were so important. Each one paid the organization $500 to join. And that's where Sammy Davis, Jr., could help. We don't want your money, Marvin said. We want your star power. We want you to headline a fundraiser.

Davis was indeed a show-biz star. He was a marquee member of the 1960s version of the Rat Pack, a group that included men seen as the entertainment world's most exciting, casually hard-drinking, coolest characters. The core members were Frank Sinatra, Dean Martin, Davis, Peter Lawford, and Joey Bishop.[192] Davis was the Justin Timberlake of his day. He was a renowned singer, dancer, actor, and even impersonator. He had charisma. He didn't just sing and dance; he put on a *show*. For his sparkling, multi-talent performances, he earned the nickname "Mister Show Business."

Merely getting access to Davis, never mind hitting him up for a favor, was no small feat. On top of that, it was almost absurd of Marvin to think that Davis would have the time to help out, even if he were so inclined. After all, he was in the midst of intense rehearsals for what was intended to be a world-class musical. Under the best of circumstances, that type of production would be time-consuming and draining for a lead performer such as Davis.

This was not the best of circumstances. Unlike his Rat Pack pals, he aspired to perform on Broadway. "...Sammy Davis, Jr. had respect for the legitimate stage and the Broadway musical," wrote theater critic Peter Filichia.[193] So this was not just any show for Davis. This was a shot at boosting his self-image, a shot at heightened career respectability. Given such high stakes, Davis was doubly focused.

Additional factors contributed to this being the worst of times to introduce a distraction into Davis' life. The musical was suffering through extremely difficult birth pains. The book of the show was being adapted by celebrated playwright Clifford Odets from his own famous 1937 stage play. The play was about Joe Bonaparte, a young Italian who had switched from a career as a violinist to one as a boxer. He then fell in love with his manager's girlfriend. This being 1964, the show's creators were not going to ask audiences to accept African-American Davis as an Italian-American. But why not make the boxer black, producer Hillard Elkins wondered?[194] That had the added benefit of making race an ingredient in the dramatic tension. The audience could be forced to question its own assumptions and biases.

But before Odets finished his adaptation, he died of cancer. Music composer Charles Strouse and lyricist Lee Adams described the tragic, futile effort to help Odets complete his work: "'By the time Lee Adams and I caught [Odets], he was at the end,' Strouse said in the book *It Happened on Broadway*. 'We were in Vegas. He told us he had a terrible problem with gambling, that we shouldn't let him near the tables. Nevertheless, around midnight, we would have to pull him away and say, 'Get ye to the typewriter, because we've got to meet Sammy [Davis].' I'm an early riser, and at 6:30 the next morning, I'd pass by the casino and see an unshaven Clifford. 'I was going to quit,' he'd say, 'but I was ahead.' The first week of rehearsals, Odets died.'"[195]

A new book writer was hired. More characters were changed to blacks from Italian-Americans. Now, half a century later, it sounds like a perfectly reasonable strategy. But the altered story never worked as well as the original classic. "[T]he whole project creaked under the strain [of adapting and updating the 1937 play]. Panic set in, [and British director Peter] Coe was fired,... [Songwriter Charles] Strouse was given a bodyguard in Philadelphia because the theatre was receiving death threats, due to the love story between a black and white character," reported whatsonstage.com. The show was eventually packed off to Boston for more pre-Broadway fine-tuning.

While the production was still in Philadelphia, Marvin Gilmore arrived, unaware of details of the turmoil surrounding the musical. He made his pitch to Davis. No doubt Davis would have welcomed any brief escape from the pressures of remaking a timeless Depression-era masterpiece into a modern civil-rights era inspiration. But this was more than an unsolicited piece of good luck, a chance to get a much-needed break. Marvin's endeavor was worthy. Davis would be helping fellow blacks in need. Fittingly, that was one of the themes in *Golden Boy*.

"Sammy Davis said my request shook him up," Marvin recalled. "He said it caught him off guard."

In addition to having Marvin explain why the Life Membership Committee needed money, Davis sized up Marvin himself. He asked him personal questions – nothing inappropriate; just questions that would allow Davis to assess Marvin and assess his request. Davis sat straddling a chair, leaning his arms against the back, which was facing Marvin. The always-stylish entertainer was dressed in a blue jump suit. One question led to another, and in the course of this interview Marvin mentioned that his birthday, September 23, was approaching. Davis smiled. He spread his hands, and in that famous side-of-the mouth style of his began to serenade Marvin with a rendition of "Happy Birthday to You."

A Changing U.S.

Black History

Sammy Davis, Jr.

The Sammy Davis, Jr., performance raised a huge amount of money for the NAACP Boston branch's life membership committee. And Marvin's initiative planted another seed.

Within a few years, Sammy Davis, Jr., became chairman of the NAACP national life membership committee, filling a role that Kivie Kaplan, Marvin's longtime friend and activist in the NAACP, previously held for a period, starting in 1953.[i]

Then Davis gave Marvin what amounted to a splendid birthday gift. "He said he was moved by my zeal," Marvin said. "Right there, while I was in the room, he called Billy Daniels" – another big-name crooner, who had another role in the musical – "and asked him to fill in for a show or two of *Golden Boy*. Daniels said yes, and Davis turned to me and said he would do the fundraiser. He refused to take any fee – that was his

Sidebar notes
[i] S. Norman Feingold, "Two Friends Touch A Legend," *Kivie Kaplan: A Legend In His Own Time*, edited by Dr. S. Norman

gift to the Committee – and he paid for his own transportation and hotel room, where he dressed for the performance. He came with his wife May Britt. When I left the theater, I was very excited."

The Show Went On

Once Marvin had his star attraction, he had to organize the fundraiser itself.

Feingold and Rabbi William B. Silverman (New York, N.Y.: Union of American Hebrew Congregations, 1976), p. 6. Cynthia Yeldell, "NAACP Lifetime Membership Program Celebrates 100th Anniversary," *The Crisis,* 117, no. 2 (2010), pp. 58-115.

One key challenge was to lock up a performance location. His own club, the Candlelight Lounge, was too small. "It could only hold 50 people, and I needed a place that could hold 150 to 200 people," Marvin said. Renting a larger commercial venue would eat into the event's precious proceeds.

Marvin wondered if any civil rights supporter with a large suburban home might be willing to make his residence available. He thought of Morton and Sylvia Grossman. Morton was vice president, credit controller, and mortgage finance manager of Grossman Lumber. The New England-New York lumber and building products chain had been founded by Morton's grandfather. Now Morton and Sylvia were friends of Marvin. Their home in Brookline – the suburban Boston town where Mr. and Mrs. H.H. White, for whom a teenage Marvin had reluctantly washed cars – had spacious grounds and had often been the site of sizable parties. "They had a beautiful home," Marvin said. "A garden party there would provide a very classy setting, which would be suitable for a major artist like Davis."

Marvin knew the Grossmans well enough. He had enjoyed dinner on several Friday nights, the start of the Jewish Sabbath, at their home. Sylvia was the daughter of Kivie Kaplan, a longtime friend of Marvin, who had long been active in the NAACP. Kaplan had joined the organization in 1932, had been elected to the national board of directors in 1954, and would serve as elected president from 1966 to 1975.[196]

And the Grossmans had taken up Kaplan's commitment to civil rights. "My granddad had everyone in the family as a member of the NAACP," said Ma'ayan (formerly known as Amy) Sands, the second of the Grossman's four offspring, who is now a rabbinical student. "And when we married, our spouses became national life members of the NAACP like us, and so did our children."[197]

When Marvin got back to Boston, he told Kaplan that Sammy Davis, Jr., had generously agreed to headline a fundraiser, and he asked Kaplan what he thought about seeing if Mort and Sylvia Grossman would host the event. Kaplan agreed it was a fine idea.

So Marvin asked the Grossmans. They immediately said yes, enthused about the opportunity to help Marvin raise money for the local branch's life membership committee and charmed by the idea of hosting bigger-than-life entertainer Davis at their home.

The Grossmans' home was in a neighborhood of large homes with ample grounds, all flanked by the relatively open spaces of the Pine Manor College campus, The Country Club (the oldest country club in the United States), and Brookline's municipal golf course.

"It lent itself very naturally to parties," said Ma'ayan Sands. "My parents were, number one, gracious people. And, number two, the house was totally set up for entertaining. My marriage took place there. Sometimes we had a tent. There were times we put a tent in the driveway. We had an attached garage, which was perpendicular to the house, where caterers could set up. We also had a large patio out back, with awnings that rolled in and out for the seasons. My parents did a lot of entertaining there. And the back yard sloped down, away from the house. We used to ski there."

The Sammy Davis, Jr., fundraiser took place on the splendidly sunny afternoon of August 19. Guests sat in folding chairs arranged in neat rows, facing the back of the Grossman home. A small band set up their instruments on the patio, to the left of the rear entrance to the house.

Sands was six years old. Her generation was fans of pop and rock singers who were younger than Sammy Davis, Jr., but she understood who Davis was and was aware of her parents' peers' excitement about getting this close-up experience with an entertainer they enthusiastically enjoyed.

"Guests parked along the street and maybe nearby streets," Sands said. "I think – I'm not sure – the tent was alongside the house."

Sands' recollection is that the crowd was perhaps 85% white. Kivie Kaplan, a veteran public speaker, addressed the audience before Davis' show. For a time while he spoke, Davis sat at a bridge table off to one side with Marvin and branch president Kenneth Guscott. The three men leaned inward toward each other, listening to Kaplan and engaging in their own conversation.

Guscott and Marvin also addressed the attendees.

Davis had brought a quartet to provide music. He was backed by a pianist, saxophonist, drummer, and bass player. Davis and the band began to perform in the late afternoon, once the heat of the summer day had begun to subside. Since this was 1964 – the "Mad Men" era – a sense of style and class pervaded the entire affair. Men wore suits or sport coats with narrow neckties. Ladies wore smart cocktail party dresses. As a bonus, Davis circulated among guests after his show, and attendees enjoyed the opportunity to shake hands and chat briefly with this entertainment superstar as much as the show itself.

"The garden party started around noon, I think," Marvin said. "And it took the whole day. Sammy Davis played and then stayed the whole afternoon, talking with people. He made no effort to rush out. I admit I was drunk with having produced a man of his stature. Sammy Davis stayed until the evening. It was a huge success."

All day long, in front of the performance area, propped up against a low row of bushes for the audience to see was a placard that showed the face of Myrlie Evers, the young widow of civil rights activist Medgar Evers, who had been assassinated a mere 14 months earlier in Jackson, Mississippi, where Marvin had ventured just the month before with Bill Russell. In the photo, a large tear trailed down Myrlie's left cheek. The placard also bore her words: "You can kill a man but you can't kill an idea."

That idea was equality. And this garden party where people of different races mixed, joining forces in common cause to raise money for the fight for freedom, was a celebration of that idea.

Chapter 10

Fighting the Civil Rights Battles of the 1960s

On a sultry July evening in 1964, Marvin Gilmore pulled his sleek sports car to the curb on Massachusetts Avenue in Boston, just a few yards from the intersection with Columbus Avenue. This was a prime location in Boston's South End, then a mixed but largely minority neighborhood, along the boundary with Roxbury, which was well on its way to becoming a solidly African-American neighborhood, abutting growing black neighborhoods in Dorchester and Mattapan.[198] Marvin parked, and then walked across the street into the red-brick townhouse offices of the Boston branch of the NAACP.

Marvin liked to park right there. It was convenient. And from inside the branch offices he could glance out at the street to make sure his car was undisturbed. It was, after all, an eye-grabber: a stylishly silver Jaguar XJ6. Marvin took a lot of pride in those wheels. For the benefit of anyone who could not identify the make and model, Marvin's license plate spelled it out: "XJ6."

Marvin was early. As usual. It was 5 p.m., and his meeting inside would not start until 6:30. This would give him time to review his paperwork, chat with colleagues, think through issues, consider

A Changing U.S.

Black History

Mayhem in Mississippi

In the darkest days of the civil rights struggle, racist repression in America was most brutal in three locales – Mississippi, Alabama, and southwest Georgia, according to modern African-American history expert Charles Payne.[i] Mississippi segregationists' bloodlust alone captured the nation's attention on several occasions in the pivotal 1950s and '60s, Payne wrote.

There was the 1955 torture, mutilation, and lynching of Emmett Till, a 14-year-old black boy strategies, and consult his crystal ball – ponder where each of several possible courses of action regarding tonight's topic could lead. It didn't matter whether it was his life membership committee, a fundraising group, a school-desegregation brainstorming discussion, or a skull session for some other subject such as the Civil Rights Act of 1964, which had been enacted just days before. This was typical Marvin. Most of his colleagues were elsewhere, grabbing an early dinner before gathering at the NAACP offices for their evening meetings. Not Marvin. He would eat later, after his meeting, maybe at Estelle's or the Red Fez or one of the small jazz clubs nearby.

In this colorful neighborhood there were several restaurants and clubs that served dinner late, which was uncommon in most of straight-laced Boston's neighborhoods. In fact, restaurants that offered late-night dining were so rare in still-puritanical Boston that the few after-hours establishments attracted an exotic, multiethnic, multiracial Noah's Ark of Boston's nocturnal creatures. In one or two late-night spots, Marvin – who was an habitual night owl from his earliest days as a musician – was used to seeing characters from Boston's white organized crime world, on dinner break after a evening of collecting tribute throughout the metro area from sundry bookies, bordellos, bars, numbers rackets, night clubs, and the like. "They were friendly and talkative, but I always kept my distance," Marvin recalls.

who was kidnapped and killed for whistling at a white man's wife.[ii] One of Medgar Evers' first NAACP assignments was investigating Till's homicide; he succeeded in digging up witnesses and evidence.[iv]

There was also the 1959 abduction of Mack Charles Parker from a jail cell. Accused of raping a pregnant young white woman, Parker was dragged down stairs, beaten, shot, and thrown from a bridge to his death.[v]

In the mid-1960s there was the abduction, beating, and murder of three voter-registration workers – 21-year-old black Mississippian James Chaney and two white New Yorkers, Andrew Goodman, 20, and Michael Schwerner, 24. Aided by local police, a gang of Ku Klux Klansman shot the three young men to death, then buried them in an earthen dam.[vi]

So this night, like all meeting nights, Marvin was here early, trying to stay one move ahead of everyone, adversaries and allies alike, on the NAACP issues at hand.

Tonight Marvin's nose-to-the-grindstone approach would pay extra dividends. Shortly after Marvin arrived, the girl at the branch's switchboard took a call from an out-of-town man. It was Charles Evers, brother of civil rights activist Medgar Evers, who had been assassinated in Mississippi 13 months earlier by a fanatical white supremacist. Charles had taken over his martyred brother's job as field secretary for the NAACP in Mississippi. And now Charles fervently needed help from up North.

He needed African-Americans to come to test the new law's implementation and trigger enforcement actions if needed. People had to keep the pressure on Mississippi. And he desperately needed help bolstering the morale of local blacks and local civil rights workers. A virtual civil war was underway in Mississippi and other parts of the South, with white supremacists using threats and violence – shootings, bombings, and even murder – to discourage blacks from agitating for voting rights and broader civil rights.

So Charles Evers introduced himself to the girl who answered the phone. *Was any branch officer handy,* he asked. Before she even looked up, the girl knew the answer. This was meeting night. She knew one branch officer who certainly would be there. She looked around for Marvin.

Segregationists also weaved a complex web of rules to prevent blacks from voting. For example, one legacy of post-Civil War Southern white bitterness against Abraham Lincoln's Republican Party was the strong, longtime allegiance of Mississippi whites to the Democratic Party. Democratic candidates routinely predominated in election results. And for decades blacks were excluded from running and voting in the Democratic primary, which came to be known as the white primary.[vii]

That practice was not ruled unconstitutional by the Supreme Court until 1944. Yet lax federal law enforcement allowed the white primary to remain in use until 1956. In 1946 Medgar Evers and a group of friends, all wearing their World War II military uniforms, were barred from registering to vote at the Decatur,

Martyred in Mississippi

In the spring of 1963, Medgar Evers was the target of hate-mongers. He made himself even more vulnerable to murder when he broke one of his own safety rules.

Evers had promised his wife Myrlie that every time he drove home he would get out of his car on the passenger side.[199]

That's because getting out on the driver's side would put him next to the road, exposed, where an assassin could have a clear shot, where a drive-by shooter would be able to mow Medgar down.

And there was no shortage of people who wanted to kill him. He had been appointed the first National Association for the Advancement of Colored People (NAACP) field secretary for Mississippi, part of America's heart of darkness in that year of 1963. Many Mississippians were among the most rabid segregationists in the United States.

Yet incredibly Evers was making headway in his lonely campaign to bring equal rights to the Magnolia State. His progress was in modest steps, one at a time, rather than in dramatic leaps, but it was forward motion. He was registering voters. He was organizing boycotts of segregated businesses. He was campaigning for voter rights. He was spotlighting murder and terrorization of Mississippi blacks, in pursuit of justice and to help break the cycle of intimidation. Even if Evers' progress was glacial, many segregationists saw his persistence as a mortal threat to the Jim Crow status quo.

Mississippi, courthouse by a heavily armed mob of 15 to 20 white men.[viii]

Other tactics were used to prevent blacks from registering to vote. Through the 1940s, Mississippi rigorously enforced a two-year residency requirement and a $2 poll tax, which many poor blacks could not afford, to keep African-Americans from voting. By 1954 some 22,000 blacks were registered to vote, but that was only about 4% of the number eligible, Dittmer wrote. And six counties with black majorities were among the 14 statewide that did not have a single black registered to vote.[ix]

White hostility was hardly limited to black voting. It showed up as militant resistance to most any form of equality. On May 31, 1963, hundreds of black youths met at the Farish Street Baptist Church in Jackson, Mississippi, to

So with each voter he registered, he made enemies. With each rally he organized or attended, he made enemies. With each witness to white-on-black violence he interviewed, he made enemies. With each day that he continued to breathe, even, he made enemies. In May 1963 one of them had tossed a Molotov cocktail – a fire bomb – at his home.

Now it was June 12, 1963, and another fanatical foe was nearby, stalking him. Ardent segregationist Byron De La Beckwith was hiding 200 feet away in a honeysuckle thicket across the street.[200] De La Beckwith's mother's father had served in the Confederate cavalry. De La Beckwith hated blacks and Jews. On occasion he passed out leaflets criticizing racial integration. Some people said he carried a pistol to church on Sundays in case any blacks tried to worship there.[201]

This night he was armed with a powerful Enfield hunting rifle. He laid down on the ground next to a sweet gum tree. Then he waited.

Shortly after midnight, Evers arrived home. He pulled his 1962 light blue Oldsmobile into the driveway of his simple, ranch-style home in Jackson, Mississippi. He scooped up an armful of T-shirts that read, "Jim Crow Must Go." And he opened the car door and got out. On the driver's side. Evers got out on the wrong side because on this spring night he was weary. He was coming home from a civil rights rally and from a strategy organize boycotts of white-owned businesses, part of a campaign to persuade the state's capital city to address grievances such as the lack of black policemen and the segregation of public facilities. The city's idea of negotiating was to assemble what Dittmer described as "a wall of Jackson police, backed by sixty shotgun-toting state troopers." As the black youths emerged from the church waving American flags and chanting, "We want freedom!" authorities arrested 450 of them "and carried them in garbage trucks to a makeshift prison at the state fairgrounds."[x]

Some blacks were told they could not vote or register because they belonged to the NAACP. In 1959 Medgar Evers encouraged five blacks to complain to the U.S. Department of Justice about being prevented from registering to vote meeting after that. A big chunk of his day had been spent leading efforts to get the city to hire black police officers.[202]

The 37-year-old was part way up the driveway when De La Beckwith pulled the trigger on his Enfield. The rifle recoiled, driving its scope into De La Beckwith's eye, bruising him.[203] The rifle did worse to Evers. The bullet tore into his back, striking just below his right shoulder blade. It ricocheted around inside his chest, tearing up his body, his wife recalled years later.[204] Evers staggered up to the steps of his house. Then he collapsed.[205]

An instant after knifing into Evers and tearing out his life, the bullet was still hurtling onward with deadly force.

The slug rocketed through a front window of the Evers home, penetrated an interior wall, tore a tile off that wall, caromed, slammed into the refrigerator door leaving a dent, and struck a coffee pot.[206] The battered bullet was found beneath a watermelon on a kitchen cabinet," Claude Sitton reported in the *New York Times* in 1963.[207]

Inside the house, Myrlie was watching President John F. Kennedy on TV deliver an important civil rights speech to America. She sat on a bed with her eight-year-old daughter Reena and three-year-old son James Van Dyke, known as Van. Nine-year-old son Darrel was nearby. The children were being allowed to stay up late so they could greet their father when he got home.[208]

because of their race. But the FBI and Justice Department failed to pursue the complaints, Crosby wrote. Whites continued to discourage blacks from registering and voting into the 1960s.

Also, blacks were discouraged from joining the NAACP – or from remaining members of the civil rights organization – by sustained, widespread acts of intimidation, harassment, violence, economic sanctions, threats of job loss, and actual firings.[xi] Whites burned a cross at the end of NAACP officer Ernest Jones' driveway, according to historian Crosby, who said Jones lamented that in the 1950s people who had joined his branch of the NAACP quickly quit or were too afraid to attend meetings.

White leaders also thwarted attempts at school integration.[xii]

The children heard the gunshot and reacted as Medgar and their mom had taught them. Reena dropped to the floor alongside Darrel, pulling down young Van, then dashing for the tub in the bathroom.[209] The two older children left Van in the relative safety of the tub. "And then we stopped and ran down the steps and begged our father to get up," Reena told National Public Radio in 2013.

Screaming, "Daddy! Daddy! Daddy!", they found their father in the carport, laying in a pool of his own blood.[210]

Evers was taken to a hospital, where he died within the hour.

Reportedly, sniper De La Beckwith bragged subsequently about committing the murder at a Ku Klux Klan rally.[211] He was eventually sentenced to life in prison. His conviction more than 30 years after the slaying symbolized the very thing he had fought so hard to prevent – the transformation of Mississippi into a more tolerant society.

Medgar Evers was buried with full military honors in Arlington National Cemetery. His murder helped focus broad public political opposition to segregation, culminating in enactment the next year of the Civil Rights Act of 1964 (please read sidebar "Black History: Civil Rights Act of 1964" in this chapter). His death helped bring about the very thing that his assassin and everyone who hated him had hoped to prevent – the beginning of the end of Jim Crow rule.

And in 1956 the state legislature created the Sovereignty Commission, whose job was "to protect the sovereignty of the state of Mississippi ... [from] encroachment thereon by the Federal Government."[xiii] In plain English, the Commission was a secret police force, allied with the Citizens' Council, a white supremacy group.[xiv] Its mission was to spy on citizens. It kept dossiers on opponents of segregation, recruited espionage moles inside black organizations, warned white officials of impending federal investigations, and aided the campaign to bolster white supremacy, Crosby wrote. It kept at it until it ceased to operate in 1973.

The history of the civil rights movement shines a permanent spotlight on his name. His legacy also lives on in the Medgar & Myrlie Evers Institute in Jackson, Mississippi, which champions civil rights by encouraging education and reconciliation. The City University of New York named one of its four senior colleges for him. In 2011 the U.S. Navy christened one of its vessels for the slain civil rights leader, who was a World War II veteran. Like Marvin Gilmore, he had participated in the invasion of German-occupied France, willing to risk his own life and safety in pursuit of a freer world.

Passing the Baton

In the aftermath of Medgar Evers' death, his brother Charles Evers replaced him as the NAACP's field secretary in Mississippi. Charles Evers was as colorful and flamboyant as Medgar had been straight-laced and rule-abiding.

Charles was Medgar's older brother. Both had been born in Decatur, Mississippi – Charles in 1922, Medgar in 1925. Charles graduated from Alcorn College in 1951, and then moved to Philadelphia, Mississippi. Charles worked at a series of jobs. He was a teacher, mortician, cab driver, and disc jockey. As flexible as he was in the ways he earned a living, he was steadfast at one particular thing. He persistently advocated for black voting rights. And that angered Philadelphia whites, who bankrupted him and forced him to leave the state, according to

---

A Changing U.S.

Black History

"Freedom Summer"

How dangerous was it for Marvin and Bill Russell to journey to Jackson, Mississippi? Extremely.

With the civil rights movement struggling to gain momentum and pledging a summer voter registration offensive in the then-ironically nicknamed Hospitality State, segregationists vowed to fight back. The head of the state's White Knights of the Ku Klux Klan ordered his group's members to counterattack selected targets.[xv]

The Klan and like-minded extremists, including many law officers, went on a binge of terrorism.[xvi] Their aim was to discourage blacks and civil rights activists from pressing for voter

historian John Dittmer.[212]

From 1956 until 1963, Charles lived in Chicago. At times, he lived on the edge, surviving on day-old bread and chicken necks in a basement apartment plagued by cockroaches and leaking water pipes. At night in bed, rats ran over him. But Evers never cracked, and he gave new meaning to the word "hustle." He made a living however he could, saving money to invest in one opportunity after another. Several of his enterprises were shady, but to Evers they were just ways to earn a buck in a white world that often didn't like to see a black man get ahead. He catalogued his jobs in his biography: he hauled slabs of meat in a slaughter house and was a washroom attendant, petty thief, and bartender. He sold booze from a hotel washroom. He got a job as a numbers runner, then started his own numbers running racket. He ran a liquor store and a tavern – three taverns, in fact, at least one of which paid bribes to the police so it could operate after hours – and was a jukebox operator. He was a bootlegger and school teacher – physical education and history. He even bought a 24-unit residential building, which generated income for him and Medgar.[213]

One day when Charles was working as a washroom attendant, hotel magnate Conrad Hilton strolled in and in the course of conversation offered advice: "'Own everything you can, and run nothing.'" As soon as he could, Evers followed that advice. He concessioned several of his

rights and an end to segregation.

"[T]he summer of 1964 was the most violent since Reconstruction,..." wrote historian John Dittmer. He chronicled the mayhem: there were 35 shootings; 65 homes, businesses, and other buildings were burned or bombed, including 35 churches; 1,000 voter-registration activists were arrested; 80 activists suffered beatings.[xvii] Four activists were murdered.[xviii]

It would not matter whether Gilmore and Russell actually accomplished anything. It would not matter if they broke the color barrier at any restaurant, or whether their church meetings, civil rights rallies, NAACP strategy sessions, and basketball clinics achieved any real strategic threat to segregation. It would not matter whether more people registered to businesses – a liquor store, grocery store, and restaurant – to other merchants. They ran the businesses, paying Evers a rent-like commission and keeping the balance of any profits as their own. His shrewd maneuvering earned him an invaluable reward: financial independence, especially from white people.[214]

When his brother was murdered, Charles returned home and declared himself the NAACP's new field secretary in the state. Wary of his checkered past, the NAACP national leadership was ambivalent about being represented by Charles. But rather than risk negative, divisive publicity over an ugly public battle with the brother of their martyred Mississippian, the organization let Charles step in. After all, if he slipped up, they could find a way to replace him later.[215]

Charles Evers provided no such excuse for ouster. He was a classical American entrepreneur. He kept his eyes peeled for opportunities, and he was not afraid to wrestle with any challenge. His style differed from his brother's. But he knew how to work at a puzzle until he could solve it. Bringing freedom and equality to Mississippi was no different. It was not an easy task. And his progress was sometimes slow. But Charles Evers kept at it just as diligently as his brother had.

When Congress finally enacted the Civil Rights Act of 1964, Evers knew the battle to bring equality to his state was not over. It was one thing for the federal government to pass a law. It was quite vote, whether voter activists became better motivated or more effective, or whether any white boys decided not to hate black boys because of an afternoon of hoops at the gym. The mere fact that their presence threatened to accomplish any of those goals placed them in the crosshairs of white supremacists.

All that mattered was skin color and the *appearance* of a threat to white supremacy.

Anyone who seemed to pose a threat to the rule of Jim Crow law in the South was in trouble, vulnerable to harsh, inhumane savagery. That was the fate of Henry Hezekiah Dee and Charles Eddie More.

On May 2, 1964 Klansmen abducted the two 19-year-olds, who were hitchhiking in Franklin Country in southwest Mississippi. The Klansmen had seized the two because the another to persuade Mississippians to accept and follow it.

The sooner that the law could be used to challenge segregation practices, the better. That was the thinking of activists like Evers, who were at ground zero.[216] Once establishments that had barred blacks had served them, they'd be less likely to revert to segregation. The psychological barrier would already be crossed. As for businesses whose owners would rather close permanently than comply, good riddance. The only businesses that mattered were those that continued to operate in defiance of the new law. And federal law authorities would be most likely to enforce the new rules in the immediate aftermath of enactment, when the bright glare of saturation news coverage could be counted on to publicize prominent law breakers. But over time, news coverage would dissipate. Federal back bone might go limp. So, yes, it would be better to test the new law right away.

But how? Who would test the new law? Who would be willing to risk limb and life by entering establishments that had remained segregated up to that moment? An African-American seeking service in many of those hotels, motels, restaurants, schools, and other places of public accommodation would be met by potentially loud, angry, violent whites intent on preserving the racial exclusivity of those businesses. Many of those passionate separatists would use violence. Civil rights activists since World War II had learned painfully that people who tried to integrate hotels, motels, restaurants, lunch counters, and rest rooms risked retaliation ranging from

head-bandana-wearing Dee had recently visited Chicago and the Klansmen believed – mistakenly – that the two young blacks were members of a militant group bringing weapons into the county, where they planned an armed insurrection. In fact, no such plot existed, and Dee and Moore were not members of an insurgency troop.[xix]

Determined to learn details about the rumored uprising plot, the Klansmen tied Dee and Moore to trees and beat them unconscious, nearly to death, with poles and trees limbs. Then the abductors taped the young men's mouths, wrapped them in plastic, tossed them into the trunk of a car, and drove them 150 miles into Louisiana. They put the men into a boat and took them onto the Mississippi River. They tied Dee to an engine block. They strapped Moore to a getting tossed out of a job and being boycotted economically to being beaten or killed. Local blacks faced the gravest threats. White supremacists knew them and could reach them, their families, their homes, their businesses at most any time.

So a key role would have to be played by Northern blacks who were willing to go to the South and dare white establishments not to serve them. They had to be able to afford such a journey, take time away from their own jobs, and be prominent enough to deserve news coverage during their visit.

Charles Evers needed precisely such people. Marvin and other key figures in the Boston branch of the NAACP were eager to pitch in. And it would be far more dangerous than the milestone mission to Mississippi that Kenneth Guscott, president of the Boston branch, had participated in just days earlier.

Call for Help

The highlight of that earlier excursion had occurred on the morning of Sunday, July 5, 1964. Kenneth Guscott became the first African-American since Reconstruction[217] to register as a guest at a "white" hotel in Mississippi.[218] When his registration was accepted at the Heidelberg Hotel in Jackson and the desk clerk handed a room key to Guscott, integration had checked into the previously segregated hotel.

Guscott and eight leaders of the NAACP's national organization stayed in railroad tie and iron weights. Then they dumped both men overboard.

Authorities — who were searching for civil rights workers who had been kidnapped and murdered — found parts of Dee and Moore's bodies by chance in mid July. Badly decomposed, one body seemed to have been cut in half; the other was decapitated.[xx]

Segregationists' paranoia was fueled by that summer's voter-registration drive.

In a campaign run by civil rights organizations including the Congress on Racial Equality (CORE) and Student Non-Violent Coordinating Committee (SNCC), more than 1,000 out-of-state student volunteers flooded Mississippi that summer. The drive came to be known as Freedom Summer.[xxi]

The students began to arrive in June. Labeling the campaign a Northern two Jackson hotels and a motel.[219] They were sent by the NAACP, whose national convention a week earlier in Washington, D.C., had voted to send its group to look into whether young civil rights workers were being protected from violent opponents.[220] (Thousands of young civil rights workers had flocked to the state that summer, joining native Mississippi activists, and many were threatened and beaten; a few were famously murdered. (Please read "Black History: 'Freedom Summer'" sidebar nearby.))

The NAACP traveling group's purpose broadened when it found itself departing for Mississippi just three days after Pres. Lyndon Johnson signed into law the Civil Rights Act of 1964. Now the group would also be seeing whether businesses in the state were accepting and implementing the nation's new rights legislation. The group began its journey through the state in Jackson, and its itinerary would take it through Philadelphia, Meridian, Laurel, Moss Point, Pascagoula, Greenwood, Canton, Clarksdale, and Hattiesburg.

But the NAACP – as well as Charles Evers, Marvin Gilmore and other members – realized that one tour by one group hardly guaranteed that whites in Mississippi, elsewhere in the South, and in the rest of the United States would continue to obey the new civil rights law.

What would encourage enduring compliance? The NAACP traveling group had been denied an opportunity to expose defiance when, ironically perhaps, the invasion, white supremacists continued to fight back and sought to undermine the campaign.[xxii]

The civil rights activists included two white New Yorkers, Michael Schwerner and Andrew Goodman, and James Chaney, a black Mississippian. On June 21 they were driving to investigate the burning of Mount Zion United Methodist Church, a black congregation.

They were arrested by the police on trumped-up charges, imprisoned for several hours, and then released after dark to a mob of Ku Klux Klansmen, who beat and murdered them. Much later, in court it came out that some members of Neshoba County's law enforcement had conspired with Klansmen to kill the civil rights workers.[xxiii]

Schwerner was doubly resented. Not only was he from out of state, he

Jackson Chamber of Commerce had asked local businessmen to comply with the law.[221] The Chamber did not want bad publicity. After all, the NAACP tour group was historic. Sure enough, the biracial group – which included Kivie Kaplan, a white, Jewish, retired Boston businessman who was a member of the NAACP national board and who was a friend and mentor of Marvin Gilmore – got a protective police escort. Three Jackson plainclothes detectives accompanied Guscott to the Heidelberg's front desk. His registration was peaceful and uneventful. "There was not the slightest disturbance," the *Boston Globe* reported.[222]

Yet a week earlier Guscott "would have been bitterly rejected and probably arrested for trespassing," the *Globe* noted.

The Chamber got its way. "[T]here were no crowds to watch the historic scene. There had been no advance publicity about the plans to integrate the hotels," the *Globe* indicated.

Guscott told the *Globe* reporter that he had been treated "very, very cordially."

But the NAACP was already planning to send more people south to test the new law. The NAACP even had a name for this campaign: "Hands Across the Cotton Curtain."[223] The nickname was a jibe at the South. It made the NAACP's point that racial repression in the South was akin to repression in the Cold War-era Soviet Union bloc of countries, whose European citizens were kept under control behind a boundary known as the Iron Curtain.

was Jewish. The Klan hatefully targeted Schwerner – whom its members scornfully called "Jew-Boy" – because he had organized a black boycott of a white-owned business and because he had aggressively tried to register blacks in the Meridian area to vote.[xxiv]

The civil rights trio's disappearance captivated the national public's attention, and Americans watched as investigators searched for the missing men for six weeks. When state authorities failed to pursue justice, the FBI stepped in.

Rabid segregationists, who had tried to rally support from other whites by characterizing the voter-registration activists as an invasion, now had a real one. The FBI increased its force in the state roughly 10-fold to 153. The Bureau opened its first office in the state. The manhunt was also beefed up with

And for that campaign the NAACP had already asked one of its branches – Boston – for help.[224]

A Plan Takes Shape

The NAACP national office, Charles Evers, Marvin Gilmore, and others were all thinking the same thing. More people had to go to Mississippi to test the new law's implementation and trigger enforcement actions if needed. People had to keep the pressure on Mississippi.

Evers, who brought his street-smart entrepreneurial style to politics, took action. He telephoned the Boston branch of the NAACP. Marvin, who brought his own entrepreneurial style to everything he did, had lived his life answering the door whenever opportunity knocked. This occasion was no exception. "I happened to be in the office when Evers called," Marvin said. "So I got on the phone with him and we started to talk."

The NAACP national group, which had toured Mississippi, had not stayed long in Jackson. Nor had they done much in Jackson, as far as Evers was concerned. Marvin felt the same way.

"When they [the national group] got back, I asked, 'What did you do?' They couldn't answer," Marvin said.

So he and Evers began to plot a strategy for a return trip. It would build on the national group's foray. Whoever went on this next visit would test compliance with the new Civil Rights Act. In addition, the new group would make a variety of

an influx of Justice Department lawyers and investigators and about 400 sailors (including U.S. Navy divers) from nearby Naval Air Station Meridian.[xxv]

After 44 days the trio's remains were found. They had been bulldozed into the muck of an earthen dam, just a few miles from Mount Zion United Methodist Church.

Schwerner and Goodman had been shot once in the heart. Chaney had been shot three times. More than three years later, despite FBI Director J. Edgar Hoover's reluctance along the way, federal prosecutors won convictions of seven defendants.[xxvi]

It wasn't until 2005, though, that state charges were finally brought, leading to a ringleader's conviction on three counts of manslaughter.[xxvii]

Chillingly, in the course of combing the

public appearances to boost morale among African-Americans in Jackson. These public meetings would show that blacks were free to meet and speak in public about their rights; that people of color in Jackson had friends and supporters elsewhere in the United States; that if blacks elsewhere in the United States like Gilmore were able to rise to positions of affluence and influence, so could they.

But Marvin and Evers were realists. Marvin was inspiring, but he was not a celebrity. They needed someone famous, someone who would draw people to a public gathering, someone whose presence could generate publicity, someone available.

They both knew someone who fit their bill. They were both thinking of the same person: Bill Russell, basketball superstar.

Russell would be perfect. He was even a veteran of political missions into hostile territory, masquerading as innocent basketball tours. In fact, he was just returning from a U.S. State Department-sponsored goodwill tour of All-Stars through Eastern Europe and the Middle East. The Boston Celtics' legendary coach Red Auerbach was the maestro. The team consisted of hoop royalty, including Russell, Bob Cousy, Oscar Robertson, and Jerry Lucas.

A tour of Jackson and nearby cities and towns would be similar, except more dangerous for a black athletic hero wading

state for evidence in the Chaney-Goodman-Schwerner, the investigative army found the bodies of at least seven other missing black Mississippians, whose disappearances in recent years had not been deemed worthy of in-depth investigations.[xxviii]

Those seven, plus the Chaney-Goodman-Schwerner murders, were just eight instances of the racial enmity that turned Mississippi into a cauldron, bubbling with violence and fear. Some activists called for responding to the terrorism with armed force, but the movement stuck to its pacifist tenets. Some did so for philosophical reasons. Many stuck to nonviolence to avoid being shot "in self-defense" by hostile local police if they were detained in one of the frequent harassment stops that occurred in isolated, rural into the heartland of anti-black activism.

Evers had another reason for inviting Russell. Eleven months earlier, in the wake of Medgar's murder Russell had called Charles Evers, offering to help. So after conferring with Marvin, in July of 1964 Charles took Russell up on the famously goateed star's offer. Charles asked Russell to come to Mississippi to run basketball clinics.[225]

There was just one problem. "I didn't want to go to Mississippi," Russell wrote. "I was like anyone else. I was afraid to get killed."[226]

Mississippi was filled with people who'd love to kill him, Russell told biographer Taylor Branch. "The whole state was an armed camp, full of tension, as close to open racial warfare as any place on earth,..."[227]

His wife Rose and some of his friends also feared Russell would suffer the same fate as Medgar Evers. They urged him not to go.[228]

But two additional people exhorted him to go: Marvin and Kivie Kaplan, the Bostonian who was chairman of the NAACP's national lifetime membership committee (and who would be NAACP president from 1966 until 1975).

"I knew Bill," Marvin said. "His wife was my co-chair on the Life Membership Committee [of the Boston branch of the NAACP]," Marvin said. "I used to go back and forth to his house in Reading [a town in suburban Boston] all the time. We spoke whenever he was there. I knew the man. He was a friend."

---

locations.[xxix]

So the violence remained strictly one-way – directed at blacks and civil rights activists.

This was the shooting gallery that Marvin Gilmore and Bill Russell stepped into, knowing that they were targets, far from the relative safety of their lives around Boston.

A Changing U.S.

Black History

Civil Rights Act of 1964

As if inserting themselves into the war zone created by the Freedom Summer conflict between white supremacists on one side and blacks and civil rights activists on the other was

Resolving that a man must do what he thinks is right, Russell decided to go to Jackson.[229]

Russell would be a magnet, attracting people to public gatherings. Evers would arrange public sessions at churches, black colleges, gymnasiums. At some, Russell could conduct basketball clinics. Introductory remarks at each gathering would be an opportunity for someone like Evers to talk about voter registration and voting. Privately, Gilmore, Russell, Evers, and other local activists could talk politics and strategy.

Gilmore would be pleased to be on hand, lending encouragement to foot soldiers in the civil rights war, in the location where Medgar Evers and other brave souls had been martyred. There were also strategic questions to discuss. What did the Jackson NAACP branch need? What help could Boston provide? What sort of advice could Jackson blacks offer Boston's? In battles taking shape in Boston over such issues as school desegregation, could Jackson's experience offer any lessons?

Marvin could hardly wait to go.

Into the Shooting Gallery

Evers says he wanted Marvin to visit Jackson because it would gall a lot of local white supremacists. He also wanted Marvin to visit for the sake of what it would show local blacks.

"At the time the NAACP was hated by a lot of people, particularly a lot of white

not perilous enough, a second, very large event ratcheted up tensions in Mississippi and elsewhere in the South just as Marvin and Bill Russell arrived.

On July 2, 1964, at 6:58 p.m., President Lyndon Johnson signed into law the Civil Rights Act of 1964. The enactment took place five hours after the U.S. House of Representatives approved the historic law by a vote of 289 to 126.

Johnson's signing occurred 100 years, six months, and one day after Abraham Lincoln issued the Emancipation Proclamation.

Just seven days after the Civil Rights Act's enactment, Marvin and Bill Russell boarded an Eastern Airlines aircraft, winging towards Jackson.

They were winging their way into a region where many residents bitterly opposed the bill that had been debated for a year. The new law people," he said. "And it was praised by a lot of blacks. And I felt like if we could bring in those kind of persons, show they still live and walk on this earth, then it may encourage some of us to have more respect and support for the things we were trying to do. All we were trying to do is make America the kind of America it should be: equal, equality for all – black, white, Chinese, it doesn't matter. Just give them the same chance."[230]

Marvin's brainstorming session with Evers was exhilarating. "I was just thrilled I was asked by Charles to go down," he said. "At that moment, I had no fear. I have it now. But I didn't have it then. I was totally excited. I was being given a chance to make changes directly. I knew the South. I had been trained about the South by my mother, by my uncle, by my father, and by my grandmother. My experience helped. He knew that. The Army was good training too, from Texas to Georgia to Virginia. So I knew the people down there. I knew what we were getting into."

Within days Marvin and Russell were standing at the Eastern Airlines ticket counter at Boston's Logan International Airport, buying tickets for flight 311 on Thursday, July 9, 1964.

Russell's presence in Jackson would not only draw people to gatherings. His presence boosted the odds that federal law enforcement officers would shadow and watch the Boston visitors, improving their chances of surviving the trip. And if trouble did erupt, the resulting publicity

had picked up valuable support from an American public increasingly shocked by growing violence against blacks and civil rights workers.[xxx]

In the days and hours after the new law's creation, angry whites expressed their outrage. In Jackson, the family-owned Robert E. Lee Hotel closed rather than comply with the new law, which required businesses like hotels, restaurants, and theaters to serve all customers regardless of race. The hotel also closed its coffee shop, barbershop, beauty salon and basement supper club. The *Commercial Appeal* of Memphis, Tennessee, reported that someone posted a sign on the supper club door that declared, "Closed in despair. Civil rights bill unconstitutional."[xxxi]

Mississippi Gov. Paul Johnson said business owners should refuse to would put pressure on the feds to identify and prosecute the troublemakers.

"Bill was a shield," Marvin said. "Bill was my guard, no question about that. They [white supremacists in Mississippi] couldn't kill him. There would be too much news coverage. Can you imagine what just the Boston newspapers would do? I hoped that would protect me too. But I wondered whether they would kill me instead out of frustration."

Marvin and Russell timed their arrival at Logan well. Once aboard their flight, both men dozed off. "Me and Bill had a fairly short wait at the airport," Marvin said. "Bill sat in the front seat of the plane because he was long-legged. I sat behind him. Bill was always afraid to fly, so Bill went to sleep on the flight. I slept as well because I had no one to speak with."

On arrival in Jackson, Charles and some friends picked up Marvin and Russell. "We stopped and changed cars along the way," Marvin said. "It was for safety. Each time, we looked around to see if anyone was following us. We pulled over onto the shoulder of the road and switched cars when there were no other cars around and no one was watching the switch."

The precaution was necessary. Days later, in tag-team fashion, another group of NAACP members from the Boston area flew to Jackson the day after Marvin and Russell returned home. Like Marvin and Russell, they were met at the Jackson airport by a number of Evers' security

comply with the new law. "I don't think they should," he said. "I think it should be tested in the courts. A great many people feel it is unconstitutional." He predicted that attempts by African-Americans to desegregate public accommodations would trigger violent clashes.[xxxii]

Some Mississippi whites did far more than defy the new law. They lashed out. Shots were fired from a moving car carrying four white men into a crowd of 300 African-Americans, who were holding a voter-registration rally in a Knights of Pythias hall in Moss Point, Mississippi. The bullets smashed through a window. One shot hit 17-year-old Jessie Stallworth in her left side, sending her to the hospital.[xxxiii]

The Pleasant Plain Missionary Baptist Church, a black church in Greenwood, north of Jackson, was set ablaze.

guards. And as they piled into a Volkswagen bus for the drive to Evers' home, one of the men noticed a fresh hole in the windshield. It was about six inches from the driver's head. It was a bullet hole, from a small caliber rifle.[231] Crackers were stalking them, with lethal intent.

That hunt was a continuation of the lethal game of cat-and-mouse that Marvin and Russell had played days earlier with Mississippi supremacists. And for Marvin and Russell to survive this potentially fatal contest, they had to rely on sharp wits. Tools and devices we take for granted now didn't exist then. For one thing, they could not call for help on cell phones, which would not be invented until decades later.

"Whenever we were at Evers' house, we waited for the advance guards to check out the arrival scene and phone to let us know the coast was clear," Marvin said. "The advance guards would call from a friendly person's house. They never worried about whether Evers' phone was tapped. They weren't that sophisticated in those days. And it was a very rural area for a city, even a capital city."

In strategy sessions at Evers' home during the four-day visit, Marvin and the others discussed the local group's important and dangerous agenda. They plotted schemes for registering black voters despite intimidation and threats. They mulled over ideas for convincing African-Americans, after they had registered, that it was safe for them to exercise their right to vote. They

When a fire truck arrived, its crew stood by idly while flames consumed the church, a voter-registration activist said. In Hattisburg, three civil rights workers, including a rabbi, were beaten by two white men, one of whom wielded an iron pipe. The assailants fled in a pickup truck.[xxxiv]

The Jerusalem Baptist Church and the Bethel Methodist Church, both southeast of Natchez, were burned to the ground in predawn arson raids. In Natchez, the home of 57-year-old black contractor Willie Washington was attacked with a fire-bomb (which did not ignite). [xxxv]

In Laurel, several white and black youths were injured in a July 4 street brawl, which erupted when blacks tried to enter a hamburger stand. Police seized 15 weapons, including guns, clubs, bottles, and chains. A 19-year-old black youth said

221

brainstormed about the Jackson Movement Patronage Campaign. This boycott of stores in Jackson's Capitol Street shopping district was designed to pressure stores into having their sales associates address black customers with what black Jacksonians called courtesy titles – "Mr.," "Mrs.," and "Miss" – rather than "boy," "girl," nothing, or derogatory terms. The boycott was also intended to persuade stores to let black customers try on clothes before a purchase. A key goal of the boycott was to eliminate segregated rest rooms. And a fourth goal was to persuade stores to hire black workers.

The boycott was working. In effect about six months, at least 95% of area blacks were abiding by it, and an astounding 10 businesses in downtown Jackson had closed because of the boycott's impact.[232]

In their four days in Jackson, Marvin and Evers' team also discussed how to draw attention to the murder and mayhem being inflicted on civil rights workers and black activists in Mississippi.

And the Jackson-Boston activists talked about compiling a list of reporters, editors, and broadcast producers, whom the NAACP could contact to air their side of issues and to seek publicity for events.

They also asked themselves whether there were businesses with operations in both Jackson and Boston. Some might be persuaded to contribute money or materials – like paper, copiers, and

he had been refused entry. When he returned with friends, they were attacked by white youths. "After a while the police came, but they just arrested us colored boys and none of the white kids," he later told a group of NAACP leaders.

The episode was not over. On Sunday night, two more black youths were arrested while standing peacefully on a street corner. And that Monday when some of the black youths returned to the food stand, they were met by white men in cars who pointed shotguns at them.[xxxvi]

In McComb, a home used as a dormitory for voter-registration activists was bombed with dynamite. Witnesses reported "three rapid explosions in succession like gunshots, only much louder" in the predawn incident, which heavily damaged the house and injured two people.[xxxvii]

In a similar incident in

envelopes – to the NAACP branches or to specific campaigns, such as voter registration.

And again and again they came back to the topic of helping Evers run his operation. He needed assistants; he needed assistants who knew how to run an office, run a campaign such as a voter drive or business boycott, run a public relations battle.

They also touched topics that were applicable to both Jackson and Boston: school desegregation, learning how to use the new Civil Rights Act as a legal lever, easing fear among Jackson blacks and apathy among Boston blacks, and strengthening leadership in both communities' NAACP operations.

Those and others were subjects that Marvin discussed with his colleagues, and which would continue to be topics of conversations with later delegations from Boston to Jackson.

No Armed Escort

Meanwhile, in between those skull sessions Marvin and Russell attended to their other tasks: seeking service from restaurants and hotels in Jackson to test the new civil rights law, conducting basketball clinics, and holding public meetings with area blacks to boost morale and encourage African-Americans to stand up for their rights.

The Heidelberg Hotel's whites-only policy had been shattered the prior weekend by the NAACP national office

Shaw, a home used by civil rights workers had to be evacuated late at night after a man told occupants that five white men offered him $400 to bomb the dwelling, where 19 people were living.[xxxviii]

In Longdale, just outside Philadelphia, Mississippi, a group led by NAACP officials asked to view the remains of a black church that had been burned down. They were confronted by a mob of several hundred whites, many of whom were armed and angry. The crowd pressed closer to the NAACP entourage and grew in size. Deputy Sheriff Cecil Price yelled at the NAACP's Charles Evers, "Get out of town! Get going! Get out of town." As the confrontation grew more heated, county attorney Rayford Jones addressed some members of the NAACP group as "niggers." The NAACP group departed when entourage. Within just a few years, the NAACP would hold its national convention there. But when Marvin and Russell approached it for the first time, they lacked a key protection that had shielded the national entourage. Marvin and Russell were the first blacks since Reconstruction to attempt to register without an armed escort of police. The two Bostonians were painfully aware of how exposed they were.

"I saw white guys parading around outside with their guns," Marvin said. "Some carried shotguns. I saw some with handguns tucked into their belts."

Their stomachs tightened as they approached the hotel entrance. Marvin suddenly knew how Russell felt before games. The superstar center famously got sick to his stomach before pro basketball contests.

"We didn't know if the hotel would let us in before we got there," Marvin said. "There weren't as many reporters around as when the other [national NAACP] group had come. But there were some reporters waiting to see what would happen. The hotel did let us in. I still have my room key. I began to worry more about the people still outside."

In his Cambridge home office, Marvin still keeps his Heidelberg room key, a simple key attached to a plastic oval bearing the hotel's name and the number "1029" boldly inscribed.

Marvin and Russell were in adjoining rooms. Both were traveling lightly.

local officials warned that they could not assure their safety.[xxxix]

In Pascagoula on the Gulf Coast, the Ku Klux Klan used a light airplane to drop pamphlets to scare people and foment violence by warning people that blacks would engage in "gangsterism" during the upcoming July 4 weekend. The flyers urged whites to "arm yourself and stay at home. Do not fire unless your home, your person, or family is attacked."[xl]

Similar incidents of violent defiance erupted in other Southern and border states. But the vast majority of citizens, even in the South, complied with the new law of the land.[xli]

In a nutshell, the new law barred places that serve the public, such as restaurants, lunch counters, gas stations, cinemas, theaters, concert halls, sports arenas, hotels, and motels, from refusing

Marvin's suitcase held one extra pair of pants, two shirts, underwear, and toiletries. Russell's luggage still had not arrived. Marvin dropped his luggage in his room, and the men went out for the first of their whirlwind schedule of events and huddles with the Evers team.

Each time they traveled to a location that required transportation by car, an armed group of Evers' men would pick them up. "We had lookouts," Marvin said. "Evers' people would go to the destination beforehand to scout it out. Then they would contact us by phone to let us know it looked safe. And they would tell us what part of town we should or should not drive through."

Marvin also said, "We always had reporters meet us at destinations. We never let them travel with us. We didn't know who we could trust. We didn't know if someone we trusted might accidentally reveal our travel plans. So we didn't take any chances. And we didn't let people know when we would be someplace. Times were always approximate."

Marvin and Russell were in a bind. On the one hand they wanted publicity – at least after an event, to spread their message. On the other hand, advance publicity could be fatal. "We went to some black churches at night. Those were way out in the woods. We could be shot in the dark, like Medgar. Reporters could not guard us. All they could do was get us shot. 'Here's where I'm gonna be. Come shoot me!'"

service to people on the basis of race. Other provisions prohibited racial employment discrimination and segregation of schools.[xlii]

It would be followed the next year by legislation that had comparable impact in barring discrimination in polling places, the Voting Rights Act of 1965.

In the case of the Civil Rights Act, Congressional passage and presidential signing were just the first two steps. After enactment, it was equally important to identify establishments that defied the new law so they could be brought into compliance through publicity, loss of business, or legal sanctions. Yet segregation extremists made clear that they would maim and murder and intimidate anyone trying to do that. Dead bodies and burned out buildings were proof of their determination.

It was into that

Their visits to rural black churches were usually at night for the sake of security. It was harder for white predators to spot them exiting the hotel. And it would be harder for assassins to tail them without their car headlights being spotted. And like the drive in from the airport after their initial arrival on July 9, they sometimes switched cars along the way.

Neither Marvin nor Russell carried a weapon. But their escorts were armed. "The men had guns. There were pistols in the back seats of cars. You know: extra weapons in case we came under heavy fire. It was like the war. It *was* a war," Marvin said.

And they always carried phone numbers of the FBI in case they needed to call for extra help. "We just weren't sure they would come if we called," Marvin said. "They had never shown much interest in investigating the murders of black boys down South."

All of the safety measures were necessary. "Despite everything we did to avoid being followed, the crackers did follow us," Marvin said.

Not only did the Marvin-Bill Russell entourage change cars whenever possible, as they had on the initial drive out from the airport, but they also tacked back and forth, never taking a direct route to any destination. "We'd take different directions, making random turns to see if any cars were following us," Marvin said.

Sometimes, once they arrived at a church or other destination, their guards firestorm that Marvin and Russell leaped. They would test compliance with the new law, knowing that some opponents of the new law were willing to kill integrationists if that's what it took to kill the new law itself by sparking what they hoped would be a national tsunami of defiance.

Marvin and Russell volunteered to make themselves into targets, drawing out the law-defiers and violent segregationists that the overall American public rejected, solidifying support for a new era of improved racial justice.

"Knowing what I know now about how dangerous it was to go to Jackson, it's scary that I went there," Marvin said. "But I'm glad I went. It was important for the people there. And it was important for my own kids up here and wherever they choose to live."

exited the car first, making a big deal of waving their guns. "They wanted to show that they were armed, so anyone waiting to ambush us would know they'd have a gun fight on their hands if they tried to kill us the way they had killed Medgar," Marvin said.

These clandestine gatherings were civil rights pep rallies. Some audiences included civil rights workers as well as ordinary civilians.[233] Evers talked about the importance of registering to vote and the importance of then voting. He would boost the crowd's morale by introducing Marvin and Russell, reminding each audience that the presence of these men showed that the outside world cared about freedom in Mississippi, that Mississippi blacks were not alone in their struggle.

When Marvin spoke, he explained to each crowd that more blacks elsewhere, especially outside the South, were achieving economic success and living better lives, and that this was within reach of blacks in Mississippi too. But it all began with political power, it all began with voting, he said.

White Men with Guns

After the church meetings and following any strategy sessions back at Evers' home, Marvin and Russell returned to the Heidelberg. There, white supremacists had no trouble making threats and intimidating the men from Boston. Everyone knew exactly where they

Sidebar notes

[i] Charles Payne, "Foreword," *Groundwork: Local Black Freedom Movements in America,* edited by Jeanne Theoharis and Komzi Woodard (New York, N.Y.: New York University Press, 2005), p. x.

[ii] Jason Keyser, Associated Press, "Willie Louis, witness to Emmett Till's torture and lynching," *Boston Globe,* July 25, 2013, p. B14.

[iii] Patricia Older, "FBI re-opens Mack Charles Parker lynching," *The Picayune Item,* May 9, 2009: http://picayuneitem.com/local/x2079288107/FBI-re-opens-Mack-Charles-Parker-lynching/print, accessed July 25, 2013.

[iv] Debbie Elliot, "Fifty Years After Medgar Evers' Killing, The Scars Remain," NPR.org: http://m.npr.org/news/U.S./188727790, accessed July 23, 2013. History.com, "This Day in History – June 12, 1963: Medgar Evers assassinated": http://www.history.com/this-day-in-history/medgar-evers-assassinated accessed July 23, 2013.

[v] Patricia Older, "FBI re-opens Mack Charles Parker lynching," *The Picayune Item,* May 9, 2009: http://picayuneitem.com/local/x2079288107/FBI-re-opens-Mack-Charles-Parker-lynching/print, accessed July

were. Even behind a bolted hotel room door, Marvin and Russell felt like targets in a shooting gallery.

"We saw men walking around outside the hotel with guns," Marvin said. "They carried guns openly. Armed men outside the hotel called out our names and made threats."

All the time – not just during the Marvin-Russell visit – Evers took dramatic precautions to safeguard his own life. Russell was shaken up to realize that such defensive steps were needed. "He was shocked I slept with a pistol in my hand," Evers wrote.[234]

The first night Marvin and Russell were in Jackson, every so often someone rattled each of their hotel room's doorknobs. Marvin and Russell heard unsettling noises in the alley below. It was hard to sleep, Marvin says.[235] Other nights, Marvin and Russell took turns as sentries. "Bill slept part of the night and I kept watch, then I slept while Bill listened and watched out," Marvin said.

The Russell-Gilmore double-headers began the very first day they were in Mississippi. Russell conducted basketball clinics by day; Marvin was there. At night mostly, Marvin and Russell joined civil rights meetings. Most were at churches, drawing about 100 people. They also met smaller groups of about a dozen at people's homes.

The day of their arrival, Russell went to the Y.M.C.A. that served Jackson blacks. Russell was forced to improvise because

25, 2013.

[vi] History.com, "Aug. 4, 1964: Slain civil rights workers found," http://www.history.com/this-day-in-history/slain-civil-rights-workers-found, accessed July 254, 2013.

[vii] Emilye Crosby, *A Little Taste of Freedom: The Black Freedom Struggle in Claiborne County, Mississippi* (Chapel Hill, No. Carolina: The University of North Carolina Press, 2005), p. 15.

[viii] John Dittmer, *Local People: The Struggle for Civil Rights in Mississippi* (Urbana: University of Illinois Press, 1994), pp. 1-2.

[ix] John Dittmer, *Local People: The Struggle for Civil Rights in Mississippi* (Urbana: University of Illinois Press, 1994), pp. 52.

[x] John Dittmer, *Local People: The Struggle for Civil Rights in Mississippi* (Urbana: University of Illinois Press, 1994), pp. 163.

[xi] Emilye Crosby, *A Little Taste of Freedom: The Black Freedom Struggle in Claiborne County, Mississippi* (Chapel Hill, No. Carolina: The University of North Carolina Press, 2005), pp. 64-78.

[xii] Emilye Crosby, *A Little Taste of Freedom: The Black Freedom Struggle in Claiborne County, Mississippi* (Chapel Hill, No. Carolina: The University of North Carolina Press, 2005), p. 70.

[xiii] Mississippi Department of

his workout clothes and basketball gear were on a later plane and had not arrived yet. Instead of leading boys through drills and demonstrating various basketball moves, Russell treated a group of 20 black teenagers to anecdotes.

The boys, still sweaty from playing before Russell's arrival, gathered around the Boston Celtics star as he stretched his legs on a simple bench. Russell proceeded to tell them that when he was their age, he had been a third-string member of his junior varsity high school team. He was so low on the totem pole that when it turned out his team had only 15 uniforms for 16 players, he was the one deemed unimportant enough not to get a uniform.[236]

Russell put the initially shy boys at ease with his stories, down-to-earth style, and his trademark cackle. He explained that he had recently returned from a State Department basketball tour. In games behind the Iron Curtain, frustrated opponents had tried to rough up Russell – which backfired because it only made him play harder. He had first learned to cope with adversity, he told the teens, when he was introduced to basketball at a local YMCA.

His own career had taken him to the pinnacle of accomplishment, fame, and pay, he said. But it had taken hard work to prepare for opportunities in high school, college, and in the pros. "One thing I learned," Russell said, aiming to inspire the boys, "you can never tell what will happen

Archives and History, "Sovereignty Commission Online": http://mdah.state.ms.us/arrec/digital_archives/sovcom/scagencycasehistory.php, accessed July 27, 2013.

[xiv] John Dittmer, *Local People: The Struggle for Civil Rights in Mississippi* (Urbana: University of Illinois Press, 1994), pp. 58.

[xv] Mark Potok, "Civil Rights Era Klan Murderer Dies In Prison," Southern Poverty Law Center, Aug. 3, 2011: http://www.splcenter.org/blog/2011/08/03/civil-rights-era-klan-murderer-dies-in-prison/, accessed Aug. 30, 2013.

[xvi] AtYourLibrary.org, "Murder of Civil Rights Workers While Registering Voters Shocks Nation in 1964": http://atyourlibrary.org/culture/murder-civil-right-workers-while-registering-voters-shocks-nation-1964, accessed Aug. 27, 2013. Jonathan Saltzman, "Justice follows decades of silence," Boston Globe, http://www.boston.com/news/education/higher/articles/2010/06/23/northeastern_students_aid_justice_in_64_slayings/?page=full, accessed Aug. 30, 2013.]

[xvii] John Dittmer, *Local People: The Struggle for Civil Rights in Mississippi* (Urbana: University of Illinois Press, 1994), pp. 58.

[xviii] Doug McAdam, Freedom

in the future so you have to work and be ready for the breaks when they come. And then as you keep going you can be proud of what you've done, proud of your accomplishments."[237]

Watched by Spies

That night Russell and Marvin participated in a rally at Jackson's New Jerusalem Baptist Church. Marvin spoke. So did Russell, Evers, and others. "I said I came down to help the community," Marvin recalled. "Hopefully, my presence and Bill's would be a support. That's why we were down there, to make changes. The natives could not do it themselves. We outsiders could put pressure on, say the violence and intimidation has got to stop. We could say things and do things the natives could not do because it was a little harder to attack us, to kill us. We were trying to give the natives more confidence in the fight for freedom. More strength."

The New Jerusalem Baptist Church meeting illustrated the tensions and conflicting agendas among white and black Mississippians. While Marvin, Russell, and others spoke, a spy from the Sovereignty Commission – the secret police force whose mission was to perpetuate segregation – was in the audience, taking notes. Later, he submitted a typed report to his white handlers. It detailed how officials of the NAACP reminded the church audience of the need for action by recounting their own recent experiences of being denied service at a local café and a

Summer (New York, N.Y.: Oxford University Press, 1988), p. 96.
[xix] Jonathan Saltzman, "Justice follows decades of silence," Boston Globe, http://www.boston.com/news/education/higher/articles/2010/06/23/northeastern_students_aid_justice_in_64_slayings/?page=full, accessed Aug. 30, 2013. Crimeshots Web site, "Ex-Miss. sheriff's deputy charged in '64 deaths," http://www.crimeshots.com/forums/showthread.php?t=5237, accessed Aug. 30, 2013.
[xx] Jonathan Saltzman, "Justice follows decades of silence," Boston Globe, http://www.boston.com/news/education/higher/articles/2010/06/23/northeastern_students_aid_justice_in_64_slayings/?page=full, accessed Aug. 30, 2013. Crimeshots web site, "Ex-Miss. sheriff's deputy charged in '64 deaths," http://www.crimeshots.com/forums/showthread.php?t=5237, accessed Aug. 30, 2013. Rick Emert, "Retired CSM focuses on personal moment of black history," *Fort Carson Mountaineer*, http://www.army.mil/article/17489/, accessed Aug. 30, 2013. Mark Potok, "Civil Rights Era Klan Murderer Dies In Prison," Southern Poverty Law Center, Aug. 3, 2011: http://www.splcenter.org/blog

local skating rink. The Commission spy dutifully reported Russell's amazement and outrage at having come across an army tank in downtown Jackson. The mayor had ordered it deployed to help quell any civil rights demonstrations. Other speakers made it clear that it was black Jacksonians who felt threatened during demonstrations. James Pittman told the crowd that the NAACP was running workshops to teach youngsters how to protect themselves when they are being beaten in cafés where they were seeking service.[238]

"I remember the tank," Marvin said. "It was crazy. It shows how afraid of us they were. It shows how far the Southern white crackers were willing to go, killing people, using a tank to stop demonstrators. The crackers were all carrying weapons, and your life was not worth a plugged nickel."

In the following days, Russell's itinerary of basketball clinics was cut back. Deciding that it would be unsafe for Russell to visit Canton, Meridian, and Clarksdale, trips to those cities were cancelled. Still, a total of four clinics were conducted in Jackson.[239]

On Friday, Marvin and Russell's second day in Mississippi, the then-30-year-old center who had led the Celtics to seven National Basketball Association titles – he would go on to win four more, for a total of 11 – conducted the first integrated hoops clinic in the Jackson Auditorium.[240] This integrated clinic may

/2011/08/03/civil-rights-era-klan-murderer-dies-in-prison/, accessed Aug. 30, 2013.
[xxi] History.com, "Freedom Summer": http://www.history.com/topics/freedom-summer, accessed Aug. 27, 2013.
[xxii] Rachel S. Ohrenschall, "Freedom Summer campaign for African-American voting rights in Mississippi, 1964": http://nvdatabase.swarthmore.edu/print/content/freedom-summer-campaign-african-american-voting-rights-mississippi-1964, accessed Aug. 27, 2013.
[xxiii] Borgna Brunner, "The Murders of James Chaney, Andrew Goodman, and Michael Schwerner": http://www.infoplease.com/spot/bhmjustice4.html, accessed Aug. 27, 2013. "Jackson Motel, Two Hotels Drop Racial Barriers Quietly," *Commercial Appeal* (Memphis, Tenn.), July 6, 1964, p. 1.
[xxiv] Douglas O. Linder, "The Mississippi Burning Trial": http://law2.umkc.edu/faculty/projects/ftrials/price&bowers/account.html, accessed Aug. 27, 2013.
[xxv] Claude Sitton, "Mississippi Force Expanded By F.B.I.," *New York Times*, July 11, 1964, p. 1. AtYourLibrary.org, "Murder of Civil Rights Workers While Registering Voters Shocks Nation in 1964":

have been the most satisfying for Russell. Shortly after his initial arrival in Jackson, he had said he hoped white youngsters would play with him and black youths "no matter what their parents think."[241]

Before returning to Boston, Russell would preside over two more clinics, one at Jackson State College and another at Tougaloo College.[242]

Basketball clinics were as close as the Marvin-Russell visit came to fun and games. Every time they went for a meal, the Boston duo was reminded how terrifying life in Mississippi could be for anyone who did not share segregationists' vision of a whites-on-top Mississippi.

One night, Marvin and Russell were seated for dinner in the Heidelberg's restaurant. Suddenly, they found themselves surrounded by hostile whites at other tables, carrying guns. "The people had guns everywhere – in their pockets, under their coats, in their belts – everywhere," Marvin told United Press International shortly after.[243]

Years later Marvin said, "We looked out the window and saw people walking up and down the street with guns in their hands. Inside the restaurant, they wanted us out."

Marvin and Russell finished their meal. But they stepped to a telephone and called the FBI to make sure they escaped alive, without being abducted or shot on the spot.

At such moments, all Marvin and Russell could think of was the danger they

http://atyourlibrary.org/culture/murder-civil-right-workers-while-registering-voters-shocks-nation-1964, accessed Aug. 27, 2013. History.com, "This Day in History – Aug. 4, 1964: Slain civil rights workers found": http://www.history.com/this-day-in-history/slain-civil-rights-workers-found, accessed Aug. 27, 2013.

xxvi Claude Sitton, "Mississippi Force Expanded By F.B.I.," *New York Times,* July 11, 1964, p. 1. AtYourLibrary.org, "Murder of Civil Rights Workers While Registering Voters Shocks Nation in 1964": http://atyourlibrary.org/culture/murder-civil-right-workers-while-registering-voters-shocks-nation-1964, accessed Aug. 28, 2013. History.com, "This Day in History – Aug. 4, 1964: Slain civil rights workers found": http://www.history.com/this-day-in-history/slain-civil-rights-workers-found, accessed Aug. 27, 2013. Civil Rights Movement Veterans Website, "Neshoba Murders Case — A Chronology by Arkansas Delta Truth and Justice Center": http://www.crmvet.org/info/csg.htm, accessed Aug. 28, 2013.

xxvii AtYourLibrary.org, "Murder of Civil Rights Workers While Registering Voters Shocks Nation in 1964": http://atyourlibrary.org/cultur

were in. But many of Jackson's people of color were watching them and drawing on their courage. William Kunstler, a Manhattan-based civil rights attorney who rose to prominence defending Sixties' and Seventies' political radicals, ran into Marvin and Russell in a black-owned café on North Farish Street in Jackson. Kunstler was on the scene to represent jailed Freedom Riders.

"Fear was rampant," Kunstler said. Suddenly, through the café door came Russell. The tall man had to stoop to get through the door. "Keep up the good work," Russell told Kunstler, shaking his hand. Kunstler returned the compliment, telling Russell, "Thank god you're here." "I wouldn't have missed it," Russell replied.[244]

"Nigger, Don't Move"

The most dangerous moment came that Saturday, on Marvin and Russell's final night in Jackson. The *Boston Globe* reported matter-of-factly that Marvin and Russell were denied entry to a restaurant. The details are more chilling. Marvin, Russell, and three priests tried to enter Primos, part of a chain of three restaurants owned by a father and three sons. One son, Aleck Primos, was president of the Jackson White Citizens' Council.[245] The Council was a white supremacist organization, a sort of Ku Klux Klan for white-collar workers and chamber-of-commerce members.[246]

Because the restaurant was known as

e/murder-civil-right-workers-while-registering-voters-shocks-nation-1964, accessed Aug. 28, 2013.

[xxviii] AtYourLibrary.org, "Murder of Civil Rights Workers While Registering Voters Shocks Nation in 1964": http://atyourlibrary.org/cultur e/murder-civil-right-workers-while-registering-voters-shocks-nation-1964, accessed Aug. 28, 2013.

[xxix] Veterans of the Civil Rights Movement, "Mississippi Freedom Summer Events": http://www.crmvet.org/tim/ti m64b.htm, accessed Aug. 30, 2013.

[xxx] United Press International, "South Protests to the Last Gun / Civil Rights Bill Passed; LBJ Signs Tonight," Boston Evening Globe, July 2, 1964, p. 1.

[xxxi] Kenneth Toler, "Jackson Hotel Won't Mix, Closes," *Commercial Appeal* (Memphis, Tenn.), July 7, 1964, p. 13.

[xxxii] Associated Press, "Rights Law Gets Fast Tests," *Boston Globe,* July 3, 1964, p. 1.

[xxxiii] United Press International, "Shot Fired At Rally Hits Negro Girl," *Boston Traveler,* July 7, 1964, p. 5.

[xxxiv] Associated Press, "Negro Church Fired In Race-Torn Miss." *Boston Globe,* July 11, 1964, p. 1.

[xxxv] Associated Press, "2 More Negro Churches Burned in Miss.," *Boston Evening Globe,*

a citadel of segregation, Marvin and Russell had come accompanied by allies. With them were three white Catholic priests from the North, who were in Jackson in support of local civil rights activities.

On the sidewalk outside the front door, a man described as an armed private guard shoved a gun into Marvin's belly. He said, "Nigger, don't move or I'll kill you!" Marvin recalled. "In World War II I never let an armed enemy soldier get that close to me. It was only in America that I allowed the enemy to get so close to me and put a pistol in my stomach while I was trying to get something to eat. I fought in the war to save Southern white crackers like that, and now he was threatening to kill me."

Marvin still seethes at the thought that he had spent World War II making the world safer for "a jerk like this, a nobody," yet now this nobody was threatening to blow a hole in Marvin's abdomen. "A priest with a white collar did not deter him," Marvin said. "I wasn't afraid. I had been through terrible things in the war. And I had learned how far you could push somebody, how far you could go before calling a man's bluff. I was smart enough to not make him pull that trigger. We moved back."

No one in Marvin's group had an appetite after that. "The ministers took off. Bill and I went our way," Marvin said.

Then, as abruptly as it had begun, the odyssey to Jackson was over. That Sunday

July 13, 2013, p. 3. (The report noted that neighboring white residents pledged men, money, and materials to help rebuild the churches.)

xxxvi Michael Lydon, "'But They Just Arrested Us Colored Boys,'" *Boston Globe,* July 8, 1964, p. 11. Compiled from wire services, "Jackson Motel, Two Hotels Drop Racial Barriers Quietly," *Commercial Appeal* (Memphis, Tenn.), July 6, 1964, p. 1.

xxxvii Associated Press, "2 Rights Workers Hurt in Bombing," *Boston Globe,* July 8, 1964, p. 1. United Press International, "FBI's Hoover Flying To Mississippi Today," *Boston Globe,* July 10, 1964, p. 8.

xxxviii United Press International, "Body Found, May be Miss. Victim," *Boston Globe,* July 13, 1964, pp. 1 and 2.

xxxix David Halberstam, "Hostility Meets N.A.A.C.P. On Tour," *New York Times,* July 7, 1964, p. 20.

xl United Press International, "South Mostly Complies," *Boston Globe,* July 4, 1964, p. 3.

xli United Press International, "St. Augustine to Comply With Rights Law," *Boston Globe,* July 2, 1964, p. 16. Bicknell Eubanks, "'Rights' Law In The South," *Christian Science Monitor,* July 6, 1964, p. 1. Compiled from wire services, "Jackson Motel, Two Hotels

Marvin and Russell flew home. Feeling inundated by hostile, armed whites around their hotel, the duo phoned the FBI and asked to be escorted out. The next night at NAACP branch quarters in Boston, the men held a press conference.

Jackson was a tragic locale, a small city caught in a giant, terrible time warp, where some of the true final battles of the Civil War were being waged. Only it wasn't uniformed armies of grey Confederates contesting blue Federals. It was largely a guerilla action, with plain-clothed segregation fanatics on one side and on the other side a rag-tag coalition of blacks in farmers' overalls allied with blue-jean clad college kids and civil rights workers.

Russell described the visit as four fearful days in an armed city.[247] Mississippi's blacks were getting tired of being maimed, murdered, and muscled around by armed posses of segregationists, he said, and sooner rather than later they would abandon pacifist tactics. Russell didn't have to spell it out: at that point, America would have an out-and-out race war.[248]

Meanwhile, walking through Jackson during the day is like whistling in a graveyard, he added. At night you fear for your life because everyone carries a gun.[249]

Russell said he was repeatedly shocked by seeing and hearing about church bombings, kids getting beaten up, and the lack of police protection for blacks. He had talked to a boy who had been beaten up five times. Once, he had been beaten unconscious for two weeks.[250]

Marvin spoke too. But as usual, the press devoted most of their ink to comments by the celebrity, Bill Russell. Marvin described how unsafe it was for a black man to travel alone anywhere in or around Jackson. Marvin described the open hostility of so many white men walking the streets, openly bearing firearms.[251]

Drop Racial Barriers Quietly," *Commercial Appeal* (Memphis, Tenn.), July 6, 1964, p. 1. Associated Press, "Scattered Resistance Greets Rights Testers," *Boston Globe*, July 7, 1964, p. 22. United Press International, "Testing of 'Rights' Law Continues Across Dixie," Clarion-Ledger (Jackson, Miss.), July 7, 1964, pp. 1 and 10. "Civil Rights Rundown," *Boston Globe*, July 10, 1964, p. 2. "Jackson Gets First Tests Of New Civil Rights Law," *Jackson Advocate,* July 11, 1964, pp. 1 and 3.
[xlii] David Barnett, "What Rights Law Can Do – What's Banned," *Boston Sunday Globe,* July 5, 2013, p. 14.

A second purpose for the press conference was to publicize the carnage against blacks in Mississippi. In the year since the murder of Medgar Evers, another six men had been killed, five more are missing, and a twelfth had disappeared and was presumed murdered. Blacks understood all of those men to be victims of white-on-black violence. Russell reeled off each man's name and home town.[252]

"Bill and I did what we could while we were down there," Marvin said. "We played a small role in a big battle. I hope we helped people there feel a little safer, knowing people on the outside cared about them. I didn't think about how dangerous it was until much later. But, you know, it was like World War II – the reason we fought is that freedom is never given to you. You have to fight for it."

Chapter 11

Marvin Gilmore, Impresario

Marvin was driving his sporty red Jaguar sedan along Cambridge's Western Avenue one day in the early 1960s. He was traveling a seedy stretch of street. It was pock-marked with dive bars, hangouts for prostitutes, and bookie joints. This was an area that gave Boston's notorious red-light district, the Combat Zone, a run for its illicit money.

But Marvin certainly was not there looking for a good time. He was heading somewhere else on some routine business. Still, the entrepreneur's voice in the back of his head took notice. *Look at this street,* the voice said. *It's rundown. It's a shame. But it's a place where you could buy property at a discount price.*

A second voice in the back of Marvin's mind whispered something too. This was the old voice of Marvin the musician. It was a voice that had not said much in recent years. It was a voice that had taken a back seat in Marvin's decision-making as his career had focused on real estate and away from music. But now this voice whispered to Marvin: *Yes, you could buy some place, and run it as a music club. You could treat it as a business, but it would bring you back toward music. Your first love.*

Music had proven to be too hard, too risky a way to try to make a living. There was no going back for Marvin now, not at his age. He was no longer a care-free kid, responsible to no one but himself. He was a married man with growing children. He also had a portfolio of rental properties that needed taking care of. But owning a club – that would be different. It would be one more investment, one more way to earn income for his family. Better yet, it would be a way to diversify his sources of income. It would be prudent. It would spread his financial eggs around to more baskets. And, yes, it would re-open a door on a world he had always loved, music.

A Plan Takes Shape

On this day, in his Jag, it was the zillionth time he had taken this route. He was usually on his way to one of his properties in Cambridge or elsewhere, or heading to view a potential address for purchase, or driving home, or driving to a jazz club in Boston, or motoring somewhere nearby on some other errand.

Western Avenue was – and still is – one of Cambridge's key radial thoroughfares, extending like a spoke from Central Square, a bustling hub of small locally owned stores, shops, and restaurants, where several of the city's main streets intersect. Western Avenue shoots out in a westerly direction. It jumps across the Charles River's big northerly bend, then cuts into Boston's Alston neighborhood.

And five decades ago, this part of Western Avenue was a rough stretch of bars and worse. This was where Marvin started to look for a property he could buy, a place where he could run a decent music club. And it didn't take Marvin long to focus on one property in particular.

"It was a bar at the corner of Howard and Western aves," said Marvin, referring to a location at the midpoint of the Cambridge side of the avenue. "It was a little rundown bar, a place for horse-race betting. They served just beer and wine. They didn't have a full liquor license. It was literally a dive bar."

Marvin learned what he could about the bar. After all, he owned a lot of property in the city. He knew people everywhere in the city. He knew people in city hall, although his reach there was very limited. "Cambridge was a city that simply did not want a black man to succeed," he said bluntly. White officials and white city-hall clerks and white bureaucrats spilled no secrets with Marvin. Whatever he learned was public information, public records. But Marvin was a smart man who knew how to read between the lines.

Marvin visited the bar. The bar's owner was an older woman who happened to be a member of the city's licensing commission, Marvin says. Marvin learned she was in ill health and spending a lot of time in Florida. Marvin spoke with her attorney. Just before the woman died, Marvin bought her bar. He renamed it the Candlelight Lounge.

The Hard Part

The easy work was done.

In a compact city like Cambridge, neighborhoods are both distinct and yet small. Drive just a few blocks, and you suddenly cross into another neighborhood with its own sharply defined character and dramatically different cast of residents. Especially in the early 1960s, Cambridge like Boston was a patchwork quilt of ethnic neighborhoods, each fiercely proud of its own tribal identity.

The stretch of Western Avenue occupied by the Candlelight Lounge was home turf to a struggling but proud West Indian community. "All up and down the street were small restaurants, chicken places, shoe-shine places, a car repair shop. It was a small black town along Western Ave. And there were three or four bars. Some were legal [licensed], and some weren't. I wanted something different. I tried to rejuvenate the neighborhood, provide people with a nice place to go."

But members of a church that was just a few doors down the street could not see anything positive in Marvin's endeavor. The congregation zealously tried to make Marvin's bar go away. Whether they were jarred simply by ownership changing from familiar to unfamiliar hands or were opposed to the presence of a bar of any kind in their tight-knit neighborhood, they campaigned against Marvin.

At the same time, the city fought Marvin too.

"The city took me to court, blaming me for gambling, drugs, and prostitution along the street," Marvin said. "They just didn't want blacks to have any businesses in the city." This was the same old, same old, to Marvin. White bankers' refusal to grant him loans was a big part of the reason he had led the drive to start Unity Bank & Trust (see Chapters 8 and 11).

Neighborhood residents battled him by demonstrating outside his bar. "On Sunday mornings church members marched and sang outside the bar," Marvin said. "I sang with them. I tried to reason with them. I asked them why they picked on the only black-owned bar. Why not go a few blocks up to Central Square and pick on a white-owned bar? But they wouldn't listen, and it kept a lot of young black people out of my bar."

Surrender, Or...?

Marvin faced additional hurdles in his efforts to make a go of it with the bar. For one thing, the bar was too small. It could host no more than about 70 people. That limited everything from the amount Marvin could gross from cover charges to the quality of musical bands he could afford. Another problem was that it lacked a full liquor license. It could serve only beer and wine.

He faced a simple choice. Quit or double down.

Quitting would be the logical decision. Marvin had plowed a lot of money into the Candlelight Lounge. "I bought it, fixed it up," Marvin said. "I spent a fortune to put in mahogany walls and a mahogany bar." His reward had been community opposition and demonization, as well as harassment by the city. In addition, he could see from a strictly business perspective that the site's small size made it difficult to achieve a reasonable return on his investment. So selling or folding the club would be an easy business decision.

But surrender was not Marvin's style. He had not run from Nazis or racist crackers in World War II. He had not bowed to rich white men who wanted him to accept trifling wages for washing their cars and scrubbing the floors of their mansions. He had not settled for a career as a house boy. So he was not about to cave in to city authorities who wanted to block a black entrepreneur. So giving up was out of the question when he knew he could succeed.

Doubling down was his choice. He would start anew with a bigger venue that had a full liquor license. Marvin began to look for such an opportunity.

The search took several years. All the while, he stabilized the Candlelight Lounge, preventing it from draining his time and resources too heavily. When he did finally find his second opportunity, it was across the street, just a few blocks away, closer to the river, at the corner of Putnam and Western Avenue.

It was Ernie's Lunch, a bar named for its owner. The bar, which had a full liquor license, was Ernie's sideline and vice. He also worked for Cambridge Gas & Electric Company, a utility, whose plant was just down the street. Ernie's problem was that he quaffed a lot of his own profits. Marvin came to Ernie's rescue.

"In those days you had to find a club with a license," Marvin said. "All of the available licenses had been granted. So I saw who had each license, and then I learned what I could about each one. I could tell Ernie's wasn't solid. I went down to it and thought about it. Ernie was drunk a lot. So one day I wrote a check for $150,000 and put it in my pocket. I went to Ernie's and after closing I told him I wanted to buy the club, the real estate, and the license. I pulled out the check and said, "Sign this, Ernie." He did. We carried him outside, put him into a friend's car, and sent him home. I think it was the next day when I heard from Ernie's son. I wondered whether he was going to complain about the sale. But he thanked me for getting his father away from the booze, out of a constant, drunken stupor, coming home drunk every night."

Ernie's Lunch was in as much need of an intervention as its owner had been. Marvin began to renovate the new club, but the more his contractors did, the more they discovered that had to be fixed.

"I put a fortune into the place," Marvin said. "I built a new teak bar on the first floor. It was expensive. Now, it would cost an absolute fortune to build a bar of teak. And I had to put in air-conditioning, heating, sprinklers. We ended up gutting the whole building. It took a year to finish. There's a residential building on the back side of the parcel. I refurbished that too. The apartments were cold-water flats – you know, apartments without hot water. I fixed that. I tried to operate the club while doing the repairs, but it was impossible. After a while, I closed it down to gut it and refurbish it from top to bottom."

One unintended consequence was that Marvin had deprived a lot of loyal customers from their favorite bookie joint. As a result, he got hit with a new wave of harassment by the city. "The reason I got so much heat was that Ernie's had horse-betting," Marvin said. "City workers and police stopped in there at 8 in the morning, and they were angry because I had cut off their betting."

Cambridge city hall was nearby, on the far side of Central Square.

Plowing forward, Marvin named the club the Western Front after old photographs he found in the basement. They showed First World War soldiers – known as doughboys – fighting in the contested territory between Germany to the East and the Allies to the West. That battle zone was known as the Western Front. "I put those photos on the first floor of the club," Marvin said. "And we used them on the invitations when we did a formal opening."

Blues Club

Marvin's own battle plan called for introducing something entirely new to Western Avenue. He did not want to run a dive bar. He certainly wanted nothing to do with the vices that were rampant up and down the street. Instead, he wanted to focus on music. He wanted to run clubs whose primary draw was artistic talent.

The Candlelight is remembered mainly as a blues venue. It became an outpost on the circuit of clubs played by hard-core bluesmen, who rotated among select cities and communities such as Chicago, Detroit, Harlem, Memphis, and St. Louis. Boston proper, Roxbury, and Harvard Square boasted clubs. So did the area around Central Square. "The heart of this new scene beat in central Cambridge at the Candlelight Lounge, Joe's Place, and the Speakeasy," Ted Drozdowski wrote in *Boston* magazine.[253]

James Montgomery, a Detroit native who fronts the popular James Montgomery Band, early on played places like Estelle's in Roxbury and the Candlelight. He told Drozdowski that the Candlelight is where his band was born. "The Candlelight reminded me of a place I knew in Detroit called the Decanter. It was a little neighborhood bar. The first couple of times I went there, it was all black people who lived nearby and the white band. After a while, it caught on and became a great little melting pot."

But backstage the Candlelight remained a burden to Marvin. He had to split his time between it and the Western Front, and the Candlelight could not compete with the 165-person-capacity Western Front. The Front simply enjoyed better economies of scale. And because he was unable to focus as much time as necessary on the Candlelight, Marvin could not cure its ills.

"Staff were stealing my money," he said. "The bartenders. And it never got past its early problems. I had walked into a den of iniquity."

Marvin sold the Candlelight Lounge after running both clubs simultaneously for about two years. The buyer, perhaps with fitting symbolism, later became an undertaker.

Music Came First

Focusing solely the Western Front, Marvin featured music he loved and music his audiences loved. "In an era when the blues were high, I featured blues," Marvin said. "Then blues went down. We had jazz, then that went down. Then reggae, electric music [a genre of pop music featuring electronic instruments such as synthesizers and drum machines], ska, rap, hip-hop and Latin music." Styles ebbed and flowed in popularity and in their predominance at the clubs. Reggae, in particular, came, went, and came back.

Through it all, Marvin was a different sort of club owner. For him, the music came first, says Steve Morse, who was the senior pop music at the *Boston Globe* for 30 years. Rather than making decisions based solely on profitability, Marvin made decisions based on what he enjoyed in music, what he expected his audiences to enjoy, and what would be good for the musicians too.

"The bottom line for Marvin was that he was a music lover first and foremost," Morse said. "The club was a labor of love for him. It wasn't his primary source of income. It was more like a club house. This is what made Marvin and that club so special."[254]

Late at night, usually on weekends, Marvin often grabbed a pair of maracas and jumped on stage to join the band. He may have been in his forties, fifties, or even his sixties or seventies when he made the leap. But the man who landed on stage was the same skilled musician who had proven himself a quick study at the Royal Scottish Academy of Music, the same skilled musician who majored in percussion at New England Conservatory, the same skilled musician who had led jazz bands in the early 1950s. Band musicians didn't need to worry whether Marvin could keep up with them; the real question was whether these young musicians could avoid being taken to school by the old man.

Marvin makes no apologies. "I wasn't that old then," he said. "And I knew what I was doing. Most of the bands loved it. A few opposed it. But I showed them up, some of the young drummers. Word was that if Marvin didn't play on stage, you don't come back. They didn't like it when they made a mistake rhythm-wise. Most welcomed [having me join them on stage] because it put them into the right rhythm. I know what I'm doing."

Morse saw Marvin leap into action on numerous occasions. "Some acts may not have been wildly in favor of having a club owner jump up and play with them," he said. "It was not standard operating procedure. But they quickly discovered that Marvin was an exceptional maraca player and he added to every single act he joined.

"He brought a wonderful spirit and energy to the stage, which shot a show into overdrive, and bands loved that. I don't know any band that tried to forbid him from joining in. He was smooth about it, never arrogant. Never imposing. And as soon as bands noticed that he was good, everyone would go into absolute ecstasy. He was an ecstatic personality in his club. He wanted everyone to have a good time."

Biracial Crowds

Successful clubs have distinct personalities. The Western Front's personality consisted of equal parts of Marvin himself, the musical talent he brought in, and the club's demographics. A lot of people talk about being color-blind. Marvin did much more than talk.

"What made the Western Front special was that it was a biracial crowd, for starters," Morse said. "And that was not particularly common in Cambridge, even though Cambridge thinks of itself as a multicultural city. For a long time it was not. Reggae was one of the few styles of music that had a way of uniting people. Marvin encouraged that."

Marvin also saw to it that the club appealed to people from all walks of life. "You had carpenters dancing next to Harvard students," Morse said. "There was no snobbery at his club. There was none of this condescension that some Boston clubs became famous for, prima-donna pretentious clubs. Not the Western Front. It was a festive place."

Marvin's instinct about the club's location was vindicated too. Western Avenue may have had its rough spots when Marvin bought in, but it was easy for a wide range of customers to reach, townies and gownies alike. "Marvin liked having the Harvard kids, the future generation," Morse said. "That meant a lot to him. And those kids could walk home. They could have their beer or three and get wasted, and they wouldn't have to drive home. They'd dance and party at his place, then walk home and not risk accidents."

The club was equally handy to black youths who lived in Riverside — the club's own neighborhood — and Cambridgeport, the adjacent neighborhood further south.

The club's welcoming ambience was an irresistible gravity. "I would review a rock show at a fancy Boston club like the Paradise," Morse said. "And I'd go across the river [into Cambridge] to wind down at the Western Front."

The Western Front was so comfortable to Morse that he took Nell, his future wife, there on their first date in the early 1980s.

Despite his job, Morse says that Marvin did not treat him differently than other guests. "I would only write about the place every few years,"

Morse said. "He treated me like everyone else, and *that* made me feel good. He treated everyone like a VIP. He was a life-affirming, very spiritual fellow, who just wanted everyone to get along. He just exuded that spirit of unity. *That* made the place special."

Fun-House Layout

The club also had a distinct physical personality. Its floor plan looked like it had been laid out by a group of squabbling architects. Some adjacent spaces did not flow gracefully into each other. But that's exactly why it was as much fun as an amusement-park fun house to its youthful patrons. It was as awkward as a teenager. It made you grimace, then laugh.

"The club was architecturally a mess," Morse said. "You'd walk in and there was that weird bar by the front door. There was a narrow little walkway by the bar, then you had to go up these stairs that let you off right in front of the stage. Whoever designed the club must have been out to lunch. You'd come out literally in front of the stage. The club was divided by the stairs. On one side was the bar. On the other side were some seats. Instead of the stairs being at the back or side of the club, they were in the middle. You'd come up the stairs and feel embarrassed. Everyone would be looking at you."

Still, the design quirks had some advantages. Many performers liked their proximity to the audience. "This is the type of club that provides an easy to reach audience," singer-songwriter Bruce Gray told the *Sporting Life* newspaper. "We are right up next to them. There is a great need for more clubs where people can be close to the musicians."[255]

Those and other idiosyncrasies helped make the Front lovable. As the Front carved out a niche for itself as metro area's go-to club for reggae, it reinforced that reputation by serving food that was equally reminiscent of Bob Marley's native isle.

"They had a Jamaican guy for a cook," Morse said. "He served wonderful Jamaican recipes almost right up until closing time. Most clubs shut their kitchens two or three hours before closing. This guy's pots would still be steaming, cooking up a storm. My wife and I would stop in and have a little jerked chicken. He was a phenomenal cook. The club had an ambience of authentic Jamaican cuisine that was very inexpensive. I never spent more than $5 for a plate.

"It was very cheap. Nobody ever got ripped off. The beer prices were very reasonable. Cover charges were reasonable. It was a friendly place to go. Plus, there was the whole sophisticated spirit of being biracial, cross-pollinating. There was the whole flavor of the place. You really wanted to go there."

No Fanfare

Marvin ran the club in a relatively low-key fashion. "In 1998 I wrote about the club's 30th anniversary," Morse said. "Most club owners use any anniversary to promote themselves through the roof. Not Marvin. He did it without fanfare, which I thought was remarkable. But that's Marvin. He enjoyed attracting an audience through word-of-mouth rather than having a big publicity firm promoting him. He never went in for anything that appeared condescending or snotty. He kept it simple."

That approach cost him some business, Morse says. "He was never a critics' darling. He never had the press that the Middle East [Restaurant and Night Club] or T.T. the Bear's [Place] had, clubs that were promotional minded. Marvin's was never the chic club. It provided good music, an informal, friendly, unpretentious time. If you wanted to be seen, trendy, and fashionable, you went somewhere else."

Sometimes Marvin combined business with sentimentality. When bluesman Little Joe Cook became available because of a falling out over money with Cambridge's Cantab Lounge, Marvin leaped at the chance to sign the popular entertainer. Cook had played at the Cantab for decades. "When I read about it I was really taken aback," Marvin told the *Globe's* Jim Sullivan. "I took a ride out to his home. He felt very bad how his relationship [with the Cantab] had deteriorated and he wanted to go on. There were tears in his eyes. Being a club owner and him being legendary, I can't see him be put out on the street."[256]

As a one-time musician, Marvin often identified with artists he signed, and he preferred a personal approach. "He never had written contracts," Morse said. "It was always word-of-mouth deals with musicians. That shows he was old-school. That was a very unusual, larger-than-life personality way of doing business. You treat him right, he'd treat you right. You give him your word, he'd give you his."

That jibed with Marvin's preference for signing acts personally. "We deal with each other's word," he once told Morse. "It's a lot better to talk to the bands personally, rather than through agents, because that way you find out who they are."[257]

Changing Fashions

The club typically showcased different styles of music each night. The biggest draws were featured on Friday and Saturdays. A June week in 2002, for example, saw jazz playing on Wednesday, bluesman Little Joe Cook on Thursday, reggae on Friday, and Latin on Saturday.[258] The club's musical menu would shift over time, keeping in step with its patrons' preferences and Marvin's vision. Sometimes a disc jockey would hold court on Sunday nights.

Reggae was the top draw – Saturday's headliner – from the early 1980s through the late 1990s.

Still, before he went all-in with the genre, Marvin had misgivings. "I was frightened by reggae at first," he told the *Globe* in 1985. "Reggae seemed like a bunch of war cries with frightful politics, but then I started to tune in to it more and saw its sense of love and peace. That was over three years ago. Since then we have come to live and breathe reggae here."[259]

Over the decades, Marvin hosted Jamaican bands such as Mutabaruka, Eek-a-Mouse, and J.C. Lodge, a London-born, Jamaica-raised singer, at the club. He also staged American-based reggae acts Blue Riddim, Black Sheep, and First Light, as well as local talent like the I-Tones, Loose Caboose, Magic & the Reggae Stars, Zion Initiation, Jah Spirit, Afrikan Roots, New Lions, and Cool Runnings.[260]

The night-club business had a dark side. After closing the club for the night, Marvin arrived home at 3 a.m. one cold, clear January morning in 1986. Two masked gunmen jumped him in his driveway. They pushed him to the ground and savagely beat and kicked him, breaking his right hand. They stole his wallet, watch, jewelry, and briefcase. They also grabbed his leather satchels, which held the night's cash from the club.

The thugs weren't done yet. They bulled Marvin into the trunk of his wife's Saab. Then one of them leveled a .357 magnum handgun at his chest, cocked the hammer, and pulled the trigger.

Click! The deadly weapon failed to fire. But Marvin's assailants locked him in the trunk and fled. Incredibly, despite this near-death experience, Marvin remained cool enough to kick his way out of the trunk and race into nearby Porter Square, where he rushed up to police. Against all odds, police in neighboring Somerville spotted the fleeing felons and caught them after a wild car chase.

"This is not TV," said Audrey Parr, the assistant district attorney whose prosecution put the robbers behind bars. "It's not glamorous. When you have a gun pointed in your face, what it is is traumatic.... When a person puts a gun to your head and says he'll blow your brains out, it takes a very strong person to survive that,...and that's what Marvin did.... Marvin kept his cool, and I don't know that most people could have."[261]

The Front's blues offerings included James Montgomery, Ellis Hall, and Duke & the Drivers. Webster Lewis, a jazz, soul, and disco keyboardist who also play clarinet, was a multi-genre performer at the Front.[262]

Marvin's personal favorite was jazz. The Front's lineup over the years featured more local names and fewer national names than some local competitors.[263] But Marvin occasionally brought in eye-popping giants like Duke Ellington and Louis Armstrong.

He even had the great pleasure of seeing his sons David and Marque, on their respective visits to Boston from out of town, perform from time to time with various noted jazz bands and artists. And of course Marvin would hop on stage to jam.

Hip-hop artists played an ever larger role at the Front in its final decade and a half. With that style, the club's vibe changed. "Reggae lost its appeal," Morse said. "A lot of bands broke up or moved out of town. Marvin had to book more hip-hop on weekends. That can be stressful. It has a rougher crowd than the love-and-peace reggae crowd."

Citing a desire to devote more of his time and energy to family and friends, Marvin closed the club at the end of 2013. After a run of nearly half a century, all fell quiet at the Western Front.

Marvin says he enjoyed almost everything about running the club. He loved the opportunity to get involved again in the world of professional music. He loved the musicians. He loved meeting the challenge of running a business.

The attitude of the city and many of its officials, though, was something else. "They did not want a black man to succeed," Marvin said. "I don't think they liked the fact that it was a black and white club. And they tried to blame me for everything in the neighborhood, even though it was there long before I was. I'll tell you, I ran the club with an iron fist to make sure none of that stuff [drugs, betting, and prostitution] got inside my club. I went to court, and [the city's] case lost because I wasn't doing *anything* [wrong] in the club. None of that stuff [that authorities claimed] was true."

For Marvin, the saddest part was that the racial discrimination he had fought his whole life in so many places was also right there in his home town.

Still, over the years many of the people who had obstructed Marvin were replaced, retiring from their municipal jobs or otherwise departing, not to correct bigoted behavior toward Marvin, but simply taken out with the tide of time.

In their wake, at least some newer and younger officials treated Marvin differently. In 2004 the city honored Marvin by naming the street intersection outside his club "Marvin E. Gilmore Square." In turn, Marvin paid tribute to the woman who had given him a solid foundation in life. The Marvin E. Gilmore Square street sign is inscribed, "In honor of my mother Lee Augusta Gilmore."

"Mayor" Gilmore

Marvin interacted with Cambridge officialdom in many more capacities than as a club owner and liquor license holder. Governors had appointed him to several state commissions grappling with housing discrimination and with strategies for making it easier for poor people to obtain housing. And from 1966-1972 Marvin was a member of the Civic Unity Advisory Committee for the City of Cambridge.

Marvin was no stranger around city hall. He had his conflicts with city authorities. But those did not prevent him from fighting his fights, battling for his own business interests and for the betterment of other people.

"Marvin is the 'mayor of Cambridge,'" said Charles J. Ogletree, Jr., a professor at Harvard Law School as well as founder and Executive Director of the Charles Hamilton Houston Institute for Race and Justice, who has known Marvin since the 1970s.[264] "He may not have that title officially, but he is called that because he knows everything about the city, he goes everywhere, is resilient, is part of any movement to enact meaningful change in this city. Who else can describe what Cambridge was like in 1940 from first-hand experience and is still around and can talk about it like it was yesterday?

"Marvin has been an enormous force in Cambridge, if you're talking about affordable housing, jobs, public safety. No one has been as well-known or well-versed or involved in the Cambridge community as he's been. You can see that by the people who can't afford rent because they're working on a job that only pays so much an hour, he has put thousands of people into homes. I've seen children stay in school because their families got a home – they were raised from a young age to young adults – That's what Marvin's important work has been.

"People like Ken Reeves and Denise Simmons [both former mayors of Cambridge], who serve on the city council – Marvin is somebody that everyone wants on their side. He can bring in money, votes, young people looking for jobs, and councilors admire and appreciate that.

"Look at the city council. Whether a member is white or black, gay or straight, it doesn't matter. They all want Marvin on their side. Everyone knows him, everyone wants his vote.

"Those things will be part of his legacy.... We all benefit from it and learn a lot from it and from him. His legacy of opening doors for others, of going to bat for others, is a legacy he can turn over to the next generation of leaders in this city and to leaders far beyond that in time."

Chapter 12

Community Leader

By the early 1970s, Marvin had become a perpetual motion machine.

In a typical day he combined work for state and city boards wrestling with weighty issues of housing for the poor, block busting, and racial harmony. He also tackled tasks for the Boston branch of the NAACP. He performed his duties as vice chairman of the board of directors of Unity Bank & Trust. He was director of business development and marketing of the bank. In addition, he had his real estate business to run, a full-time obligation.

Overseeing the Western Front was another full-time responsibility. A magazine profile showed how Marvin juggled all of these responsibilities.[265] The profile appeared some years later, but generally Marvin's daily routine had not changed. With the writer shadowing him, Marvin's day began as usual at 4 a.m. after three hours sleep. Tasks related to his businesses and public-service and racial justice groups consumed his morning and early afternoon. The Front grabbed hold of his schedule the rest of the day and wouldn't let go.

Throughout the day, Marvin was a one-man band – banker, property investor and manager, civic activist, club impresario. In his red Jaguar sports XJ6, he crisscrossed Cambridge and Boston, attending meetings, talking with business associates, pow-wowing with politicians.

The pace only quickened as the day advanced, leaving Marvin less and less time to square away preparations for that night's show at the Front. He returned a phone call to the jazz recordings buyer for the Boston store of Towers Records, then a huge national retail chain, to negotiate a promotional arrangement for pianist Cecil Taylor, who was performing that night. He drove across the city to a former shoe factory that he had helped redevelop into professional office condominiums and an incubator for new start-up businesses. He drove back across town to his night club, where he supervised the delivery of a piano through a wide upstairs back door, keeping a nervous eye on the instrument as it swung through the sky, tethered to the arm of a 50-ton crane.

He drove across the Charles River to a hotel to check in on Taylor, who would make magic with that piano. In his car again heading back across the river, Marvin made the first of several phone calls to his limousine service driver. Marvin didn't need a lift — he was fine transporting himself. It was Taylor he was concerned about. The driver was due to pick up Taylor shortly, but he wasn't waiting outside the hotel and he had not checked in with Marvin. Marvin suspected the driver and his paramour had slipped away to some love nest, which meant Taylor would need alternative conveyance. One more task piled onto Marvin. But first he was back at his club, 40 minutes before Taylor's first set was scheduled to begin at 8 p.m. He hopped on stage and fingered a brief melody to hear for himself if the piano had survived its airlift into the club.

Then Marvin ran back to his Jaguar and hustled downtown to the Back Bay Sheraton to make an appearance at a dinner board meeting of the Metropolitan Area Planning Council, a regional agency focused largely on economic development, housing, transportation, public safety, and safeguarding natural resources. When he was done with that, he hurriedly returned to the Front. He bounced upstairs, where he took a seat at the end of the bar. From there, he enjoyed Taylor's music and oversaw his club. When "Shirt," lead singer of the I-Tones, a popular reggae band that often plays the club, walked by, the men exchanged warm greetings.

During a break between sets, Marvin huddled with some of his staff, then took a phone call. The call was from a local politician, inviting him to a meeting — *right now* — at the Middle East Restaurant in nearby Central Square. So once again Marvin hopped into his car, keyed the engine to life, and drove to a back-room rendezvous. The sit-down was with Mel King, who was a longtime activist, one-time Boston mayoral candidate, and then instructor in MIT's urban studies program. Marvin and King were not on the best of terms, having drifted apart over some philosophical differences, but on this night King was offering to bury the hatchet if Marvin would run a fundraiser for him at the Western Front.

Marvin returned to his club a little after one in the morning, shortly after the end of Taylor's second set, as smiling patrons were reluctantly departing the Front for the night.

After a brief rest at home, Marvin would start the cycle again the next day. One key to being able to maintain this schedule was Marvin's ability to get by on just three or four hours sleep a night. "I've always been able to do that," he once said.

With small variations, Marvin generally had been following a similar daily schedule for years. From time to time, a new organization worked its way into Marvin's daily lineup. He always seemed to be adding more organizations than subtracting. His overflowing plate of activities was – and still is – a result of ceaseless networking. With each new organization that he joins, he becomes even more attractive to more suitors from additional corporations, charities, and civic boards.

In 1971, one such newcomer was the Roxbury Children's Service. Marvin became assistant executive director. "I was working at the bank. One night at a meeting with Roxbury Children's Services, they explained that they wanted a new building on Dale Street [in Boston]. I helped them get the building. Next thing I knew, they voted me in as second in command," Marvin said.

Marvin Joins the CDC of Boston

Two years later, the CDC was looking for an executive director. "My name came up in community discussions," Marvin said. "People knew me through Roxbury Children's Services and through the bank. The CDC interviewed me three times. The third time I said I'm willing to take this, but I want full control. If you can't give me that, you shouldn't hire me."

The CDC had been born not long before that. It was created in 1969 as part of the federal Model Cities Program. Overseen by the federal Department of Housing and Urban Development, the Model Cities initiative was part of campaign to reverse the deterioration of inner-city businesses and neighborhoods. Its goal was to save jobs, which would save neighborhoods.

Boston's CDC was the economic development arm of Boston's Model Cities Program. But the CDC was in big trouble by the time the organization was interviewing Marvin for its presidency. President Richard Nixon was in the process of dismantling the Model Cities Program. Nixon, a fiscal conservative, saw the Program as an expensive and wasteful boondoggle that was not producing its intended results.

Resistance to ending the program came from bureaucrats who didn't want to be cut off from Model Cities funding they were already receiving.[266] But many big-city politicians, whether they were liberals or conservatives, quickly grasped that Nixon was aiming to change how money was spent for urban community development, not end it. And, more important to local officials, Nixon's reforms would give them more control over those federal dollars.[267] So an army of local politicians nationwide supported pulling the plug on Model Cities.

By 1973 the directors of the Boston CDC knew that the end was near for the program that had given birth to their organization. That year Nixon began a moratorium on funding for Model Cities and related federal programs. The following year congress would axe the Model Cities Program outright.[268] What the CDC trustees did not know for sure in 1973 was what the future held. How could they pursue their mission of helping Boston's inner city? Yes, they could see that there would still be federal dollars for community development. But they lacked a crystal ball that could show how their organization might avail itself of new funding. They had no roadmap. No one did.

So at this moment when they were seeking a new chief executive, they asked candidates to explain how they would operate. Interviews would last for several months.

"As part of the interview process, the CDC wanted to know where I would take the CDC," Marvin said. "They wanted me to talk with neighborhood boards [which the CDC was obligated to consult]. And they wanted to know if I would take care of their friends. I told them I would talk with the neighborhood boards, which I did. I told them the CDC would help them, not hurt them, if I became president. And I told the CDC I would stop people from draining its blood. I demanded the freedom to do what needed to be done. And one of the important things I asked them was this. I asked the board if they would authorize me to keep the CDC charter, which authorized its continued existence even if its parent program, the Model Cities Program, died or was closed. And I could see that Nixon was going to do that."

The way this CDC was set up, the decision to let the CDC stay in existence would also be up to the mayor of Boston.

Marvin felt his appearance before the neighborhood board – a consultative body required by the Model Cities Program – went well. A week after his third interview with the CDC itself, Marvin was offered the CDC post, which at that time was titled general manager.[269]

"I fired most of the staff," he said. Now Marvin had to figure out what the CDC could do next.

A New Direction for the CDC

Marvin studied other CDCs, to see what lessons he could learn. He looked at other regional CDCs. And after retaining a knowledgeable consultant named Andrew Bennett, he visited CDCs across the country. "I looked at a CDC in Watts [a black neighborhood in Los Angeles], and I went to Chicago," Marvin said. "I saw that Mayor [Richard] Daley in Chicago had authorized their CDC to set up an industrial park. I asked him if he thought I could develop an industrial park in Boston. He said yes, but you'd have to deal with the politics."

After studying CDCs first-hand for a month, Marvin returned to Boston. Marvin began to oversee the Boston CDC's reorganization as an independent nonprofit economic development organization. Its focus shifted from making investments in local businesses – basically, giving loans to small businesses – to a broader, longer-range economic development strategy, one with an eye to creating an industrial park to spark job creation and business development in Roxbury, Boston's minority neighborhood.

Marvin even knew where this miracle should occur. A huge swath of barren land cut like a knife through the heart of Lower Roxbury, in an area stretching northwesterly roughly from today's Massachusetts Avenue exit off the Southeast Expressway to the Penn Central railroad right of way north of Tremont Street, near Ruggles Street. At its greatest expanse, this waste land would encompass nearly 200 acres.[270]

This open expanse was the corpse of the Southwest Corridor, land taken from largely African-American homes, businesses, and work places to build a highway to ease commuting into the city for suburbanites. But that highway plan had been killed in 1972 as a result of community opposition, in which Marvin had played a key role. What had not been flattened by planned demolition for the highway project had fallen into ruin when banks refused to invest in this no-man's land. Fires had added to the desolation.[271] Now Marvin saw a way to use that land so that it again played a nurturing role in this minority community. The CDC would help develop it as an industrial park, hosting businesses that provided jobs to local blacks.

"You've got to have uptown as well as downtown in the city," Marvin told the *Boston Globe* years later. "There used to be an uptown here, but it was destroyed. Now it's being recreated."[272]

Eventually, this development would be called CrossTown Industrial Park.

But, just as Chicago's Mayor Daley had forewarned, Marvin had to find a way to persuade Boston's key politician, its mayor, to buy in. But how?

Marvin's attempts to pitch city of Boston planning agencies on helping the CDC lure manufacturing jobs to the city went nowhere. Manufacturing employment in Boston had plummeted in recent decades. City planners were convinced that the service economy was the city's best hope for the future. Marvin's vision, they thought, was a pipedream. An official of the Boston Redevelopment Authority told a panel meeting at Massachusetts Institute of Technology, "If you ever get any industry in there, I'll eat my shirt."[273]

Desperate for money to pay its own bills and small staff, pay for planning and feasibility studies, and to cover the costs of reaching out to potential tenants of any industrial park, Marvin scrambled for support.

A small foundation in Boston gave the CDC a small grant. "It was just enough to pay the secretaries," Marvin said. "I foregoed my own salary."

Nearly at the last moment, the Ford Foundation provided a $100,000 grant.

Still, those were mere stopgap measures. Marvin went to Washington, D.C., and won a $104,000 technical assistance grant from the Department of Commerce's Economic Development Administration. But it came with a slipper string attached. The CDC had to persuade the city of Boston to match that money with a Community Development Block Grant.

The trouble was that Marvin could not get an audience with Boston Mayor Kevin White.

Marvin felt like a knight on horseback eager for a meeting with a mighty king, only to find himself locked outside the castle walls, barred from the inner court. "I tried for days to make an appointment," Marvin said. "But he wouldn't see me."

"I began to consider how to approach Mayor White," Marvin said. "What was his Achilles heel?"

Marvin finally hit on the idea of recruiting a key ally. "Kevin White's Achilles heel turned out to be Melnea Cass, the 'First Lady of Roxbury,'" Marvin said.

Melnea Cass was a civil rights dynamo. She was a tireless campaigner for better educational and economic opportunities for African-Americans in Boston. She was everywhere, working every which way. She joined well-known organizations such as the National Association for the Advancement of Colored People (NAACP). She founded several groups serving black working mothers. She helped unionize black railroad porters. She worked to assure Social Security and other benefits for black domestic workers. She helped black women register to vote and cast their first ballots after women received the franchise in 1920. She was a founder of Freedom House, a nonprofit advocacy organization for African-Americans in Boston. As her impact grew, so did her renown. She became an icon of Boston's black community. In 1950 she was the only woman appointed by Boston Mayor John Hynes as a charter member of the anti-poverty agency Action for Boston Community Development (ABCD). In 1966 the governor declared May 22 Melnea Cass Day to honor her on her 70th birthday and many years of volunteerism. More than 2,000 helped her celebrate.[274]

Best of all for Marvin, he knew Mrs. Cass from her service to the NAACP. She had been president of the Boston branch from 1962 to 1964, not that many years prior to Marvin's appointment as general manager of the CDC. He contacted her.

"Kevin [White] loved her," Marvin said. "I told Mrs. Cass what I wanted to do. She loved it. She said she would help by arranging a meeting with the mayor.

"We met White in the mayor's office. Mrs. Cass told the mayor she wanted him to do something for her boy – me – who was there to help poor citizens. So White agreed to let me keep the [charter]. He was looking for some cover anyway, because the Feds had started investigating White's use of Model Cities money."

White also agreed to match the federal Economic Development Administration funds.

Marvin still faced the arduous task of persuading potential tenants to sign on. He was trying to create something out of nothing, filling vacant lots with real businesses that would employ inner-city residents. But his pitches to corporations had to overcome the off-putting fact that the city, not Marvin's CDC, owned the land that Marvin was proposing as new business sites. The city also controlled the review and approval processes. Furthermore, even after Mayor White himself agreed to support Marvin's vision, that did not change individual city planners' skepticism about luring manufacturing to the city. It remained hard for Marvin to get troops in the planning trenches to contribute needed work.[275]

But Marvin was a man with only one gear – forward. He had bled for his country during the charge into Germany. He had defied crackers in the Army. Unarmed, he had stared down gun-toting racists in Jackson, Mississippi. He was not about to abandon this campaign for Roxbury.

Landing a Technology Giant
Still, there was no denying how difficult the goal was. Like the mythological hero Hercules grappling with his epic tasks, Marvin faced a seemingly impossible set of challenges in his campaign to solve the CDC's riddle. He had enlisted the aid of Melnea Cass, secured a green light from Mayor White, and won grants from the Ford Foundation and Economic Development Administration as well as a Community Development Block Grant.

But time was running out. It was already 1976. He needed to complete a development that would generate jobs for Boston's blacks as well as provide the CDC with an ongoing source of income so it could focus on its mission, not just on survival.

Marvin kept knocking on doors. One of those belonged to Digital Equipment Corporation. Also known as DEC and Digital, in the 1970s the fortunes of the Maynard, Massachusetts-based manufacturer of minicomputers were skyrocketing. It was becoming a giant in the computer industry.[276] At its peak in 1988, Digital would have a then-colossal $11.5 billion in annual revenues and a huge market capitalization, making it the second largest computer company in the world, trailing only International Business Machines.[277]

In 1976, as Marvin tried to blaze a new life path for the CDC, Digital was still expanding and the company was on the lookout for advantageous manufacturing sites. Marvin was offering that very thing: a new low-cost factory site. In addition, he was offering a location in the city of Boston, near a large pool of motivated labor, which was also close to the education centers of Boston and Cambridge. Universities like Harvard and MIT produced valuable research as well as fresh yearly crops of skilled young technical talent. It was a natural marriage. But that alone could not assure that a wedding would take place.

In fact Marvin's efforts to seal the deal with Digital were not succeeding. Digital president Kenneth Olsen as always had many irons in the fire. Why focus on this particular one? The last time a similar opportunity had come up, just a few years earlier, he had found many of Boston's black leaders more interested in demonizing corporations than in landing jobs for their community. He had found no such hostility in a far-more-welcoming Springfield, Massachusetts, so that's where Digital had opened its first inner-city plant anywhere, in 1972. By the time Marvin was trying to persuade Olsen that Roxbury was ready too, Digital employed 800 to 900 mostly black and Puerto Rican workers in Springfield.[278]

There were additional reasons that Olsen was proving to be a hard sell. For one, there was the complexity of the deal. The CDC did not own the land that Marvin had dangled like bait in front of this biggest of corporate fish. The Economic Development and Industrial Corp., then Boston's lead hands-on economic development arm, owned most of the land (the state owned some parcels[279]), had power of eminent domain to take and assemble parcels, and was empowered to borrow money through revenue bonds.[280] As a result of the deal with Boston that Marvin had arranged, leveraging the respect that Mayor White had for Melnea Cass, the EDIC had leased the land to the CDC. Marvin and the CDC would do all of the heavy lifting, trying to create development deals. They would have the satisfaction of any successes. Mayor White could take the political credit since his EDIC owned the land.

But what assurance did Olsen have that Marvin could make this happen? Where was his clout? In the face of so many doubts, it was imperative for Olsen like any top executive to concentrate on other Digital business, opportunities that had valuable prospects of reaching fruition.

Marvin knew he was at an impasse. The question was how to break this logjam?

Marvin turned to a friend he had made a decade earlier, Mike Dukakis. Back in the Sixties, Dukakis had been the state rep from the affluent, almost entirely white Boston suburb of Brookline. They had spent hours together in automobiles, crossing the state, exchanging ideas about how to provide housing to the poor, housing that would not turn into Dickensian slums. Marvin had earned the respect of the young state representative. And now that young public servant was Governor of the Commonwealth. Time for another phone call.

Marvin called Dukakis, explained the situation, and asked for the governor's aid. Understanding the potential reward for Boston and for the men and women who could end up as Digital employees, Dukakis contacted Olsen and advocated on behalf of the industrial development project in Roxbury.

That answered some of Olsen's key questions. Marvin had clout. He had the contacts necessary to facilitate the development and other approvals Digital would need. Boston's mayoral administration was onboard. And Marvin was willing to spend valuable political capital to help bring Digital jobs to Roxbury.

Olsen gave the go-ahead. When he decided the project made sense for his company, a special coordinating team under the Boston Redevelopment Authority's deputy director for development Stewart Forbes was assembled to line up the city's ducks and to provide a single key contact city planning, zoning, and regulatory issues.[281]

Forbes told the *Boston Globe,* "Marvin had trouble because he was promoting something over which he did not have complete control. There were inherent tensions in the roles different parties had to play."[282]

But those tensions and myriad challenges were resolved. Ground was broken on September 26, 1978, and in 1980 Digital opened its 62,000-square-foot computer keyboard assembly factory. Officially, the CDC and the Economic Development and Industrial Corporation, were co-developers.

When it opened, the keyboard plant employed 300 people. Nearly 70% lived within seven miles of the facility. Over 50% of the plant's employees were minorities. The facility's general contractor, John B. Cruz Construction, was minority owned. So was the architectural design firm, Stull & Lee. Digital was the first major occupant of CrossTown Industrial Park.

Kenneth Olsen, who was famous for avoiding the limelight and staying out of politics, described the Boston black community's new open-arms attitude as a "miracle."[283] Marvin was the mastermind behind that new stance. At the factory's opening ceremony, Marvin told a crowd of dignitaries including the governor and mayor, "I wore out four sets of tires going back and forth and around town."

Years later Marvin said, "For our goal of encouraging hiring from within the black community, that was Mission Accomplished," Marvin said.

CrossTown's Evolution

Digital's decision to build a factory served as a giant advertisement for CrossTown Industrial Park, which was the CDC's pet project. Less than a year after Digital broke ground, medical and dental supply manufacturer Healthco agreed to build a 166,000-square-foot building – more than two and a half times bigger than the Digital plant – in the Park.[284] The facility would provide jobs to 330 people.[285]

That deal did not come to fruition, but it showed how attractive CrossTown had become.

Nearby, after trying to find someone interested in developing the old Baltimore Brush Building at 801 Albany Street, directly across the street from the Digital site, the CDC itself bought the 50,000-square-foot paintbrush factory in 1984. In the early 1900s the site had been a horse-carriage factory. The locale had also housed Hurley's Log Cabin, one of Boston's most famous saloons. It was a match made in whip-and-buggy heaven. *Industry* magazine reported, "For many years the Log Cabin provided the local workers with live entertainment and cold draft beer after those long hours at the factory."[286]

The purchase price was a modest $60,000. Still, the CDC was unable to secure a conventional bank loan for the acquisition because Boston's downtown banks largely ignored Roxbury.

Marvin's mother helped out. Lee Augusta Gilmore, who always scrimped to save pennies and nickels and dimes, reached into her purse and wrote a check for $65,000.

"She loaned that money to us because no bank in Boston would lend money for a vacant building to a nonprofit in a black neighborhood," Marvin said. Lee Augusta proved to be a shrewder judge of the CDC's prospects than the banks with their professional analysts. "She was right. The banks were wrong," Marvin said. "We repaid her in about a year."

When the CDC began to renovate the two factory buildings, the activity caught the eyes of nearby Boston University School of Medicine. Needing more space for its biomedical research, B.U. partnered with the CDC to plan and create a biotechnology facility at 801 Albany Street. B.U. occupied 90% of the structure on a lease than ran until 2014. CDC took the remainder of the address for its corporate offices.[287]

In the years that followed, Boston University developed other nearby parcels.[288] While those improvements were not part of CrossTown Industrial Park, they were part of the fulfillment of Marvin's dream. His vision, his goal, was that CrossTown would be a magnet for additional investments in and around the Southwest Corridor from entrepreneurs, businesses, and other organizations, boosting property values and creating jobs there and nearby.

That's exactly what happened, and it happened repeatedly. Two years before the renovated 801 Albany Street opened in 1989, Morgan Memorial Goodwill Industries opened a 104,000-square-foot headquarters in the Park itself. Morgan Memorial is a nonprofit that provides job training and placement services to people with disabilities. The charity's multi-use facility included office, industrial, and retail space. The building was developed by the CDC and the EDIC. "The facility now provides training and work programs for individuals with disabilities, programs that promote self-reliance for youth, and a recycled goods program," the CDC reports.

Morgan Memorial's new quarters enabled the charity to operate more effectively. One of the charity's key tasks is to teach job skills.

Marvin's efforts to spur economic advancement for the black community sometimes have paid dividends at the individual level too. His collaboration with Morgan Memorial, he says, helped lead to the appointment in 1989 of Deborah Jackson as the first black president and CEO of the Boston organization or any of its 165 independent sister affiliates in the U.S. and Canada. (Jackson is now president of Cambridge College.)

Jackson was not privy to Marvin's efforts on her behalf. "But I heard second-hand that he was an advocate and excited about my candidacy," Jackson said. "And I know what my appointment signaled about diversity."[289]

And Jackson says she is certainly not the only African-American to benefit from Marvin's support. "As our city of Boston has become more progressive and diverse in some ways, we should never lose sight of people who broke ground for all of us.... Marvin is in that group.... He is in a special, small group of mentors, advocates, and community leaders. And he did this while leading a nonprofit, the CDC, while he was also running private businesses. He is an amazing role model, and an amazing entrepreneur."

801 Albany Street was also the site of Boston University and biopharmaceutical company research, much of which sought cures or treatments for diseases that ail African-Americans, such as sickle cell anemia and thalassemia, two blood disorders. B.U. School of Dental Medicine faculty did research there on restorative dental materials. NitroMed developed a drug there in the 1990s for treatment of congestive heart failure in blacks. The address has also been home to and an incubator for a number of biopharma and biotech start-up companies that sought cutting-edge treatments.[290]

"The really key aspect, and it cannot be understated, is that Marvin has been a community partner," said William Gasper, who was associate vice president for financial and business affairs of Boston University medical campus. Gasper was the university's point person for its tenancy at 801 Albany Street. He added, "Boston University as an institution is here for the long haul. We've been in [Boston's] South End as a medical school and medical campus since the 1800s. So we've been here well over 150 years. We'll be here for the next 150 years. We'll be here 300 years from now.

"Our approach can often be long-term. What's been interesting working with Marvin – look at the name of the company. It is Community Development Corporation, and it is nonprofit. It's been focused on what's good for this area. How can we make jobs? How can we make this area better?

"Ours is not just a tenant-landlord relationship. We have been partners in this never-ending effort to improve our community, improve where we work, where we study, where people live.

"And B.U. and Marvin and the CDC have often joined together, whether on small or large initiatives, in support of one another in activities or initiatives that support or improve our community."[291]

As examples, Gasper cited a number of infrastructure projects in the area. Those may sound prosaic. But in the real world they are essential. Without the right underground wiring and plumbing and above-ground street work, no developer will invest in new research labs, offices, hotels, dormitories, apartments, factories, and so on. And infrastructure does not build itself. Some gets rejected. Infrastructure that gets built has survived a brutal gauntlet of public and political review. It often happens only after respected community figures – like Marvin and like Gasper – weigh-in and ask public authorities to greenlight the work.

Gasper also cited Marvin's support for additional developments, such as CrossTown Center, a hotel-office-parking garage complex which, among other things, makes it easier for people to visit and use Boston University's medical facilities. And he cited Marvin's support for the new Albany Fellows complex that provides housing for B.U. Medical School graduate students.[292]

Gasper's point is that those and other developments would not be possible – or would be many years in the future – if Marvin had not built a foundation for improvements in the CrossTown area, starting back in the 1970s.

Gasper said, "The immediate area is undergoing a renaissance, and Marvin has been there since the beginning."

Planting Seeds

Of course, in the real world not all businesses survive and thrive. In CrossTown Industrial Park, businesses have come and gone. After flying high, Digital is no more. Its site and adjacent property have since become redeveloped as CrossTown Center, which includes Boston's first majority black-owned national-chain hotel – possibly its first black-owned hotel, period.[293] CrossTown Center also features a parking garage, retail space, and two office complexes whose tenants include a variety of hospital and medical professionals.[294]

In that too, the CDC – and Marvin – succeeded.

The CDC has also been an ally of the Newmarket Business Association, encouraging redevelopment in the Newmarket Industrial District, an industrial zone just southeast of the Southwest Corridor. "The CDC took dilapidated Newmarket buildings and turned them into textbook examples of urban revitalization," Marvin said.

The CDC reach has even been felt in Cambridge, Marvin's hometown to this day. Through the Cambridge Enterprise Collaborative, a nonprofit run by Marvin, the CDC became the developer of the Cambridge Business Center. Once up and running, the Center provided office and incubator space at 432 Columbia Street. Before its renovation, the site had been the Hyde Athletic Shoe Building. The Collaborative purchased the old sneaker factory with a $1 million grant from the U.S. Department of Human Services.

"We did it with major support from Tip O'Neill," Marvin said, tipping his hat to Thomas P. O'Neill, Jr., the powerful Cambridge-born congressman who represented his home town's district a breathtaking 34 years, from January 3, 1953 until January 3, 1987, and served as Speaker of the U.S. House of Representatives in the ninety-fifth through ninety-nine congresses.[295] "He orchestrated it. He did it for me."

The CDC of Boston also helps small businesses and start-up companies gain access to capital and business services they need to grow. The CDC of Boston does that by working with other community development corporations through the Community Business Network (CBN). The CBN also helps small businesses network with each other, form working relationships among themselves, and create partnerships with the overall business community.

The CDC of Boston has also conducted informational exchanges with businesses and developers in Canada, China, and South Africa. "We've been through a lot of the processes that those foreign organizations are encountering for the first time," Marvin said. "We can explain how we've learned to work with private businesses and government bodies to promote economic growth. These are lessons they can adapt for use back in their own homes."

Replacing the Southwest Corridor
On August 11, 1978, a hot summer Friday, U.S. Senator Edward W. Brooke – who in 1966 became the first African-American elected to the Senate since Reconstruction and the first ever elected by the direct ballot of a state's voters[296] – stood near an immense granite block wall along Columbus Avenue in Boston's largely black Roxbury. Painted on that wall behind Brooke, giant graffiti block letters shouted, "STOP I-95."[297]

The graffiti's anonymous artist could rest easily. The battle was won. Federal interstate highway 95, known locally as the Southwest Corridor, had been stopped, choked to death by a constrictor python of public opposition and waning political support. And now, in that unwanted eight-lane road's place, a huge new development was taking shape.

Instead of a single-purpose highway ramming its way through the community and ignoring the neighborhood's needs, a multidimensional concept was taking shape that would bring jobs to the area and provide mass transit to other jobs, services, and recreation nearby. This replacement project would include improved new housing, a community college, park-like outdoor public space, and a new local road. Before all was done, the undertaking would also lead to antidiscrimination changes in state and city of Boston minority hiring rules for construction projects.

And groundbreaking for the new Digital Equipment Corporation plant, part of the Crosstown Industrial Park that was a key segment of the Southwest Corridor, was just weeks away.

"It's a great day for the community," said Senator Brooke. Standing nearby were a host of public figures, including Brock Adams, U.S. Secretary of Transportation since January 23, 1997, who had come to Boston to deliver the first $44.6 million installment for the $607 million project. The federal share of that budget, $486 million, was the largest single award in the Department of Transportation's history.[298]

The mass transit and rail aspects alone were huge. The project would relocate the Orange Line of the Massachusetts Bay Transportation Authority's (MBTA) subway system to the Amtrak (successor to the Penn Central) right-of-way. It would hide the new part of the Orange Line below street level, and it would eliminate the old southwesterly portion of the Orange Line, which was elevated on steel stilts, straddling Boston's Washington Street. The elevated structure had deteriorated into an aged eyesore, which cast a baleful shadow on the street, sidewalk, businesses, and pedestrians below it. Old rail embankments – such as the stone one behind Brooke, Adams, and the other gathered dignitaries – that had become barriers between the black and white communities, reminiscent of walls imprisoning residents of an old-world Jewish ghetto, would be torn down. Nine new transit stations would be built here and elsewhere along the subway system. Three new railroad tracks would be introduced to the Amtrak right-of-way, for use by Amtrak and local commuter trains.

On this day that Senator Brooke led cheerleading along Columbus Avenue, an MBTA official said about 13,000 construction jobs would be created during the five years it was scheduled to take to build the subway and railroad portions of the new Southwest Corridor project, and that 2,500 permanent transportation jobs would follow.

It was a grand day indeed, and the public figures from Senator Brooke and Transportation Secretary Adams on down had every right to congratulate themselves. Savvy public servants one and all, every single one of the participants understood that the unprecedented, huge federal infusion of dollars was the grease that made all of the parts slip into place. Uncle Sam's checks made possible all of the benefits, including state funds, that were about to flow.

Marvin Gilmore, standing among the smiling celebrants, could take special pride. He had played a key role – perhaps *the* key role – in securing those federal dollars, even as he was hard at work persuading Digital Equipment to become the first tenant of CrossTown Industrial Park. Here's how it happened.

A Better Idea Emerges

Before CrossTown Industrial Park was born, the area was home to a living, breathing, largely African-American neighborhood. Unfortunately for its residents, businesses, and workers, it found itself in the crosshairs of an old-fashioned urban renewal project. Between 1966 and 1970 the Massachusetts Department of Public Works bulldozed the nearly 200-acre neighborhood flat to make room for the Southwest Expressway, an eight-lane, 10-mile, divided highway. That road would connect downtown Boston to Interstate Highway 95 in suburban Canton, Massachusetts.[299]

"Stop I-95" became the war cry of a United Nations of diverse people and groups from the neighborhood, elsewhere in Boston, and the suburbs as well as antihighway environmentalists, all of whom joined the battle to stop the Expressway, which became known as the Southwest Corridor.

Against mounting political opposition and skepticism about urban redevelopment projects that displaced poor people, Governor Francis Sargent declared a moratorium in 1970 on highway construction within Rte. 128, the state highway that loops around Greater Boston and is home to many technology companies among other types of businesses. After having a major regional transportation analysis done, Gov. Sargent killed the Southwest Corridor outright in 1972.

But severe damage had already been done. One thousand thirty-nine families, almost all in Boston, had been forced from their homes as 416 residences were destroyed along with 156 businesses. The federal government had spent $38 million just to acquire the land.[300]

And now the question was what would be done with this vital, large tract of urban land, strategically located close to downtown Boston and the Mission Hill, Back Bay, South End, Roxbury, and Dorchester neighborhoods? It was blessed with rail and mass transit links. It was adjacent to the crucial Southeast Expressway. It was not far from the Massachusetts Turnpike. Its next-door neighbors included Boston City Hospital and Boston University Medical Center Hospital.

The state formed the Southwest Corridor Land Development Coordinator's Office, headed by Anthony Pangaro, to guide planning and development. When local groups didn't like something that was being run up the proverbial flag pole, even the smallest group got a larger voice by virtue of being in the Southwest Corridor Land Development Coalition, an umbrella group formed by 50 community organizations to keep an eye on the tract and to provide grassroots feedback about development proposals.

But what to do with the Southwest Corridor was not entirely a mystery. Remember that regional transportation study ordered by Gov. Sargent? That study, the Boston Transportation Planning Review, concluded not only that the long-planned Southwest Expressway should not be built. It also concluded that the relocation of the Orange Line rapid transit branch should proceed, full speed ahead.[301] The old elevated subway line, which had thrown a dark frown onto Washington Street for a long time and had decayed into a rusting pigeon roost, would be torn down. Sunshine would be allowed to return to Washington Street, and the subway would be moved to a parallel route several blocks north as part of the sunken, out-of-sight railroad right-of-way.

Commuters coming and going to the relocated line's spanking new mass transit stations would spark urban renewal and redevelopment around each station, like grains of sand giving birth to pearls. "New stations typically become catalysts for renewal, attracting people who spend money in surrounding stores, restaurants, and retail establishments, invigorating nearby businesses," said Anthony Pangaro, now head of the Boston office of Millenium Partners-Boston, a major development firm, who in the mid-1970s was the Southwest Corridor project coordinator – basically the ringmaster of the show.[302]

And quite a show it was shaping up to be. It would include a new local arterial road, housing, and provisions for training youths in everything from construction to architecture. Marvin was hard at work trying to make a reality of the CrossTown Industrial Park. Before long, broad consensus had been reached among local residents and city and state planners. And a new worldview dominated the entire, sprawling enterprise. The old highway proposal had been guided by an old-fashioned, top-down model of decision-making. Planners acted as if they knew what was best for everyone else. But the new Southwest Corridor project embraced a consensus-building model. Decisions were not imposed on local residents and business people. Residents and business people were brought into the decision-making process.

But debate could not be allowed to drag on forever. At some point decisions did in fact have to be made, votes taken, and construction contracts drawn up. Then everyone had to move on to the next decision that needed to be made.

"It was a process with an incredible number of moving parts," Pangaro said. "We held hundreds of community meetings. For each transit station, we had to make decisions about design, functional details inside each station, elements on the street, a park plan. We had to do that for each of nine stations, over and over. So the permutations were extreme. And that process went on, even once construction began. We kept elaborate minutes of every meeting, and we mainlined them to everyone involved. It was important to keep the process moving, even when new people joined the process and old people left. That applied to public members and public officials, who changed all the time. So it was important that newcomers who joined the process late could not reopen issues that had already been settled."

Marvin, Pangaro says, played a crucial role in keeping the process moving.

"Marvin was good at saying to newcomers who wanted to rehash old issues that we already talked about that and settled it," Pangaro said.

"Marvin could be as passionate as anyone about his favorite details. But he was practical and fair. He did not let newcomers hijack the process."

Marvin was just as willing to tell a newcomer that the group had been there, done that, regarding some issue, whether the new person was a powerful public figure or a little-known resident of a nearby neighborhood.

"One pivot point was when Ed King beat Mike Dukakis in the Democratic primary at the end of the first Dukakis administration," Pangaro said. "King campaigned on a platform of building expressways, and everyone wondered whether he was going to come in and resurrect the old Southwest Corridor or something like it. But he stopped talking about that during the campaign. Marvin was one of the people who went to King's advisers and said forget that, at least here. You will roll back a lot of progress and economic potential and you will create turmoil by advocating for a return of that highway."

Breaking a Logjam

Even before helping to influence the new governor's stance on the Southwest Corridor, a major logjam had developed. The federal administrators whose interstate highway had been turned into political road kill refused to sign off, releasing their respective agencies' funds and rights to the turf. And why should they? They were Feds. They were in far-off Washington, D.C. They didn't care what the local public officials in Massachusetts were saying. And it began to seem as if no one would be able to change their minds.

Without their sign-offs, no alternative plan could move forward. Their obstinacy also bottled up federal funding for any alternative plan.

"On the federal level, there was a lot of bureaucratic inertia working against us," Pangaro said. "We had turned an approved plan on its head. Massachusetts had upset those bureaucrats, and they were powerful heads of federal agencies. They were used to getting their way. They didn't like being told, No."

It was a stalemate. The federal bigwigs ignored the Bay State delegation's pleas for action.

Even if Massachusetts somehow had succeeded in persuading just one of federal officials to collaborate, it would not have been enough, explains Frederick Salvucci, who was then state secretary of transportation in the Dukakis administration. "Tony Pangaro was in charge of the process on the Massachusetts end," Salvucci said. "He was having a substantial problem getting cooperation from the federal government because land in the Southwest Corridor came under three separate federal jurisdictions. One was the Federal Highway Administration because federal highway funds had been used to buy houses there and knock them down. This was Alice in Wonderland stuff. Even though those former residents were gone, that money gave the highway people a reason to be involved.

"Another jurisdiction was the Federal Highway *Commission*. The land had been taken to build a federal highway, and now we wanted to build something else, so we needed the permission of the Commission. And the Commission hated us for the major humiliation of stopping an interstate highway and proposing to substitute rail, which they also hated. So *they* stonewalled us.

"The third jurisdiction was the Urban Mass Transportation Administration, which is now the Federal Transit Administration, because at the end of the day this would involve urban mass transit funding to build a transit line, do work on what is now the Amtrak line, and build commuter rail and stations.

"So you had three agencies within the U.S. Department of Transportation, with guidelines and regulations that weren't always consistent with each other, and you needed all three to agree to transfer the land, primarily away from a federal highway administration and into the hands of private developers and local government agencies and so on. So we were badly stuck, and it was getting frustrating."[303]

At one of the countless community and task force meetings, attendees demanded that Pangaro explain why progress was bogging down. Pangaro explained that the federal transportation czars had set up roadblocks. People in attendance began to talk over one another. Order began to break down in the room. Then, Pangaro's explanation sank in. As the meeting's participants began to understand their lack of power, a gloomy silence settled over the gathering. Then Pangaro heard Marvin speak up.

Salvucci describes what Marvin said: "Tony told me later that Marvin basically said, 'If you're having trouble with the federal government, I can help.'"

The next day at his office, Marvin made three phone calls. One was to Senator Brooke. The other was to Senator Edward Kennedy. Marvin considered both men his friends. Marvin explained to both that he needed to arrange a meeting with U.S. Secretary of Transportation William T. Coleman, Jr., Brock Adams' predecessor. These were political courtesy calls. "That was the protocol that you used," Marvin said. "I was their constituent, and I was going to call someone in the [President's] Administration. Ed Brooke especially was a close friend of mine. If I could bring in additional political clout by getting the senators involved, I would."

The third call was to Coleman. Shortly before this, in 1975, President Gerald Ford had appointed Coleman as Secretary of Transportation, making him only the second African-American to hold a cabinet-level position. That was merely the latest in a string of firsts by Coleman. After law school, he was appointed U.S. Supreme Court Associate Justice Felix Frankfurter's law clerk, becoming the first African-American to clerk for the high bench. Before that, he had been selected as the first black man to serve on the board of editors of the *Harvard Law Review.*[304]

It was while he had been a student at Harvard Law School – before and after serving in the Army during World War II – that Coleman, unable to find university housing because he was black, had become a tenant of Lee Augusta Gilmore, Marvin's mother, in Cambridge. Now nearly 30 years later, he was very pleased to hear from his old friend Marvin.

Brooke had already called President Ford, but it was overkill. Coleman was only too glad to arrange a meeting in his office with his old friend Marvin and other representatives of the Southwest Corridor project from Massachusetts as well as the foot-dragging federal highway bureaucrats.

"We were sitting in the office," Salvucci said. "I was there, Tony Pangaro was there, Senator Brooke attended, and Marvin and about eight other black people. And Secretary Coleman said he had never had the three federal agency heads – the head of federal rails, the head of federal transit, and the head of federal highways – in the same room at the same time. But he looked at the three of them and said my friend Ed Brooke here says he's having a problem, and no one's getting out of this room until the problem is settled. That was it. In 10 seconds the intransigence was resolved. Everything moved forward after that. To me, it was a memorable occasion. If it weren't for Marvin, we'd still be arguing with the federal highway administration about whether we could transfer that land. It was Marvin's connection to Brooke and Coleman that broke the log jam and allowed the thing to move forward."

It was a project well worth the effort, says Dukakis. He refers to the Southwest Corridor as the Melnea Cass Corridor, for the park-flanked boulevard that became part of the new, multimodal project. The road was named for Cass, the defiant community and civil-rights activist who helped Marvin get his hearing with Mayor Kevin White.[305] Cass Boulevard traverses the Corridor, serving local residents and businesses, unlike the originally planned interstate highway that crushed the neighborhood in order to whisk white suburbanites past it as fast as possible.

"I became interested in the potential of the Melnea Cass Corridor as a job-creating and economy-building project, benefiting people in the South End, Roxbury, and Dorchester," Dukakis said. "And Marvin was deeply involved in making the new Corridor happen, both in the planning stages and in his work at the CDC, creating the CrossTown Industrial Park. He argued all along that the Corridor was an ideal place to develop new businesses and jobs."

Legacy of Help for Working Men and Women

An additional layer of community oversight was provided by creating task forces – special interest groups – for each of the planned subway stations. A task force was also created for a 5.6-acre site along the planned subway line known as Parcel 18. The heart of Parcel 18 would become the Ruggles Station, at Ruggles Street. It also included nearby land that would be the temporary new home of the Massachusetts Registry of Motor Vehicles before becoming Northeastern University's Renaissance Center. The parcel also included what became the new site of the Boston police department headquarters. Because it would be concerned with these additional nearby site as well as Ruggles Station itself, this task force was named Parcel 18+ Task Force.

Minority developers found themselves competing with white developers for tracts within the Southwest Corridor. This became a political issue as minority developers complained about a lack of reciprocity. They were in effect locked out of competing for development rights elsewhere in the city, especially downtown. But they had to share the emerging bounty on their home turf. It wasn't fair, they complained.

Sure, downtown opportunities had nothing to do with the Southwest Corridor. But the minority developers complained that a combination of politics – was it discrimination? – and higher costs for bigger projects in choice downtown sites barred them from those downtown opportunities.

The Parcel 18 Task Force, the most vibrant of the station-area task forces, developed an alliance with Asian-American developers. With Marvin as its chairman, the Parcel 18 Task Force hit on the strategy of requiring certain downtown developers to team up with minority developers. By the 1980s, the Task Force had won support from the Boston Redevelopment Authority, Mayor Raymond Flynn, and Governor Michael Dukakis.

Linkage first played out in development of the downtown Kingston-Bedford multilevel parking garage adjacent to Chinatown in Boston's financial district. The "majority" developer had to team up with minority partners. Developers' fees, net operating income, net refinancing proceeds and net resale proceeds would have to be divvied up among the majority developer, the Chinatown community (where the garage was located), and the Roxbury community.

In Roxbury, a similar share-the-wealth formula was applied to the Ruggles Street Station along the newly built subway line and the adjacent Ruggles Center office site.

The linkage policy succeeded in making sure that black entrepreneur-community advocates got a slice of publicly funded development pies. Philip Hart, who had been on the board of the CDC of Boston, described the linkage arrangement decades later in a professional journal: "The 45 minority investors from the African American, Asian American, and Latino communities walked away with a substantial return on their investment. The four community development corporations realized upward of $1 million each. Roxbury and Chinatown community trusts received $15 million in community benefits, some of which was to be invested in affordable housing.

"After fits and starts, the parcel-to-parcel linkage plan thus far has yielded a 36-story office tower in Boston's financial district, a nine-story office building in Roxbury and a multilevel parking structure, nearly $20 million in community benefits, several new minority millionaires, a rejuvenated Roxbury, and a positive working relationship among three key racial and ethnic groups in a city still addressing its image problems."[306]

Entrepreneurs weren't the only African-Americans to benefit from the linkage policy. Professionals like engineers did too.

"Pangaro hired some young guys, Stull and Lee, as architects," Salvucci said. "Their firm got the master contract for urban design of the whole Corridor to establish the 'vocabulary' of how [transit] stations would look, where bike paths would go, and so on. They were also given the actual architectural work to design Ruggles Station. So the Southwest Corridor became a place where minorities participated in the construction, engineering, and design of the physical development of transit, housing, and office structures. Marvin played a key role in getting that done."

Marvin was also a key advocate for creating benefits for minority construction workers, not just in the Southwest Corridor but on an ongoing basis, Salvucci says. In talks with the Parcel 18 Task Force and groups like United Community Workers, the state agreed to what became known as the Altshuler Plan – a goal of setting aside 30% of construction jobs to blacks.[307] Later, that agreement inspired Boston and the state to adopt minority-worker allocation targets for publicly-funded and large private construction elsewhere in the city and state. Today Boston requires at least 25% of the pay for such work to go to minorities, for example.[308]

"Dukakis extended it to all state construction, and Mayor White extended it to all city construction," Salvucci said. This ended an era in which blacks were largely shut out from big construction jobs in Boston and Massachusetts.

Unique Contribution

Boston's African-American community has had many advocates. Two things make Marvin's contribution unique. One is that he was effective. Some other advocates have been louder and have garnered more attention. But Marvin's batting average is peerless. His tireless efforts got results.

The other thing that is distinct about Marvin's contribution is that his focus is not on handouts, but on creating jobs. Jobs put money into people's pockets, jobs are the mortar that binds together the bricks of a community. Jobs and earned income flower into dignity and hope. Jobs and earned income are the life blood of freedom.

And he did it in the face discrimination and hostility.

275

"Marvin has done what was, especially at the time years ago, the toughest thing an African-American could do," Dukakis said. "He went out as an entrepreneur and succeeded in the white community. There weren't many folks of color who could do that, especially in those days, but he did it.

"And having actually done it, accumulating some affluence for himself and his family, what does he do? He comes to Roxbury and uses his business tools and skills to help the poorest part of the city find and build employment. That's pretty unusual.

"If you think back to that time, how many people could do that? How many people actually did do that? And he started out as a percussionist yet. What he's accomplished has been an amazing thing.

"He's very unselfish. His work is serious and hard. Yet he's a guy who finds time to be a mentor, who *loves* being a mentor. He takes the time and makes the effort to sit with young people and provide guidance.

"And there is his musical interest. He created a real estate empire. He recreated the CDC. He fought in a war. He fought discrimination. He helped make everything in the Melnea Cass Corridor possible. And he still found time to pursue his musical interest by running his club. Marvin comes as close to being a Renaissance man as anyone I know.

"And I've got to say, on a personal level, he's always a fun guy, an interesting guy, and he is always interested in not just what he was doing but in what *you* were doing. I don't remember anyone quite like him, at least in Boston back then. Marvin is a guy who has opened that door to many young people today."

You can't show me anyone else who's done so much, Dukakis says.

Adds the two-time governor of the Commonwealth of Massachusetts: "Marvin is a special guy, who's had a special impact on so many people in so many places."

Chapter 13
More Giving Back

On a trip to Cuba with a charity group, Marvin put up with dirty hotel towels, government snitches, and iffy drinking water. Welcome to the people's tropical paradise!

His hotel provided him with a single towel at a time. Sometimes room service replaced his used face cloth with a fresh one, sometimes it simply took away his used one without replacing it. "When that happened, I washed myself with the towel," he said.

Some "fresh" towels weren't. "You could smell an odor everywhere because nothing was that clean. Some towels came with brown stains. And sometimes there was no toilet paper in the room, so I had to use a towel. The spies figured I was sick," Marvin said, referring to the autocratic government's stooges who kept tabs on tourists to prevent them from doing anything that might undermine the dictatorship's rigid rule. "They check everything. They report everything to the ministry of health."

There were problems with water, too. The water pressure in his hotel was frustratingly weak. Throughout much of the day it didn't matter; he didn't want to shower or bath because there was no hot water except early in the morning. He got around that problem by rising very early each day. The other problem with water: it was unsafe to drink. "Their tap water would kill you," he said. "I had to buy water in bottles."

Clean water was in such short supply that conservation was encouraged. A meter in his room tracked the use of every drop.

Secret Police?

Some aspects of the August 2012 visit read like a Cold War espionage novel. Cuba and the U.S. are merely 90 miles apart. But relationships between the two nations often seem as treacherous as the shark-infested Caribbean currents that separate them. The two countries have not had formal diplomatic relations since 1961. The State Department staffs what is called the U.S. Interests Section in the former U.S. embassy in Havana. A State Department official met with Marvin and his traveling friends at their hotel. She offered advice about how to find various places and people. And she reminded them to mind their Ps and Qs because they would be under constant surveillance.

"She told us several dos and don'ts. The main thing was, *Don't talk politics!* The government liked what we were doing. We were there to help people. But the warning was, *Don't talk politics,*" Marvin said.

For Marvin, who has never shied away from fights, political or military, heeding that advice took discipline. But as someone who has never hesitated to stand up for rights, he has also learned the importance of picking the right time and method to take on an adversary. On this trip to Cuba, he could protect his opportunities for delivering desperately needed supplies by avoiding head-on beefs with the authoritarian regime.

The situation also reminded him why he never gambles. "There's no point in playing a game where the house stacks the odds in its own favor," he said. Politics in Cuba are like gambling in a casino. The game is rigged in favor of the house.

"The woman from the State Department was very careful, like the room might be bugged," he said. "The message about surveillance was very clear. The whole visit, I kept my mouth shut. I minded my own business. I did what I had to do. But we got the message. They [the Cuban government] check on you. The walls are bugged."

Sticking to the Mission

For all of the journey's difficulties and the jolt of finding themselves under the eyes of a nasty regime, Marvin did not regret his visit. He went with a charitable group named Acceso, whose mission was to donate musical instruments and other items that are hard to get on the island that has been impoverished by the dictatorship's choke hold on economic freedom. Preventing everyone else from amassing money and influence helps perpetuate the government's monopoly on power.

"We had about 100 clothes bags," Marvin said. "They were filled with books, medical equipment, musical instruments and parts. We had strings for violins and guitars, reeds for saxophones. They don't have any horse hair strings for bows in Cuba.

"We brought cases of vitamins, aspirins, and toys – teddy bears for the little children. And dresses and clothes.

"Bringing instruments was my job. And parts. It can cost $85 per bow for string. I got rosin; strings for violas, violins, cellos; reeds; DVDs of orchestras. I asked the Guitar Center in the Fenway for supplies, but they did not donate. I spent around $1,000 of my own. Hey, the music stores have it tough too. Most of the stores in Boston have closed. Daddy's in front of Berklee College is closed. The only one left is the Guitar Center."

Like Santa and his elves, Marvin and his friends assembled their stockpile and went to Tags, a hardware store in Cambridge's Porter Square, for bags to carry their goodies. The store owners pitched in and helped Marvin's group pack and seal their bags. Then the charity's volunteers brought the bags to Boston's Logan International Airport for a flight to Miami. From Miami, the charity travelers would bring the bags to Cuba.

In Cuba, the group's game plan was to visit a pre-determined list of churches, schools, and libraries to deliver its valuable cargo. "We traveled all over," Marvin said. "At each stop we left three or four bags."

Schools got mostly books. Music schools got mostly instruments. To say that recipients were grateful would be a gross understatement. "I was told to keep a few musical parts in my [luggage]. I gave the girls in the hotel, who played for us at breakfast, strings for their guitars. They kissed my feet," said Marvin, who sounded embarrassed by the girls' show of gratitude and awed by their desperation. "People were so happy to receive stuff, tears were coming down their eyes."

Losing Their Shadows

Each day, the group had planned one or more destinations. One day the charitable group made a delivery to the national library. For whatever reasons – either politics or simple logistics or safety issues – several times Marvin's group's itinerary was changed. "Sometimes we went someplace that wasn't on the original schedule," Marvin said. "We took some bus rides that were 100 miles away to get away from where we were supposed to go. I didn't ask, but I got the feeling that sometimes it was to avoid people who were following us or who were watching the people we were going to visit. We drove halfway across that country a couple of times. By the time we got back to the hotel, it was 11:30, midnight. I was dead tired. But the driver and tour guide took a chance."

Drives around Cuba were draining. "The buses were clean, but they were old," Marvin said. "You know all those stories about old American cars on the streets of Cuba. Most of the people can't afford new ones. Same thing with the buses. They were old, and you could feel the springs poking up through the seats. And the buses broke down. The air-conditioning did. Or you'd get a bus where they'd only run the air-conditioning for 10 to 15 minutes at a time so the bus engine wouldn't overheat. So we got a little relief every so often, then it would get hot and humid inside the bus again. But it was well worth it. We weren't there to be pampered. You had to enjoy what you saw outside the bus more than the discomfort inside the bus."

One night members of the group planned a fun outing to Havana's Tropicana, a cabaret and nightclub dating to 1939 that is famous for its Cuban show and dance music with a mix of Afro-Cuban music. "Once the show begins, the stage and verdant surroundings become an orgy of light, color, spectacular costumes, and pulsating movement," says Frommer's online travel guide.[309] But Marvin passed on that excursion.

"I didn't go to the Tropicana, where all the beautiful ladies dance," he said. "I've been there before. Mainly, I was tired. We had been driving all that day. The Tropicana show started at 1 a.m., and I had to get up early the next morning and drive four and a half hours to a library and school for children."

Haves and Have-Nots

As he mingled with Cubans, Marvin was struck by two things: How friendly the people were, and the sharp divide between the haves and the have-nots.

"When you walk on the streets, people come out of their homes, which have iron gates," Marvin said. "Their apartments are bare except for chairs and sofas, which they bring right out to the edge of the sidewalk.

"Then in one part of Havana you see beautiful homes. You see mansions owned by communist party officials."

His hotel, despite its shortcomings, offered television like most every hotel on earth. "I was able to see CNN," he said.

And he couldn't help notice that hotel doormen doubled as security. "They watched the doors carefully, to keep unauthorized people out," he said.

Each day's bus expedition took seven volunteers like Marvin from back home, plus a tour guide, a driver and an extra driver, for a total of 10 pilgrims. Many of the volunteers were veterans of such visits to Cuba, and several had made friends and close contacts on previous journeys. "Sometimes we picked up local friends of people in our group," Marvin said.

"Wherever we went, we stopped and bought sandwiches. And bottled water. Always bottled water. And we traveled halfway across Cuba. Each trip was long and tiring."

Marvin's sharpest impressions are of people on the streets.

"The people are like you and me: beautiful and colorful," Marvin added. "You see horses pulling carts. You see old cars with new engines or rebuilt engines under the hood. People have those old Chevies from the 1950s [before the Cuba revolution]. People painstakingly keep them looking almost new. You also see old bicycles pulling old carts.

"You see girls in modern short, short, short dresses. Their hair is fixed beautifully. But it's not all postcard stuff. The streets are run down. And you've got to stay on the main streets. People are desperate. Kids will rob you and disappear. If you go on side streets, you've got to go with a group for protection.

"There are a lot of contrasts. You see thousands of kids on the street. You see women thumbing for rides. But you don't hear of rape. It's the kiss of death if you try that. Very harsh punishment.

"Buses are jammed full of people like cattle cars. How do they breathe? I don't know. You see old-fashioned trucks with wooden side rails like prisons on wheels."

The visit was not designed for tourists expecting to be pampered. "Whenever we went to a restaurant, it was hot," Marvin said. "I don't mean hip. I mean it was hot inside. And it seemed like I had to climb three flights of stairs to reach each one. You'd wait to be seated on the second floor, where they had air-conditioning. They'd feed you on the third floor. No air-conditioning. But the drinks were good. Lots of mojitos, Cuba libras. Lots of drinks with sugar in them."

But the bottom line was the people. Marvin said, "Wonderful people, very friendly, very courteous."

Helping Others Help Themselves

That 2012 visit to Cuba was Marvin's fourth. He had been there at least once with his wife Lorna. On his most recent visit, in December 2013, Marvin met with owners of music clubs to explore the possibility of arranging musical exchanges – Cuban musicians would come to perform in the U.S., and Americans would play in Cuba. "It could help club owners, but the big beneficiaries would be the musicians, both American and Cuban," Marvin said.

After a lifetime of hard work to provide for his family and of nearly nonstop fights for liberty and civil rights – his own and for others – these days Marvin can afford to spend more time helping others in a variety of ways.

When people are not in a position to help themselves, charity can be the quickest way to provide their needs. That's was the case with each of Marvin's visits to Cuba. It was also the case in the wake of the tragic 2010 earthquake that caused death, destruction, and dislocation in the Caribbean island of Haiti. Marvin hosted a fundraiser for earthquake survivors at the Western Front on February 14 of that year.

And it's been the case in his ongoing philanthropic work.

Over the years he devoted time, expertise, and resources to various charities, many with a focus on children: the Board of Directors of Greater Boston Legal Services; Board of Directors, Cambridge YMCA; Board of Directors, Roxbury Multi-Service Center; Board of Corporators, Mount Auburn Hospital, in Cambridge; Board of Directors, Dimock Community Health Center, in Boston; Cambridge Boys and Girls Club, as its President; Home, Inc., as its President; Roxbury Children's Services, as Assistant Executive Director; Board of Directors, NAACP Boston branch; Board of Directors, Traditional Childbearing Group; Board of Directors, Junior Achievement; Boston Chamber of Commerce, as a member; Board of Directors, Youville Hospital in Cambridge.

Some, like Youville Hospital, Marvin has outlived.

Marvin also remains a strong believer that the best way to help people in the long run is by helping them earn a living so they remain in charge of their own lives. That's the root of his commitment to the CDC's mission of creating jobs.

"You create jobs by creating businesses," Marvin said. "That's what attracted me to the CDC, that's why accomplishing the CrossTown

Industrial Park was important, that's why it was so important to encourage development of the Newmarket Industrial District, that's why it was so important to build up the area around B.U. Medical School, that's why it was so important to open a black bank. Yes, it was important for African-American businessmen to be able to get loans. But it was also important for black people to be able to work for a bank. That was my whole focus."

And it's what fuels his commitment to helping young people get an education.

Brandeis University

One evening when Marvin was running his catering business, back in the days shortly after graduation from New England Conservatory, he was standing near the front door as a guest arrived at this particular function. The new arrival handed his coat to Marvin. Maybe it happened because Marvin was standing near the check room. Maybe it was because he is black.

In any case, Marvin thought to himself, "Hell, no, I am not destined to check coats, I am going to be a successful business leader," recalls Frederick Lawrence, president of Brandeis University.[310] That exchange was part of what convinced Marvin to decline an offer at that same event to become butler for Abram Sachar, who was then Brandeis' president.

The good news for the university was that its loss then was only temporary. Marvin maintained his connection to Brandeis and eventually became a supporter of the nonsectarian, Jewish community-sponsored university.

One strand of Marvin's tie to Brandeis was through Kivie Kaplan, the Boston businessman and officer in the national NAACP, who was a friend and mentor of Marvin. Kaplan was a supporter of Brandeis, who discussed Brandeis with Marvin. Kaplan's son Edward, who became a member of the Brandeis faculty and a professor of French literature, comparative literature, and religious studies, also became a friend of Marvin and kept Brandeis on Marvin's radar screen.

"The first memory I have of meeting Marvin was at an NAACP meeting in [Denver] Colorado [in the 1960s]," Edward Kaplan said. "I went with my father. And I remember we got into a car with Marvin and someone else and went sightseeing in the hills. Marvin was a charming and interesting guy."[311]

One reason the occasion sticks in Kaplan's memory is that the NAACP gathering, the 1965 national convention, was one of the more pleasant civil rights gatherings he attended during that decade.

Kaplan said: "My dad, myself, and Louis Grossman [Edward's nephew and son of Morton Grossman, who hosted the Sammy Davis, Jr., fundraiser at his home in suburban Boston; see Chapter 9] went to the [March 1965] march on Montgomery," Kaplan said, referring to the historic 54-mile march from Selma to the state capital of Alabama, led by Martin Luther King., to demand voting rights. "We got up at four or five in the morning, and took a chartered plane from Boston to LaGuardia [in New York City] and then to Selma. We went under the auspices of the Union of American Congregations, which is now the Union for Reformed Judaism. People on the airplane had a lot of energy. It was very exciting. But when we reached Alabama it was frightening. There were people along the march route with signs that said, 'Martin Luther King Is A Communist' and 'Martin Luther Coon.' When it was finally over and we were getting into the airplane to fly back, Martin Luther King came aboard and greeted my father by name. He asked about my mother Emily. I was introduced to him and shook his hand."

Kaplan kept up his relationship with Marvin. He and his parents socialized with Marvin and Lorna. Sometimes the couples dined at Boston area restaurants, other times the Gilmores visited Kivie Kaplan's home in Newton, a suburb of Boston, or the Kaplan's getaway on Martha's Vineyard, the resort island off the southern coast of Cape Cod. They also participated together in various charitable activities.

Edward Kaplan introduced Marvin to Tony Williams, who invited Marvin to speak with Brandeis students. Lawrence said, "Tony always sought out positive role models for his students," Lawrence said. "Marvin was and is an inspiration to the students. When he speaks, he emphasizes the importance of believing in oneself, persisting, and not being afraid to take a different path."

Marvin was only too happy to oblige Williams. "Tony was a black professor, who knew what I was doing in the community and invited me to give a motivational talk to kids," Marvin said. "I must have made an impression, because they wanted me to come back. I spoke there two or three times a year. Tony Williams wanted African-American kids to learn what it takes to be somebody in the community, to hear about the other side of life, the successful side."

The more that Marvin spoke at Brandeis, the more that Williams wanted him to come back. "I not only spoke to classes. They invited me to graduations, picnics with the kids, lots of events," Marvin said.

Kaplan introduced Marvin to the possibility of helping Brandeis assist youngsters financially in 2001. "In the spring of 2001, Ed Kaplan, his wife Janna, and [Brandeis] President Jehuda [Reinharz and his wife] Shula went dancing at Marvin's club, the Western Front. It was there that Ed first introduced Marvin to Jehuda and the conversation gradually elevated over time," Lawrence said.

Helping students at Brandeis made sense to Marvin for several reasons. "It was the only university trying to do something right for African-American kids," he said. In addition, Marvin had numerous strong personal relationships with Jews. Lorna, his wife, was Jewish. Kivie and Edward Kaplan and the Grossmans were Jewish. And he was developing friendships with the Reinharzes and other figures at Brandeis. His friendship with Tony Williams was yet another bridge to the university.

Marvin also felt a bridge, although it was indirect, to Brandeis through certain real estate professionals. Part of the link was based on the fact that the real estate men were Jewish. "I think of them as members of the Jewish community," Marvin said. "Brandeis gets most of its support from that community. I've learned some important things from members of that community. Seeing their interested in Brandeis made me look into Brandeis, and I've seen how it helps a lot of young people in need, including black kids."

One of those real estate professionals was Samuel Poorvu, a successful commercial real estate investor. Poorvu was founder of the Bullfinch Companies, a prominent commercial real estate investment firm now specializing in the development, acquisition, repositioning and management of properties in Greater Boston. Learning Marvin's reputation as a caterer, Poorvu hired Marvin to provide food and refreshments for some dinner parties and other social gatherings at his home in suburban Boston.

In Poorvu, Marvin recognized a kindred spirit. Both were self-made men. Both rose out of modest beginnings. Poorvu – who was Jewish, nearly two decades older than Marvin, and much further along in his career – had first arrived in the United States from Lithuania with only $8 in his pocket. Poorvu had taken whatever jobs were available to earn a living and, he hoped, bring his parents as well as seven friends to the U.S., so he worked as a grocery clerk. He also went to night school. He managed to help finance his sister's medical education. And he eventually began to work as a bricklayer. Family legend puts a modest spin on how he rose to foreman. The story goes that he was so bad as a bricklayer that his boss promoted him so he wouldn't handle bricks and mortar.[312]

Poorvu went on to build his fortune by constructing post offices in more than 100 communities throughout the U.S. That prompted the *Wall Street Journal* to nickname him "the Post Office King of America." Along the way Poorvu developed a reputation as a reliable man of his word.[313]

Marvin learned from Poorvu not by speaking with him but by listening to what the developer's friends and party guests said about him and by researching whatever he could about Poorvu's work.

"I watched Sam," Marvin said. "I didn't learn by talking with him. Sam was famous for post offices. I learned by listening and talking with people at the parties, sometimes at the real estate board. Sam didn't learn about development from book teaching. He learned by doing."

Marvin was especially struck by the fact that Poorvu built his own success. He saw the signs that pointed to Poorvu having risen from poverty. Marvin understood the discipline and hard work that Poorvu needed to do that. "At the parties I saw that Sam never ate with a fork, only with his hands," Marvin said. "That's not criticism; he was very clean. But he was from the old country. And if he could do that and become a millionaire and a very respected man, then he was a person I should learn from."

The Poorvu role model was reinforced years later by an acquaintanceship with William Poorvu, a cousin of Samuel's father. William Poorvu was a real estate investor and Harvard Business School adjunct professor of entrepreneurship, who also taught real estate courses. For a research project into community development corporations around the country, Poorvu asked the CDC of Boston for information. In the course of conversation, Poorvu invited Marvin to Harvard.

"I got invited to Harvard to listen to William speak," Marvin said. "I listened carefully and tried to pick up pointers."

"I learned a lot about ethics from Jews," Marvin said. "Samuel Poorvu taught me about working hard and doing things right. He taught me, *Don't leave a stone unturned*. And he taught me the value of controlling land. He bought the land that the government put buildings on. I tried to apply that lesson to the Southwest Corridor. Even though I didn't own the land, I tried to work with the folks who did own the land. Sam Poorvu's lessons helped me move out of residential real estate into commercial real estate. I never forgot the training I got from Sam. Decades ago I thought maybe I can do the same thing when it comes to helping other people get started in their careers."

An opportunity to do exactly that emerged as Marvin talked with President Reinharz, then-Director of Donor Relations Raquel Rosenblatt, and other Brandeis figures. The chief result was that in December 2010 Marvin donated money to establish the Marvin E. and Lorna J. Gilmore Endowed TYP Scholarship.

The scholarship helps pay college costs for a graduate of the program, whose formal name is the Myra Kraft Transitional Year Program. The TYP is akin to a prep-school program, which annually offers 20 students courses that help them get ready for college as well as some actual Brandeis undergraduate courses. Some participants need income and have to work long hours while attending school. Others are refugees from countries where domestic conflict has disrupted their educations. Many are from under-resourced high schools in the U.S. The bulk of the graduates go on to complete their undergraduate degrees at Brandeis.

Lawrence said, "If TYP had existed 70 years ago, Marvin would have been the ideal candidate. He was motivated, ambitious, eager to learn and up to just about any challenge. Now, through [this scholarship], the Boston civil leader is helping to ensure that promising students will have the opportunity to pursue a Brandeis degree by completing TYP's unique one-year academic preparation program."

Marvin bottom-lined his interest this way: "These kids have to have the perfect attitude. They must have goals. They must have a vision of where they want to go in life. They've got to be ready to work hard. To me, this is an investment in the future."

University of Massachusetts, Boston

UMass Boston is another university that benefits from Marvin's support. He has been a member of the Board of Visitors, which is an advisory group for the university and its chancellor or chief executive, since October 19, 2011. Marvin has also contributed to a scholarship fund named for Chancellor J. Keith Motley. And he frequently appears on campus at various events and to speak with students.

The campus sits on Columbia Point in Boston's Dorchester neighborhood. Its location is a peninsula, created from a landfill, which juts into Dorchester Bay and looks out the length of Boston Harbor to the ocean beyond. The John F. Kennedy Presidential Library and Museum, serving the memory of the 35th President of the United States, is a neighbor on Columbia Point. Many UMass Boston students are residents of the city and its immediate environs, and their ability to attend school hinges on the fact that UMass Boston is a relatively low-cost state university.

One of Marvin's key impacts is as a role model for UMass students, says Chancellor J. Keith Motley. "Marvin is a veteran, and so are many of our students. We have 200 veterans on campus. We are a vet-friendly school, and they are proud that Mr. Gilmore is a member of that special club. And he went into the Army even though he had not yet finished school. He had the discipline to finish school at an older age. He is a powerful symbol of what young people can do if they choose."

Marvin often meets with students. Motley says he has a knack for meaningful conversations. "Students disconnect when they think you're bragging about yourself," Motley said. "They tune you right out. I never hear about that happening to Mr. Gilmore. He makes students drag *him* out. Then they're pleasantly surprised that he's shared so many of their experiences."

Marvin is also a valuable Visitor for this largely inner-city school because he has fought on behalf of inner-city residents, Motley says. "Mr. Gilmore never turned his back on the city of Boston or Cambridge," he said. "He's always working for both economic development and development of opportunities for individuals, whether helping develop the Southwest Corridor or one of his babies, the Western Front. He's somebody who doesn't sit around. He likes to be part of the beginning of new things. Like starting Unity Bank in Roxbury.

"My selfish reason for having him [as a Visitor] is understanding the value of exposing our students to one of the most important people around here, a giant like Marvin Gilmore Jr., who can share his life experiences the way he can."

Part of Marvin's value as a role model has to do with style. At a time when many young people avoid what they consider an Establishment look and sound, Marvin shows that you can be black and look successful without looking like a rebel. "I've known him since he was a community leader in the 1970s, for example, stopping the Southwest Corridor highway," Chancellor Motley said. "You saw Senator Ed Brooke; he was dressed up in a suit. When you saw Mr. Gilmore, you knew he was dressed for business. He was always chasing some dream. He looked ready to do that. And that told you that he would catch that dream.

"Today it's the same thing. You can't help but notice him. He looks the same now as he did then in the 1970s. He is always suave and debonair and cool, and always looks ready to do business. And it's certainly not just for show. Joining the Army, the Southwest Corridor, the Western Front, Unity Bank – he has dreamed and implemented more in one lifetime than most people, and he never stops."

Also, the chancellor has very worldly, pragmatic reasons for valuing Marvin's presence. Those reasons are especially helpful now while the school is less than one-third of the way through a 25-year master plan that calls for redeveloping its campus. Several complex, costly, new facilities are on tap.

"Mr. Gilmore knows construction," Motley said. "And now we're in the construction business. We're building an integrated science center, an academic center, chemistry labs and performing arts in the same building. So he's been part of our thinking about that. He's had to build complex facilities. We're facing construction of building complex facilities. When he built Newmarket, you had a little of everything there: hotels, research facilities, food, food processing, all in one area. So he's a multidimensional thinker. And he understands financing. We're facing complex financial questions. He reminds us not to frontload debt into a project. Instead, he tells us, build debt out over the life of a project. Mr. Gilmore is exactly the sort of person we need."

Marvin also strikes Motley as someone who is easy to work with. That no doubt stems from years of learning to not irritate the fragile egos of politicians who control public projects. Motley said, "He knows what sorts of questions to ask. He's smart. And he lets you learn. He offers his advice, then he gets out of the way and doesn't hound me. He's an asset, not a liability. Some elders have to have their fingerprints on everything. He prepares us by interacting with us, then letting us make the right decisions."

The Board of Visitors meet monthly, Motley says, "but I speak with Mr. Gilmore every week or two weeks. He is very generous with his time."

And Motley does not hesitate when asked what the most unique thing is about Marvin's contribution to UMass Boston. "We're in a world-class community. We are surrounded by experts in various fields. But Mr. Gilmore is an expert in *many* fields. Where else could I find someone who can talk about music, the arts, about development, finance, running a club, politics, and how each of those things plays a role in society and in economic development?

"Mr. Gilmore can connect the dots in his life, in *your* life, and talk about things that matter to a campus community."

New England Conservatory

On a brightly sunny October Saturday in 2011, a day when many colleges throughout New England and the rest of the nation celebrated alumni homecoming with rousing intercollegiate football games, New England Conservatory marked its annual reunion with several ceremonies featuring that institution's favorite pastime, music.

One highlight was the alumni association's awards luncheon in Brown Hall, inside the Jordan Hall building. In between courses of nourishment for the body, recognition was given to alumni and faculty of various ages for their contributions to the nourishment of the soul through music. As the program got underway, the six recipients would range from American light lyric opera soprano Amanda Forsythe, who earned a masters in 2001, to baritone Ernest Triplett, Jr., class of 1961, who has mastered formats including opera, theater, and church.

At a round table along one side of the room, two young attendees introduced themselves to each other. Both were undergraduates at NEC and among the few young people in the hall. In near whispers they confessed to each other that they had limited familiarity with the work of most of the award recipients. "I don't know the Western Front guy," one told the other. "But I've been to the club."

So Marvin, who was receiving the Florence A. Dunn Alumni Award for Distinguished Service from NEC President Tony Woodcock, had an actual fan and paying customer in the audience that day.

Woodcock paid tribute to Marvin that day for serving on the NEC Board of Oversees since 1995.

In addition, Marvin helps individual students directly by mentoring several each year. He listens to the young students perform and provides them with feedback. He makes them his guests at various music-related functions. He introduces them to industry professionals.

Marvin learned the hard way that it can be tough to make a living in music. He does what he can to help musicians from NEC get make their way. During 2009 and 2010, NEC celebrated the fortieth anniversary of its first-in-the-nation Jazz Studies program. That ongoing celebration spotlighted NEC faculty, alumni, and students each weekend in concerts in New York and Boston. Clinics and community events surrounded many of the performances.

Marvin supported the program by making the Western Front one of the participating venues. Headliners for the overall program included marquee jazz names like Wayne Shorter and Ran Blake.

"During the Jazz 40th, Marvin created some lovely opportunities for our musicians," Woodcock said. "He takes a keen interest in them. When we did something at the B.B. King Blue Club in New York, there was Marvin. He came up from Boston to support us and support B.B. King."[314]

Marvin has gone farther than Manhattan in support of NEC. As part of NEC delegations, he has journeyed to Venezuela, most recently to review the work of El Sistema, a program that has enabled thousands of children from impoverished backgrounds to get music educations. The NEC group visited *nucleos*, or music centers, where music is studied and performed and where instruments are made. NEC also runs a Sistema Fellows Program. It pays for 10 participants to learn how to run a Sistema-style program in the U.S.

"The Sistema program in Venezuela uses the power of music to teach kids in a dedicated after-school program," Woodcock said. "It has touched the lives of millions of impoverished kids and families from all over Venezuela. We went to learn about it and see what we could transcribe to

America. Marvin was in our group. Every day he got up early in the morning, sat on a bus, watched kids, and he was as moved as all of us. He did this at age 82 or 83. He lent his support, enthusiasm, and entrepreneurship."

And Woodcock touches on one more aspect of Marvin's support, something that goes beyond his mere presence and his material backing. "Whenever I see him at meetings or concerts, I am reminded how diligent he is about coming to everything we do," Woodcock said. "I am delighted about his making the effort. He demonstrates initiative, his generosity to everyone including students he might be mentoring, and he will have a great time listening to them and supporting them.

"He has a sparkle in his eye all the time. When you look at him, there is something in his eyes that denotes huge energy. That sparkle is about him seeing the lighter side of life. Despite all of his experiences going back to D-Day in France, he still has a sense of humor. He's a remarkable human spirit."

Chapter 14
Twinkle in His Eye

Raheem W. and Monroe B. were two young men who admitted they were supposed to be somewhere else. "Like in school?" they were asked. Grinning sheepishly, they took the Fifth, refusing to say one way or another. They also declined to reveal their last names. But this was a Thursday morning, May 20, 2010, not yet summer break. And here these two teens stood, inside Gardner Auditorium in the Massachusetts State House.

Raheem wore a green and white satin Boston Celtics warm-up jacket. Beneath that, a white shirt and a green tie. Monroe was more casually attired in a black windbreaker over a white t-shirt. They looked like a million other high school boys, except for where they were and Raheem's necktie nod to decorum.

Asked why they were in Gardner Auditorium, Raheem – who, like Monroe, is African-American – said his grandfather had been an American soldier in World War II, who married a woman from France. His grandfather had told him that a fellow black veteran named Marvin Gilmore was going to be honored today for his U.S. Army service in France during World War II. Raheem decided it would be cool to check out the ceremony, since he thought of himself as slightly French – when he said that, his eyes actually darted left and right, as if he was embarrassed.

"I don't know, so maybe I'm a little curious about this guy," he said, referring to Marvin. "Like maybe he helped France. And he was a soldier like my granddad."

Monroe nodded solemnly. He said he was just hanging out with his buddy Raheem. And they had nothing better to do, he said.

So the two teens were inside Gardner Auditorium instead of outside in the spring sunshine, where they could have been hanging out on, say, Boston Common, people watching, checking out the girls, or roaming around Downtown Crossing, or doing whatever struck their fancy.

A lot of other people had also come to Gardner Auditorium that day, creating a standing-room-only throng. And the vast majority was there more intentionally. They were friends and family of Marvin or somehow participants in the ceremony that was about to take place, a ceremony in honor of Marvin. Not bad for a high school dropout from Cambridge.

Defying Jim Crow

Marvin, at age 86, was getting back a little of the love he had shown more than 67 years earlier. On a December day in 1942 he had enlisted in the Army. He was just a little beyond his 17th birthday. He was still a senior at Cambridge Latin High School. Theoretically, he would not be eligible for the draft for another nine months. And he was even safer, even further insulated from military service than that if he had chosen. That's because in the America of 1942, a Jim Crow mindset still held sway. One of its many foolish rules was a prohibition against drafting African-Americans into the Armed Forces.

At the loud demand of African-Americans eager to show they were ready and willing to fight for their country, for a better democracy, and against a foreign tyrant who held African-Americans in contempt precisely because of their race, the barrier against blacks participating in the military draft would be breached for the first time the next year.

But in late 1942 Marvin could have stayed in Cambridge Latin School, graduated, and even gone on to college if he wanted to. No one would have forced him to don a military uniform. On the contrary. The last thing that many Americans wanted to see were African-Americans armed with assault weapons, especially on U.S. soil, trained to fight, and wearing the uniforms of Uncle Sam's service branches.

Marvin was having none of that nonsense. He got signed parental permission to enlist and donated his services to the U.S. Army.

"High Esteem"

Fast forward to May 2010. Marvin found himself in Gardner Auditorium being honored for that 1942 decision and for the quality of his military service through his discharge in 1946. On that day in Gardner Auditorium, the crowd cheered as Christophe Guilhou, France's consul general in Boston, presented Marvin with his nation's prestigious Legion of Honor award with its highest degree, Chevalier. The Legion was created in 1802 by Napoleon Bonaparte to acknowledge services rendered to France by persons of great merit.

The decoration was signed by the Nicolas Sarkozy, President of the French Republic, who was Grand Master of the National Order of the Legion.

Pierre Vimont, French Ambassador to the United States, wrote a note to Marvin that read, "This award testifies to the President of the French Republic's high esteem for your merits and accomplishments. In particular it is a sign of France's true and unforgettable gratitude and appreciation for your personal, precious contribution to the United States' decisive role in the liberation of our country during World War II."

France bestowed its prized Legion of Honor on Marvin not just because he had served in the campaign to liberate France from Nazi domination, but because of what Marvin had endured in the course of that service.

He was subjected to harsh racism by white soldiers, his own comrades in arms, while training in the South, and while fighting in the field in continental Europe, and while rotating through Scotland. He had seen buddies killed in training and in combat. During training in the States, he did his part to defuse the notorious race riot at the Army's Camp Stewart in Georgia in June 1943. He landed in Normandy in the great D-Day invasion. In combat with his anti-aircraft unit against Germans, he suffered wounds by shrapnel, which speared into the left side of his abdomen and knifed into his left eye. In the crazed atmosphere of a field hospital, he had to fight off assailants – fellow G.I.s – with a handgun that he had kept hidden. He faced constant death threats from black-market operators during the war. And he was a virtual one-man army, doing it all and seeing it all.

On D-Day and several times after that, he carried dead and wounded comrades from the field. Without advance preparation, he was shuffled into the soon-to-be famous Red Ball Express, the nonstop conveyor belt of trucks – whose drivers and mechanics were largely by black troops like Marvin – that ferried men and supplies to the battle fronts.

Once Marvin was sent back to his front-line anti-aircraft outfit, he fought through the bloody, gory, key battle for Aachen, the gateway into Germany that the *wehrmacht* defended with renewed passion.

When Marvin was reassigned to Scotland, white military police tried to ambush him because...he was black. And when he was finally ordered back to the United States and a return to civilian life, he was barred from boarding his assigned ship by a white sergeant who brusquely explained, "Only white solders can board this ship."

The blocked passage embarrassed Marvin in front of a large group of Scottish friends and well-wishers, who had accompanied him to the dock to see him off on what they all expected would be his voyage home. His thin consolation was that he got to remain with his new foreign friends for several additional months. When he was finally allowed to steam home, it was aboard a smaller ship that tossed uncomfortably on the rough North Atlantic seas the entire voyage.

Paying Tribute

Decades later, in 2010, no one could erase the memories of war and racial affronts. But France could make plain its gratitude for what Marvin had been through and for what he had helped accomplish, the liberation of France, despite the discrimination he had endured.

In preparatory remarks, Counsel General Guilhou said, "Marvin Gilmore's heroic service in World War II alone is enough to recommend him for the Legion of Honor. But his bravery and dedication in the face of discrimination make Marvin a true hero."

As Marvin stood on the podium of the stage in Gardner Auditorium, Guilhou pinned the red-ribbon decoration on Marvin's left lapel. A smiling Marvin became the first African-American in New England to receive the Legion of Honor award. As the Counsel General shook Marvin's hand, the assembled crowd of friends, family, and supporters rose to its feet in applause.

In his acceptance remarks, Marvin recalled the bigotry that had divided America and its soldiers, sailors, and Marines. "We were not allowed to fight together," he said. "We were two armies, one black, one white. That prejudice permeated all throughout Europe."

But he also saluted his fellow men and women in arms who endured hardship together, spurring each other through pain and suffering, sadness and death, often leaning for support on one another, in pursuit of a shared goal. "I take this honor for all my fellow veterans who have passed away, the ones that fought with me on Normandy beach," Marvin said. "If you live in America, if you live in France, you just don't know what war was like. I went through hell."

The challenge was met, Marvin said. Freedom was restored to France. Europe was liberated from the yoke of Nazi terror. America was kept safe. "We are free," he added.

And we are freer than Americans were during and before the war. That was a point proclaimed by other speakers at the Legion of Honor ceremony, who cited the impact that Marvin and his generation of veterans had as they participated in the postwar civil rights struggle, which expanded American liberty. Speakers also high-fived Marvin for his endeavors in creating jobs, both for African-American workers and for black entrepreneurs.

Rev. Charles Stith, Director of the African Presidential Archives and Research Center at Boston University and former U.S. ambassador to Tanzania, said Marvin's family had been helping him since he first moved to Boston in the 1970s and found housing as a tenant of Marvin's mother, Lee Augusta Gilmore. He thanked Marvin for his battles against discrimination and for his efforts to create jobs for African-Americans. "Thank you for opening the doors of opportunity," Marvin said. "And for making sure once you got through, you left the doors open for us to follow through."

Continuing an African-American Legacy

Prof. Charles J. Ogletree, Jr. – who taught both Barak and Michelle Obama at Harvard Law School, is a longtime confidant of the president, and is a prominent civil-rights lawyer – said Marvin personified a tradition of African-Americans fighting for civil rights and equal economic opportunity, which included former slaves fighting for the Union and their freedom in the Civil War. Black men fought in Vietnam only to return home, unable to find jobs, he said. Marvin has focused on the fight for economic freedom as much as the fight for equal rights, Ogletree said. "That's what makes [black soldiers] so important – not that they were veterans, but that they sacrificed for our freedom," he added, referring to Marvin.

In an interview for this biography Ogletree said, "He has been through so much, and he has opened doors and helped keep them open for others. "[315]

The roster of attendees and guests was evidence of how appreciated Marvin is. Seated at the dais above the presentation podium were luminaries such as Governor Deval Patrick; State Representatives Timothy Toomey, Marie St. Fleur, Linda Dorcena Forry, Willie Mae Allen, Gloria Fox, and Alice Wolf; Cambridge Vice Mayor Henrietta Davis, Cambridge City Councilors Denise Simmons and Kenneth Reeves; and Boston City Councilor Charles Yancey.

Cambridge Mayor David Maher applauded Marvin for his charity, jobs creation, and civic concern in the university city. "This man has been a philanthropist and has given so much throughout his career and his lifetime," he said. "We are extremely grateful and very proud of him."

Deval Patrick and Timothy Murray, governor and lieutenant governor of the Commonwealth of Massachusetts, awarded Marvin a Governor's Citation for his military service and in recognition of being the first African-American from New England to receive the Legion of Honor medal.

The decoration ceremony coincided with the 75th annual Massachusetts Lafayette Day. The observance is held every May 20, the anniversary of the death of General Lafayette, the French aristocrat and military officer who served in the Continental Army under General George Washington during the American Revolution. His military prowess was especially helpful to the American cause during battles in New England and at the victory-clinching battle of Yorktown. When he was buried in Paris in 1834, a grateful American public provided soil from the historic battlefield of Bunker Hill in Boston.[316]

Participating in the overlapping celebrations were Count Gilbert de Pusy Lafayette, Lafayette's sixth-generation grandson; Senator-Mayor Jean Pierre Leleux of Grasse, France; Alan Hoffman, President of the Massachusetts Lafayette Society. All spoke in honor of the occasions. Hoffman further tied the celebrations together by noting Lafayette's commitment to racial equality.

Musical grace was added to the Legion of Honor ceremony by Marvin's son, David, who played guitar accompanied by singers Robert Honeysucker and Yuriko Nonako.

After the formal Legion of Honor presentation, the throng retired to the Union Club, close by the State House on Beacon Hill's Park Street, for a celebratory luncheon. Marvin and key participants made a short detour to the nearby Lafayette Monument on Boston Common. There, they laid a wreath in honor of the 176th anniversary of the general's death. The Regiment Saintonge provided a musketry salute.

Then it was on the luncheon. More speeches were made. Resolutions by various government bodies were presented. And in a day filled with commemorations of long-past events – some decades in the rearview mirror, some more than a century prior – one last set of honors was conferred on Marvin.

Sterling MacLeod, colonel of the Massachusetts Army National Guard field artillery, accompanied by the 54th Massachusetts Voluntary Regiment Honor Guard presented Marvin with six medals that the U.S. Army had never quit gotten around to awarding in the previous decades.

Participation by the honor guard of the 54th reflected the anti-segregation spirit of that May day. The regiment's roots run back to the Civil War. It was born as the first military unit consisting of black soldiers to be raised in the North during the Civil War. But the regiment's creation was controversial, even in abolitionist Boston. The federal government caved in to national white public pressure. Secretary of War Edwin Stanton appointed white officers to command the regiment. And its black troops quickly understood exactly how much danger they put themselves into by joining the Army.

Confederate President Jefferson Davis issued a proclamation that equated black Union soldiers with slaves in revolt. That meant that any captured black troops could be tossed into slavery – or executed on the spot. They were stripped in advance of whatever protection they were supposed to receive as prisoners of war.[317]

As the war dragged on, executions and atrocities against black Union troops were common, according to historian Donald Shaffer. Some black POWs were used as forced labor by the Confederates. Some were forced to be personal servants of rebel soldiers. Some were sent into slavery on rebel soldiers' farms and plantations. Following one 1864 battle, many African-American soldiers were massacred as they attempted to surrender. The relatively "lucky" captured black troops throughout the war were merely carted off to prison camps, which were generally notorious hell holes.

Still, the regiment fought with distinction in South Carolina and Georgia. Their valor encouraged President Abraham Lincoln to enlist more African-Americans into the Union army.[318] The regiment's heroism in the face of adversity was portrayed in the 1989 film *Glory*, whose cast included Denzel Washington and Morgan Freeman.

The regiment and its leadership have also been memorialized in a dramatic, famous monument created by the renowned American sculptor Augustus Saint-Gaudens. On their way from the State House to the Lafayette Memorial, Marvin and the Lafayette Society contingent passed by the famous memorial, which sits at the peak of Boston Common.

At the luncheon, the medals that Col. MacLeod conferred on Marvin were the Good Conduct Medal; the American Campaign Medal; the European-African-Eastern Campaign Medal & Bronze Star Attachment (the four stars indicate that Marvin was in four major campaigns); the World War II Victory Medal; the Honorable Service Lapel Button (WWII); and the Sharpshooter Badge & Rifle Bar.

Well and good. But why so many decades after Marvin's discharge? Was the Army embarrassed into catching up on these awards to a veteran, whom France saw fit to decorate before the Army paid homage to one of its own?

"That was how they treated black soldiers," Marvin said. "They tried to ignore us during the war, and France finally forced them to remember who I was. Better late than never. I accepted the medals for all of the men who fought with me, for all of the men who died. None of *them* should ever be forgotten."

Saying Thanks

While the U.S. Army was tardy in showing its appreciation to Marvin for his service, France's cup of gratitude was running over. After France conferred its Legion of Honor decoration on Marvin in May, in September of 2010 the French city of Grasse invited Marvin, Massachusetts Lafayette Society President Alan Hoffman, Consul General Christophe Guilhou, and seven members of the Marblehead, Massachusetts-Grasse Sister-City Committee to a three-day series of celebrations and ceremonies in Grasse.

The happy occasion was the birthday of the 18th-century Admiral Francois Joseph Paul Compte de Grasse, a member of the family for whom the French city is named. The admiral, like Lafayette a friend of the American rebels in their fight for liberation from Britain, commanded a French fleet that helped seal victory over British forces in the decisive siege and battle at Yorktown, Virginia.

Also among the participants was Vice Admiral Harry Harris, Jr., Commander, U.S. 6th Fleet in the Mediterranean and Commander of NATO's Striking and Support Forces.

"The French were outstanding hosts," Marvin said. "They made me feel like visiting royalty. They made me feel like the entire celebration was in honor of me. Of course it was not. I was flattered to be invited. It was just nice to know that this city still remembered how American troops, including black soldiers, had sacrificed for their freedom."

Marvin's Karma

"Karma" means payback. It is the Hindu equivalent for the American saying about chickens coming home to roost. In the long run, you get what you deserve. And it works two ways. A nice person ends up having good karma. An evil person creates his own bad karma.

In the year 2000, Marvin was visited by some decidedly good karma.

In April of that year, as the annual anniversary of the World War II D-Day invasion approached, Marvin finally got his high school diploma. In a Massachusetts Department of Veterans' Services program called Operation Recognition, Cambridge Rindge & Latin School, the successor to Marvin's old Cambridge Latin, awarded the then-75-year-old Army veteran his diploma. The program empowers high schools to grant diplomas to veterans who left school to enlist in the military or because they were drafted.

Marvin says the better-late-than-never public high school diploma is one of his prized possessions. That ceremony also helped renew Marvin's relationship with his old school. He visited again from time to time over the following years, and one of his fondest possessions is a thank-you note sent to him by students he spoke with in March 2012.

He told the youngsters about growing up in their city, and he told them about the rigors of war.

"Boys like me from Cambridge went to war so youngsters like them would not have to," Marvin said.

In their group note, the students thanked Marvin for sharing his experiences. One of the students, named Natalie, understood the big picture. She understood that Marvin not only fought for what is right during World War II but also year by year after that, right up to the present.

"Dear Marvin," she wrote in a sky-blue ink. "I found your stories very inspiring! Anytime I pass Marvin Gilmore Square or Dudley Square I am reminded of the many things you went through and how you never stopped. Even at the age of 87!!"

Tom Brokaw

In May of 2000, Marvin's karma continued to deliver good things to him.

He was featured on an "NBC Nightly News" segment. Anchorman Tom Brokaw's topic was about the sacrifices, risks, and rewards of minority veterans like Marvin during World War II.

Day of Honor

On May 25, Marvin participated in the Day of Honor 2000 program.

The program paid homage to minorities veterans – African-Americans, Asian-Americans, Hispanic Americans, Native Americans, Pacific islanders, and Native Alaskans, whose World War II service is often overlooked by mainstream society. "Sometimes the contributions of minorities was overlooked because of prejudice," said William "Smitty" Smith, project executive of Day of Honor and now founding executive director of the National Center for Race Amity.

The morning of May 25 Marvin represented black World War II veterans in the Laying of the Wreath at the Tomb of the Unknown Soldier at Arlington National Cemetery. Later he joined President William Clinton at the White House for a ceremony in which the president signed a proclamation recognizing the contributions of minority veterans in the Second World War. Marvin was among the guests who were invited to stand behind President Clinton, witnessing the moment as he signed the document.[319]

Clinton's proclamation noted that by the war's end, some 15 million Americans had served in the U.S. Armed Forces. Their ranks included more than 1.2 million African Americans, 300,000 Hispanic Americans, 50,000 Asian Americans, 20,000 Native Americans, 6,000 Native Hawaiians and Pacific Islanders, and 3,000 Native Alaskans.

The proclamation pointed out that minority veterans fought important battles against America's enemies, as well as "battles against prejudice, ignorance, and discrimination. Many gave their lives on foreign soil for the freedom they had never fully shared at home. Many of those who survived returned home from the war and worked to make real in America the ideals for which they had fought so hard and for which so many of their comrades in arms had died."

The proclamation continued, "On this Day of Honor, we have the opportunity – and the responsibility – to acknowledge the contributions our minority veterans have made to the peace and freedom we enjoy today. I ask my fellow citizens to join me in saluting the [minority soldiers] who served so valiantly in our Armed Forces during World War II and to remember those who died in service to our country. Their extraordinary devotion to duty is a reminder to us all that our Nation's diversity is not a cause for division, but rather one of our greatest strengths."

To further celebrate Marvin's award, the Republic invited him for a three-day tribute in France in September 2010. The culmination was an event attended by Vice Admiral Harry Harris, Jr., Commander, U.S. 6th Fleet and Commander of NATO's Striking and Support Forces.

Encore

Marvin latest visit to France was in June 2014. The highlight was a ceremony that marked the solemn 70th anniversary of the invasion that began to pry Nazi Germany's chokehold from around the throat of Europe. Marvin was among the veterans who were invited to the commemoration by President Barak Obama and French President Francois Hollande. The observance was at the Normandy American Cemetery and Memorial in Colleville-sur-Mer on the morning of June 6.

The cemetery overlooks the Omaha beach invasion section, the bloodiest of the Normandy landing sites. It is the final resting place of 9,387 American soldiers who died in Europe during the Second World War. Most of those perished during the D-Day landings and operations that followed. Its one million annual visitors make it the most visited American military cemetery on foreign soil.

On the morning of June 6, 2014, 70 years after a young Marvin had stormed a murderous Normandy shore with tens of thousands of his comrades, Marvin was up early as usual. On this day he dressed and at 5 a.m. left his hosts' home, the Chateau de Tocqueville, with friends for a return visit to the broad sandy beach. On Marvin's first visit to this shore, 70 years earlier, the mud flats and sand had been transformed into a bloody cutting board by the slashing, searing, screeching heavy weapons of its German occupiers, who fired from inside their steel and concrete bunkers and trenches.

When Marvin reached the ceremony area, he was escorted to the stage where he joined other veterans and dignitaries including President Obama, President Francois Hollande, and Queen Elizabeth. This anniversary observation was special. The veterans are in their late eighties and nineties. This was the last time that many of these elderly survivors will be able to attend such a gathering. Each day now 555 are passing away.[320] In five more years, many more of those still alive will be too frail to travel from the U.S. to Normandy. This beach again will be a mortal challenge to these men.

At the end of the ceremony, Marvin got to shake hands with Obama and Hollande and to mingle with his fellow veterans. It was a farewell as much as a fond hello.

Marvin's hands – impressions of them, anyway – will remain in Normandy as part of a memorial to the American soldiers who began the liberation of Europe. Marvin's hand prints were engraved in concrete modules shaped like picture frames, which focus on a particular site on Utah Beach. They frame the precise location where G.I.s first breached defenses erected by the German army along the Normandy beach, which were known as the "Atlantic Wall." Marvin's hand prints are among those of a number of still living veterans' prints used in the modules, which were created by French artist Milene Guermont.

French Connection

In the days leading up to the commemorative event and in the days following, Marvin stayed mainly at the Chateau Alexis de Tocqueville, the ancestral home of its namesake, who was a renowned 19th century French political thinker and historian. He is best known to Americans for his *Democracy in America*, published in 1835. After traveling through the United States, de Tocqueville wrote his book. The work is an admiring look through foreign eyes at the attitudes of Americans, whose young republic was still taking shape. The chateau, whose earliest sections were built in the 1500s, is in the western end of Normandy, east of Cherbourg.

The chateau now is the home of Count Jean-Guillaume, the great-great-great-grand nephew of Alexis de Tocqueville, and his wife, Countess

Stéphanie de Tocqueville d'Hérouville, and their children. Marvin spent time with the Count and Countess, and they autographed a copy of the chateau's brochure. Their inscription reads, "For my friend Marvin Gilmore / With respect and gratitude".

During his Normandy visit, Marvin attended receptions, including one at the Chateau de Count Jean D'Aigneaux. This occasion was another reminder that France backed the insurgent American colonists in their fight for independence from George III with guns and bullets and ships, imperiling their own limbs and lives. D'Aigneaux's is a sixth generation descendant of a French soldier who fought with Lafayette at Yorktown, the decisive battle of the American Revolution.

Marvin attended numerous dinners, concerts, and film exhibitions. (Amazingly, at one concert he ran into an old college chum from his days at New England Conservatory.) No matter what type of gathering he was at, Marvin became a center of attention. Even at concerts and movie exhibitions, Marvin's side comments to his companions caught the ears of other audience members. Realizing Marvin was a veteran and was speaking about war events from first-hand experience, more and more people gathered around to hear his comments and stories before and after the scheduled performances. When Marvin was introduced to audiences, people burst into applause.

One gathering that Marvin attended was for the showing of a film about Robert Murphy, a soldier from Boston who reportedly was the first pathfinder for the 82nd Division. Murphy's job included marking drop zones for paratroopers that would follow. At one point, the film's producer introduced Marvin to the audience. The audience, which included many people who had come to Normandy for the 70th anniversary events, was famished for first-hand accounts of soldiers, so Marvin was bombarded by questions during the ensuing question-and-answer period, he says. He was also swarmed by people asking him to autograph their copies of DVDs of the film and war-related books.

David Hooke, a music-oriented missionary based in London, was in Normandy during the 70th anniversary events with his five-person ensemble, which was performing at local churches.[321] He heard Marvin describing his wartime experiences with fellow visitors to the Airborne Museum in the village of Sainte-Mere-Eglise. The museum is devoted to American paratroopers of 82nd and 101st Airborne Divisions, who played key roles in the Normandy invasion – and who suffered horrific losses in one of the invasion's key battles.

"There was a film showing at the museum," Hooke said. "At the end of it, I happened to notice Marvin at the back of the cinema. I saw him stand and turn to people behind him. I could tell that he was apologizing for being emotional during the film. He explained that he had been involved in the invasion, and that the film brought back memories."

Hooke wanted to talk with Marvin but an appropriate moment never presented itself. Later that day, Hook and his wife and in-laws entered a café for lunch. By chance, he spotted Marvin at a nearby table. Not wanting to lose this second chance, Hooke introduced himself and got to hear more about Marvin's wartime experiences. Hooke made a point of inviting Marvin and his companions to a concert that Hooke's ensemble would give the next day at Sainte-Mere-Eglise, a church bearing the same name as its village.

That church had been in the center of a fierce fire fight in the earliest hours of the D-Day invasion. American paratroopers had descended on the strategic location, but they took tragically heavy casualties. By coincidence, buildings in the village happened to be on fire. Their flames lit the night sky, making the slowly falling paratroopers easy targets for German troops who were overlooking the fire-fighting effort. The parachute of one G.I., John Steele, got caught on the church spire. He had watched the slaughter while hanging helplessly, until he had been taken prisoner.

Seventy years later, Hooke described the Friday-night concert by his ensemble, which is sponsored by the Asaph Christian Trust. He said, "It was a privilege to have met Marvin. I invited him and his party to our concert. He certainly did not have to attend, but he did. Our theme spiritually was that light shines in the darkness, even in the darkness of war. We made a reference to the light coming to the European continent through D-Day and we made a point of asking Marvin to stand and honoring him and his involvement in the invasion and the war."[322]

At one point a German nun who is based at the French church approached Marvin. "It was so neat that things had come full circle," Hooke said. "I remember the nun going up to Marvin. I wondered what she was going to say. How do you respond to the fact that the whole D-Day thing (commemorating a crucial defeat of German forces) is so big in

Normandy? But the first thing that the nun said to Marvin was, 'Thank you ever so much for liberating my people from Adolf Hitler.'"

Hooke says he came away with several vivid impressions of Marvin: "Number one, it was a privilege to have met him. Number two, it was a privilege to have him show up at our concert. Number three – I was struck by this and said this to him: he is about to turn 90, and he looks better at 90 than I feel at 53. He just seemed to have boundless energy, enthusiasm, and enthusiasm for life."

Hooke says that he was so astonished that he googled Marvin when he got home to London days later. Hooke said, "I was impressed by what he had done in terms of his life, his career. The thing I never got an answer to was the whole dynamic about being African-American. What was it like in the Army? Things were very different in the States toward African-Americans then and even toward African-Americans who fought in the war. They would have been in the minority. I never got to ask how he felt about being African-American at a time when attitudes were quite different."

Charles J. Ogletree, Jr., the Harvard Law School professor, provides one answer:

"Marvin has lived through segregation. He has been treated differently and called names and been the victim of slurs and racism throughout his career. But he fought many [of the people who discriminated against him and insulted him] by smiling and getting past the episode, and by having a tough skin and proving people wrong. That's his biggest weapon: proving people wrong.

"He shows that if he gets a piece of the [economic] pie, he shares it and makes sure the pie is available to all members of society.

"He's my hero because of what he has been able to do throughout his life.

"I can't imagine having the patience or tolerance in the face of the vile and racist things he has put up with and the inappropriate remarks he's heard and been subjected to and directed at him, trying to keep him down.

"Marvin doesn't complain about the past. He complains about overcoming obstacles and about needing to be strong and forward looking and being talented at what you do despite things they [bigots] says about you and other people of color."[323]

Micqueen Clerger spent time with Marvin in Normandy during June 2014 as an assistant to the organizer of Marvin's traveling group. Clerger, who was a 21-year-old about to enter her senior year at UMass Boston, says her time with Marvin taught her the value of sticking up for your beliefs. She heard many of Marvin's stories about not backing down from injustice during his many years in war and in peace. Turning the other cheek would have been easier for him many times. But justice itself would have suffered. She understood the connections to her own life.

"Not only was I able to listen to Gilmore's accomplishments, I was also able to listen to what he had endured being on the front line and being an African-American in this intricate world," she said. "I think he has come a long way, and today he taught me a lot. He taught me to always remain firm, and stand up for what I believe in. Never walk away from a fight, never show your weakness."[324]

The best summary of Marvin's life's work comes from Marvin, the nonstop fighter, the nonstop entrepreneur, the philanthropist, the fearless civil rights agitator: "It all boils down to helping people get treated fairly. Sometimes that means helping people get jobs. Sometimes it means helping people live free from fear of dictators or crackers. I was never afraid to fight for what I believed in. Sometimes I wonder whether I should have been afraid. I was young. I was lucky. Maybe I should have been afraid sometimes. But you know what? I'd do it all again."

The Power of Friendship

A lot of what Marvin means to the community was captured in a warm-spirited barbecuing of the man, who allowed himself to be a piñata for puns and punch lines as the guest of honor in a roast conducted to raise money for Boston's Whittier Street Health Center, in April 2001.

With 3,000 generous friends and contributors on hand at Boston's Hynes Auditorium, Marvin endured being poked fun of – all in an atmosphere of appreciation and good-humor – by a skewering gallery of Boston power brokers, many from the African-American community. Edward W. Brooke, who served in the U.S. Senate from 1967 until 1979, summarized how much the people and organizations in attendance valued what Marvin had done for each of them over the decades with the closing words of his limerick: "You are many things to many people / And on that good note I shall end / Blessed with the knowledge that, like others, I have you as a friend."

Next Phase

As his ninetieth birthday in September 2014 approached, Marvin made plans to retire from the Community Development Corporation of Boston. That gear shift would enable him to devote more time to community, education, and philanthropic activities. It would also give him the flexibility to spend more time with family and friends.

"I want to work a little less. I want to smell the roses," he said.

But working less on various projects and causes does not mean no work at all. With a mischievous smile, he joked, "Maybe I'll cut back to a 16-hour day!"

Says Marvin's friend, the writer Andrew Szanton: "Marvin shifts gears so easily. One moment he's laughing and his eyes are twinkling. The next he is dead serious. Marvin is a fearless speaker. He says what's on his mind. Then he might stop, look at you, and pause. You can practically see the mental gears turning. He's silent, but there's a lot going on inside. He may be silent, but he's really thinking, 'What's my next project?'"

Appendix A

Who Owned Marvin's Ancestors?

In Chapter 1 we looked at Marvin's family tree, tracing his relatives back in time. On his mother's side of the family, for example, the tree goes back to Kizzie Rowell, Marvin's great great grandmother, who lived in rural Alabama and was born in Virginia in 1812.

And we learned what some of Marvin's ancestors did for a living. For example, Jerimiah Rowell, Kizzie's son, was a tenant farmer or sharecropper. We also saw that his worldly possessions were worth a total of $125 in 1870. That was a pittance compared to the $18,000 in personal property owned by white neighbors like Burrell Barrow.

But none of that answers this big question: Before the end of slavery, who owned Kizzie and Jerimiah and his wife Milly?

If any ownership documents exist, they have not yet been found. In fact, it is difficult to find records of any sort for slaves before 1865 because little such paperwork existed. Slave-owning society refused to treat African-Americans as human beings. In Chapter I we pointed out that federal census records, for example, rarely identified slaves by name. The 1790, 1800 and 1810 censuses show only the total number of slaves an owner held. The

A Changing U.S.

Black History

Origins of American Slavery

It was impossible. Yet Jonah did it. He emerged intact from the belly of a beast. So too Marvin's family survived something huge and threatening, which made every attempt to consume them. They survived an evil institution that goes back nearly 500 years.

After first appearing earlier elsewhere in the New World, slavery came to what would become the United States in 1526.[i] Spanish colonizer Lucas Vasquez de Allyon brought the first African slaves to the future U.S.

next three censuses listed slaves by sex and age range.

The 1850 and 1860 censuses added slave schedules. Those owner inventories of slaves typically listed slaves only by gender and age, not by names. Slave schedules were as impersonal as an inventory list of tools in a work shop. Some schedules also detailed whether any of slaves were fugitives on the run from their owner, had been released from slavery (known as "manumitted"), and were deaf or mute (which was called "dumb"), blind, insane, or "idiotic."

The refusal to acknowledge a slave's humanity was endemic, extending to nearly all forms of record-keeping. Exceptions were made only for the convenience of slave owners. For instance, one or more particular slaves could be identified by name for the sake of clarity in some business or legal transactions such as the sale or bequest of a black person.

So figuring out who owned Kizzie, Jerimiah, and Milly requires detective work.

Picture Puzzle

Start by looking at the evidence. Marvin's family kept some birth records, but none that go as far back as Kizzie.

What about government paperwork? Census lists are one of the most useful tools for tracking family connections. But before the Thirteenth Amendment ended slavery in 1865 throughout the United States, censuses generally did not count

when he landed at present day Georgetown, South Carolina, on Winyah Bay at the mouth of the Pee Dee River to start the first colony in the Carolinas, San Miguel de Guadalupe.[ii]

Ironically, this site of the first black slaves on what would be U.S. soil was also where the first slave revolt erupted. As illness decimated the colonists' ranks, the surviving slaves rebelled and fled.

Unfortunately, slavery fared better elsewhere. By the 1800s roughly 20 million Africans had been kidnapped from homes in western and southeast Africa for sale into bondage and shipment to the Americas. Half died before they reached the African coast for shipment across the ocean.[iii] Of the survivors, slavers brought about 645,000 to today's United States.[iv]

The brutal voyage across the Atlantic

312

and identify slaves by name. Former slaves first show up by name in post-Civil War censuses. The first federal one to do that was in 1870.[325]

So when you try to find out who owned Kizzie, Jerimiah, and Milly, you run into a stone wall.

But that does not mean there are no clues whatsoever. At first glance, that 1870 census report looks as indecipherable as a jigsaw puzzle before the pieces are put together. None of the dozens of lines of information seem related to each other. It looks random and chaotic.

But it isn't. A fascinating picture emerges when you take time to piece together individual names, facts, and figures. Snap together pieces of the puzzle and they form a picture that shows you more than seemed to be there in the first place.

Marvin's great-great grandfather Jerimiah Rowell and Marvin's great-great grandmother Milly appear in the 1870 U.S. census for Macon County, Alabama. The census records called their community "Notasulga Beat." That referred to the municipality of Notasulga as well as its environs.[326]

The Rowells were the 96th family in the 93rd home visited by the census taker in that district. They appear halfway down page 11 of the July 7 tally. It looks like they lived on today's Country Road 60, probably west of Country Road 31, or on CR 31 itself as it bends southeast toward Wolf Creek.

became known as the Middle Passage. It was the middle leg of a three-part journey.

The first leg departed from any of several European ports, with the ship bearing a cargo of goods such as iron, cloth, brandy, firearms, and gunpowder. A Public Broadcasting Service (PBS) Web site describes the rest: "Upon landing on Africa's 'slave coast,' the cargo was exchanged for Africans.

Fully loaded with its human cargo, the ship set sail for the Americas,… The African slave boarding the ship had no idea what lay ahead…. [In the Americas] slaves were exchanged for sugar, tobacco, or some other product.

The final leg brought the ship back to Europe."[v]

The slaves' voyage was hellish. Slaves were branded like cattle with hot irons. They were restrained with shackles.

313

In this farming district, one resident after another listed his or her occupation as farmer or farm hand. A few said they are keeping house; they are homemakers. Youngsters were listed as students or, already, farm hands. A small number had some occupation such as wagon driver. Jerimiah, who was listed by his nickname Mia, and his wife Milly identified themselves as farm hands. So Jerimiah did not own his own farm. He was a tenant farmer or sharecropper. That was common for newly freed black men. A man who owned his farm was identified as a farmer, not farm hand.

The Rowells had four children. Walter was one year old. Caleb was five. Edmond was eight. The oldest was Sophronia, 11 years old, who was also listed as a farm hand.

When Sophronia grew up, she would become Marvin's grandmother. It was Sophronia who sat with Marvin on an outdoor bench in Central Square in Cambridge, Massachusetts, enjoying a day in the sun, while she told him tales of her childhood as a slave and in the years soon after the Thirteenth Amendment outlawed slavery. She also told Marvin the horror stories about slavery that she witnessed and that were told to her by older relatives.

All of those cautionary tales were filed away permanently in Marvin's memory. They shaped his personality. They helped shape him into a man who has spent a lifetime fighting for his own

They were packed aboard wooden ships, typically crammed below decks, often with less than five feet of headroom. Three to four hundred abductees were sardined into tight quarters with little ventilation and often no buckets for human waste. Disease was rampant.

Slaves were treated as if they were nothing. But they were in fact valuable. The PBS site elaborates: "A slave who tried to starve him or herself was tortured. If torture didn't work, the slave was force fed with the help of a contraption called a *speculum orum*, which held the mouth open."

Still, the horrid conditions slew an estimated 10% to 20% of the slaves during transportation.

Importation of new slaves was federally outlawed after 1807, but illegal smuggling continued.[vi] And slavery rights and for the rights of others.

But that's not the end of the clues we can glean from the 1870 census report.

If you look closely, you'll notice that a second "family" also resided at home number 93, where Jerimiah and his family lived. In that second family were two people: Elizabeth Clough and Kizzie Rowell.

Who are they? What's their connection to Jerimiah and Milly? The census taker dutifully noted that Kizzie was 58 years old. Her occupation was keeping house. At her age, relatively elderly for that day, she was too old to work farm fields, so she was a homemaker.

Jerimiah (Mia) and Milly Rowell were 32 and 30 years old. Kizzie was 26 years older than Mia, had the same last name, lived at this very same location, but was counted as part of a different "family." Why? Because Mia and Milly were a married couple with kids. Kizzie, then, was Mia's mother.

Family Ties

We care about the Rowells because they are Marvin's great-great grandparents. We know this by backtracking through each U.S. census after 1870 as well as documents like birth, death, and marriage records, military draft forms, voter registrations, a family tally of births and a few deaths that was tucked for safe keeping into a bible for decades, and so on. Step by step, decade by decade, it leads in a straight line back to Marvin Gilmore.

itself remained legal in the United States until adoption of the Thirteenth Amendment to the Constitution late in 1865. With rare exceptions, each newborn black added to the ranks of slaves. So by 1860 the number of slaves approached 4 million.[vii]

Today's African-Americans are almost entirely descendants of Africans dragged against their will into the U.S. and its predecessor territory, mainly from 1526 through 1807 plus some additions until 1865 as well. With key waves of white immigration not taking place until after the Civil War, the average African-American has been in the United States about 100 years longer than the average European American.[viii]

Still, slavery was not exclusively a Southern institution. It existed in the North as well, but

And that makes Kizzie, Mia's mother, Marvin's great-great-great grandmother.

So this trunk of the family lineage started with Kizzie. Her son Jerimiah married Milly Cluff. They had three sons and a daughter, Sophronia. Sophronia eventually married Ruse Onel, later also identified as Reese Oneal, Reece O'Neal, and Reason O'Neal. Sophronia and Ruse had 10 children, six girls and four boys. One of their daughters was listed on the 1900 census as Agusta Onel. Census takers wrote down names as they sounded. By the 1920 census Agusta was listed as Legusta Oneal. She was Marvin Gilmore's mother, Lee Augusta O'Neal.[327]

The 93rd Home

You can mine more golden nuggets of information from that 1870 census page. Notice what else the census taker felt compelled to do on this sheet of paper. He drew a bracket connecting all of the Rowells as well as Elizabeth Clough and their next door neighbor, Nancy Clough, and next door to her, Hal Thrasher. Why did the census taker do it? Because they were the only black people on this page.

And there's another intriguing detail. Census takers often recorded nicknames instead of proper names. That's how Jerimiah got listed as Mia. (We know they are the same person because so many of their vital records are exact matches.) Census takers often spelled names phonetically based on what they heard or

state by state its abolition was voted between 1777 and 1804.[ix]

Even after that, slavery was not restricted to the Confederacy. Slavery was legal in five other states as well. In the 1860 federal census, slaves were counted in Delaware, Kansas, Kentucky, Maryland, Missouri, and Nebraska. Three of those had sizable numbers of humans languishing in bondage. In Kentucky more than 225,000 blacks were enslaved by more than 39,000 owners. In Maryland more than 87,000 souls were held against their will. And the ranks of slaves topped 115,000 in Missouri.

Surprisingly, some slave owners were black.[xi] Some were free blacks, especially in the South, who could only liberate their family members by buying them. A few were free blacks who bought African-Americans to thought they heard. That's why Lee Augusta was first listed as Agusta. And census takers often guessed at how names should be spelled. Marvin's grandmother shows up in various records as Sophronia, Saphronia, Saffronia, and Sofronia.

A similar thing happened to Milly Cluff, Jerimiah's wife. In other official documents her first name was spelled Millie.

Now look again at Elizabeth Clough's name. Remember, Clough lived at the same address as the Rowells. Elizabeth Clough was 35, five years older than Milly. Since she lived under the same roof as the Rowells, virtually shared a family name with Milly, and was close in age to Milly, in all likelihood Elizabeth was Milly's sister! One version of their family name – either Cluff or Clough – is the correct spelling; the other is a phonetic imitation, a haphazard guess by a weary, maybe even lazy and disdainful bureaucrat census taker.

Looking along this census route, we find more pieces of the jigsaw that fit together.

The Rowells, Elizabeth Clough, and Kizzie Rowell lived under one roof. Right next door, five-year-old Nancy Clough lived with David and Mary McCloud. The census form clearly identifies both McClouds as white. So was Nancy Clough living with the McClouds because she had been born into slavery under them? Or was Nancy Clough the illegitimate daughter of David McCloud?

profit off their toil and sweat as venally as any white slave owner. Yet others were of mixed race, including many whose mothers were black slaves and who got a jump start towards a life of relative luxury by being set up with land and money by their wealthy white fathers.

Demand (especially by white farmers) for slaves in the South got a key boost from the invention of the cotton gin – "gin" is short for engine – a device that greatly increased the efficiency of combing seeds from harvested cotton and which amped up the profitability of cotton cultivation. If cotton was king, the gin was its throne.

Largely due to each slave's role in producing the profits that sprang from cotton, the value of a prime field hand by 1860 was $1,800. That price had skyrocketed five-fold since 1800.[xii]

Elizabeth might have been Nancy's biological mother. Milly also might have been her mom. If David McCloud was her father, then the McCloud household was a snapshot of the power white slave owners had over their black slaves.

But there are more reasons we care about David McCloud. For one thing, he needed farm hands. In the 1870 census he is identified as a farmer and land owner, whose farm was worth $400. That's equivalent to $7,110 today. It was enough land to produce nearly $100,000 of annual income in today's money.[328]

For another thing, he was born in North Carolina. His wife was a native of Georgia. Ring any bells? Mia Rowell was born in Georgia. (His mother, Kizzie, was born in Virginia.) You can't help but wonder if Mia Rowell had been part of Mary McCloud's dowry, and if the McClouds had owned Mia before 1865.

Following the Clues

To learn that a particular person owned a specific slave, it helps to find a document such as a deed, bill of sale, receipt, or will that recorded the transfer of ownership of a specific slave from one white person to another. Those documents often named the slave. But no such evidence has been found in an archive or attic or dusty antique footlocker, showing who owned Jerimiah.

Yet there are tantalizing clues. The first is Jerimiah's last name. It was common for a freed slave to take the last

Just compare that to Jerimiah Rowell's personal worth of $125 in 1870. The price of a slave in 1860 was more than 14 times higher than all the money and personal property Jerimiah had managed to save in five years of labor as a free man.

Slave ownership required wealth. Not everyone could afford to own slaves. Less than 6% of free people in what were about to declare themselves the Confederate States of America were slave holders in 1860.[xiii] In states with slavery outside the soon-to-be Confederacy, such as Kentucky, Maryland, and Missouri, less than 3% of the free population owned African-Americans. But the benefits of slavery to slave owners, their families, and other free household members was widespread. Nearly 25% of Southern households name of his former owner. And many white, farm-owning Rowells lived in the community. There was Albert H. Rowell. Remember him? As we learned in Chapter 1, he was the well-to-do white farmer who lived in the Notasulga area with his fine family and who, in 1860, owned 15 slaves.

But when he was deprived of the free labor of slaves after the Civil War, he fled to Texas to start over again.

Still, Albert does not appear to have been Jerimiah's owner. How do we know? None of Albert Rowell's slaves was the same age as Jerimiah. That year, 1860, Jerimiah would have been 22 years old, based on his 32 years of age listed on the 1870 census. That means he was born in 1838. But in 1860, none of Albert Rowell's slaves, male or female, was 22. The closest in age was a 25-year-old male.

However, 10 years later – in the 1880 U.S. census – Jerimiah's year of birth is listed as "about 1835."[329] If 1835 was the correct year of Jerimiah's birth, then he would have been 25 years old in 1860, the same age as another one of Albert Rowell's male slaves. Was that accurate? It seems more likely that the 1870 census was correct. It would be easier for the census taker to get Jerimiah's right age when the black farm hand was younger, had a good memory, was fewer years removed from his birthday, and was being counted for the first time.

And that 1880 rendition of Jerimiah's age was contradicted a second time. The 1900 federal census lists his birth month

owned slaves in 1860.[xiv] That's one in every four families. It ranged from 20% – one in five – in Arkansas to 49% in Mississippi.[xv]

And among recruits in 1861 to the Rebel army, almost one of every two lived with slaveholders.[xvi]

"Nor did the direct exposure [to slave ownership] stop there," *The Atlantic* explained in August 2010, describing how widespread the cancer of slavery was in the Southern corpus, including its military. "Untold numbers of enlistees rented land from, sold crops to, or worked for slaveholders. In the final tabulation, the vast majority of the volunteers of 1861 had a direct connection to slavery. For slaveholder and nonslaveholder alike, slavery lay at the heart of the Confederate nation. The fact that their paper notes frequently depicted scenes of slaves demonstrated the and year as March of 1833.[330] That would have made him 27 in the year 1860. Albert Rowell's two male slaves closest in age were 24 and 30 years old. No match.

A second reason to doubt that Albert Rowell owned Jerimiah involves geography. The white Rowell was born in Virginia on January 11, 1821.[331] By 1830 he appears to have moved to Lowndes County, Alabama with his father.[332] And Albert became sheriff of Tallapoosa County, Alabama, in 1842.[333] There's no indication that he relocated to Georgia before that. Yet Jerimiah Rowell was born in Georgia in 1838.

Still, there's another Rowell-to-Rowell connection that provides circumstantial evidence pointing to one or more white Rowells as having been owners of Jerimiah and Kizzie. Remember that Jerimiah's mother Kizzie was born in Virginia in 1812. It turns out that Albert Rowell's father, Howell, was born in that same state in October 1795.[334]

So did the elder white Rowell, Howell, own Kizzie back in Virginia? Was Kizzie born into slavery on Howell Rowell's farm in Greensville, Virginia? And did Howell later bring Kizzie to Alabama? Very possible.

Did Howell Rowell Own Jerimiah?

It's also possible that Howell initially owned Jerimiah as well. Perhaps Jerimiah was born while Howell Rowell and Kizzie were travelling between Alabama and Virginia after Howell had moved to the institution's central role and symbolic value to the Confederacy."

But the South was not populated exclusively by rich plantation plutarchs who lorded over vast estates with expansive fields preened over by battalions of black workers in bondage. Just the contrary. While owning even a single human being is outrageous, on average each slaveholder possessed 10 slaves.[xvii] That was an appalling injustice, although it fell short of the impression many people have that all slave-worked farms were grandiose plantations like Tara in the fictional *Gone with the Wind*, large-scale agricultural factories whose fields, work shops, kitchens, stables, and more hummed with the activity of countless slaves.

Still, there was an agricultural aristocracy for sure. The topmost,

Cotton State. At some point, Howell Rowell could have given or sold Jerimiah to a member of his own family.

In fact, Howell had 10 children.[335] His first was Albert, who was born in Virginia and moved to Alabama. Some of his next nine children may have been born in Virginia. All ended up living in Alabama.

We've already seen that Albert did not own any slaves whose age matched Jerimiah's. What about Albert's nine siblings? One of them was a daughter named Georgia Ann. She was born in 1842, four years after Jerimiah. If we assume that Howell would have been more likely to give a slave to one of his children who was older than Jerimiah, then Georgia Ann would have been an unlikely recipient of Jerimiah.

Four more of Albert's siblings were born from 1831 to 1837. None would have been at least 10 years older than Jerimiah. So, they too would have been less likely recipients of Jerimiah, although it's not out of the question.

That leaves four more of Albert's siblings. Each was at least 10 years older than Jerimiah: Catherine was born in 1822, Robert Edward was born in 1824, Isaac Rowe was born in 1827, and William Douglas was born in 1828. They seem to be the best bets among Howell Rowell's offspring to have received Jerimiah as a gift from dear old dad.

We can eliminate Isaac straight off. He died at age one.[336]

Catherine E. Rowell had the means.

crowning class of land barons presided over stunning numbers of slaves. In 1860, 20% to 30% of the total number of slaves were enchained by farm moguls who owned 200 or more slaves each, according to researcher Tom Blake.[xviii] The biggest single holder of slaves within one county was the estate of Joshua J. Ward of Georgetown, South Carolina. His 1,130 slaves were the largest group of slaves within any one county anywhere in the U.S. (The last U.S. census slave count, in 1860, was compiled by county.) Blake found another 15 owners of 500 to 999 slaves each. Together, those 16 were the largest American slaveholders in 1860.

Blake included a slaveholder in this top 16 only if he held more than 500 slaves in a single location. He limited his tallies in that way because he could not be

She married Edmund Webb around 1843, and the 1860 census shows that he was a wealthy man. The Virginia-born farmer's land was worth $4,000. His other assets were worth $21,000.[337] That would be $586,000 in today's money.[338] He even lived within a few farms of William Douglas Rowell and a man named William W. Webb – a brother, maybe? – who was born in Georgia, like Jerimiah Rowell. And the Webbs owned slaves – 10 of them in 1860.[339] None of them was around Kizzie's age. One male slave was age 24. Close to but not quite an age match for Jerimiah, who would have been 22 in 1860. One of Webb's female slaves was 19, close in age to Milly, Jerimiah's wife and Marvin's great-great grandmother, who would have been 20.

If the census taker was careless and slightly mistaken about ages, we're looking at Jerimiah and Milly's owners. But the age discrepancies cloud the possibility of ownership by Catherine (Rowell) and Edmund Webb. What about Robert Edward Rowell and William Douglas Rowell? Could either have owned Jerimiah?

While not as wealthy as William Webb, Robert Edward Rowell was a successful farmer and owner of 12 slaves. None was anywhere near Kizzie's age. But one of them was a male and 22 years old in 1860, the right age to have been Jerimiah.[340] Still, Robert Rowell had already moved to Marion County, Texas by 1860, taking his slaves and family with

sure that listings of slaves under the same owner's name in different places, even within a single county, were in fact holdings of the same person. They could have been different owners with the same name.

In the few cases where he had evidence that different farm operations were owned by the same person, he included that slave owner in his list if the combined number of slaves warranted it. That's why "Jno. Robinson" of Madison County, Mississippi, who owned five separate plantations, each with a different overseer, whose slave rolls totaled 550, is in Blake's top 16, for instance.

Collectively, those top 16 owners' 11,406 slaves accounted for about one of every 346 slaves in the U.S. Their bondage fueled enterprises in South Carolina, Mississippi, Louisiana, Alabama, him.[341] When war erupted, he joined the Confederate Army, becoming part of the 18th regiment of the Texas Infantry, company DFS. Coming from wealth and having an education, he served as a surgeon.[342]

That leaves William Douglas Rowell. Unlike his brother Robert, in 1860 William lived in the right place, Macon County, Alabama. That's where Jerimiah lived after the Civil War. William was 32 years old and single.[343] He owned six slaves.[344]

None was close in age to Kizzie. None was near Jerimiah's. One girl was two years younger than Milly. Certainly no strong indication that William owned any of Marvin's ancestors.

Unless...

William's 1860 slave schedule lists a 28-year-old male. That *could* have been Jerimiah, but only based on Jerimiah's age in the 1900 U.S. census, not the 1870 census, which we've been assuming is more likely to be correct because it was earlier. Yet the 1900 census *could* be correct. That census listed Jerimiah's birth month and year as March of 1833. That would have made him 27 in 1860 up until March. After March in 1860, he would have been 28 – the exact same age as that male slave owned by William Rowell.

But how do we explain the fact that Jerimiah was born in Georgia? One likely scenario: Jerimiah was born while his mother was traveling with whichever Rowell owned her between Virginia and Alabama.

The slave owner Rowell could have

Arkansas, and Georgia.

"Everybody knows slavery was big business," Marvin said. "But most people have no idea just how huge its scope was, how widely it permeated life in the U.S. and especially the South. It is hard not to get angry about it. It's a miracle my ancestors survived. It says something about their guts and passion and strength."

Sidebar notes

[i] Herbert Aptheker, *American Negro Slave Revolts* (New York: Columbia University Press, sixth edition, 1993), p. 163.
[ii] J.D. Lewis, "Lucas Vasquez de Allyon," http://www.carolana.com/Carolina/Explorers/lucasdeallyon.html, accessed Aug. 17, 2012.
[iii] WGBH, "People & Events / The Middle Passage: c.1600 – 1800":

had lots of business and family reasons to shuttle between the two states. Many people did. And in the post-Civil War period there was a major thoroughfare that took travelers from Virginia to the very part of Alabama where the Rowells resided. The segment known as the Great Wagon Road dated back to the colonial era, and it ran from Virginia south to Augusta, Georgia.

That, other roads, and other forms of transportation facilitated the relocation of an incredible number of slaves, reaching almost 300,000, in the 1830s. Alabama and Mississippi alone received 100,000 each.[345]

Jerimiah was among them or he arrived soon after. He may well have traveled along a similar byway, the Old Federal Road, which extended the Great Wagon Road westward through Macon, Montgomery, and Lowndes Counties in Alabama.[346] Those places are exactly where Jerimiah and the many white Rowells resided. Those roads were nineteenth-century dirt versions of today's multilane interstate highways. They were busy, important commercial links among Southern states.

And how did the Rowells come to possess Kizzie? A strong clue appears in some of Howell Rowell's slave schedules. No female slave matching Kizzie's age is in his slave schedule of 1820. But in 1830, when Kizzie would have been 18, Howell reports owning two female slaves who were between 10 and 24 years old.[347] Kizzie could have been one of them. If that

http://www.pbs.org/wgbh/aia/part1/1p277.html, accessed Aug. 18, 2012. Alistair Boddy-Evans, "How Many Slaves Were Taken from Africa?" About.com: http://africanhistory.about.com/cs/slavery/a/slavenumbers.htm, accessed Aug. 18, 2012.

[iv] Graziella Bertocchi and Arcangelo Dimico, "Slavery, Education, and Inequality," http://morgana.unimore.it/bertocchi_graziella/papers/slaveryweb.pdf, accessed Oct. 6, 2012.

[v] WGBH, "People & Events / The Middle Passage: c.1600 – 1800": http://www.pbs.org/wgbh/aia/part1/1p277.html, accessed Aug. 18, 2012.

[vi] Schomberg Center for Research in Black Culture, New York Public Library: http://abolition.nypl.org/essays/us_constitution/5/, accessed Aug. 18, 2012.

[vii] The Civil War Home Page, "Results from the 1860 Census": http://www.civil-war.net/pages/1860_census.html, accessed Aug. 18, 2012.

[viii] Pamela Oliver, African-Americans: History & Politics": http://www.ssc.wisc.edu/~oliver/soc220/Lectures220/AfricanAmericans/African%20Americans%20rev07.pdf, accessed Aug. 16, 2012.

[ix] WGBH, "The Battle for Abolition," American Experience:

was the case, then Howell got Kizzie sometime between her 1812 birth and 1830. He could have bought her or received her as a gift, maybe from his own father. The Kizzie-age female slave shows up again in Howell Rowell's 1840 slave schedule.

Yet another possibility is that Kizzie and/or Jerimiah started out as the property of someone outside the Rowell family. The Rowells were close to many other wealthy white land owners in Alabama. Albert Rowell married Tabatha (spelled Tabitha in some records) Driskell, eldest daughter of the rich and powerful Peter Driskell, on Nov. 11, 1845 in Macon County.[348] In 1850, Peter Driskell, who was about 50 years old, reported owning 15 female and another 15 male slaves on his federal census slave list.[349] One male was 12 years old, Jerimiah's age that year. Five years earlier Driskell easily could have afforded to gift his newlywed daughter and his new son-in-law with one or more slaves. Just as easily, Driskell could have provided slaves by sale or gift to other white Rowells in those years prior to Emancipation.

There is something extremely important we know for sure about Mia Rowell. He valued freedom. On the auspicious date of July 5, 1867, one day after Independence Day and about two years after the end of the Civil War, he registered to vote in Macon County.[350]

"If some cracker was voter registrar, it probably killed him to add Jerimiah's

http://www.pbs.org/wgbh/americanexperience/features/general-article/lincolns-abolition/, accessed Aug. 18, 2012.

[x] The Civil War Home Page, "Results from the 1860 Census": http://www.civil-war.net/pages/1860_census.html, accessed Aug. 18, 2012.

[xi] Wikipedia, "Slavery in the United States," http://en.wikipedia.org/wiki/Slavery_in_the_United_States, accessed Aug. 23, 2012.

[xii] Feross Aboukhadijeh, "Chapter 16: The South and the Slavery Controversy, 1793-1860," StudyNotes.org, Nov. 17, 2012: http://www.apstudynotes.org/us-history/outlines/chapter-16-the-south-and-the-slavery-controversy-1793-1860, accessed Aug. 8, 2012.

[xiii] Author's calculation using data at : http://www.civil-war.net/pages/1860_census.html, accessed Aug. 18, 2012.

[xiv] Andy Hall, "Small Truth Papering Over a Big Lie," The Atlantic, Aug. 9, 2010: http://www.theatlantic.com/national/archive/2010/08/small-truthpapering-over-a-big-lie/61136/, accessed Aug. 19, 2012.

[xv] The Civil War Home Page, "Results from the 1860 Census": http://www.civil-war.net/pages/1860_census.html, accessed Aug. 18, 2012.

[xvi] Andy Hall, "Small Truth

name to the voter list," Marvin chuckles all of these decades later. "I get a real kick out of that. And I'm sure the rest of my entire family, my kids, my relatives, cousins – everyone – does too!"

Papering Over a Big Lie," *The Atlantic,* Aug. 9, 2010: http://www.theatlantic.com/national/archive/2010/08/small-truthpapering-over-a-big-lie/61136/, accessed Aug. 19, 2012.

[xvii] Author's calculation using data at: http://www.civil-war.net/pages/1860_census.html, accessed Aug. 18, 2012.

[xviii] Tom Blake, "The Sixteen Largest American Slaveholders from 1860 Slave Census Schedules": http://freepages.genealogy.rootsweb.ancestry.com/~ajac/biggest16.htm, accessed Aug. 19, 2012.

Appendix B
Slavery's Brutal Enforcement

Just as the Confederacy was willing to wage war in defense of slavery, so too individual supporters of slavery helped perpetuate the institution with a perpetual war against African-Americans in bondage. It took that violence and threats of violence to sustain slavery.

The evil institution's horrors were engraved in the memoir of a South Carolina slave who escaped from his masters around the age of 22.[351] His experience was reported by Reverend Joshua Leavitt in the *Emancipator*, a newspaper of the American Anti-Slavery Society that Leavitt edited. The *Emancipator* published the narrative in installments from August 23 to October 18, 1838. Presumably to protect the runaway slave from retribution or worse, Leavitt did not identify him by name.[352]

Those *Emancipator* installments are safeguarded in the same University of North Carolina library that preserves the original manuscript of *Twelve Years A Slave*. Its author, Solomon Northup, was a free black man from New York, who was kidnapped in Washington, D.C. and sold into slavery in Louisiana. One hundred sixty years later, his memoir was turned into a movie, which won the Academy Award for Best Picture.[353]

The *Emancipator's* unnamed slave was born around 1816 in a place called Four Holes, about 25 miles from Charleston. He was owned by a widow, who hired him out to neighboring plantations. When the boy was 14, the widow died and her son inherited the slave. Five years later, his new owner sold him.

Two years after that he ran away for the first time. In one month's time he was captured and sent to Sugar House in Charleston, a jail for slaves. Sugar House served two purposes. One was as a short-term lock-up where captured runaway slaves were penned up until claimed by their owners. To earn their keep while in custody, and as punishment, slaves were forced to walk on a treadmill to grind corn for use in the jail. "This constantly turning treadmill often injured and maimed the slaves and at times their bodies or body parts would end up in the ground corn," according to researcher Lewis Powell IV.[354]

Sugar House also functioned as a sadistic reformatory, where owners paid to have miscreant slaves punished and taught to work obediently. Sugar House's name may conjure sweetness and pleasure, but its bitter tools were whippings and torture.

Some slaves' Sugar House sojourns were brief if painful. Widowed women, lacking the muscle or mindset to beat a person, brought their slaves every week to be whipped for routine disciplining or as punishment for offenses real or imagined. Some widows went into the whipping room, reprimanding their slave while they watched. "They would say, '[H]ow does that feel? Which would you rather do, have that, or mind your business?'" the *Emancipator* reported.

Beatings were inflicted one after another, like an assembly line, until every slave awaiting punishment had been flogged. Sometimes it went on until late at night.

Other slaves were imprisoned for extended periods. Leavitt's anonymous survivor was locked up for months.

To prevent escapes, the jail was surrounded by a very high brick wall. Above the gate, the wall bristled with sharp pointed iron bars. Everywhere else, sharp broken glass was imbedded along the top of the wall.

A would-be escapee's way was blocked by a gate, a thick iron door, an equally formidable wooden one, and chains that forced the doors to open and shut together. The walls were built of impregnably thick stone and brick.

Sugar House's severe treatment almost killed the *Emancipator's* unnamed correspondent, wrote Zachary Hutchins in a modern introduction to the memoir, which is preserved by the University of North Carolina at Chapel Hill. Fretting that the slave would be less productive due to his wounded health, his owner Davey Cohan sold him for $700, a $500 loss, in June 1837 to John Fogle. In turn, Fogle leased his new slave to contractors building the Hamburg and Charleston Rail Road.

Things got worse for the slave. The contractors worked their laborers mercilessly. Female slaves, nearly naked, strained to push wheelbarrows awkwardly weighted down with dirt and rocks up narrow wooden planks, sometimes 10 to 20 above the ground. Many women fell and were injured. Male slaves hacked soil out of the ground, and struggled to bull heavy, fully loaded wheelbarrows from pits up to where the new rail roadway was being built. It was backbreaking labor.

Sometimes a pit was close to the new road, but often a pit was some distance. The slaves emptied their barrow loads. Young boy and girl slaves threw the dirt and rocks into place, helping to form the new road bed and ballast. Adult male slaves also ripped up heavy old metal railroad rails, and laid new rails.

Nearly every single day slaves got crippled or killed, Fogle's rental slave later told Rev. Leavitt. Whippings were constant, and often for petty reasons. And they were calculated to inflict maximum pain and flesh-ripping damage. Fogle's slave several times saw overseers tie a slave's hands together and put a pole between his legs to make his skin tight before lashing him 20 or 30 times.

Whippings were just one form of discipline and punishment that Fogle's slave had seen and endured himself through the years up to this points.

Owners could question slaves at will. Slaves, their quarters, and their belongings were subject to search at any time, with or without reason. A slave who was traveling on his master's behalf was subject to the same search and interrogation by any white person, on or off the owner's property. Woe to the slave who could not produce a document showing that he had permission to be out and about.

Either routinely or just from time to time, some owners allowed their charges to roam the local community during their limited off hours. Those slaves could trade with each other for goods and services. A slave might even earn cash by performing work. And some slaves could attend religious services. Other slaves had no such leeway and were always confined to their quarters when not at work.

Rev. Leavitt's eventual confidant said some masters would whip a slave just for asking permission to attend a prayer meeting. He called a travel document a ticket. When he could not get one, sometimes he would sneak away to attend a service. If the religious gathering was for whites, slaves were generally barred from entering the church unless they were caring for white children. Otherwise, slaves stayed outside behind the church. If they were lucky, there were seats for them to sit on.

Even then, as soon as the service ended a white slave patrol would accost the blacks, demanding to see each one's ticket. Any slave without a ticket would be tied to a tree and whipped, he recalled. He added, "I never could understand what the minister was preaching about. I heard a mighty [hollering] and that was all. I knew a woman once who was whipped for praying. The overseer used to creep round behind the camp at night to listen and find out what we were talking about. He heard the woman praying, and in the morning she was whipped for it."

Dreading the lash, many slaves tried to talk or beg their way out of such punishment. The pain was awful. A severe whipping could kill a person. Many slaves succumbed later to infected wounds. And it's hard to imagine that masters and overseers did not count on the horrendous scars that often erupted from deterring that slave and others from future misbehavior.

Rev. Leavitt's anonymous slave recounted an encyclopedia's worth of tortures whose aim was to discipline and punish slaves. He learned to recognize as many different types of flogs as an Inuit recognizes forms of snow. There were paddles and whips, and several varieties of both. A smooth paddle would blister and peel its victim's skin. After being wetted and rubbed in sand, a paddle peels off even more skin – like peeling a potato, the slave recalled. As for whips, torturers used everything from horse whips to cat-o'-nine tails, to cowskins. The whip called a bluejay has two lashes, each very heavy and full of knots. "It is the worst thing to whip with of any thing they have," the slave told Rev. Leavitt. "It makes a hole where it strikes, and when [the torturer is done] it will be all bloody."

Victims were restrained with ropes or chains. Often the restraints painfully stretched a slave. Also, victims' clothes were often removed before whipping. That deprived them of protection that was liable to be pathetically flimsy and threadbare. Afterward, victims were often washed down with salt water – whose sting could be excruciating – to help heal their wounds and hasten their return to labor in the fields or elsewhere.

One time, an old slave named Peter was caught stealing wood, perhaps fallen tree branches, from his owner's land. Peter wanted to sell the wood. Instead, he was carried to his hut and tied to the ceiling so his feet could not reach the ground. A log was tied to his feet to stretch him and keep his flesh taut, then he was whipped until he passed out. One overseer said Peter probably would die from his wounds.

Still, after his whipping he was washed with brine and locked into stocks in the lightless basement of his owner's home. A chain was wrapped around his neck, locked in place, and fastened to a beam. His feet were bolted between two wooden ankle restraints. His hands were

330

tied. He spent the night on his back, unable to move any part of his body except his head. Some slaves who had stolen something or attempted to escape were locked up like this for two or three weeks, with periodic whippings. Rev. Leavitt's narrator did not say whether Peter survived.

Whipping was the most frequent punishment, Rev. Leavitt's narrator recalled. But he witnessed other torments as sinister as anything from a medieval dungeon. One day his owner sent him on an errand to a neighbor's plantation, where he saw an overseer lock a man inside a barrel. The overseer had driven nails into the barrel, which he then rolled around the yard. The supervisor laughed while the trapped man howled with each nail that punctured him.

Several times he saw slaves tied by their heels and hung upside down over a burning pile of corncobs. After a while the fire was put out, and the slave was left hanging over the smoking embers like a side of meat being cured.

He also saw men locked for long periods inside coffin-sized boxes with a single breathing hole.

Despite these tortures, if any slave tried to escape he would have to elude white slave patrols and any other suspicious whites he encountered. In the countrywide chances were good that he would be pursued by hounds led by armed men on horseback. If caught, he faced beating and execution.

A man named Jess repeatedly tried to escape from his owner, a minister named Stephen Williams. One time after Jess was caught, the anonymous slave learned that Jess had been tied down atop a big nest of ants, which stung him while he was whipped. The message from Jess's owner was painfully clear; the price of attempted escape would be insufferably high. Yet through his torture Jess must have responded in a manner that prompted his owner to conclude that he had failed to break Jess, that he had failed to persuade the man not to flee again, because Jess was taken into the woods and shot to death.

"Nobody can tell how badly the slaves are punished," the anonymous slave told Rev. Leavitt. "They are treated worse than dumb beasts. Many a time I have gone into the swamp, and laid down and wished I was a dog, or dead."

Still, the worst torture, the toughest deterrent to running away or any misbehavior, may have been the fear of being torn apart from your family.

In 1838 or shortly before that, the anonymous slave escaped from his railroad construction gang and made his way to Charleston. Around the harbor he mixed in with black work gangs, posing as a slave whose owner let him hire himself out. Loading cotton aboard a ship, he hid in a cargo hold. When the ship reached Boston, he went ashore to freedom.

His narration ends with, "I am now as well situated as I wish to be, and have no fears of being carried back to slavery."

Photo Album

Marvin Gilmore (left) and his brother Lester in about 1929.

**Uncle "Cap" visiting Marvin (right) and Lester in 1930
outside the apartment building on Cambridge's Pleasant St.
where the Gilmores lived.**

Private Marvin Gilmore in 1942.

Marvin Gilmore's anti-aircraft artillery unit hit Normandy beach on D-Day, rolling off landing ships like these.

Marvin and Lorna cut the cake at their 1959 wedding.

Marvin Gilmore, Sr. at Marvin and Lorna's wedding.

Marvin and Lorna at their wedding celebration, flanked by Lee Augusta (left), Wanda, and Marvin Sr.

**Lester Gilmore (left) and Sylvia (right) join Marvin and Lorna
at their wedding reception.**

The Gilmores (from the left): Marvin, Marque, David, and Lorna at David's Brooklyn, N.Y. apartment in about 1998.

Lisa A. Gilmore

Marvin's grandmother Sophronia during a visit to Cambridge in about 1932.

Marvin Gilmore (right) and Bill Russell flew to Jackson, Miss. in July 1964 to test enforcement of the new Civil Rights Act of 1964. They also strategized with civil rights leaders, including Charles Evers, and rallied with local African-Americans.

In a press conference at the Boston branch of the NAACP the night after their return from Mississippi, Marvin (right) and Bill Russell (center) told the press about their frequently frightening visit and the violence that was often used to discourage African-Americans from exercising their rights. (Seated left: NAACP branch president Kenneth Guscott.)

Marvin (in 2013) with the key to room 1029 of the Heidelberg Hotel in Jackson, Miss., a souvenir from his visit with basketball star Bill Russell.

Sammy Davis, Jr. (right, seated at table), conferred with event producer Marvin Gilmore (center at table) and NAACP branch president Kenneth Guscott as Kivie Kaplan (standing) addressed the audience for the August 1964 fundraiser for the branch's Life Membership Committee, chaired by Gilmore. The fundraiser was hosted by Morton and Sylvia Grossman at their suburban Boston home.

It was essential for Marvin Gilmore (left) to win the trust of Digital Equipment Corporation headman Kenneth Olsen (right) to get CrossTown Industrial Park off the ground.

Breaking ground for Digital Equipment's factory in CrossTown Industrial Park in Boston's Roxbury neighborhood in 1978. Front, from the left: State Senator William Owens, Marvin Gilmore, Lt. Gov. Thomas P. O'Neill Jr., Mayor Kevin White.

Marvin spoke with Gov. Michael Dukakis (left) during a campaign event for Dukakis' 1988 presidential run. Dukakis later signed the photograph, "To Marvin / Many thanks / Mike".

Pres. Bill Clinton (seated), signing his Day of Honor 2000 proclamation at the White House, May 24, 2000. Standing behind the president (from the left): Floyd Dade, 761st Tank Battalion veteran (largely hidden from view); Rep. Sheila Jackson Lee; Secretary of Veterans Affairs Togo West; Sen. Edward Kennedy (who autographed the photo); unidentified veteran; Marvin Gilmore; Terry Shima, 442nd Regimental Combat Team; representative of Native American veterans; Lloyd A. Barbee, Navy veteran.

Photo credits: Pictures of Marvin E. Gilmore, Jr., family, and wedding are courtesy of Marvin E, Gilmore, Jr.; Lisa A. Gilmore picture, courtesy of Lisa A. Gilmore; D-Day landing on Normandy beach, courtesy of the Library of Congress; Marvin E. Gilmore, Jr., with Hotel Heidelberg room key, courtesy of Paul Katzeff; Sammy Davis, Jr., fundraiser, courtesy of Marvin E. Gilmore, Jr.; Marvin E. Gilmore, Jr. with Bill Russell, courtesy of Getty Images/Boston Globe; Marvin E. Gilmore, Jr. with Kenneth Olsen, courtesy of CDC of Boston; groundbreaking for Digital Equipment Corp. factory, courtesy of CDC of Boston; Marvin E. Gilmore, Jr., with Michael Dukakis, courtesy of Marvin E. Gilmore, Jr.; Day of Honor 2000 presidential signing ceremony, courtesy of Day of Honor 2000 Project.

ENDNOTES

[1] The 458th had been officially disbanded just weeks earlier on April 24, 1944. But the men still thought of themselves as members of the 458th. The outfit's breakup is detailed in Chapter 6.

[2] Marvin shared his thoughts in 76 formal interviews conducted by the author between December 2010 and spring 2014, in addition to several dozen informal conversations during that period.

[3] Christopher Paul Moore, *Fighting for America / Black Soldiers – The Unsung Heroes of World War II*, 1st edition (New York, N.Y.: The Random House Publishing Group, 2005), p. 176. In addition to the 1,800 black troops who landed in Normandy, another 3,200 were aboard ships of the Allied invasion armada. Altogether, 156,000 Allied troops of all races landed on June 6, according to the D-Day Museum: http://www.ddaymuseum.co.uk/d-day/d-day-and-the-battle-of-normandy-your-questions-answered, accessed April 7, 2013. Some 1.1 million blacks served the U.S. armed forces in the war, according to African Americans in World War II: http://www.lwfaam.net/ww2/, accessed April 8, 2013, and Florida State University Institute on World War II and the Human Experience: http://ww2.fsu.edu/African-American, accessed April 8, 2013.

[4] By D-Day, Allied air power had whittled the German air force to a fraction of its peak power, but the *luftwaffe* still existed and fought. The German air command dispatched 319 sorties over the Normandy area. America and the Royal Air Force countered with 14,674 sorties. (See Oberst Walter Gaul, "The G.A.F. [German Air Force] And The Invasion of Normandy 1944," The Navy Department Library: http://www.history.navy.mil/library/online/gaf_invasionnormandy.htm, accessed June 5, 2014; Christer Bergstrom, "Luftwaffe Aces KIA in Normandy in 1944," 12 O'Clock High website: http://forum.12oclockhigh.net/showthread.php?t=625, accessed June 5, 2014; "D-Day Figures," The Battle of Normandy: http://www.dday-overlord.com/eng/dday_figures.htm, accessed June 5, 2014; Randy Wilson, "American Airpower In Support Of The Normandy Invasion," Dispatch Archive: http://rwebs.net/dispatch/output.asp?ArticleID=46, accessed June 5, 2014.)

[5] U.S. paratroopers began their assault earlier, soon after midnight.

[6] http://www.8thwood.com/320th_barrage_balloon_battal.htm, accessed April 13, 2013.

[7] Stephen Ambrose, *Citizen Soldier* (New York, N.Y.: Simon & Schuster, 1997), p. 19.

[8] Like most soldiers, Marvin had trained with a full-size M1 rifle. But non-infantry combat troops like Marvin were armed in war zones with weapons such as the .30-caliber M1 carbine, which was a shorter, smaller, lighter weapon than the M1 rifle. See report about M1 carbines:
http://www.rt66.com/~korteng/SmallArms/m1carbin.htm, accessed April 1, 2013; Pete Kuhlhoff, "Lightweight Carbine," *Popular Science,* June 1942, pages 79-80: http://books.google.com/books?id=RicDAAAAMBAJ&pg=PA79&dq=popular+scien ce+1930&hl=en&ei=vvbJTp6GD4KWtwe11eX4Cw&sa=X&oi=book_result&ct=resul t&resnum=8&ved=0CE0Q6AEwBzgy#v=onepage&q=popular%20science%201930 &f=true, accessed April 1, 2013.

[9] New Jersey State Library, Unit 12 World War II: "The Struggle for Democracy at Home and Abroad, 1940-1945":
http://slic.njstatelib.org/NJ_Information/Digital_Collections/AAHCG/unit12.html, accessed April 8, 2013.

[10] David P. Colley, "On The Road To Victory: The Red Ball Express":
http://www.historynet.com/red-ball-express, accessed Jan. 24, 2014.

[11] From time to time Marvin has been cited as among the Boston area's most stylish men. (See Julie Hatfield, "A Sartorial Symphony / An Ear For Music, Eye For Fashion At Hayes Gala," *Boston Globe,* Feb. 5, 1996, p. 30.)

[12] Interview with author, Oct. 7, 2013.

[13] Interview with author, June 26, 2014.

[14] 1870 U.S. census, *Notasulga, Macon, Alabama*: http://search.ancestry.com/cgi-bin/sse.dll?rank=1&new=1&MSAV=0&gss=angsc&
gsfn=sophronia&gsln=rowell&msbpn__ftp=Notasulga%2c+Macon%2c+Alabama%
2c+USA&msbpn=26807&msbp
n_PInfo=8-
|0|1652393|0|2|3246|3|0|1843|26807|0|&msypn__ftp=Alabama%2c+USA&m sypn=3&msypn_PInfo=5-
|0|1652393|0|2|3246|3|0|0|0|0|&uidh=mc7&pcat=CEN_1870&h=12856854& db=1870usfedcen&indiv=1&ml_rpos=12, accessed June 29, 2014.

[15] Some documents spell his first name "Jeremiah."

[16] Sharecropping was a business relationship between a land owner, who almost always was white, and someone – typically black – who paid for access to farm land because he (or she) could not own any. Sharecropping proliferated after the Civil War. Because the relationship between land owner and farmer commonly was much more favorable to the white land owner, sharecropping was often a thinly disguised substitute for slavery. Sharecroppers tended to be poorer than tenant farmers. Tenant farmers usually rented land and sold their harvest, or they were paid a wage – customarily a desperately low amount. The landlord kept all or most of the crop. Tenant farmers often could afford to own a mule and

equipment. Sharecroppers worked another man's farm and shared the produce. They rarely owned mules, horses, or gear.

[17] No evidence indicates that Jerimiah Rowell had been a free black prior to the Thirteenth Amendment. On the contrary, his poverty (all of his possessions were worth only $125 in 1870) and his location in a rural section of Alabama are strong signs that he had not been free. Southern blacks who were free before the Thirteenth Amendment tended to reside in cities because that's where most jobs were, according to Harvard professor Henry Louis Gates Jr., director of the W. E. B. Du Bois Institute for African and African American Research, at the Web site The Root: http://www.theroot.com/articles/history/2013/07/free_blacks_precivil_war_whe re_they_lived.4.html, accessed May 1, 2014.

[18] Productions of Agriculture in Notasulga, Macon County, Alabama, Schedule 3, July 6-7-8, 1870.

[19] 1860 U.S. census, *North Division, Macon, Alabama:* http://search.ancestrylibrary.com/iexec?htx=View&r=5542&dbid=766&iid=42111 87_00403&fn=Burrell&ln=Barrow&st=r&ssrc=&pid=11808678, accessed Oct. 13, 2012.

[20] From the money-value calculator at http://www.measuringworth.com/uscompare/relativevalue.php, accessed Aug. 4, 2012.

[21] 1870 U.S. census, *Notasulga, Macon, Alabama:* http://search.ancestrylibrary.com/cgi-bin/sse.dll?h=12857385&db=1870usfedcen&indiv=try, accessed Aug. 4, 2012.

[22] 1860 U.S. census slave schedule, *North Division, Macon, Alabama:* http://search.ancestry.com/iexec?htx=View&r=an&dbid=7668&iid=ALM653_3203 34&fn=A+H&ln=rowell&st=r&ssrc=&pid+291138, accessed June 28, 2012.

[23] 1860 U.S. census, *North Division, Macon, Alabama:* http://search.ancestry.com/iexec?htx=View&r=an&dbid=7668&iid=4211187_004 08&fn=A+H&ln=rowell&st=r&ssrc=&pid=11808865, accessed July 15, 2012.

[24] Howell Rowell family tree: http://trees.ancestry.com/tree/14713929/person/150454437, accessed Aug. 15, 2012.

[25] 1870 U.S. census, *Notasulga Beat, Macon, Alabama:* http://search.ancestrylibrary.com/iexec?htx=View&r=5542&dbid=7163&iid=4257 603_00420&fn=Kizzie&ln=Rowell&st=r&ssrc=&pid=13227126, accessed Oct. 13, 2011.

[26] 1923 Ohio marriage record: search.ancestrylibrary.com/content/viewerpf.aspx?h=1227249&db=CuyahogaOH marriages&iid=32365_225741-00271&sp=0, accessed Oct. 13, 2012.

[27] For clarity, Marvin's family tree shown here is pared down. It does not, for example, show the many siblings of his parents, grandparents, and other ancestors. Nor does it show those ancestors' offspring. For each person who is included, the family tree shows the most likely year of birth when documents provide conflicting birth dates.

[28] 1870 U.S. census, *Poplar, Orangeburg, South Carolina:* http://interactive.ancestry.com/7163/4275973_00386/11848002?backurl=http%3a%2f%2fsearch.ancestry.com%2fcgi-bin%2fsse.dll%3frank%3d1%26new%3d1%26MSAV%3d0%26gss%3dangs-c%26gsln%3dGilmore%26msbdy%3d1869%26msbpn_ftp%3dcalhoun%252c%2bSouth%2bCarolina%252c%2bUSA%26msydy%3d1870%26msypn_ftp%3dsouth%2bcarolina%26uidh%3dmc7%26pcat%3d35%26h%3d11848002%26db%3d1870usfedcen%26indiv%3d1%26ml_rpos%3d31&ssrc=&backlabel=ReturnRecord#?imageId=4275973_00385, and http://interactive.ancestry.com/7163/4275973_00386/11848002?backurl=http%3a%2f%2fsearch.ancestry.com%2fcgi-bin%2fsse.dll%3frank%3d1%26new%3d1%26MSAV%3d0%26gss%3dangs-c%26gsln%3dGilmore%26msbdy%3d1869%26msbpn_ftp%3dcalhoun%252c%2bSouth%2bCarolina%252c%2bUSA%26msydy%3d1870%26msypn_ftp%3dsouth%2bcarolina%26uidh%3dmc7%26pcat%3d35%26h%3d11848002%26db%3d1870usfedcen%26indiv%3d1%26ml_rpos%3d31&ssrc=&backlabel=ReturnRecord#?imageId=4275973_00386, both pages accessed June 30, 2014.

[29] Samuel M. Gilmore was listed as Monroe S. Gilmore in the 1870 U.S. Census.

[30] 1870 U.S. census, *Poplar, Orangeburg, South Carolina:* http://search.ancestry.com/Browse/print_u.aspax?dbid=7163&iid=4275973_00385&pid=10070249, accessed Dec. 6, 2011.

[31] 1880 U.S. census, *Poplar, Orangeburg, South Carolina:* http://search.ancestrylibrary.com/cgi-bin/sse.dll?db=1880usfedcen&indiv=try&h=12963435, accessed Dec. 3, 2011.

[32] 1880 U.S. census, *Poplar, Orangeburg, South Carolina:* http://search.ancestrylibrary.com/cgi-bin/sse.dll?db=1880usfedcen&indiv=try&h=12963435, accessed Dec. 3, 2011.

[33] http://eh.net/encyclopedia/article/haines.demography, accessed Aug. 16, 2012.

[34] Emilye Crosby, *A Little Taste of Freedom: The Black Freedom Struggle in Claiborne County, Mississippi* (Chapel Hill, No. Carolina: The University of North Carolina Press, 2005); John Dittmer, *Local People: The Struggle for Civil Rights in Mississippi* (Chicago: University of Illinois Press, 1994); Doug McAdam, *Freedom Summer* (New York: Oxford University Press, 1988); Jack Mendelsohn, *The*

Martyrs: Sixteen Who Gave Their Lives for Racial Justice (New York: Harper & Row, 1966).

[35] "Cracker" is a slang put-down for bigoted whites, especially those from the rural South.

[36] The death record for Isaac Gilmore lists his birth date as Sept. 8, 1897 (http://www.death-record.com/1/125599778/Isaac-Gilmore, accessed Oct. 28, 2012). Other documents show dates for Isaac's birth ranging from 1897 to 1901: 1910 U.S. census, *Lyons Township, Calhoun, South Carolina:* http://interactive.ancestry.com/7884/4449781_01156/153789294?backurl=http%3a%2f%2fsearch.ancestry.com%2fcgi-bin%2fsse.dll%3fdb%3d1910USCenIndex%26h%3d153789294%26indiv%3dtry%26o_vc%3dRecord%253aOtherRecord%26rhSource%3d6061&ssrc=&backlabel=ReturnRecord, accessed July 1, 2014; 1920 U.S. census, *Pine Grove, Calhoun, South Carolina:* http://interactive.ancestry.com/6061/4383808_00360/42980889?backurl=&ssrc=&backlabel=ReturnRecord, accessed July 1, 2014; "A Memorial Tribute for Relatives and Friends," Walker Funeral Home, Geneva, Ohio, Dec. 23, 1977.

[37] Lee Augusta had 17 siblings in total, according to Marvin. That's more than the number listed on various U.S. census reports because many of Lee Augusta's mother' children died in childbirth, infancy, or childhood, before being enumerated in a once-a-decade census.

[38] The dialogue between Isaac Gilmore's heirs and the county sheriff was still taking place nearly a year after Isaac's death. It is recounted in a Nov. 1, 1978 letter from attorney Stephen B. Angel to the heirs, whom he represented.

[39] Fresh Air from WHYY, "Great Migration: The African-American Exodus North," National Public Radio interview with Isabel Wilkerson, author of *The Warmth of Other Suns,: The Epic Story of America's Great Migration*, Sept. 13, 2010: http://www.npr.org/templates/story/story.php?storyId=129827444, accessed April 27, 2013.

[40] "Great Migration: The African-American Exodus North," transcript of a "Fresh Air" from WHYY broadcast, Sept. 13, 2010: http://www.npr.org/templates/story/story.php?storyId=129827444, accessed April 27, 2013.

[41] Lee Augusta provided many details of her life in an autobiographical essay. This book uses a typewritten version of her essay, which is slightly longer and more detailed than other versions. Her funeral's memorial tribute includes an abbreviated version.

[42] Marriage Records and Indexes, Cuyahoga County, Ohio, 1810-1973: search.ancestrylibrary.com/content/viewerpf.aspx?h=1227249&db=CuyahogaOHmarriages&iid=32365_225741-00271&sp=0, accessed Oct. 13, 2012. The marriage

record listed Lee Augusta's occupation as housework. Marvin says that his mother always said she worked as a nurse's aide.

[43] The first name of the candy manufacturer and retailer is spelled "Fanny." The first name of Fannie Merritt Farmer, the innovative cookbook author and cooking school director, is spelled differently. Her heirs licensed her name to the candy shops company. See: CooksInfo.com Web site, "Fannie Merritt Farmer:" http://www.cooksinfo.com/fannie-merritt-farmer, accessed July 28, 2014.

[44] James Grossman, "Great Migration," *Encyclopedia of Chicago:* http://www.encyclopedia.chicagohistory.org/pages/545.html, accessed April 27, 2013.

[45] New Jersey State Library, Unit 11 The 1930s: "The Great Depression": http://slic.njstatelib.org/NJ_Information/Digital_Collections/AAHCG/unit11.html, accessed Nov. 26, 2012.

[46] Interview by author, Sept. 17, 2011.

[47] Interview by author, Sept. 17, 2011.

[48] Interview by author, March 31, 2011.

[49] Interview by author, Sept. 4, 2012.

[50] Edmund J. O'Neal, *The Story of My Life / An Autobiography,* p. 2. The memoir is undated but apparently completed in late 1927. Edmund autographed Lee Augusta's copy, writing, "To my 'Baby Sister' Lee Augusta O'Neal Gilmore," and dated it December 1927.

[51] U.S. military draft registration card, World War I, June 5, 1917: http://search.ancestrylibrary.com/Browse/print_u.aspx?dbid=6482&iid=MS-a682706-0568&pid=22222407, accessed Oct. 22, 2011.

[52] Tuskegee Institute evolved into today's Tuskegee University. It was founded in 1881 in Tuskegee, Alabama, to provide higher education to African-Americans, who were being excluded from white schools.

[53] David Wheelock, "The Great Depression," Federal Reserve Bank of St. Louis: http://www.stlouisfed.org/greatdepression/qa.html, accessed June 9, 2013.

[54] History.com, "Bank Run": http://mercatus.org/sites/default/files/Barth_ResolvingTBTF_v1.pdf, accessed June 9, 2013.

[55] James R. Barth and Apanard Prabha, "Resolving Too-Big-To-Fail-Banks In The United States," Working Paper No. 13-05, March 2013, Mercatus Center, George Mason University, p. 3: http://mercatus.org/sites/default/files/Barth_ResolvingTBTF_v1.pdf, accessed June 9, 2013.

[56] Detailed in emails May 14 and 15, 2013, from Alyssa Pacy, archivist, Cambridge Public Library, working from a series of Cambridge city directories.

[57] Program for Annual Gala 2012, Asian American Civic Association, p. 6.

[58] Program for Annual Gala 2012, Asian American Civic Association, p. 6.

[59] Biography Channel Web site, "Nat King Cole": http://www.biography.com/people/nat-king-cole-9253026, accessed May 19, 2013.

[60] Freya Petersen, "Nat King Cole's widow, Maria Hawkins Cole, dies of cancer, aged 89": http://www.globalpost.com/dispatches/globalpost-blogs/hollyworld/maria-hawkins-cole-nat-king-cole-natalie-cole-cancer-dead-jazz, accessed May 19, 2013.

[61] Program for Annual Gala 2012, Asian American Civic Association, p. 6.

[62] Window Shop description is in email on May 29, 2013 to author from Alyssa Pacy, archivist, Cambridge Public Library.

[63] North Carolina Department of Cultural Resources, "Nat 'King' Cole's Widow Maria Cole Visits Charlotte Hawkins Brown Museum": http://news.ncdcr.gov/2008/06/11/nat-king-coles-widow-maria-cole-visits-charlotte-hawkins-brown-museum/, accessed May 26, 2013.

[64] From Lee Augusta's memoir. In 1954 the family bought 72 Dana St. and moved there.

[65] In her memoir, Lee Augusta wrote: "During my fifty one years as a resident here, it was both challenging and rewarding to be able to cope with the economics of the times. In order to operate my apartments by charging reasonable prices – and to ensure the security of the family, I found for example that a lot of money could be saved by shopping for fresh meats and vegetables at Haymarket Square [a colorful outdoor farmer's market in Boston, near Quincy Marketplace and Fanueil Hall].

"I have enjoyed my work as a business woman and as a missionary to my fellow man. I was chaplain for a local chapter of the V.F.W. Auxilliary for thirty years, and for one term the president. Over a period of twenty years, I visited hospitals, nursing homes, and private homes of the sick. Through God's blessing my goals have been reached.

"It is my desire to continue to work with the sick, and to relate to people who high moral standards. One cannot expect that every relationship will be in complete harmony, but only a few have let me down. We must take chances sometimes – often what appears to be a loss may actually result in a double gain."

Whenever the memoir is quoted in this book, it is done so verbatim except for a small number of minor typographical corrections for clarity.

[66] Steven Watts, *The Magic Kingdom: Walt Disney and the American Way of Life* (Columbia, Mo.: University of Missouri Press, 2001), p. 101: http://books.google.com/books?id=NgARIndAbjAC&pg=PA101&lpg=PA101&dq=robert+d+feild+harvard&source=bl&ots=3OOFi-7ND8&sig=ep0esg1K0wAyqX49CQ9qyctJWBc&hl=en&sa=X&ei=FRPSUJbQF9Lh0w

G50oAo&ved=0CEYQ6AEwAw#v=onepage&q=robert%20d%20feild%20harvard&f=false, accessed Dec. 20, 2012.

[67] Filmsite Movie Review, *Fantasia:* http://www.filmsite.org/fant.html, accessed Dec. 21, 2012.

[68] Steven Watts, *The Magic Kingdom: Walt Disney and the American Way of Life* (Columbia, Mo.: University of Missouri Press, 2001), p. 101: http://books.google.com/books?id=NgARIndAbjAC&pg=PA101&lpg=PA101&dq=robert+d+feild+harvard&source=bl&ots=30OFi-7ND8&sig=ep0esg1KOwAyqX49CQ9qyctJWBc&hl=en&sa=X&ei=FRPSUJbQF9LhOwG50oAo&ved=0CEYQ6AEwAw#v=onepage&q=robert%20d%20feild%20harvard&f=false, accessed Dec. 20, 2012.

[69] Steven Watts, *The Magic Kingdom: Walt Disney and the American Way of Life* (Columbia, Mo.: University of Missouri Press, 2001), pp. 101-102: http://books.google.com/books?id=NgARIndAbjAC&pg=PA101&lpg=PA101&dq=robert+d+feild+harvard&source=bl&ots=30OFi-7ND8&sig=ep0esg1KOwAyqX49CQ9qyctJWBc&hl=en&sa=X&ei=FRPSUJbQF9LhOwG50oAo&ved=0CEYQ6AEwAw#v=onepage&q=robert%20d%20feild%20harvard&f=false, accessed Dec. 20, 2012.

[70] History.com, "This Day in History – Aug. 9, 1936: Jesse Owens wins fourth gold medal": http://www.history.com/this-day-in-history/owens-wins-4th-gold-medal, accessed June 15, 2013.

[71] History.com, "This Day in History – Nov. 11, 1942: Draft age is lowered to 18": http://www.history.com/this-day-in-history/draft-age-is-lowered-to-18, accessed June 3, 2013.

[72] The "Air Force" was actually the U. S. Army Air Forces, the aviation wing of the Army. It had been called the Army Air Corps until June 1941. The U.S. Army Air Forces became a separate branch of the military on Sept. 18, 1947, when the U. S. Air Force was created.

[73] Prejudice against blacks kept the ranks of American airmen lily white even after U. S. entry into World War II. But political pressure and the merciless math of military manpower needs finally opened the door to black combat aviators. In a program that many people inside and out of the military continued to oppose, African-Americans began to train at Tuskegee Army Air Field (TAAF) in Tuskegee, Alabama, in July 1941 as single- and multiengine pilots. The first aviation cadet class completed training in March 1942. These were America's first black military airmen, according to the Tuskegee Airmen National Historical Museum. Black navigators, bombardiers and gunnery crews were trained at military bases elsewhere in the U. S. Mechanics were trained at Chanute Air Base in Rantoul, Illinois until facilities were in place in 1942 at TAAF, the museum Web site says. Tuskegee Airmen, as they came to be known, notched impressive combat records.

Black aviators who eventually trained at bases other than TAAF were subjected to racist restrictions, the Web site says. When black officers tried to enter the whites-only officers' club at Freeman Field in Indiana in early 1945, a disturbance erupted and 103 black officers were arrested. See: "The Tuskegee Airmen," Tuskegee Airmen National Historical Museum Web site": http://www.tuskegeeairmennationalmuseum.org/history/who-were-they, accessed June 16, 2013.

[74] History.com, "This Day in History – Nov. 11, 1942: Draft age is lowered to 18": http://www.history.com/this-day-in-history/draft-age-is-lowered-to-18, accessed June 3, 2013.

[75] New Jersey State Library, Unit 12 World War II: "The Struggle for Democracy at Home and Abroad, 1940-1945": http://slic.njstatelib.org/NJ_Information/Digital_Collections/AAHCG/unit12.html, accessed April 8, 2013.

[76] Handbook of Texas Online, published by Texas State Historical Association, "Camp Wallace": http://www.tshaonline.org/handbook/online/articles/qbc30, accessed June 23, 2013.

[77] U.S. Army discharge report, Jan. 16, 1946.

[78] New Jersey State Library, Unit 12 World War II: "The Struggle for Democracy at Home and Abroad, 1940-1945": http://slic.njstatelib.org/NJ_Information/Digital_Collections/AAHCG/unit12.html, accessed April 8, 2013.

[79] Steven D. Smith and James A. Zeidler, *A Historic Context for the African American Military Experience* (Champaign, Ill.: U.S. Army Corps of Engineers, Construction Engineering Research Laboratories, 1998): pp. 187-246.

[80] National WWII Museum, "African Americans in World War II," http://www.nationalww2museum.org/assets/pdfs/african-americans-in-world.pdf, retrieved April 8, 2013. Also: Leon Litwack and Winthrop Jordan, *The United States: Becoming a World Power*, 7th edition, Vol. II (Englewood Cliffs, N. J.: Prentice Hall, 1991), p. 708-710. And: Christopher Paul Moore, *Fighting for America / Black Soldiers – The Unsung Heroes of World War II*, 1st edition (New York, N.Y.: The Random House Publishing Group, 2005), pp. 27-30. And: New Jersey State Library, Unit 12 World War II: "The Struggle for Democracy at Home and Abroad, 1940-1945": http://slic.njstatelib.org/NJ_Information/Digital_Collections/AAHCG/unit12.html, accessed April 8, 2013.

[81] Christopher Paul Moore, *Fighting for America / Black Soldiers – The Unsung Heroes of World War II*, 1st edition (New York, N.Y.: The Random House Publishing Group, 2005), p. 95.

[82] Ulysses Lee, United States Army in World War II / Special Studies / The Employment of Negro Troops, Chapter XII, "Harvest of Disorder," (Washington, D.C.: Center of Military History United States Army, 1966): http://www.history.army.mil/books/wwii/11-4/chapter12.htm, accessed Feb. 22, 2011; title page and index: http://www.history.army/mil/books/wwii/11-4/index.htm, accessed Feb. 22, 2011.

[83] Ulysses Lee, United States Army in World War II / Special Studies / The Employment of Negro Troops, Chapter XII, "Harvest of Disorder," (Washington, D.C.: Center of Military History United States Army, 1966): http://www.history.army.mil/books/wwii/11-4/chapter12.htm, accessed Feb. 22, 2011.

[84] Christopher Paul Moore, *Fighting for America / Black Soldiers – The Unsung Heroes of World War II,* 1st edition (New York, N.Y.: The Random House Publishing Group, 2005), p. 96.

[85] John Dittmer, *Local People: The Struggle for Civil Rights in Mississippi* (Urbana, Ill.: University of Illinois Press, 1994), pp. 14.

[86] National WWII Museum, "African Americans in World War II," http://www.nationalww2museum.org/assets/pdfs/african-americans-in-world.pdf, retrieved April 8, 2013; Leon Litwack and Winthrop Jordan, *The United States: Becoming a World Power,* 7th edition, Vol. II (Englewood Cliffs, N. J.: Prentice Hall, 1991), p. 708-710; New Jersey State Library, Unit 12 World War II: "The Struggle for Democracy at Home and Abroad, 1940-1945": http://slic.njstatelib.org/NJ_Information/Digital_Collections/AAHCG/unit12.html, retrieved April 8, 2013; "Race In World War II": http://www.shmoop.com/wwii/race.html, retrieved April 8, 2013; Florida State University Institute on World War II and the Human Experience: http://ww2.fsu.edu/African-American, retrieved April 8, 2013; Jerrold M. Packard, "Jim Crow & WWII," Command Posts: http://www.commandposts.com/2011/07/jim-crow-wwii/, retrieved April 8, 2013; Stephen Ambrose, *Citizen Soldier* (New York, N.Y.: Simon & Schuster, 1997), pp. 345-350.

[87] Ulysses Lee, United States Army in World War II / Special Studies / The Employment of Negro Troops, Chapter XII, "Harvest of Disorder," (Washington, D.C.: Center of Military History United States Army, 1966): http://www.history.army.mil/books/wwii/11-4/chapter12.htm, accessed Feb. 22, 2011.

[88] Ulysses Lee, United States Army in World War II / Special Studies / The Employment of Negro Troops, Chapter XII, "Harvest of Disorder," (Washington, D.C.: Center of Military History United States Army, 1966):

http://www.history.army.mil/books/wwii/11-4/chapter12.htm, accessed Feb. 22, 2011.

[89] "1 Killed, 4 Shot At Camp Stewart," *New York Age,* June 19, 1943, page 1.

[90] Army spies were not a figment of Marvin's imagination. In "'Ain't Slavery Grand' – School Days Army Style," the *Chicago Defender* newspaper of Chicago, Ill., on Aug. 21, 1943, reported that on July 29, 1943, Brig. Gen. E. A. Stockton of Camp Stewart had issued a 12-page directive, "Educational Program for Colored Troops." The document advised black soldiers to accept segregation in Georgia because it was the law. The general also suggested to unit commanders that they set up networks of spies and informants to root out trouble before it starts. The general advised his officers, "Select as secret agents qualified and patriotic men in each barracks. Instruct these men carefully and secretly. Give them code names and have them mail their reports to you except in emergencies." He also told officers to check their troops' reading material. Gen. Stockton added, "Some of it, often innocently appearing, may be seditious and highly inflammatory."

[91] Daniel Kryder, *Divided Arsenal* (Cambridge, U.K.: Cambridge University Press, 2000), p. 194.

[92] Ulysses Lee, United States Army in World War II / Special Studies / The Employment of Negro Troops, Chapter XII, "Harvest of Disorder," (Washington, D.C.: Center of Military History United States Army, 1966): http://www.history.army.mil/books/wwii/11-4/chapter12.htm, accessed Feb. 22, 2011.

[93] John Jasper, "Were Slaves," *Afro-American* (Washington, D.C.), Aug. 14, 1943, p. 1.

[94] Ulysses Lee, United States Army in World War II / Special Studies / The Employment of Negro Troops, Chapter XII, "Harvest of Disorder," (Washington, D.C.: Center of Military History United States Army, 1966): http://www.history.army.mil/books/wwii/11-4/chapter12.htm, accessed Feb. 22, 2011.

[95] John Jasper, "Were Slaves," *Afro-American* (Washington, D.C.), Aug. 14, 1943, p. 1.

[96] "Comments on General Stockton's Order to Soldiers at Camp Stewart, Ga.," *Afro-American* (Washington, D.C.), Aug. 21, 1943, p. 1.

[97] Communicated by Brig. Gen. O.L. Spiller, Camp Stewart, to the 458th AAA AW Battalion, and 13 additional anti-aircraft battalions, on July 16, 1943.

[98] Special Order by Lt. Col. Keller of the 458th AAA AW Battalion, Camp Stewart, Dec. 23, 1943.

[99] "Historical Data," Records of the Adjutant General's Office, 1917-(Record Group 407), general orders 1943-1944, TAG card for the 458th Automatic Weapons Anti-Aircraft Battalion (AWBN).

[100] At the Quartermaster Replacement Training Center, the Army taught soldiers how to store, transport, and dish out essentials ranging from fuel, food, and other supplies, as well as handle mortuary duties and laundry services. The center trained more than 300,000 officers and enlisted soldiers for service in both the European and the Pacific theaters, says Encyclopedia Virginia.(See Bradford A. Wineman, "Fort Lee," Encyclopedia Virginia: http://www.encyclopediavirginia.org/Fort_Lee, accessed Jan. 12, 2014.)

[101] Robert F. Jefferson, "African Americans in the U.S. Army During World War II," *A Historic Context for the African American Military Experience,* edited by Steven D. Smith and James A. Zeidler (Champaign, Ill.: U.S. Army Corps of Engineers, Construction Engineering Research Laboratories, 1998): pp. 235-236.

[102] Richard L. Baker, Senior Technical Information Spec. GS-11, U.S. Army Military History Institute, Army Heritage and Education Center, Carlisle, Penn., email to author, Dec. 26, 2013.

[103] Records that would clarify details in Marvin's military service were lost in a 1973 fire at the National Archives' National Personnel Records Center in St. Louis. The fire destroyed 16-to-18 million files of military personnel, including Army veterans who served from Nov. 1, 1912 to Jan. 1, 1960. See the U.S. National Archives and Records Administration, "The 1973 Fire, National Personnel Records Center": http://www.archives.gov/st-louis/military-personnel/fire-1973.html, accessed Jan. 12, 2014.

[104] Amanda N. Neal, Army Heritage Center Foundation, Carlisle, Penn., email to author, Jan. 8, 2014.

[105] Robert F. Jefferson, "African Americans in the U.S. Army During World War II," and Keith Krawczynski, "African American Navy, Marine, Women's Reserves, and Coast Guard Service During World War II," *A Historic Context for the African American Military Experience,* edited by Steven D. Smith and James A. Zeidler (Champaign, Ill.: U.S. Army Corps of Engineers, Construction Engineering Research Laboratories, 1998): pp. 187-246.

[106] Combined Arms Support Command, "The Second Camp Lee," Fort Lee Web site: http://www.lee.army.mil/pao/history.aspx, accessed Jan. 12, 2014.

[107] Bradford A. Wineman, "Fort Lee," Encyclopedia Virginia: http://www.encyclopediavirginia.org/Fort_Lee, accessed Jan. 12, 2014.

[108] Amanda N. Neal, Army Heritage Center Foundation, Carlisle, Penn., email to author, Jan. 8, 2014.

[109] Robert F. Jefferson, "African Americans in the U.S. Army During World War II," *A Historic Context for the African American Military Experience,* edited by Steven D. Smith and James A. Zeidler (Champaign, Ill.: U.S. Army Corps of Engineers, Construction Engineering Research Laboratories, 1998): p. 194.

[110] "1944 World War II Troop Ship Crossings": http://www.skylighters.org/troopships/1944.html, accessed Jan. 11, 2014.

[111] Mildred A. MacGregor, "The Troopship Queen Mary," (chapter 1 of *World War II Front Line Nurse*): http://www.press.umich.edu/pdf/9780472033317-ch1.pdf, accessed Jan. 5, 2014.

[112] "The Gray Ghost: The Queen Mary during WW2": http://www.sterling.rmplc.co.uk/history/wartime.html, accessed Jan. 5, 2014. "The History Behind the Queen Mary," QueenMaryShadows.com: http://www.queenmaryshadows.com/history.html, accessed Jan. 5, 2014. Mildred A. MacGregor, "The Troopship Queen Mary," (chapter 1 of *World War II Front Line Nurse*): http://www.press.umich.edu/pdf/9780472033317-ch1.pdf, accessed Jan. 5, 2014.

[113] "The Gray Ghost: The Queen Mary during WW2": http://www.sterling.rmplc.co.uk/history/wartime.html, accessed Jan. 5, 2014. "The History Behind the Queen Mary," QueenMaryShadows.com: http://www.queenmaryshadows.com/history.html, accessed Jan. 5, 2014. Mildred A. MacGregor, "The Troopship Queen Mary," (chapter 1 of *World War II Front Line Nurse*): http://www.press.umich.edu/pdf/9780472033317-ch1.pdf, accessed Jan. 5, 2014.

[114] "The History Behind the Queen Mary," QueenMaryShadows.com: http://www.queenmaryshadows.com/history.html, accessed Jan. 5, 2014. Mildred A. MacGregor, "The Troopship Queen Mary," (chapter 1 of *World War II Front Line Nurse*): http://www.press.umich.edu/pdf/9780472033317-ch1.pdf, accessed Jan. 5, 2014.

[115] US Army Quartermaster Foundation, "The History of Rations": http://www.qmfound.com/history_of_rations.htm, accessed Jan. 24, 2014.

[116] Jerrold M. Packard, "Jim Crow & WWII," Command Posts: http://www.commandposts.com/2011/07/jim-crow-wwii/, accessed April 8, 2013; Florida State University Institute on World War II and the Human Experience: http://ww2.fsu.edu/African-American, accessed April 8, 2013; Karen Hodges, "Continuity or Change: African Americans in World War II," http://www.umbc.edu/che/tahlessons/pdf/Continuity_or_Change_African_Americans_in_World_War_II(PrinterFriendly).pdf, accessed April 8, 2013; "Race In World War II": http://www.shmoop.com/wwii/race.html, accessed April 8, 2013.

[117] "Race In World War II": http://www.shmoop.com/wwii/race.html, accessed April 8, 2013.

[118] New Jersey State Library, Unit 12 World War II: "The Struggle for Democracy at Home and Abroad, 1940-1945": http://slic.njstatelib.org/NJ_Information/Digital_Collections/AAHCG/unit12.html, accessed April 8, 2013; National WWII Museum, "African Americans in World War

II," http://www.nationalww2museum.org/assets/pdfs/african-americans-in-world.pdf, accessed April 8, 2013.

[119] "Race In World War II": http://www.shmoop.com/wwii/race.html, accessed April 8, 2013; New Jersey State Library, Unit 12 World War II: "The Struggle for Democracy at Home and Abroad, 1940-1945": http://slic.njstatelib.org/NJ_Information/Digital_Collections/AAHCG/unit12.html, accessed April 8, 2013.

[120] "Race In World War II": http://www.shmoop.com/wwii/race.html, accessed April 8, 2013.

[121] Jerrold M. Packard, "Jim Crow & WWII," Command Posts: http://www.commandposts.com/2011/07/jim-crow-wwii/, accessed April 8, 2013.

[122] National WWII Museum, "African Americans in World War II," http://www.nationalww2museum.org/assets/pdfs/african-americans-in-world.pdf, accessed April 8, 2013.

[123] "Race In World War II": http://www.shmoop.com/wwii/race.html, accessed April 8, 2013.

[124] Stephen Ambrose, *Citizen Soldier* (New York, N.Y.: Simon & Schuster, 1997), p. 345.

[125] Leon Litwack and Winthrop Jordan, *The United States: Becoming a World Power,* 7th edition, Vol. II (Englewood Cliffs, N. J.: Prentice Hall, 1991), p. 708.

[126] New Jersey State Library, Unit 12 World War II: "The Struggle for Democracy at Home and Abroad, 1940-1945": http://slic.njstatelib.org/NJ_Information/Digital_Collections/AAHCG/unit12.html, accessed April 8, 2013.

[127] Stephen Ambrose, *Citizen Soldier* (New York, N.Y.: Simon & Schuster, 1997), p. 19.

[128] Skylighters.org Web site, "The Cigarette Camps / The U.S. Army Camps in the Le Havre Area": http://www.skylighters.org/special/cigcamps/cigintro.html, accessed Jan. 23, 2014.

[129] Distance Calculator Web site, "Measuring the Distance from Cherbourg France to Le Havre France": http://www.distance-calculator.co.uk/distances-for-cherbourg-to-le_havre.htm, accessed Jan. 24, 2014.

[130] USArmyModels.com Web site, "U.S. Army Field Rations": http://www.usarmymodels.com/ARTICLES/Rations/rationsintro.htm, accessed Jan. 24, 2014.

[131] "Buck sergeant" was the lowest rank of sergeant (The Free Dictionary, "Buck Sergeant": http://www.thefreedictionary.com/buck+sergeant, accessed Jan. 24, 2014). In this quote, Marvin was using the term loosely, in reference to various

drill instructors and sergeants he had in training camps as well as during overseas deployment.

[132] David P. Colley, "On The Road To Victory: The Red Ball Express": http://www.historynet.com/red-ball-express, accessed Jan. 24, 2014.

[133] U.S. Army Transportation Museum, "The Red Ball Express, 1944": http://www.transchool.lee.army.mil/museum/transportation%20museum/redbal lintro.htm, accessed Jan. 24, 2014.

[134] David P. Colley, "On The Road To Victory: The Red Ball Express": http://www.historynet.com/red-ball-express, accessed Jan. 24, 2014. U.S. Army Transportation Museum, "The Red Ball Express, 1944": http://www.transchool.lee.army.mil/museum/transportation%20museum/redbal lintro.htm, accessed Jan. 24, 2014. Steven D. Smith and James A. Zeidler, *A Historic Context for the African American Military Experience* (Champaign, Ill.: U.S. Army Corps of Engineers, Construction Engineering Research Laboratories, 1998): pp. 238.

[135] David P. Colley, "On The Road To Victory: The Red Ball Express": http://www.historynet.com/red-ball-express, accessed Jan. 24, 2014. U.S. Army Transportation Museum, "The Red Ball Express, 1944": http://www.transchool.lee.army.mil/museum/transportation%20museum/redbal lintro.htm, accessed Jan. 24, 2014.

[136] David P. Colley, "On The Road To Victory: The Red Ball Express": http://www.historynet.com/red-ball-express, accessed Jan. 24, 2014. U.S. Army Transportation Museum, "The Red Ball Express, 1944": http://www.transchool.lee.army.mil/museum/transportation%20museum/redbal lintro.htm, accessed Jan. 24, 2014.

[137] Mike Miller, "Black Market": http://www.armchairgeneral.com/forums/showthread.php?t=114357, accessed Jan. 25, 2014. David P. Colley, "On The Road To Victory: The Red Ball Express": http://www.historynet.com/red-ball-express, accessed Jan. 24, 2014. Brandon Lindsey, "African American Soldiers in World War II," ABC-CLIO Web site: http://www.historyandtheheadlines.abc-clio.com/ContentPages/ContentPage.aspx?entryId=1289447&currentSection=128 8543&productid=18, Jan. 25, 2014.

[138] Vehicle Technologies Office, U.S. Dept. of Energy, "Historical Gas Prices, 1919-2004": https://www1.eere.energy.gov/vehiclesandfuels/facts/2005/fcvt_fotw364.html, accessed Jan. 26, 2014. Mike Miller, "Black Market": http://www.armchairgeneral.com/forums/showthread.php?t=114357, accessed Jan. 25, 2014. Television History – The First 75 Years, "What Things Cost in 1944": http://www.tvhistory.tv/1944 QF.htm, Jan. 26, 2014. David P. Colley, "On The

Road To Victory: The Red Ball Express": http://www.historynet.com/red-ball-express, accessed Jan. 24, 2014.

[139] U.S. Army Transportation Museum, "The Red Ball Express, 1944": http://www.transchool.lee.army.mil/museum/transportation%20museum/redballintro.htm, accessed Jan. 24, 2014. JCS-Group.com Web site, "Something About Everything Military / Red Ball Express": http://www.jcs-group.com/military/war1941tomorrow/redball.html, accessed Jan. 25, 2014. David P. Colley, "On The Road To Victory: The Red Ball Express": http://www.historynet.com/red-ball-express, accessed Jan. 24, 2014.

[140] David P. Colley, "On The Road To Victory: The Red Ball Express": http://www.historynet.com/red-ball-express, accessed Jan. 24, 2014.

[141] Brandon Lindsey, "African American Soldiers in World War II," ABC-CLIO Web site: http://www.historyandtheheadlines.abc-clio.com/ContentPages/ContentPage.aspx?entryId=1289447&currentSection=1288543&productid=18, Jan. 25, 2014. U.S. Army Transportation Museum, "The Red Ball Express, 1944": http://www.transchool.lee.army.mil/museum/transportation%20museum/redballintro.htm, accessed Jan. 24, 2014. David P. Colley, "On The Road To Victory: The Red Ball Express": http://www.historynet.com/red-ball-express, accessed Jan. 24, 2014.

[142] Robert F. Jefferson, "African Americans in the U.S. Army During World War II," *A Historic Context for the African American Military Experience,* edited by Steven D. Smith and James A. Zeidler (Champaign, Ill.: U.S. Army Corps of Engineers, Construction Engineering Research Laboratories, 1998): p. 238.

[143] V2Rocket.com Web site, "Antwerp, 'City of Sudden Death'": http://www.v2rocket.com/start/chapters/antwerp.html, accessed Jan. 27, 2014. BBC Web site, "Fact File : Battle for Scheldt Estuary": http://www.bbc.co.uk/history/ww2peopleswar/timeline/factfiles/nonflash/a1143442.shtml, accessed Jan. 27, 2014.

[144] Robert F. Jefferson, "African Americans in the U.S. Army During World War II," *A Historic Context for the African American Military Experience,* edited by Steven D. Smith and James A. Zeidler (Champaign, Ill.: U.S. Army Corps of Engineers, Construction Engineering Research Laboratories, 1998): p. 238.

[145] Peter C. Xantheas, "Aachen (North Rhine-Westphalia, Germany)," *Northern Europe: International Dictionary of Historic Places,* edited by Trudy Ring, Noelle Watson, Paul Schellinger (New York, N.Y.: Routledge, 2013), p. 4.

[146] Peter C. Xantheas, "Aachen (North Rhine-Westphalia, Germany)," *Northern Europe: International Dictionary of Historic Places,* edited by Trudy Ring, Noelle Watson, Paul Schellinger (New York, N.Y.: Routledge, 2013), p. 1.

[147] Peter C. Xantheas, "Aachen (North Rhine-Westphalia, Germany)," *Northern Europe: International Dictionary of Historic Places,* edited by Trudy Ring, Noelle Watson, Paul Schellinger (New York, N.Y.: Routledge, 2013), p. 4.

[148] Charles B. MacDonald, "Sweep to the Elbe," Chapter XVII, *The Last Offensive:* http://www.ibiblio.org/hyperwar/USA/USA-E-Last/USA-E-Last-17.html, accessed April 6, 2014.

[149] Charles B. MacDonald, "Sweep to the Elbe," Chapter XVII, *The Last Offensive:* http://www.ibiblio.org/hyperwar/USA/USA-E-Last/USA-E-Last-17.html, accessed April 6, 2014.

[150] John T. Correll, "The Invasion That Didn't Happen," *Air Force Magazine,* June 2009, Vol. 92, No. 6: http://www.airforcemag.com/MagazineArchive/Pages/2009/June%202009/0609invasion.aspx, accessed Feb. 5, 2014.

[151] Now known as the Royal Conservatoire of Scotland.

[152] Brig. Gen. Koenig, Special Order No. 68, part 108, Sept. 6, 1945.

[153] "Citizen's Diary," *Evening Citizen,* Nov. 22, 1945, p. 2. "G.I.s' Turkey And Pie Day," *Evening Citizen,* Nov. 22, 1945, p. 3.

[154] John T. Correll, "The Invasion That Didn't Happen," *Air Force Magazine,* June 2009, Vol. 92, No. 6: http://www.airforcemag.com/MagazineArchive/Pages/2009/June%202009/0609invasion.aspx, accessed Feb. 5, 2014.

[155] U.S. Department of Veteran Affairs, "The GI Bill's History," Feb. 9, 2012: http://www.gibill.va.gov/benefits/history_timeline/, accessed Oct. 20, 2013.

[156] Judith Bellafaire, "The Women's Army Corps: A Commemoration of World War II Service," U.S. Army Center of Military History: http://www.history.army.mil/brochures/WAC/WAC.HTM, accessed April 16, 2014.

[157] National Montford Point Marine Association, "Welcome": http://www.montfordpointmarines.com/, accessed April 17, 2014. President Harry S. Truman issued Executive Order #9981, ending segregation in the military. In 1974 the camp was renamed in honor of Sgt. Major Gilbert Johnson. It is the only Marine Corps installation named in honor of an African-American.

[158] National Montford Point Marine Association, "Defense Battalions": http://www.montfordpointmarines.com/, accessed April 17, 2014.

[159] Navy Department Library, "Battle for Iwo Jima, 1945": http://www.history.navy.mil/library/online/battleiwojima.htm, accessed April 17, 2014.

[160] Col. Joseph H. Alexander, "Closing In: Marines in the Seizure of Iwo Jima," *Marines In World War II Commemorative Series:* http://www.ibiblio.org/hyperwar/USMC/USMC-C-Iwo/, accessed April 17, 2014.

[161] Lester's sons are Sanford, Geoffrey, and Stephan.

[162] Massachusetts Audubon Society, "Nature and People at the Boston Insane Hospital in the Late 1890s": http://www.massaudubon.org/Nature_Connection/Sanctuaries/Boston/Healing-Landscape/BIH-1900.php, accessed Oct. 21, 2013.

[163] Robert Preer, "Specters of old state hospitals vanish as new uses take shape," *Boston Globe*, July 8, 2007: http://www.boston.com/realestate/news/articles/2007/07/08/specters_of_old_state_hospitals_vanish_as_new_uses_take_shape/, accessed Oct. 21, 2013.

[164] Interview with author, Oct. 5, 2011.

[165] Ron Newman, "Old Howard Theatre," Cinema Treasures: http://cinematreasures.org/theaters/10901, accessed Dec. 7, 2013.

[166] American Immigration Law Foundation, "John J. Cullinane": http://www.ailf.org/awards/benefit2001/ahp_0102_jcullinane.htm, accessed Dec. 25, 2013. Mark Hall, "The 10 IT People Who Mattered in the Past 40 Years (but You May Not Know Why)," *Computerworld*, July 9, 2007: http://www.computerworld.com/s/article/295941/The_10_IT_People_Who_Mattered_in_the_Past_40_Years_but_You_May_Not_Know_Why_, accessed Dec. 25, 2013.

[167] Interview with author, Dec. 27, 2013.

[168] Email to author, Dec. 29, 2013, following up on interview.

[169] Mary Moore, "Black & White: And it's all over for area nonprofit," *Boston Business Journal*, Nov. 10, 2008: http://www.bizjournals.com/boston/stories/2008/11/10/story10.html?page=all, accessed Dec. 25, 2013.

[170] Fox Butterfield and Constance L. Hays, "A BOSTON TRAGEDY: THE STUART CASE - A SPECIAL CASE; Motive Remains a Mystery In Deaths That Haunt a City," *New York Times*, Jan. 15, 1990: http://www.nytimes.com/1990/01/15/us/boston-tragedy-stuart-case-special-case-motive-remains-mystery-deaths-that-haunt.html?pagewanted=all&src=pm, accessed Dec. 25, 2013.

[171] Patricia Cantor, "Massachusetts Rent Control," National Housing Institute, March/April 1995: http://www.nhi.org/online/issues/80/massrent.html, accessed Nov. 17, 2013. Timothy Taylor, "When Rent Control Ended in Cambridge, Mass.," Conversable Economist: http://conversableeconomist.blogspot.com/2012/10/when-rent-control-ended-in-cambridge.html, accessed Nov. 17, 2013.

[172] "Judge Orders 3 Demerit Suits Be Combined," *Boston Daily Globe*, Dec. 15, 1955.

[173] "Claims Court Power Usurped / Driver Tests Assessment of Demerits by Registrar," *Boston Daily Globe*, Dec. 1, 1955, p. 39.

[174] "State Jolted On Demerits," *Boston Daily Record*, Dec. 22, 1955, p. 1. "Demerit Row To High Court," *Boston Traveler,* Dec. 23, 1955, p. 1.

[175] "High Court Test Of Demerits Due," *Boston Daily Record,* Dec. 22, 1955, p. 3.

[176] "$6 Demerit Repealer Bill Signed By Herter," *Boston Daily Record,* Feb. 9, 1956, p. 4.

[177] Interview with author, Oct. 28, 2011.

[178] Marvin Gilmore, interviews with author. Vassar College, *Tenth-Year Class Notes,* "Langer, Lorna June (Mrs. Marvin E. Gilmore, Jr.)," p. 70. *Boston Globe* Web site, "Gilmore, Lorna J.": http://www.legacy.com/obituaries/bostonglobe/obituary.aspx?n=Lorna-Gilmore&pid=86551333, accessed Dec. 10, 2013. Vassar College, bachelor of arts diploma, Lorna June Langer, June 2, 1952. Kathy Markey, "Faculty and Students Assemble In The Chapel for Convocation," *Vassar Chronicle,* Sept. 29, 1951, p. 1.

[179] Email to author, Dec. 11, 2013.

[180] 1930 U.S. census, Brooklyn, Kings County, New York City, New York: http://search.ancestry.com/cgi-bin/sse.dll?rank=1&new=1&MSAV=0&gss=angs-g&gsfn=Lillian&gsln=Langer&mswpn___ftp=New+York+%28Bronx%29%2c+Bronx%2c+New+York%2c+USA&mswpn=10119&mswpn_PInfo=8-|0|1652393|0|2|3244|35|1652382|378|10119|0|&uidh=mc7&mssng0=Robert&mssns0=Langer&mscng0=Lillian&mscns0=Langer&pcat=ROOT_CATEGORY&h=39117663&db=1930usfedcen&indiv=1&ml_rpos=2, accessed July 6, 2014.

[181] 1940 U.S. census, Assembly District 8, Bronx, New York City, Bronx, New York: http://familysearch.org/pal:/MM9.1.1.KQMV-39X, accessed Dec. 11, 2013.

[182] Interview with author, Feb. 13, 2011.

[183] Editors of Encyclopædia Britannica, "Pogrom," *Encyclopædia Britannica*: http://www.britannica.com/EBchecked/topic/466210/pogrom, accessed Dec. 8, 2013.

[184] M.A. Leonard, "Poland Border Changes," PolandGenWeb, Sept. 3, 2007: http://www.rootsweb.ancestry.com/~polpomor/borders.htm, accessed Dec. 21, 2013.

[185] Answers.com Web site, "Howard Thurman": http://www.answers.com/topic/howard-thurman, accessed Jan. 22, 2014.

[186] Lorna J. Langer and Lewis L. Engel, "Human Placental Estradiol-17B Dehydrogenase: Concentration, Characterization, and Assay," *Journal of Biological Chemistry,* 1958, 233: 583-588. Lorna J. Langer, Joyce A. Alexander and Lewis L. Engel, "Human Placental Estradiol-17B Dehydrogenase: II. Kinetics and Substrate Specificities," *Journal of Biological Chemistry,* 1959, 234: 2609-2614.

[187] "Uncle Remus Tales," The Wren's Nest Blog: http://www.wrensnest.org/about_stories.php, accessed Dec. 15, 2013.

[188] Interview with author, Oct. 5, 2011.

[189] Richard Halverson, "Boston's Black Bank That Faltered Gets Boost on Road Back," Christian Science Monitor, May 8, 1972, p. 5.

[190] John Atlas and Peter Drier, "Public Housing: What Went Wrong?" National Housing Institute, Shelterforce Online, Issue 74, September/October 1994: http://www.nhi.org/online/issues/77/pubhsg.html, accessed Dec. 25, 2013.

[191] Interview with author, Oct. 7, 2013.

[192] Larry Kart, "Sinatra, Martin, Davis Get Their Act Together," *Chicago Tribune*, March 13, 1988: http://articles.chicagotribune.com/1988-03-13/entertainment/8802290191_1_sinatra-martin-davis-frank-sinatra-rat, accessed Oct. 13, 2013.

[193] Peter Filichia, "Golden Days / As Encore! presents *Golden Boy*, Filichia remembers seeing the original production with Sammy Davis, Jr. out of town," TheaterMania.com: http://www.theatermania.com/new-york-city-theater/news/03-2002/golden-days_2028.html, accessed Sept. 8, 2013.

[194] Peter Filichia, "Golden Days / As Encore! presents *Golden Boy*, Filichia remembers seeing the original production with Sammy Davis, Jr. out of town," TheaterMania.com: http://www.theatermania.com/new-york-city-theater/news/03-2002/golden-days_2028.html, accessed Sept. 8, 2013.

[195] Andrew Gans and Robert Simonson, "London's Greenwhich Theatre Presents *Golden Boy* Musical June 19; Strouse Adds Songs," Playbill.com: http://www.playbill.com/news/article/79869-Londons-Greenwich-Theatre-Presents-Golden-Boy-Musical-June-19-Strouse-Adds-Songs, accessed Sept. 8, 2013.

[196] American Jewish Archives, "Kivie Kaplan Papers": http://americanjewisharchives.org/collections/ms0026/, accessed Oct. 20, 2013.

[197] Interview with author, Oct. 11, 2013.

[198] Gerald Gamm, *Urban Exodus: Why Jews Left Boston and the Catholics Stayed* (Cambridge, Mass.: Harvard University Press, 1999), pp. 11-95.

[199] DemocracyNow.org, "Wednesday, June 12, 2013 / Medgar Evers' Murder, 50 Years Later: Widow Myrlie Evers-Williams Remembers 'A Man for All Time'": http://www.democracynow.org/2013/6/12/medgar_evers_murder_50_years_later, accessed July 22, 2013.

[200] Federal Bureau of Investigation, "Civil Rights in the 60s / Part 1: Justice for Medgar Evers": http://www.fbi.gov/news/stories/2013/june/civil-rights-in-the-60s-justice-for-medgar-evers, accessed July 23, 2013. Barry Saunders, "Saunders: 50 Years ago, a death in Mississippi and a defining story of the Civil Rights Movement," NewsObserver.com: http://www.newsobserver.com/2013/06/12/2956334/saunders-50-years-ago-a-death.html, accessed July 23, 2013.

[201] Charles Evers and Andrew Szanton, *Have No Fear: The Charles Evers Story* (New York, N.Y.: John Wiley & Sons, 1997), pp.127-128.

[202] Barry Saunders, "Saunders: 50 Years ago, a death in Mississippi and a defining story of the Civil Rights Movement," NewsObserver.com: http://www.newsobserver.com/2013/06/12/2956334/saunders-50-years-ago-a-death.html, accessed July 23, 2013.

[203] Federal Bureau of Investigation, "Civil Rights in the 60s / Part 1: Justice for Medgar Evers": http://www.fbi.gov/news/stories/2013/june/civil-rights-in-the-60s-justice-for-medgar-evers, accessed July 23, 2013.

[204] DemocracyNow.org, "Wednesday, June 12, 2013 / Medgar Evers' Murder, 50 Years Later: Widow Myrlie Evers-Williams Remembers 'A Man for All Time'": http://www.democracynow.org/2013/6/12/medgar_evers_murder_50_years_later, accessed July 22, 2013.

[205] Federal Bureau of Investigation, "Civil Rights in the 60s / Part 1: Justice for Medgar Evers": http://www.fbi.gov/news/stories/2013/june/civil-rights-in-the-60s-justice-for-medgar-evers, accessed July 23, 2013.

[206] Barry Saunders, "Saunders: 50 Years ago, a death in Mississippi and a defining story of the Civil Rights Movement," NewsObserver.com: http://www.newsobserver.com/2013/06/12/2956334/saunders-50-years-ago-a-death.html, accessed July 23, 2013. Debbie Elliot, "Fifty Years After Medgar Evers' Killing, The Scars Remain," NPR.org: http://m.npr.org/news/U.S./188727790, accessed July 23, 2013.

[207] Barry Saunders, "Saunders: 50 Years ago, a death in Mississippi and a defining story of the Civil Rights Movement," NewsObserver.com: http://www.newsobserver.com/2013/06/12/2956334/saunders-50-years-ago-a-death.html, accessed July 23, 2013. (Barry Saunders' report in the Raleigh, N. C. *News and Observer's* Web site on the 50th anniversary of the assassination quoted the 1963 *New York Times* account.)

[208] Glen Justice, "'The Word Is Free' : For the three children of civil rights martyr Medgar Evers, the conviction of their father's murderer after 30 years has finally ended a lifetime in limbo. Quietly, each is fulfilling their father's dreams by living out their own," *Los Angeles Times*: http://articles.latimes.com/1994-03-20/news/vw-36537_1_medgar-evers, accessed July 23, 2013.

[209] Debbie Elliot, "Fifty Years After Medgar Evers' Killing, The Scars Remain," NPR.org: http://m.npr.org/news/U.S./188727790, accessed July 23, 2013.

[210] Barry Saunders, "Saunders: 50 Years ago, a death in Mississippi and a defining story of the Civil Rights Movement," NewsObserver.com: http://www.newsobserver.com/2013/06/12/2956334/saunders-50-years-ago-a-death.html, accessed July 23, 2013.

[211] Borgna Brunner, "The Murder of Medgar Evers / Byron De La Beckwith was convicted of murdering Evers in 1994, 30 years after the fact," Information Please: http://www.infoplease.com/spot/bhmjustice2.html, accessed July 23, 2013.

[212] John Dittmer, *Local People: The Struggle for Civil Rights in Mississippi* (Urbana: University of Illinois Press, 1994), pp. 177-178.

[213] Charles Evers and Grace Halsell, *Evers* (New York, N.Y.: World Publishing Co., 1971), pp.102-108.

[214] Charles Evers and Grace Halsell, *Evers* (New York, N.Y.: World Publishing Co., 1971), pp.106-107.

[215] Emilye Crosby, *A Little Taste of Freedom: The Black Freedom Struggle in Claiborne County, Mississippi* (Chapel Hill, No. Carolina: The University of North Carolina Press, 2005), pp. 165-167.

[216] Charles Evers Interview with author, Oct. 19, 2011.

[217] Reconstruction is the name of the period when the United States attempted to transform the South in part by enforcing freedom from slavery for African-Americans. Reconstruction is generally viewed as having occurred after the Civil War. It is often described as the period from 1865 to 1877, although some historians mark its beginning as 1863 with the Emancipation Proclamation. Black rights advanced, but many historians feel Reconstruction ultimately failed because of widespread poverty that occurred in the postwar South and the rise of Jim Crow laws that made blacks second-class citizens.

[218] Michael Lydon, "Hub Negro Wins in Miss.," *Boston Globe,* July 6, 1964, p. 1.

[219] A ninth man in the group was a public relations person. Guscott remained in Mississippi one day before returning to Massachusetts.

[220] Gretchen Cassel Eick, *Dissent in Wichita: The Civil Rights Movement in the Midwest, 1954-1972* (Urbana, Ill.: University of Illinois Press, 2001), p. 88.

[221] Michael Lydon, "Hub Negro Wins in Miss.," *Boston Globe,* July 6, 1964, p. 1.

[222] Michael Lydon, "Hub Negro Wins in Miss.," *Boston Globe,* July 6, 1964, p. 1.

[223] Michael Lydon, "Hub Negro Wins in Miss.," *Boston Globe,* July 6, 1964, p. 2.

[224] Michael Lydon, "Hub Negro Wins in Miss.," *Boston Globe,* July 6, 1964, p. 2. Richard Neff, "Race-Amity Gain In Jackson Cited," *Christian Science Monitor,* July 10, 1964, pp. 1-2.

[225] Charles Evers and Andrew Szanton, *Have No Fear: The Charles Evers Story* (New York, N.Y.: John Wiley & Sons, 1997), pp.135.

[226] Bill Russell and William McSweeny, *Go Up For Glory* (New York, N.Y.: Coward-McCann, 1966), p. 211.

[227] Bill Russell and Taylor Branch, Second Wind: The Memoirs of an Opinionated Man (New York, N.Y.: Random House, 1979), p. 184.

[228] Bill Russell and William McSweeny, *Go Up For Glory* (New York, N.Y.: Coward-McCann, 1966), p. 211.

[229] Bill Russell and William McSweeny, *Go Up For Glory* (New York, N.Y.: Coward-McCann, 1966), p. 211.

[230] Charles Evers Interview with author, Oct. 19, 2011.

[231] Thomas Atkins (Executive Secretary, NAACP Boston branch), memo to Kenneth Guscott (President, NAACP Boston branch), summarizing activities of visit to Jackson, Miss., by Atkins and three other men that began July 13, 1964, "Memorandum," Library of Congress, NAACP Records III. box C61. The memo is undated but presumably was submitted to Guscott within a month of the trip that began July 13; in all likelihood, the memo was written and submitted within days of July 13.

[232] Thomas Atkins memo to Kenneth Guscott.

[233] Don Fair, "My Most Dangerous Experience / Russell: 'In Dixie'," *Seattle Post-Intelligencer,* April 22, 1974, p. C3.

[234] Charles Evers and Andrew Szanton, *Have No Fear: The Charles Evers Story* (New York, N.Y.: John Wiley & Sons, 1997), pp.135. A Feb. 19, 2011 report in the *Seattle Times* describes Evers as spending one night in Russell's hotel room, providing one last line of defense against potential intruders by sleeping in a chair facing the door, cradling a rifle in his lap. Asked about that report, Marvin did not recall the episode. He said he believed it would have been difficult to conceal a weapon as large as a rifle. He said that a black man trying to enter the Heidelberg Hotel in July 1964 with a rifle would have triggered an extremely aggressive response by the hotel, by police who would have been summoned, and by white supremacists in the vicinity. Evers would have been placing his life at risk with such an attempt, Marvin said. See "Medgar Evers' assassination in 1963 inspired Bill Russell to offer help in Mississippi": http://seattletimes.nwsource.com/html/stevekelley/2014271665_kelley20.html, accessed Jan. 4, 2012.)

[235] Bill Russell and William McSweeny, *Go Up For Glory* (New York, N.Y.: Coward-McCann, 1966), p. 212.

[236] Michael Lydon, "Russell Wows Boys in Miss.," *Boston Globe,* July 10, 1964, p. 1.

[237] Michael Lydon, "Russell Wows Boys in Miss.," *Boston Globe,* July 10, 1964, p. 4.

[238] Miss. Dept. of Archives and History, Sovereignty Commission Online, SCR ID #9-31-2-2-1-1-1: http://mdah.state.ms.us/arrec/digital_archives/sovcom/result.php?image=images/png/cd10/073548.png&otherstuff=13|36|0|25|1|1|1|72610|, accessed Aug. 25, 2013.

[239] Mark Mulvoy, "'Everyone Is Carrying Guns'; Fears Trouble This Summer," *Boston Globe,* July 14, 1964, p. 1. A United Press International photo caption in the *Chicago Daily Defender*, July 14, 1964, p. 24, refers to Russell running a basketball clinic at the "College Park auditorium" in Jackson. The name of the

venue makes it sound like a fifth clinic. But it's actually the site of the clinic at Jackson State College, one of the four that were held. College Park Auditorium (its proper name) is on the Jackson State campus.

[240] Bill Russell and William McSweeny, *Go Up For Glory* (New York, N.Y.: Coward-McCann, 1966), p. 212.

[241] Michael Lydon, "Russell Wows Boys in Miss.," *Boston Globe,* July 10, 1964, p. 4.

[242] UPI, "Celts Star Gets Cool Reception," *Delta Democrat-Times* (Greenville, Miss.), July 12, 1964, p. 8.

[243] UPI, "Bill Russell Says 12 Missing Since Evers," *Chicago Daily Defender,* July 15, 1964, p. 24.

[244] William M. Kunstler, "Bill Russell," *Sport,* December 1986, p. 39.

[245] Michael Lydon, "Russell Shut Out at Restaurant," *Boston Globe,* July 13, 1964, p. 21. John Dittmer, *Local People: The Struggle for Civil Rights in Mississippi* (Urbana: University of Illinois Press, 1994), p. 46.

[246] Martin Luther King Research and Education Institute, Stanford University, "Martin Luther King, Jr., and the Global Freedom Struggle: White Citizens' Council": http://mlk-kpp01.stanford.edu/index.php/encyclopedia/encyclopedia/enc_white_citizens_c ouncils_wcc/, accessed Aug. 25, 2013.

[247] Mark Mulvoy, "'Everyone Is Carrying Guns'; Fears Trouble This Summer," *Boston Globe,* July 14, 1964, p. 1 & 4.

[248] Frank McGrath, "Celts' Star Tells of Miss. Visit / Dixie Explosive—Russell," *Record American* (Boston), July 14, 1964, p. 5.

[249] Mark Mulvoy, "'Everyone Is Carrying Guns'; Fears Trouble This Summer," *Boston Globe,* July 14, 1964, p. 4.

[250] Mark Mulvoy, "'Everyone Is Carrying Guns'; Fears Trouble This Summer," *Boston Globe,* July 14, 1964, p. 4.

[251] Frank McGrath, "Celts' Star Tells of Miss. Visit / Dixie Explosive—Russell," *Record American* (Boston), July 14, 1964, p. 5. Mark Mulvoy, "'Everyone Is Carrying Guns'; Fears Trouble This Summer," *Boston Globe,* July 14, 1964, p. 4.

[252] United Press International, "Bill Russell Says 12 Missing Since Evers," *Chicago Daily Defender,* July 15, 1964, p. 24. Mark Mulvoy, "'Everyone Is Carrying Guns'; Fears Trouble This Summer," *Boston Globe,* July 14, 1964, p. 1.

[253] Ted Drozdowski, "Getting the Blues," *Boston Magazine,* February 2003: http://www.bostonmagazine.com/2006/05/getting-the-blues/, accessed Jan. 19, 2014.

[254] Interview with author, Jan. 13, 2014.

[255] Kay Bourne, "What's in a friendship?" *Sporting Life,* Jan. 27, 1977, Vol. 1, No. 3, p. 1.

[256] Jim Sullivan, "Dropping In; A Blue Icon Moves to Western Front," *Boston Globe*, May 23, 2002, Calendar section, page 9.

[257] Steve Morse, "Gilmore's the Leader at the Western Front," *Boston Globe,* Nov. 6, 1985, Arts section, p. 51.

[258] Jim Sullivan, "Dropping In; A Blue Icon Moves to Western Front," *Boston Globe*, May 23, 2002, Calendar section, page 9.

[259] Steve Morse, "Gilmore's the Leader at the Western Front," *Boston Globe,* Nov. 6, 1985, Arts section, p. 51.

[260] Steve Morse, "Gilmore's the Leader at the Western Front," *Boston Globe,* Nov. 6, 1985, Arts section p. 51.. Steve Morse, interview with author, Jan. 13, 2014.

[261] Paul Katzeff, "The Other Marvelous Marvin," *Boston Sunday Herald,* July 2, 1989, magazine section, p. 16.

[262] Steve Morse, interview with author, Jan. 13, 2014. Find A Grave Memorial, "Webster Lewis": http://www.findagrave.com/cgi-bin/fg.cgi?page=gr&GRid=8633564, accessed Jan. 21, 2014.

[263] Steve Morse, "Western Front's Weekday Variety," *Boston Globe,* Nov. 24, 1994, Calendar section, p. 23.

[264] Interview with author, April 30, 2014.

[265] Paul Katzeff, "The Other Marvelous Marvin," *Boston Sunday Herald,* July 2, 1989, magazine pp. 5-7, 16.

[266] "Nixon and the New Urban Landscape," Richard Nixon Foundation: http://blog.nixonfoundation.org/2013/09/nixon-new-urban-landscape-continued/, accessed Feb. 23, 2014.

[267] Donald R. Larrabee, "Nixon May Scrub Model Cities Concept," *Bangor* [Maine] *Daily News*, Jan. 2, 1973, p. 4.

[268] Alexander Von Hoffman, *House By House, Block By Block* (New York: Oxford University Press, 2003), p. 12.

[269] Marvin's title was changed to President and Chief Executive Officer in September 1993.

[270] Philip Hart, "Boston's Parcel-to-Parcel Linkage Plan," *Urban Land,* July 2005, p. 24.

[271] Philip Hart, "Boston's Parcel-to-Parcel Linkage Plan," *Urban Land,* July 2005, p. 24.

[272] Charles Radin, "Housing proposed for Southwest Corridor site," *Boston Globe,* Oct. 7, 1986, p. 29.

[273] Daniel Golden and David Mehegan, "The Boston Potential: Industrial Growth Called Key to New Boston Jobs," *Boston Globe,* Sept. 23, 1983, p. 1.

[274] Bonnie Hurd Smith, "Melnea A. Cass," Boston Women's Heritage Trail: http://bwht.org/melnea-cass/, accessed March 8, 2014.

[275] Daniel Golden and David Mehegan, "The Boston Potential: Industrial Growth Called Key to New Boston Jobs," *Boston Globe,* Sept. 23, 1983, p. 1.

[276] Minicomputers were popular because they were smaller and less expensive than mainframe computers but could do many data processing tasks needed by small and mid-sized businesses. Starting in the 1990s they were made obsolete by the rise of microcomputers – which today we call desktop computers, and which gave rise to servers. (See WiseGeek Web site, "What Is A Minicomputer?": http://www.wisegeek.org/what-is-a-minicomputer.htm, accessed Feb. 23, 2014.)

[277] *Boston Globe* Web site, "A look back at Digital Equipment Corp.," Boston.com: http://www.boston.com/business/technology/gallery/dectimeline?pg=12, accessed Feb. 22, 2014. Denis Pombriant, "Digital Equipment Corporation," Feb. 8, 2011: http://beagleresearch.com/tag/digital-equipment-corporation/, accessed Feb. 22, 2014.

[278] Ronald Rosenberg, "Digital a tenant at Roxbury park," *Boston Globe,* July 15, 1980, p. 31. Jonathan Fuerbringer, "Digital Corp. plans new plant near City Hospital," *Boston Globe,* Aug. 24, 1977, p. 1.

[279] Alan Lupo, "It's a Catch-22. We can't market the land without controling it, but the BRA says come up with the tenants first...," *Boston Evening Globe,* June 25, 1976, p. 3.

[280] Jane White, "Industrial park gets first tenant," *Boston Ledger,* Sept. 2, 1977, p. 6.

[281] Daniel Golden and David Mehegan, "The Boston Potential: Industrial Growth Called Key to New Boston Jobs," *Boston Globe,* Sept. 23, 1983, p. 1.

[282] Daniel Golden and David Mehegan, "The Boston Potential: Industrial Growth Called Key to New Boston Jobs," *Boston Globe,* Sept. 23, 1983, p. 1.

[283] Ronald Rosenberg, "Digital a tenant at Roxbury park," *Boston Globe,* July 15, 1980, p. 31.

[284] Viola Osgood, "2d tenant to build in industrial park," *Boston Sunday Globe,* July 8, 1979, p. 29.

[285] City of Boston, *Crosstown industrial park, parcel 2: a neighborhood development,* Urban Development Action Grant application to the U. S. Department of Housing and Urban Development, July 31, 1979, p. 27: https://archive.org/details/crosstownindustr00bost, accessed March 9, 2014.

[286] Joseph James Perez, "Reversing the urban job tide," *Industry,* May 1979, p. 21. Philip Hart and William Gasper, "Incubating Inner-City Biotech," *Urban Land,* September 2006, p. 167.

[287] Philip Hart and William Gasper, "Incubating Inner-City Biotech," *Urban Land,* September 2006, p. 167.

[288] Philip Hart and William Gasper, "Incubating Inner-City Biotech," *Urban Land,* September 2006, p. 167.

[289] Interview with author, July 25, 2014.

[290] Philip Hart and William Gasper, "Incubating Inner-City Biotech," *Urban Land,* September 2006, p. 168.

[291] William Gasper, interview with author, May 18, 2012.

[292] Marvin describes the Fellows Street project as a property that the CDC bought, and eventually sold at a profit to a developer that sold it to B.U. The CDC thus helped guide the destiny of the site and did so in a way that benefited the CDC and its future activities.

[293] Kirk Sykes, President, Urban Strategy America Fund, key investor in Crosstown Center, interview with author, March 17, 2014.

[294] Tyrone Richardson, "Opening marks Roxbury milestone," Urban Planet: http://www.urbanplanet.org/forums/index.php/topic/4941-minority-owned-hotel-opens-in-roxbury/, accessed March 16, 2014. Philip Hart and William Gasper, "Incubating Inner-City Biotech," *Urban Land,* September 2006, p. 168. CrossTown Center Web site, "Building business in a dynamic cityscape": http://crosstowncenterboston.com/index.html, accessed March 16, 2014. The CDC of Boston was not involved in the post-Digital redevelopment.

[295] Biographical Directory of the United States Congress, "O'Neill, Thomas Philip, Jr. (Tip), 1912-1994": http://bioguide.congress.gov/scripts/biodisplay.pl?index=o000098, accessed Aug. 2, 2014.

[296] U.S. House of Representatives Web site, "Brooke, Edward William, III": http://history.house.gov/People/Detail/9905?ret=True, accessed Feb. 29, 2014.

[297] Michael Fields, "U.S. earmarks $607 million for the Southwest Corridor," *Bay State Banner,* Aug. 17, 1978, p. 3.

[298] Michael Fields, "U.S. earmarks $607 million for the Southwest Corridor," *Bay State Banner,* Aug. 17, 1978, p. 3.

[299] Mark Browne, "Boston's land of opportunity: Who controls the Corridor?" *Boston Ledger,* Jan. 11-17, 1980, pp. 4-5 & 14. Viola Osgood and Arthur Jones, "Boston expecting a reborn Corridor," *Boston Globe,* Feb. 1977, p. 3. Philip Hart, "Boston's Parcel-to-Parcel Linkage Plan," *Urban Land,* July 2005, p. 24.

[300] Viola Osgood and Arthur Jones, "Boston expecting a reborn Corridor," *Boston Globe,* Feb. 1977, p. 3.

[301] Philip Hart, "Boston's Parcel-to-Parcel Linkage Plan," *Urban Land,* July 2005, p. 24.

[302] Anthony Pangaro, interview with author, June 28, 2013.

[303] Frederick Salvucci, interview with author, June 21, 2013.

[304] HistoryMakers Web site, "William T. Coleman": http://www.thehistorymakers.com/biography/william-t-coleman-41, accessed March 6, 2014.

[305] Bonnie Hurd Smith, "Melnea A. Cass," Boston Women's Heritage Trail: http://bwht.org/melnea-cass/, accessed March 8, 2014.

[306] Philip Hart, "Boston's Parcel-to-Parcel Linkage Plan," *Urban Land,* July 2005, p. 26.

[307] Anthony Pangaro, email to author, March 12,m 2014.

[308] City of Boston, "Employment Standards": https://www.cityofboston.gov/brjp/emplo_stand.asp, accessed April 26, 2014.

[309] Frommer's Web site, "Tropicana: Havana": http://www.frommers.com/destinations/havana/nightlife/235140, accessed May 18, 2014.

[310] Interview with author by email, Feb. 21, 2014.

[311] Interview with author, May 17, 2011.

[312] New England Real Estate Journal, "Samuel W. Poorvu," 1967: http://nerej.com/images/professional-profiles/ne/SamuelPoorvu1967.php, accessed May 24, 2014. Julie Carrick Dalton, "Family affair Bulfinch Cos., now in its 3d generation of family ownership, has assets of $250 million and manages 3 million square feet," *Boston Globe*, July 4, 1999, p. J1: https://secure.pqarchiver.com/boston/doc/405298765.html?FMT=ABS&FMTS=ABS:FT&type=current&date=Jul%204,%201999&author=Julie%20Carrick%20Dalton,%20Globe%20Correspondent&pub=Boston%20Globe&edition=&startpage=J.1&desc=Family%20affair%20Bulfinch%20Cos.,%20now%20in%20its%203d%20generation%20of%20family%20ownership,%20has%20assets%20of%20$250%20million%20and%20manages%203%20million%20square%20feet, accessed May 24, 2014. Bullfinch Companies, "Investing In The Future Of Real Estate Since 1936": http://www.bulfinch.com/company/history, accessed April 19, 2014.

[313] Bullfinch Companies, "Investing In The Future Of Real Estate Since 1936": http://www.bulfinch.com/company/history, accessed April 19, 2014.

[314] Interview with author, Nov. 25, 2013.

[315] Interview with author, April 30, 2014.

[316] Massachusetts Lafayette Society web site, "General Lafayette Biography": http://www.lafayettesocietyma.com/biography.htm, accessed June 1, 2014.

[317] Donald Shaffer, "Jefferson Davis' Infamous Proclamation," Civil War Emancipation: http://cwemancipation.wordpress.com/2012/12/26/jefferson-davis-infamous-proclamation/, accessed June 4, 2014.

[318] Massachusetts Historical Society web site, "54th Regiment!": http://www.masshist.org/online/54thregiment/essay.php?entry_id=528, accessed June 3, 2014. Alexander Bielakowski, editor, *Ethnic and Racial Minorities*

in the U.S. Military: An Encyclopedia (Santa Barbara, Calif.: ABC-CLIO, 2013), p. 202.

[319] In a Dec. 28, 2013 interview with the author, William Smith described the effort to rally congressional support for creation of the Day of Honor 2000. Smith and Thomas Wynn, of the National Association of Black Veterans, presented the proposal to Sen. Edward Kennedy, a liberal, who then asked colleagues for their support. Sen. Strom Thurmond, a conservative, told Kennedy he would support the proposal if he could be a cosponsor, Smith said. Kennedy agreed. The proposal got similar liberal-conservative support in the House when Rep. J.C. Watt, a young black Republican, told Democratic Rep. Sheila Jackson Lee would support it as a cosponsor. Once Day of Honor was created and the president said he would have a signing ceremony in his office, Smith, Wynn, and the House and Senate cosponsors began to consider veterans who could participate as representatives of minority service members from the war. Marvin was quickly selected because Smith knew him as someone who had previously taken an interest in Smith's media projects exploring the wartime experiences of black veterans and public attitudes toward them. Marvin had Kennedy's support because the senator respected Marvin for his work on the CDC of Boston and CrossTown Industrial Park, for the NAACP Boston branch, on civil rights in general, and for various state, city, and regional agencies.

[320] National World War II Museum, "WWII Veterans Statistics: The Passing of the Greatest Generation": http://www.nationalww2museum.org/honor/wwii-veterans-statistics.html, accessed June 15, 2014.

[321] The ensemble is an arm of the Asaph Christian Trust. "The aims are to use musical means to communicate aspects of the Christian faith," Hooke said. "We work through different churches that want to use a classical music concert to reach out to the community. So the concerts have a clear Christian theme in them."

[322] Interview with author, July 3, 2014.

[323] Interview with author, April 30, 2014.

[324] Interview with author, July 7, 2014.

[325] Alabama History and Archives Department, email to author, July 10, 2012.

[326] 1870 U.S. census, *Notasulga Beat, Macon, Alabama*: http://search.ancestrylibrary.com/iexec?htx=View&r=5542&dbid=7163&iid=4257 603_00420&fn=Kizzie&ln=Rowell&st=r&ssrc=&pid=13227126, accessed Oct. 13, 2011.

[327] 1870 U.S. census, *Notasulga Beat, Macon, Alabama*: http://search.ancestrylibrary.com/iexec?htx=View&r=5542&dbid=7163&iid=4257 603_00420&fn=Kizzie&ln=Rowell&st=r&ssrc=&pid=13227126, accessed Oct. 13, 2011; 1900 U.S. census, *Notasulga, Macon, Alabama*:

http://search.ancestrylibrary.com/iexec?htx=View&r=5542&dbid=7602&iid=0041 19998_00049&fn=Agusta&ln+Onel&st=r&ssrc=&pid+34593511, accessed Oct. 13, 2011.

[328] From the money-value calculator at http://www.measuringworth.com/uscompare/relativevalue.php, accessed July 7, 2012.

[329] 1880 U.S. census, *Notasulga, Macon, Alabama:* http://search.ancestry.com/iexec?htx=View&r=an&dbid=6742&iid=42397820021 9&fn=Mirra&ln=Rowel&st=r&ssrc=&pid+6129345, accessed July 15, 2012.

[330] 1900 U.S. census, *Precinct 9, Notasulga, Macon, Alabama:* http://search.ancestry.com/iexec?htx=View&r=an&dbid=7602iid=004119998_000 49&fn=Jeremiah&ln=Rowell&st=r&ssrc=&pid+34593482, accessed June 28, 2012.

[331] Howell Rowell family tree: http://trees.ancestry.com/tree/14713929/person/150454437, accessed Aug. 15, 2012.

[332] 1830 U.S. census, *Lowndes, Alabama:* http://search.ancestry.com/iexec?htx=View&r=an&dbid=8058&iid=4409667_005 49&fn=Hawell&ln=Rowell&st=r&ssrc=&pid=1018115, accessed July 25, 2012.

[333] Albert Henry Rowell family tree: http://trees.ancestry.com/tree/14713929/person/150454437, accessed July 15, 2012.

[334] 1860 U.S. census, *Beat 5, Tallapoosa, Alabama:* http://search.ancestry.com/iexec?htx=View&r=an&dbid=7667&iid=4211198_000 24&fn=Howell&ln=Rowell&st=r&ssrc=&pid=12704997, accessed July 25, 2012.

[335] 1850 U.S. census, *Township 20, Tallapoosa, Alabama:* http://search.ancestry.com/iexec?htx=View&r=an&dbid=8054&iid=41915400050 7&fn=Howell&ln=Rowell&st=r&ssrc=&pid=16804373, accessed July 25, 2012.

[336] Howell Rowell family tree: http://trees.ancestryinstitution.com/tree/1760625/person/-1226285013?ssrc=, accessed Aug. 15, 2012.

[337] 1860 U.S. census, *Northern Division, Macon, Alabama:* http://search.ancestrylibrary.com/iexec?htx=View&r=5542&dbid+7667&iid=4211 187_00435&fn=Edmund&ln=Webb&st=r&ssrc=&pid=11809935, accessed Oct. 13, 2012.

[338] From the money-value calculator at http://www.measuringworth.com/uscompare/relativevalue.php, accessed Sept. 30, 2012.

[339] 1860 U.S. census, *North Division, Macon, Alabama:* http://search.ancestryinstitution.com/cgi-

bin/sse.dll?rank=1&new=1&MSAV=1&msT=1&gss=angs-i&gsfin=edmund&g,, accessed Aug. 15, 2012.

[340] 1860 U.S. census slave schedule, *Beat 2, Marion, Texas:* http://search.ancestryinstitution.com/cgi-bin/sse.dll?1860slaveschedules&rank=1&new=1&MSAV=1&msT=1&gss, accessed Aug. 15, 2012.

[341] 1860 U.S. census, *Beat 2, Marion, Texas:* http://search.ancestryinstitution.com/cgi-bin/sse.dll?rank=1&new=1&MSAV=1&msT=1&gss=angs-i&gsfin=robert+edw, accessed Aug. 15, 2012.

[342] 1860 U.S. Civil War soldiers, 1861-1865: http://search.ancestrylibrary.com/cgibin/sse.dll?MS_AdvCB=1&rank=1&new+1M SAV=2&msT=1&gss=angsg&gsfn=robert&gsfn_x=1&gsln=rowell&gsln_x=1&gskw= confederate&gskw_x=1&catBucket=rstp&uidh=ije&pcat+ROOT_CATEGORY&h=54 94171&recoff=5+7&db=NPS_civilwarsoldiers&indiv=1, accessed Oct. 13, 2012.

[343] 1860 U.S. census, *Northern Division, Macon, Alabama:* http://search.ancestry.com/iexec?htx=View&r=an&dbid=7667&iid=4211187_004 35&fn=W+D&ln=Rowell&st=r&ssrc=&pid=11809950, accessed Aug. 15, 2012.

[344] 1860 U.S. census slave schedule, *Northern Division, Macon, Alabama*: http://search.ancestry.com/iexec?htx=View&r=an&dbid=7668&iid=ALM653_3203 43&fn=w+d&ln=rowell&st=r&ssrc=&pid=291733, accessed Aug. 15, 2012.

[345] http://en.wikipedia.org/wiki/Slavery_in_the_United_States, accessed Aug. 24,2012.

[346] http://en.wikipedia.org/wiki/History_of_Troy,_Alabama, accessed July 15, 2012.

[347] 1830 U.S. census, *Lowndes, Alabama:* http://search.ancestry.com/iexec?htx=View&r=an&dbid=8058&iid=4409667_005 49&fn=Hawell&ln=Rowell&st=r&ssrc=&pid=1018115, accessed July 25, 2012.

[348] 1850 Alabama marriage records, 1800-1969: http://search.ancestrycgi-bin/sse.dll?db, accessed July 15, 2012.

[349] 1850 U.S. census slave schedule, *District 21, Macon, Alabama:* http://search.ancestry.com/cgi-bin/sse.dll?db=1850slaveschedules&o_vc=Record%3aOtherRecords&rhSour { pk check rest }, accessed July 15, 2012.

[350] Alabama 1867 Voter Registration Records Database: http://www.archives.alabama.gov/voterreg/images/46_V1_PG069.pdf, accessed June 14, 2012.

[351]*The Emancipator,* "Recollections of Slavery by a Runaway Slave," Aug. 23, Sept. 13, Sept. 20, Oct., 11, Oct. 18, 1838, electronic edition transcribed by Monique Prince, first edition 2003: http://docsouth.unc.edu/neh/runaway/runaway.html,

accessed Aug. 24, 2012. The document is in the "Documenting the American South" collection, the University of North Carolina at Chapel Hill: http://docsouth.unc.edu.

[352] Zachary Hutchins, summary of "Recollections of Slavery by a Runaway Slave," *The Emancipator,* Aug. 23, Sept. 13, Sept. 20, Oct., 11, Oct. 18, 1838, electronic edition transcribed by Monique Prince, first edition 2003: http://docsouth.unc.edu/neh/runaway/summary.html, accessed Aug. 24, 2012. The document is in the "Documenting the American South" collection, the University of North Carolina at Chapel Hill: http://docsouth.unc.edu.

[353] The memoir was also the basis for a 1984 Public Broadcasting System film.

[354] *The Emancipator,* "Recollections of Slavery by a Runaway Slave," Aug. 23, Sept. 13, Sept. 20, Oct., 11, Oct. 18, 1838, electronic edition transcribed by Monique Prince, first edition 2003: http://docsouth.unc.edu/neh/runaway/summary.html, accessed Aug. 24, 2012. Lewis Powell IV, "Layers on the dark history cake – Charleston's Old City Jail," *Southern Spirit Guide,* Oct. 22, 2011: http://southernspiritguide.blogspot.com/2011/10/layers-on-dark-history-cakecharlestons.html, accessed Aug. 25, 2012.

INDEX

Y

CPSIA information can be obtained at www.ICGtesting.com
Printed in the USA
BVOW09s0044190914

367458BV00007B/17/P